Chinua Achebe
A Biography

Chinua Achebe
A Biography

Ezenwa-Ohaeto

James Currey
OXFORD

Indiana University Press
BLOOMINGTON & INDIANAPOLIS

First published in Britain and the Commonwealth by
James Currey Ltd
73 Botley Road, Oxford
OX2 0BS

and in North America by
Indiana University Press
601 North Morton Street
Bloomington, Indiana 47404

Copyright © Ezenwa-Ohaeto, 1997
First published 1997
1 2 3 4 5 01 00 99 98 97

British Library Cataloguing in Publication Data
Ezenwa-Ohaeto
 Chinua Achebe : a biography.
 1. Achebe, Chinua, 1930- - Biography 2. Novelists, Nigerian -
 20th century - Biography 3. Poets, Nigerian - 20th century -
 Biography
 I. Title
 823

ISBN 0-85255-546-6 (James Currey Cloth)

Library of Congress Cataloging-in-Publication Data
Ezenwa-Ohaeto
 Chinua Achebe : a biography / Ezenwa-Ohaeto.
  p.   cm.
 Includes bibliographical references and index.
 ISBN 0-253-33342-3 (alk. paper)
 1. Achebe, Chinua—Biography.   2. Authors, Nigerian—20th century—
 Biography.   3. Nigeria—Intellectual life.   I. Title.
 PR9387.9.A3Z66   1997
 823—dc21
 [B]   97-10961

1 2 3 4 5 02 01 00 99 98 97

Typeset by
Long House Publishing Services, Cumbria, UK
in 9/11 Melior
Manufactured in
the United States of America

To the memory of
Ven. Michael Ogbonnaya Ohaeto
and also for
Rebecca N. Ohaeto
with gratitude

Contents

Contents

Acknowledgements

THIS biography could not have been written without the help of numerous people. The author is grateful to the Alexander von Humboldt Foundation, Bonn, Germany, the University of Bayreuth, and the Institute for Ethnology and African Studies of the University of Mainz, Germany for research facilities. The author is also grateful to Chinua Achebe for permission to undertake a biography, although he made it clear then that he would not be involved in the work (I nevertheless managed to trouble him several times for clarifications). In addition to a response to a request for memories of encounters with Chinua Achebe published in the *ALA Bulletin*, Bernth Lindfors supplied much of the material needed when other research items could not be found. I am very grateful to this distinguished researcher and academic. Ngozi Ohaeto had to return to Nigeria in order to track down some of the research items I needed urgently. It was a task that was combined with several matrimonial responsibilities and I am deeply grateful for that invaluable service. Chukwuemeka Ike and Chike C. Momah kindly gave me permission to make liberal use of their published reminiscences in *The Umuahian*.

I am grateful for interviews and conversations with: Chinua Achebe, Chinwe Christie Achebe, Ikechukwu Achebe, Chinelo Achebe, Frank O. Achebe, J. C. I. Achebe, Zinobia Uzoma Ikpeze (née Achebe), Chukwuemeka Ike, Bimpe Ike, C. C. Momah, Godwin Momah, Edwin and Mrs Nwogwugwu, C. C. Ifemesia, Obiora Udechukwu, D. I. Nwoga, S. N. C. Okonkwo, Akunwata Ugoka, Augustine Akwuba Agogbua, G. D. Killam, C. L. Innes, B. C. Uzochukwu, Alan Hill, Alastair Niven, Don Burness, Obi Maduakor, B. N. Igwilo, Ralph Opara, E. O. Aghanya, Ulli Beier, Mabel Segun, Gabriel Okara, Cyprian Ekwensi, Chijioke Abagwe and Arthur Nwankwo.

In the course of this study I derived much insight from the works of G. T. Basden, Robert Wren, C. K. Meek, K. O. Dike, Thurstan Shaw, Bernth Lindfors, John Okparaocha, Amma Ogan, F. C. K. Ekechi, Victor Uchendu, C. L. Innes, David Carroll, Chinua Achebe, E. N. Obiechina, Ada Ugah, Toyin Falola, Julius Ihonvbere, Patricia Wright, Patricia Morris, Karen J. Winkler, Conor Cruise O'Brien, Auberon Waugh and Suzanne Cronje, Frederick Forsyth, Stanley Diamond, Simon Gikandi and Cornelius Ogu Ejimofor.

Acknowledgements

My sense of Achebe's life was greatly enriched by the reminiscences of Jacob Ade Ajayi, Abiodun Iluyomade, John Munonye, Leon Botstein, Flora Nwapa, Ben Obumselu, Pius Okigbo, Abel Oshevire, Kenneth Mellanby, Jane Mellanby, Ngugi wa Thiong'o, Geoffrey Parrinder, Alex Rogers, J. P. Clark-Bekederemo, Wole Soyinka, James Currey, Keith Sambrook, Alex Olu Ajayi, Chukwuma Azuonye, Harvey Swados, Adiele Afigbo, Ulli Beier, Peter Enahoro, Kaye Whiteman, Emmanuel Ngara, Emmanuel C. Okafor, Chimere Ikoku, Edith Ihekweazu, M. J. C. Echeruo, Dennis Brutus, Lewis Nkosi, Chidi Amuta and G. G. Darah.

I gratefully acknowledge the information derived from Chinua Achebe's published interviews and interviews about him conducted by Ernest and Pat Emenyonu, Bernth Lindfors, Richard Priebe, Ian Munro, Reinhard Sander, J. O. J. Nwachukwu-Agbada, Robert Serumaga, D. I. Nwoga, Charles Rowell, M. Wilson, Karen Morell, Ulli Beier, Jane Wilkinson, Suzanne Hayes, Kalu Ogbaa, Okey Ndibe, Yusuf Hassan, Anna Rutherford, Chuzzy Udenwa, Biodun Jeyifo, Chinweizu, Bill Moyers, Mike Awoyinfa, Kirsten Holst Petersen, Rosemary Colmer, Chudi Uwandu, Jim Davidson, Rajat Neogy, Raymond Apthorpe, Paul Theroux, Quincy Troupe, Tom Hayes, Jonathan Cott, William Lawson, Ossie Enekwe, Phanuel Egejuru, Afam Akeh, G. G. Darah, A. P. J. van Rensburg, Robert Wren, Valerie Wilmer, George Adams, Conor Cruise O'Brien, Michael Smith, Harry Cowen, Angela Jackson, Robert Moss, Chris Searle, Lawrence E. Baugh, Karen J. Winkler, Jerome Brooks and Bradford Morrow.

For research material and technical assistance I owe a great debt to Robert Fraser, Betty Sue Flowers, Bernth Lindfors, A. E. Clarke (academic registrar) and the University of Southhampton, Jules Chametzky, Chuks Iloegbunam, Dan Uwandu, Austin Okereke, Suzanne Hayes, Gareth Griffiths, Susan Whyte (BBC, London), Stewart Brown, Chimalum Nwankwo, Marie Umeh, Rosemary Colmer, Mary Speilicy and the University of Massachusetts at Amherst, the registrar and the University of Prince Edward Island, Canada, H. H. Anniah Gowda, Eckhard Breitinger, Okezie Ugbor, Ifeanyi Obiakor, Anene Nwuzor, C. J. E. Okonkwo, Flora Veit-Wild, G. D. Killam, Cheryl Ennals and the Mount Allison University; I. Dike Ogu (the public relations officer) and the University of Nigeria, Nsukka, Niyi Osundare, Franz A. Nowothy and Fitchburg State College of Massachusetts; Mary Ellen Timbol (assistant to the executive vice-president for academic affairs) and Georgetown University, Washington, DC; H. Hübner, Ulla Schild, Claudia Laraher (administrative assistant to the president) and Colgate University of Hamilton, New York, Jeanne M. Julien (public affairs director) and Westfield State College, the Open University of Great Britain, Kathleen A. Wiater (assistant to the president) and Skidmore College of Saratoga Springs, New York, Robert A. Gates (vice-president and secretary) and the New School for Social Research, New York, Marguerita J. Greco (associate dean for academic affairs) and Marymount Manhattan College of New York; Provost Hobart and William Smith College of Geneva, New York, Charles Owen Jr., Joseph Cary, Eleazer Uzoalor, and David Lavallee (the provost) and the City College of the City University of New York.

Finally, I wish to thank Chinualum, Nnedi, Onyedika Ikechukwu, Ugonma, Chinelo and Uchenna as well as Aunt Mercy Ukwu-Echefu.

Preface

T H E research and writing of this book commenced in the early 1980s, once Chinua Achebe had granted his permission. As an undergraduate and later as a graduate student, I had many opportunities of meeting Chinua Achebe, but my acquaintance with him then was slight and superficial. I used to feel elated when he acknowledged my greeting, remembered my name, and asked how I was getting on; but I cannot pretend to have been ranked even in the outermost circle of his friends. I was merely a young man who had written some short stories and poetry, and was intensely interested in literature. Thus it took a great effort to summon the courage to write to him, in the course of 1983, asking timidly for permission to write his biography. When I confided in a friend my intention to write this biography he smiled with a hint of scepticism. In my letter to Achebe I had only stated that I had not much to recommend me except that I was once his student and that I have access to the Igbo language and culture which nurtured him.

The response did not come immediately but I met Achebe in 1984 when I had cause to go to Nsukka and he greeted me warmly. He invited me to his office where he verbally gave me permission to commence work, although he made it clear that he would not be involved. He remarked that he had kept forgetting to reply to my letter; on the occasions he remembered he was either in a plane or in a foreign country. I enquired if he was engaged in the production of his autobiography and if there were other writers engaged in a project similar to mine. He answered that he had not contemplated an autobiography and that he did not see anything wrong in several writers working on the same project independently. A year later, when I asked Chinua Achebe to give me a letter of authority indicating that I was working on his biography, the enormity of the task dawned on me.

> Ezenwa-Ohaeto who was my student and is now a lecturer has informed me of his desire to write my biography. I have no doubt that he will bring to both research and writing a sense of seriousness. I have therefore given my general approval to his project.

It was not that I had anticipated that biography writing would be an easy task. Achebe's statement concerning seriousness had a sobering effect, for he never gives praise recklessly. It made me a little more thorough, more sensitive, and more persistent in digging out the facts. Fortunately, Achebe had interacted with many people, and many of those who had benefited from his goodwill, advice, friendship and critical direction had publicly acknowledged that positive influence.

I found Achebe's manner to be devoid of the glitter associated with famous men and women; he had a habit of putting people at ease. In appearance he might be taken for an average well-to-do man, for there was nothing Bohemian about him. He was neither fat nor thin, neither too tall nor too short, and he carried himself erect, walking with confident strides. His voice was remarkably mellow but capable of modulation, his laughter moderate and infectious. In addition he was both witty and humorous in making and appreciating fun.

The motivations for this biography were varied, but the prominent one was the fact that writers from Africa and elsewhere had come to define themselves on the basis of Chinua Achebe's books. It struck me that any man who could elicit such reactions should be examined not just in terms of literary contributions but also in terms of the social, historical and cultural milieu that influenced and inspired him. Nevertheless the aim of this biography is not only to cast light on its subject but also to place an inspirational life in its proper perspective. If in the final analysis I have succeeded in presenting a rounded life of this remarkable personality I would feel immensely rewarded for the time, energy and resources my task has demanded.

Ezenwa-Ohaeto
Bayreuth and Mainz, Germany
Awka and Owerri, Nigeria

Christopher Okigbo, Chinua Achebe and Alex Olu Ajayi, c. 1959
Photo: with permission of Chinua Achebe

University Herald Editorial Board, 1952-3, from left to right, Chinua Achebe,
Chukwuemeka Ike, Mabel Segun, D. Oforiokuma, Agu Ogan and Akio Abbey
Photo: with permission of Chinua Achebe

Old Boys' Reunion, July
1953; standing: D.E.U.
Ekong, S.C.O. Aranoto,
M.O. Okoye, A.C. Achebe,
M.O. Egwuronu,
M.C. Adiele, E.A. Onuoha;
sitting: M.A. Nwabuko,
A.A. Agha, I.D. Erekosima,
The Acting Principal,
Chief M.W. Ubani,
B.O.N. Eluwah,
H.S. Ubozoh, M.O. Ebizie
*Photo: Government College,
Umuahia Magazine*

Chinua Achebe as Director
of Voice of Nigeria,
Lagos, 1964
*Photo: with permission of
Chinua Achebe*

Chinua and Christie
Achebe in the early sixties,
soon after their marriage
*Photo: with permission of
Chinua Achebe*

Chinua Achebe in the
sixties
Photo: Mark Gerson

Harvey Swados and Chinua
Achebe in Biafra, 1969
*Photo: with permission of Chinua
Achebe and New Letters*

Chinua Achebe receiving
honorary doctorate at
Dartmouth College, Hanover,
NH, 1972
*Photo: with permission of
Chinua Achebe*

A damaged photo of
J.P. Clark, Chinua Achebe
and Wole Soyinka after
their plea to General
Babangida for leniency for
Vatsa and other alleged
coup plotters, 1986

Ezenwa-Ohaeto and
Chinua Achebe at Awka,
1987
Photo: Ezenwa-Ohaeto

Chinua and Christie Achebe on their silver wedding anniversary with Nwando,
Chidi and Ikechukwu, September, 1986
Photo: Mike's Photos, Nsukka, with permission of Chinua Achebe

Chinua Achebe at the University of
Nairobi, 1988

Doug Killam and Chinua Achebe, Guelph,
1985. Achebe was Senior Commonwealth
Practitioner at the University of Guelph
for three months
Photo: Doug Killam

Doug Killam, Chinua Achebe and Bernard Fonlon, the University of Guelph,
12 June 1985. Chinua Achebe received an Honorary D. Litt
Photo: Illustration Services Dept, University of Guelph

Chinua Achebe and his daughter Chinelo (to his left) at an informal launching of
Anthills of the Savannah, Guelph, 1987
Photo: Doug Killam

Chinua Achebe, CBC Radio International, Toronto, recording 'Letter to Nigeria',
22 June 1985
Photo: with permission of Doug Killam

Caricature by Ake Didi Onu, *The Guardian*, Lagos, 11 November 1989
Caricature by Cliff Ogiugo, *The Guardian*, Lagos, 18 November 1989

Caricature by Tony Olise of *The Guardian*, Lagos

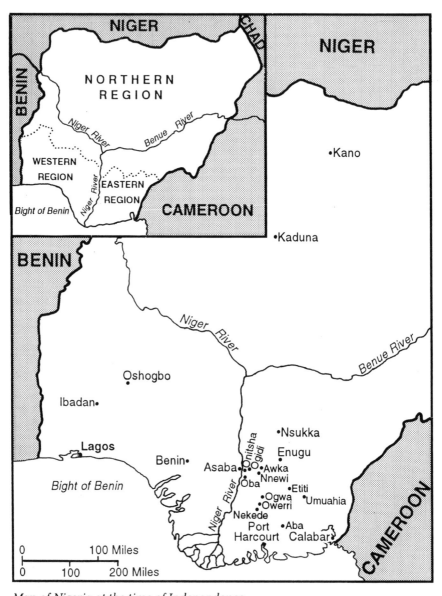

Map of Nigeria at the time of Independence

1

The Catechist's Son
Missionaries & Masquerades
1930–5

On the next day all the masked *egwugwu* of Umuofia assembled in the market-place. They came from all the quarters of the clan and even from neighbouring villages. The dreaded Otakagu came from Imo, and Ekwensu, dangling a white cock, arrived from Uli. It was a terrible gathering. The eerie voices of countless spirits, the bells that clattered behind some of them, and the clash of matchets as they ran forwards and backwards and saluted one another, sent tremors of fear into every heart. For the first time in living memory the sacred bull-roarer was heard in broad daylight.[1]

T H E beginning of the twentieth century was the period of the crossroads of cultures in Igboland. It was also a period of sweeping and complex changes in the area later to be known as Nigeria, particularly in the eastern parts of the country. The colonial power, after several expeditions, was entrenching its authority over the society; the missionaries, too, were consolidating their spiritual influence after the efforts of their pioneers; the economy was being reordered to reflect new commercial interests; and Western education was seen increasingly as providing opportunities for the acquisition of power and prestige. Although these changes were proceeding, there were still areas in which a large number of people retained and preserved their traditions. It was obvious, however, that these customs were disappearing gradually in the wake of fundamental change in the economic, social, political and cultural life of the community.

In the midst of change, farming and trading remained the major occupations; there were also still musicians, hunters, blacksmiths, builders, carvers and, to a lesser extent, fishermen along the streams and rivers. The festivals associated with various communities, often based on religious rites, were still held, although the zeal of some converts to the Christian religion, and the resistance of adherents to the old traditions, sometimes met in conflict. Interestingly, various groups of converts and traditionalists were also active participants in the market place, engaging there in numerous commercial transactions.

Recreational activities centred on the community continued to link individuals, their neighbours and their kinsmen. Wrestling was popular, often attracting competitors who represented their clans, quarters, villages or towns. Of course, communal activity was closely associated with captivating music and dance. Under normal circumstances dances were organized in elaborate detail either by the men or the women, sometimes in connection with traditional festivals. Adherents to the Igbo traditions were still in the majority at the beginning of the twentieth century, and these festivals often accorded due reverence to custodians of the gods and oracles like the priest of Udo in Ikenga, one of the villages of Ogidi.

The major festival in Ogidi was *Nwafor*, which survived the initial inroads made by the advent of Christianity and the policies of the colonial administrators. *Nwafor*, which may be likened to Christmas, takes place in the midst of the rainy season. In the past it was an event that every Ogidi indigene respected and many people from other districts attended, especially those who had relatives in Ogidi. These visitors came bearing kegs of palm wine and were given large portions of meat on their departure. It was a time for relaxation when all the major farm work had been done and people cast aside the depression induced by the rheumy weather. Young men, however, took advantage of the *Nwafor* festival not only to drink a lot of wine and make merry, but also to flog people who had earned their displeasure. Even the Christians joined in for the fun of it in later years, which is probably why the festival has survived. A major characteristic was its numerous masquerades; this was the time at which young boys were initiated into these rites.

The large number of masks paraded during the *Nwafor* festival in those days included the Bull-roarer, which normally appeared at night to the great alarm of women and children especially. *Ulaga*, *Ogolo* and *Ojionu* were among the many other masks. *Akataka* and *Agaba Idu* were powerful masks with a youthful following; most of their attendants were hefty, stalwart men. *Agaba* is another word for 'lion' and *Agaba Idu* means 'the lion from *Idu*' – a distant, mythical land. *Akataka*, on the other hand, is an onomatopoeic word that signifies a terrible being. These masks also appeared during funerals, imposing their presence on important occasions in the daily life of the people.

The presence of the missionaries of the Church Missionary Society (CMS), who arrived in Ogidi from Onitsha in about 1892, could not negate this festival, although they did win converts in the town. These early converts did not constitute a population large enough to threaten the major traditions of the people. This first generation of Christians sometimes demonstrated their faith in very aggressive ways, however; they violated the customs of the village, which invariably led to skirmishes. Fortunately the presence of the converts did not affect festivals like *Nwafor*, or even the powerful night masquerades. The latter effectively monitored the moral consciousness of the society, exposing abnormal acts publicly albeit under the cover of darkness. Their performances were enhanced by the *Ayaka* chorus.

The desire of the CMS to establish a station at Ogidi may have had something to do with the refinement of morals, but the primary aim was to extend its area of influence beyond its operational headquarters in Onitsha. When the first missionaries arrived in Ogidi they responded to the Igbo tradition that strangers must pay their respects to prominent local personalities, among them Chinua Achebe's great-grandfather, Udo Osinyi:

> He had taken the highest but one title that a man of wealth and honour might aspire to, and the feast he gave the town on his initiation became a byword for open-handedness bordering on prodigality. The grateful and approving community called him henceforth Udo Osinyi – Udo who cooks more than the whole people can eat.[2]

The story of the man in *Things Fall Apart* who set 'before his guests a mound of *foo-foo* so high that those who sat on one side could not see what was happening on the other, and it was not until late in the evening that one of them saw for the first time his in-law who had arrived during the course of the meal and had fallen to on the opposite side'[3] must have been inspired by Udo Osinyi. Chinua Achebe adds:

> The first missionaries who came to my village went to Udo Osinyi to pay their respects and seek support for their work. For a short while my great-grandfather allowed them to operate from his compound. He probably thought it was some kind of circus whose strange presence added lustre to his household. But after a few days he sent them packing again. Not, as you might think, on account of the crazy theology they had begun to propound, but on the much more serious ground of musical aesthetics. Said the old man: 'Your singing is too sad to come from a man's house. My neighbours might think it was my funeral dirge.'[4]

The missionaries departed from the compound of Udo Osinyi without bitterness. Among those who watched them go was a young man who had been attracted by their ideas and theology. An orphan whose parents had died early, he was the grandson of Udo Osinyi. Although he was no more than average in stature, the young man had acquired an enviable reputation as an excellent masquerader, an accomplishment that was valued highly in the community. He became one of the early converts of Rev. S. R. Smith and was given the name Isaiah Okafor Achebe. It must have been in the year 1904 that Isaiah Achebe was baptized, but as early as 1901 Rev. Smith could report 40 pupils in the school, 70 people attending the Sunday services and 18 candidates registered for baptism. In the following year, 15 young men were baptized at Ogidi, and subsequently the influence of the CMS became pronounced in the town, enjoying the support of Walter Amobi, one of the first persons in the region to receive a Western education.

By 1904 Isaiah Okafor Achebe had become one of the reliable young converts of the CMS, whose executive committee included him in the junior group sent to the recently established Awka College for training as a teacher and catechist. At that time most workers in the employment of the church combined priestly duties such as conducting church services with the responsibility of imparting knowledge as teachers. It is interesting that the wealthy and powerful Udo Osinyi did not object to this development, enhancing his reputation as a tolerant man.

It was probably at the new Teacher Training College at Awka that Isaiah Okafor Achebe came into contact with the missionary, amateur anthropologist and teacher G. T. Basden, who had been instrumental in the establishment of the college. Basden was a man who not only made fairly reasonable assessments of his Igbo acquaintances but also accorded recognition to the culture of the people, which was why he attracted respect wherever he visited. The respect was mutual, for the sensitive Basden confessed that

> a missionary has unique opportunities of becoming acquainted with village life, for from the very nature of things the soundest policy is for him to live in the closest communion with the people whom he seeks to influence. So it comes about that he enters freely into the life of the natives, their huts are always open to him and he goes in and out more or less as one of themselves. In like manner they expect the missionary's house to be free to them and to come and go as they please.[5]

Perhaps it was this ability to understand the 'natives' which later made Basden a welcome visitor and a man to treat with respect in the home of Isaiah Achebe.

The young man from Ikenga village in Ogidi, who went to the Teacher Training College in Awka as one of its first students, had imbibed the cultural injunction of respect for one's acquaintances. Moreover, he was convinced by the ideas of the new religion and devoted himself to his profession with commendable but dignified zeal. He became known as 'Achebe 1904', just as another Ogidi townsman, Isaiah's friend and fellow catechist, was known as 'Ofoedu 1908'. Isaiah Achebe was at Awka College a year before the Agbala oracle was destroyed by the colonial government because it served as a medium for the exploitation of several communities and the destruction of numerous human lives. The influence of this oracle was aided by the activities of many Awka indigenes, like the Nkwelle people, who travelled extensively as skilled blacksmiths and spread the fame of Agbala as its unofficial emissaries. The manner in which the secret of the oracle was guarded and the subtlety with which the gullibility of the supplicants was manipulated closely resembled the activities associated with the 'Long Juju' of Arochukwu. Those who acted on behalf of the oracle carefully extracted all the necessary information before they guided supplicants to the grove of Agbala at Awka, enabling the oracle, primed with this information, to make impressive and often accurate pronouncements that astounded the supplicants.

The events associated with the destruction of the oracle must have served as further reinforcement for the hold of the new religion on the mind of the young Ogidi man. But there were other activities of a more pleasant nature in the Awka environment. On one of their evangelical trips Isaiah met a young girl known as Janet Anaenechi, whose family name was Iloegbunam, the daughter of a blacksmith from Umuike village in Awka. Later, he informed his relatives of his intention to marry her. After the essential traditional enquiries, the relatives made the necessary arrangements and Isaiah and Janet were married according to the custom of their peoples. Chinua Achebe provides a vivid description of Janet Anaenechi's life at the time of her marriage to his father:

> My mother, after she was betrothed to my evangelist father at the turn of this century, was sent to the newly founded St Monica's Girls' School in our district, the first of its kind in Igboland. As a special favour she went to live with the Principal, Edith Ashley Warner, and her small team of English teachers. She performed domestic chores in return for her education and keep. The daughter of a village blacksmith, she found her new life strange, exciting and sometimes frightening. Her most terrifying experience was discovering one night in a bowl of water her mistress's dentures or, in my mother's words, her *entire jaw*.[6]

Achebe also tells us that

> One evening Miss Warner told my mother to eat the food in the dish and afterwards to wash it carefully. She was apparently learning the Igbo language and used it on this occasion. She said, 'Awakwana afele', which should mean 'Don't break the plate', except that Igbo verbs are sometimes quite tricky.

What the lady actually said meant something like 'Do not break (yourself) on the plate.' Achebe adds that his mother

> unable to contain her amusement gave way to a barely suppressed giggle which proved to be a great mistake. The Victorian lady was not amused. She picked up a

huge stick and walloped her good and proper. Later on she called her and gave her a lecture on good manners. 'If I speak your language badly, you should tell me the right way. It is wrong to laugh at me', or words to that effect. My mother told that story many times to my hearing and each time we would all laugh because *awakwana afele* is incredibly funny under any circumstances.[7]

But it was the moral in this anecdote that Janet Achebe stressed to her children.

Janet established such good relationships with the white women who taught at St Monica's that one of them later became the godmother of her first daughter, Zinobia. Her wedding took place in 1909 at the Ebenezer Church, Ogidi. It was an impressive ceremony, conducted by the distinguished and powerful Dr G. T. Basden and attended by many of the white missionaries in their finery and bearing gifts. Udo Osinyi was impressed by the ceremony although it did not move him to adopt the new religion. The presence of Basden was enough to attract attention: he had become one of the best-known missionaries in the region, on the basis of which he later sat as Igboland's representative in the Legislative Council for many years.

Appreciation of Basden's political role was commemorated in the various titles he was awarded by Igbo communities. Onitsha conferred the title of *Omesilincha* which means 'the one who accomplishes his duties or tasks completely'; the Ogidi community gave him the title of *Onu nekwulu ora* – 'the mouth that speaks on behalf of the people'; and the Awka community called him *Omezuluoke*, 'the one who fulfils his responsibility satisfactorily'. The Nkwelle Ogidi community honoured him with the gift of an elephant tusk and a staff, items expressing great respect. These titles and gifts emphasized Basden's roles as advocate, hard worker and responsible pioneer, clearly illustrating his personal dynamism and enterprise, and especially his willingness to use dialogue rather than force or intimidation in his dealings with people.

In his subsequent missionary work, Isaiah Okafor Achebe demonstrated many of the same qualities as he spread the gospel and imparted knowledge as a teacher. He was the first person who taught Bible reading at St Paul's Church, Ogidi. It was the beginning of a career in the opening of new missions and new schools, and in the taming of new environments on behalf of the missionaries, the church and the people. Meanwhile the family of Isaiah and Janet Achebe displayed the cohesion characteristic of most of the marriages of the early Christian converts, who practised what they preached. No one in the village could remember a public disagreement between the couple. Isaiah's commitment to Christianity was complete: as soon as he was converted he ignored all those aspects of his tradition that conflicted with the Christian religion, including the masquerades at which he had excelled in his youth. Chinua Achebe recalls his father telling him that when he was a boy there was a masked spirit in his village called Evil Forest. His carved headpiece was unevenly balanced, with a disproportionate part behind him, and he had the habit of asking people to say which part of his headpiece was greater, the one behind or the one in front. In their ignorance, people would base their answers on the evidence of their eyes: what was behind was indeed greater. To which Evil Forest would rejoin: '*Nkiruka* – what is in front is always greater.'[8] Isaiah had no dealings with the traditional medicine men and their concoctions, although in his native Ikenga village there were medicine men reputedly able to terminate the lives of their enemies. In those days the people of Ogidi had an aphorism which encapsulated their opinion of Isaiah: 'We know the people who are Christians, people like Isaiah Achebe, we know them.'[9] Isaiah also earned a reputation as a saviour of souls. Janet Achebe was fond of quoting Psalm 34, verse 11: 'Come my sons, I will teach you the fear of Yahweh.'

Isaiah was not a great talker but that does not mean that he was always silent. He 'spoke when he had to and his words were carefully chosen; the same with his sermons'.[10] They tended to be brief and to the point. In spite of his life as a devout Christian of the first generation, he retained a respect for the tradition he had left. He would perform the traditional ritual of breaking the kola nut, but end by introducing the name of 'Jesus Christ Our Lord', like the character Odogwu in *No Longer at Ease* who prays thus: 'Bless this Kolanut so that when we eat it, it will be good in our body in the name of Jesu Kristi.'[11] But Isaiah was much more adept and Achebe cites prayers that are very interesting combinations of the Christian and the traditional forms. Yet he was very strict and would not agree with a view he rejected in order to be polite. Instead he would voice his misgivings, especially in matters of his faith. He extended the same strictness and discipline to his children. But in such matters as land disputes Isaiah was most unwilling to quarrel with people, preferring to lose the land rather than commence a tragic conflict. Perhaps his weakness was to trust people excessively. Janet Achebe, on the other hand, was the leader of the women of the church. In addition she was a farmer who planted cocoyams, cassava and vegetables. Such supplementary roles were clearly essential to the welfare of Isaiah Achebe's family.

After teaching at the Ebenezer Church, Uru Ogidi, Isaiah Achebe served the CMS at places such as Ogbunike, Awkuzu, Oraifite, Obosi and Nnewi during the time of Rev. Spencer. He was also at Atuma, a town on the western reaches of the Niger. During these years he and his understanding wife were also bringing up a family. The first surviving child, a son, was named Frank Okwuofu; he was followed by John Chukwuemeka Ifeanyichukwu, Zinobia Uzoma and Augustine Nduka. Isaiah Achebe was teaching at St Simon's Church, Nneobi, when his fifth surviving child and fourth son was born on 16 November 1930. He was christened Albert Chinualumogu. When he was baptized, one of the godfathers was Amos Nwajudo.

Although his family had grown and time had taken its toll on his physique, catechist Isaiah Achebe still devoted his time and energies in the service of his employers. He was transferred to Umudim Alor, from there to the town of Uke, and later served at St Stephen's Church, Oba. In this period the last surviving child and second daughter arrived, to be christened Grace Nwanneka. In 1935, about five years after the birth of Albert Chinualumogu, who was to become known internationally as Chinua Achebe, the family returned to settle in Isaiah Achebe's ancestral village of Ikenga, Ogidi, where henceforth he would live in semi-retirement.

2

Starting at the Crossroads
Primary School
1936–43

ISAIAH Okafor Achebe had succeeded in building an impressive zinc house in his village, continuing a family tradition by distinguishing himself in the eyes of the community in Ikenga, Ogidi. It was not an easy achievement: times had changed since the days of his late guardian, the legendary Udo Osinyi. His standing in the community ensured that catechist Achebe was not unduly troubled when the time came to proceed to his village on retirement. Moreover, Igbo people expect that a traveller, at the end of all his journeys, will return home to reside with his own people. Whatever the extent of his prosperity in foreign lands, his fame will rest mainly on what he has been able to accomplish at home.

His children were still growing up, although the first son, Frank Okwuofu, had graduated from the Dennis Memorial Grammar School at Onitsha and gone on, in 1935, to obtain a first class in Magnetism and Electricity, sitting the examination set by the City and Guilds of the London Institute through the Post and Telecommunications School in Lagos (he also obtained second-class passes in both Grade I Telegraphy and Preliminary Telecommunications).

Meanwhile, Janet Achebe, with the help of her elder daughter Zinobia Uzoma, nursed and took care of the young Albert Chinualumogu and Grace Nwanneka. The Igbo names that Isaiah and Janet Achebe gave their children were a significant reflection of how their views of life now hinged on their adopted religion; their own family name, an abbreviation of *Ani chebe* which means 'May mother earth preserve', stands in sharp contrast. In naming their children, the Achebes had started with the name Okwuofu ('New word'); then came Chukwuemeka ('God has performed well'), Ifeanyichukwu ('Nothing is beyond God'), Uzoma ('The good path', derived from the proverb that when a path is good it encourages one to walk on it again), and Nduka ('Life is more important', usually a shortened form of the phrase *Ndukaku* - 'Life is more important than wealth').

Thus they came to Chinualumogu ('May God fight on my behalf'): in effect, the name was a prayer, and a philosophical statement in the Igbo tradition, reflecting both a concept of life and a desire for stability in that life. Occasionally some of Chinua's fellow infants would say to him, 'Chinualumogu, come and fight for me', and he would answer them, 'Tell my brother to fight for you, I'm

7

too tired.' Sometimes Janet Achebe would exclaim, in the course of a discussion with her acquaintances and especially when she was given shocking news: '*Chinualumogu-o!*' Her son, thinking that his mother was referring to him, would retort: '*Mamanualumogu-o!*' ('May Mama fight on my behalf!') This was the retort of a child, but also an early indication of verbal agility in the bearer of the name Chinualumogu, later shortened to Chinua, a form that retains the original meaning.

When Chinua Achebe was a child, entertainment for children, especially if designed to quieten them or keep them busy, was conducted through games and the narration of stories. Each mother or older child found it necessary to garner several stories for such purposes. Zinobia Uzoma, who had the responsibility for taking care of Chinua and Grace, was a very good mimic and would dramatize the characters in her stories. One of the tales she narrated was about a man known as Amanile who bought a 'goat' not knowing it was a tortoise. Amanile would get up each day to procure grass for the 'goat', but it would not eat. Whenever the man went out, however, tortoise ate his *alibo,* a local delicacy made of cassava flour. Other stories were narrated by Chinua's mother, whose experience of a different but related Igbo culture at Awka gave her access to their myths, legends, folktales and stories centred on events and people. These storytelling sessions were part of Igbo tradition and fired the imaginations of gifted children. In later life Zinobia recollected that her younger brother Chinua had a retentive memory and would remind her of the stories he wanted to hear once more.

Another wellspring of Chinua Achebe's early education was the walls of his father's house.

> My father filled our walls with a variety of educational material. There were Church Missionary Society yearly almanacs with pictures of bishops and other dignitaries. But the most interesting hangings were the large paste-ups which my father created himself. He had one of the village carpenters make him large but light wooden frames onto which he then gummed brown or black paper backing. On this paper he pasted coloured and glossy pictures and illustrations of all kinds from an old magazine he had acquired somehow. I remember a most impressive picture of King George V in red and gold, wearing a sword. There was also a funny-looking man with an enormous stride. He was called Johnnie Walker. He was born in 1820 according to the picture and was still going strong. When I learnt many years later that this extraordinary fellow was only an advertisement for whisky I felt a great sense of personal loss.[1]

Other familiar images were a picture of Miss Warner and a framed motto of St Monica's School in blue letters: 'Speak True, Live Pure, Right Wrong, Follow the King'. Figuring out the meaning of 'Right Wrong', Achebe remembers, was among his first self-inflicted educational assignments.

When the Achebe family returned to Ogidi in 1935 the cultural crossroads faced by their society was plainly apparent. The storytelling sessions of the oral tradition existed side by side with book-reading sessions in the schools. The hymn-singing, Bible-reading members of catechist Achebe's family, on one side, faced his traditionalist kin on the other. Although there were several Christians who seemed to operate on the basis that everything in the traditional society was bad or should be suppressed, there were also a few others who were more tolerant. Isaiah Achebe, who was quite strict in matters of his religion, and who did not hesitate to flog his children if they misbehaved, became less rigid as he grew older. He would sometimes criticize a masquerade that was not well turned out. This less rigid approach to cultural issues coincided with his semi-retirement.

Chinua Achebe's recollection of those days of crossroads cultural activities finds another focus in the journey by lorry which brought the family back to Ogidi. Travelling through a changing world or at home in the village, he found himself in the stimulating position of seeing two worlds at once, finding both interesting in their different ways, and gradually becoming better able to record what he was seeing. He was moved by the Christian message, especially the hymns in church and even the poetry of the litany. At the same time he was also moved by the traditional religion that Christianity was attempting to suppress. His developing faculty of observation and recall took in not only the human elements but also the environment with its bush paths, mud houses, shrines and festivals. His father told his children from memory 'the genealogy of the entire village, the family tree of the whole town; from the man who founded it, the number of children and their descendants and how all the kindred families were related'.[2] It was the responsibility of all Igbo fathers to perform such duties and that was how knowledge was passed on, since the elders did not keep diaries. In this way the little Chinua Achebe gained glimpses of earlier generations and their customs, and was able to compare these with customs that were still practised.

Many people wavered between two worlds, like Isaiah Achebe's brother who underwent many conversions and reversions. Nevertheless, there was a certain distance between the 'people of the church' and the 'people of the world'. Achebe tells us that

> the boundary between them had very many crossings. The average Christian enjoyed the sights and sounds of traditional festivities. Non-Christians for their part observed us closely and treated some of our practices with indulgent amusement. In the most celebrated song of those days – *Egwu obi,* song of the heart – they mimicked our singing in tonic solfa: '*Ukwe ndi uka,* sss ddd mrd mr-e-e – the song of the people of the church, sss ddd mrd mr-e-e'.[3]

He did not take this distance between the two groups in the village for granted, unlike many of his companions at that time. Those whose parents were regarded as heathens would take many of the traditional activities for granted, while Chinua, with his Christian background, was not expected to participate. Yet when there was a festival, in spite of the injunction that the children of Isaiah Achebe must not visit the neighbours because they were likely to be given food offered to the idols, the curious Chinua always managed to attend, taking with him his younger sister Grace. These visits did not require a great effort, since the houses of the village were constructed quite close to each other and usually had nebulous boundaries which it was easy for the children to cross. It is interesting that Chinua crossed those boundaries in spite of the fact that he was

> such a thorough little Christian that often at Sunday services, at the height of the grandeur of *Te Deum Laudamus,* I would have dreams of a mantle of gold falling on me as the choir of angels drowned the mortal song and the voice of God himself thundering: 'This is my beloved son in whom I am well pleased.'[4]

This was not a matter of spiritual agony or undue distress but a 'fascination for the ritual and the life of the people on the other arm of the crossroads of cultures'.

Eating those festival foods he never found 'the rice and stew to have the flavour of idolatry' or to be greatly different from the rice and stew he ate at home.

Thus the crossroads of cultures was often traversed, privately and publicly. One of the public instances was an incident which fascinated many of his companions. Chieka Ifemesia, the historian from the Achebe village of Ikenga, and Augustine Akwuba Agogbua, who was Chinua Achebe's classmate in the primary school and also his childhood friend, recollected the incident.[5] It was the 'killing' of a masquerade which depicted an old woman. This happened at the Afor-Igwe, an important, busy square situated between Ogidi, Umunya, Umudioka and Ogbunike, where it used to move from one stall to another begging. An irritated market-goer pushed the masquerader off. The 'old woman' fell down and was presumed 'killed'. It was an abomination to desecrate a masquerade and the news spread throughout the district. From every quarter mighty masquerades came out, by day and by night, to mourn in a ritual called *Ibe Oye*. The matter went to the customary court after the traditional judgement at the *Mpuke Rulu* shrine. In ancient times judgements at the shrine were so frightening that interested parties often made use of charms to protect themselves. The idea was that no one who went for judgement ever returned unscathed, and proceedings were headed by a dangerous and dreadful masquerade known as *Onyekaozulu* ('For whom is it sufficient or well?') The case of the desecration was entitled *Ikpe Nneosua,* and whenever it was scheduled at the customary court it became an event in itself to watch the splendour and terror of the masquerades on the highway. Spirit masks of all imaginable shapes and dimensions converged. One of them had a pot on its head with smoke oozing out, and a piece of thread hanging from its head on which a spider crawled up and down. There was another one from Azu Ogbunike which had no arms. Some possessed abnormal features, like the one that had a very long penis and another known as *Orikaobue* which flaunted its excessively large stomach. Children peeped at these monsters from the safety of their homes.

Chinua Achebe had no recollection of this incident, which must have occurred between 1930 and 1940. But the legend of the desecration of a masquerade associated with the incident must have entered his consciousness. Certainly the future writer was fascinated by masquerades as a child. Although Chinua was technically excluded from the *Nwafor* festival, he nevertheless experienced the traditional sights and sounds associated with it. A local preacher at that time 'was well known for taking to the pulpit at the time of the village feasts to warn true believers against the great evil of accepting gifts of food surreptitiously over their compound wall from heathen neighbours'.[6] But Chinua, like all the other children, looked forward to this major holiday of the traditional year when

> ancestral masquerades of all kinds left their underground homes through ant-holes to visit the living. For eight whole days we saw them, from a reasonable distance, because they and their attendants carried bundles of whips with which they occasionally punished themselves to prove their toughness and certainly punished you if you were available. We would keep count of the masquerades we saw every day and tally the figures at the end of the eight days and then compare our grand total with the previous year's. In a good year the number could be well over one hundred. And the rule was that even if you saw the same masquerade ten times (as might happen with the livelier ones) you only counted it once.[7]

Achebe remembers the esoteric language of the masquerades in which people are referred to as bodies: 'The body of so-and-so, I salute you!' The masquerades represented

> the range of human experience from youth to age; from playfulness to terror; from the delicate beauty of the maiden spirit, *agbogho mmuo*, to the candid ugliness of *njo ka oya*, ugliness greater than disease, from the athleticism of *Ogolo* to the legless and armless inertia of *ebu-ebu*, a loquacious masquerade that has to be carried from place to place on the head of its attendant from which position it is wont to shout: Off we go! *(Ije abulu ufia)*; from masquerades that appear at every festival to the awesome ancestors that are enticed to the world by rare crises such as the desecration of a masked spirit; from the vast majority that appear in daytime to the dreaded invisible chorus, *ayaka*, and the night-runner, *ogbazuluobodo*.

There was a 'masquerade whose name was *Omanu kwue* ('If you know, speak'). This was a dare, of course, and nobody was about to take up the challenge.' Achebe adds that

> this masquerade was of such towering height that there was only one man in the whole of Ogidi, perhaps even in the whole world who could carry it; the same man, incidentally, whose brief career as a policeman at the beginning of the century had left a powerful enough legend for him to be represented in his uniform in an *Mbari* house in faraway Owerri and simply called Ogidi.[8]

These masquerades still flourished when Chinua Achebe started school at St Philip's Central School, Akpakaogwe Ogidi in 1936. He was asked to proceed to the 'religious class' where there was singing and sometimes dancing of the catechism, the chanting of various English rhymes, and general entertainment. The boy cried and refused to go there; he wanted to go with his elder sister Zinobia to her class in the senior primary school. After Chinua had spent a week in the religious class, however, Rev. Nelson Ezekwesili sent him to the higher infant school because the child exhibited signs of intelligence. The teacher in charge of the infant school at that time was Alphonsus Ojukwu. Chinua, who was quite small, cried again because he was afraid to sit in a strange class. But he soon got used to the tempo of school activities. Achebe recalls that

> one of the earliest short stories I wrote was called 'Chike's School Days' and it ended like this: 'The first sentences in his New Method Reader were simple enough and yet they filled him with a vague exultation: "Once there was a wizard. He lived in Africa. He went to China to get a lamp." Chike read it over and over again at home and then made a song of it. It was a meaningless song. "Periwinkles" got into it, and also "Damascus". But it was like a window through which he saw in the distance a strange, magical new world. And he was happy. And so the young African boy enthusiastically opened his heart and mind to the exciting, wider world unfolding around him. That boy was me!'[9]

St Philip's Central School, Akpakaogwe was made of mud blocks and constructed in the shape of a T. The school building was surrounded with mango trees which provided snacks for the pupils whenever mangoes were in season. The rooms were well ventilated and the pupils washed the floors and scrubbed the walls on Fridays. The school was proud of its football field, reckoned to be one of the best in the Onitsha district. There was also a school farm which provided the venue for agriculture practicals under S. N. Ojemeni, and a musical band in which Chinua Achebe participated.

The young Chinua never missed Sunday school, with its songs and choir practice, and participation in the school band was thus a further exhibition of his interest in music. Once a month there was an evangelical service in the place of regular Sunday school, and Chinua would carry his father's bag as they walked to the selected site where the villagers had gathered. The primary aim was to convert a few more villagers, and they would sing and preach to those they regarded as pagans. These evangelical services were well attended but not very successful. Several of the people who turned up were those who had joined the church but then given it up, and they often put embarrassing and disconcerting questions to the catechist or the pastor, some of which Achebe captures in *Things Fall Apart*. The exchange between the missionaries and the villagers, concerning whether God had a wife and the birth of Jesus Christ, probably drew on a controversy that blighted an evangelical service conducted in the Ogidi of the 1930s.

It was at the Anniversary celebrations that Isaiah Achebe featured most prominently; on these occasions he would narrate the story of the advent of the missionaries, telling his listeners of the early trials of the church, of the suspicion of the people that the white men were freaks of nature, and of the problems those white men encountered in the acquisition of land. The Anniversary was the annual commemoration of the coming of the gospel to Igboland on 27 July 1857. Achebe provides the social context:

> It is reported that Bishop Adjai Crowther and his missionary team who arrived in Onitsha on that day were heavily beaten by rain and as a result every Anniversary celebration ever since has been ruined by bad weather. The good news is that school children were always fed new yams and stew at the Anniversary celebration. For most people it was their first taste of new yam for the year.

The white priests who were in the upper reaches of the church hierarchy seldom visited the hinterland even on those Anniversary days; their authority was felt at a distance, like that of the British Resident for Onitsha Province, Captain O'Connor, who had an Ogidi age grade named after him. The then bishop on the Niger, Rt. Revd Bertram Lasbery, visited St Philip's Church, Ogidi about once in two years. Achebe confesses that as a child 'his sermon left me disappointed. I don't know what I expected, perhaps I thought that if mere teachers and pastors could do as well as some that I knew, a bishop must set a congregation ablaze.'[10] It did not help his cause that Bishop Lasbery preached through an interpreter.

Thus the interests of the growing Chinua Achebe centred on the church, his family home, and the school. At home he was quite handy as the son available to perform household chores. He was often asked to get kola nuts from his mother Janet for the numerous visitors who called to pay their compliments to Isaiah. He could not avoid listening to the conversations of visiting elders and neighbours; he heard the village gossip; he noted the intrigues in the village and the tribulations of the missionaries; and he was exposed to the full cast of characters who made up the village, with their individual mannerisms and, especially, styles of talking. Sometimes he visited the home of his friend Augustine Akwuba Agogbua, whose father Agogbua Kpajie often told them stories of past events in the village. But he did not spend all his time listening to stories. He accompanied his mates to fetch water at Isi-mili Iyienu Ogidi, the only spring in the vicinity. The path to it was very rough and strewn with stones, which caused many children to fall down and break their waterpots. Violent struggles were common among the press of people who went to fetch water. Augustine Agogbua insists that Chinua never engaged in these, perhaps because he was not only young but small, and many of the older men and women would have maltreated him physically.[11] His teacher in the primary school, Sylvanus Ndubuisi Chikezie Okonkwo alias S. N. C., recollects that Albert Chinua Achebe was very young and that he had a constantly running nose which he used the left hand to wipe while continuing to write with the right hand.[12]

S. N. C. Okonkwo came to the school under the headship of Mr Okongwu. He was quite young, and the big boys and girls would playfully give him knocks on the head, complaining that such a young man should not be teaching them. Thus it was easy for S. N. C. Okonkwo to relate to the little Chinua Achebe as they worked under the influence of Mr Okongwu, a strict headmaster who came to Ogidi on transfer from St Peter's School, Enugu. The strict nature of Okongwu and his adherence to discipline was immediately established when he addressed the teachers and pupils, enumerating a list of prohibitions which he stressed with the refrain, 'A raa eme ya eme!' – 'It is never done!' That phrase became the nickname of the new headmaster and one day, soon after the public address, as he was going to the Iyienu hospital to give the Europeans there some lessons in Igbo, some pupils began shouting, 'It is never done! It is never done!'[13]

The next day Mr Okongwu gathered the pupils after the morning service at the school. After locking the doors he produced some canes with which he proceeded to flog every child to punish the offenders that no one was willing to identify. Despite his severity, the headmaster instilled pride in his pupils by sticking to his principles. He was a man who wanted his students to perform better than all others in both academic and social activities. There was the occasion when the school played a football match against the Central School, Abagana and was defeated by two goals. Mr Okongwu was very unhappy and wanted to flog everyone, even the teachers. Thereafter, however, he organized two football teams and trained them himself for two weeks. Then he asked for a return match with Central School, Abagana – and this time his players won by four goals. Headmaster Okongwu also set high standards in the school, awarding prizes for punctuality, cleanliness and class performances. This emphasis on cleanliness must have affected Chinua Achebe because his elder sister Zinobia recollects that he never allowed his school uniform to get dirty, a habit that endeared him to the teachers who quite often desired to know his parents.

Chinua Achebe was in Standard Two when the Second World War began. He confirms that 'the rest of my Primary education happened against its distant background. But it got close one morning when two white people and their assistants came to the school and conscripted the Art teacher.' There was also a pupil in the school who wrote a letter to Adolf Hitler. Headmaster Okongwu pointed out, 'almost in tears, that the boy was a disgrace to the British Empire, and that if he had been older he would surely have been sent to jail for the rest of his miserable life'. The headmaster called the pupil 'an offspring of Satan and flogged him before the whole school'. Perhaps this pupil, like Obi Okonkwo in *No Longer at Ease*, felt sorry for Hitler and did not enjoy going into the bush every day to pick palm kernels as part of the 'Win the War Effort': according to Achebe 'our headmaster told us that every kernel we collected in the bush would buy a nail for Hitler's coffin'.

13

Several songs were sung by the pupils: 'We sang "Rule Britannia" but the really popular song was "Germany Is Falling"':

Germany is falling, falling, falling
Germany is falling to rise no more

If you are going to Germany before me
Germany is falling to rise no more
Tell Hitler I'm not coming there
Germany is falling to rise no more

If you are going to Italy before me
Tell Mussolini I'm not coming there

If you are going to Japan before me
Tell Hirohito I'm not coming there.'

Achebe explains that 'the enemy list concluded, you moved on to friends whom you were naturally prepared to visit':

If you are going to England before me
Tell Churchill I am coming there

If you are going to America before me
Tell Roosevelt I am coming there

If you are going to Russia before me
Tell Stalin I am coming there

If you are going to China before me
Tell Chiang Kai Shek I am coming there

If you are going to Abyssinia before me
Tell Haile Selassie I am coming there.

He remarks that 'sung lustily in an arrangement for cantor and chorus, "Germany Is Falling" was as stirring as "Onward Christian Soldiers" and other evangelical war songs'.[14]

In the midst of these activities the pupils continued to be engaged by their academic work. S. N. C. Okonkwo, who taught Achebe between 1939 and 1941, from Standard Two upwards, was an inspiring teacher. He remembers teaching the biography of J. K. Aggrey, and stressing that Aggrey was a man who acquired twelve degrees. Okonkwo says that Chinua was usually quiet and attentive, and possessed the best handwriting in the class. He was also the best English reader and during dictation lessons, in which the teacher read out passages to the pupils, Chinua would normally get excellent marks. Okonkwo felt that the boy's grounding in the reading of the Igbo version of the Bible was a tremendous help. Chinua also performed well in recitations, especially when reciting either poems or essays on stage. But whenever the teacher wanted him to write on the blackboard, it would be lowered to accommodate his small size. In all the subjects that S. N. C. Okonkwo taught – dictation, reading, writing, history, geography, arithmetic, abridged biographies, hygiene, religious knowledge, and nature study – Chinua scored the highest marks. It was only in handiwork that he performed poorly, which Okonkwo attributes to his age. Okonkwo recollects that if he awarded the boy only eight marks out of ten in any of the other subjects, he would cry throughout the day. He expected Achebe to go on to study mathematics at university, since he demonstrated such sound logic in arriving at his answers.[15]

Chinua was not very sporty in primary school, although during break he could be found kicking a ball around on his own. In class, he would often burst into laughter when the older boys made mistakes. This sometimes elicited their displeasure. Other pupils were displeased when he did not allow them to copy from his answer books; they threatened to beat him up later, but he normally gained the protection of the teacher. Augustine Agogbua recalls that sometimes pupils would go to Chinua to seek clarification; they regarded him as their second teacher and affectionately abbreviated his name to Alba. Achebe confesses that his admirers nicknamed him 'Dictionary'. He was expected to take the first position in class and Okonkwo cannot recollect any other pupil getting the better of him. His sister Zinobia confirms that while other pupils wondered what would happen to them after the examination, nobody doubted that Chinua Achebe would be successful. According to Okonkwo, the only competitor Chinua had in his class was Aaron Ifekwunigwe from Nando, who later became a consultant physician, although there were other bright pupils like Dennis Okongwu, who one day would be a solicitor-general. Interestingly, Achebe never featured on the list of school offenders, nor was he outstanding in public affairs. The constant fact was that his academic performance usually gave the indication that any class in which he found himself was too low for his academic level. Headmaster Okongwu did not encourage very young pupils to be given double promotion, though he made concessions for the older boys in the school.

A major school event at that time was the Empire Day celebrations on 24 May, the birthday of Queen Victoria. The celebrations took place at the provincial headquarters, and for pupils in Ogidi that was at Onitsha, about seven miles away. On such days, Achebe explains, 'School children from all over the district would march in contingents past the British Resident, who stood on a dais wearing a white ceremonial uniform with white gloves, plumed helmet and sword.' The day's events usually ended with a sports competition among the schools. In 1940, when Chinua Achebe was in Standard Three, his parents judged him old enough to make the trip to Onitsha and back.

> I did it [the journey to Onitsha] all right but could hardly get up for one week afterwards. And yet it was a journey I had looked forward to so eagerly and which I cherished for years. Onitsha was a magical place and did live up to its reputation. First of all, to look down from a high point on the road at dawn and see, four miles away, the river Niger glimmering in the sky took a child's breath away. So the river was really there! After a journey of two thousand, six hundred miles from Futa Jalon Mountains, as every school boy would tell you. Well, perhaps not every one. I was particularly fortunate in having parents who believed passionately in education, in having old school books that three older brothers and an older sister had read and moved on from.

That day's adventure left Chinua with two distinct memories. The first locates notions of freedom and folly in the scaled-down setting of childhood.

> Cut free from my village moorings and let loose in a big city with money in my pocket, I let myself go, go so far, in fact, as to consume a half-penny worth of groundnuts. For a couple of years afterwards the very mention of groundnuts turned my stomach.

15

Fortunately, Achebe assures us,

> my other memory is much happier. I saw with my own eyes a man who was as legendary as Onitsha itself, an eccentric Englishman, Dr J. M. Stuart Young, who had been living and trading in Onitsha since the beginning of the twentieth century. I saw him walking down New Market Road bareheaded in the sun, just as legend said he would be. The other thing legend said about Stuart Young was that he had been befriended by the mermaid of the River Niger with whom he had made a pact to remain single in return for great riches. Later I was to learn that J. M. Stuart Young's story contained a few doubtful details such as whether or not he did have a doctorate degree. But it was certain that he had first come to Nigeria (after residing in Conakry and Liberia) and then turned merchant, intent on challenging, with African support, the monopoly of European commercial cartels.[16]

This white man also wrote and published poetry and fiction, while acting as the moving spirit of the Onitsha Literary Club formed by a future president of Nigeria, Nnamdi Azikiwe, and his colleagues. Stuart Young encouraged them and was instrumental in the flowering of Azikiwe and Dennis Osadebay as poets. The sight of this man at Onitsha registered in Chinua Achebe's mind with enduring power.

Some of the books used in the Central School, Akpakaogwe Ogidi at that time include *New Method Reader, Shilling Arithmetic,* an informative work entitled *Commonsense* and the popular *Azu Ndu.* Most of these books were read by Frank, John, Zinobia and Augustine, for it was the practice in most families for the older children to pass on to the younger ones their discarded books. In the home of the Achebes, Chinua found several other useful and captivating books. He remembers

> A Midsummer Night's Dream in an advanced stage of falling apart. I think it must have been a prose adaptation, simplified and illustrated. I don't remember whether I made anything of it. Except the title. I couldn't get over the strange beauty of it. A Midsummer Night's Dream. It was a magic phrase – an incantation that conjured up scenes and landscapes of an alien, happy and unattainable land. I remember also my mother's *Ije Onye Kraist* which must have been an Igbo adaptation of *Pilgrim's Progress.* It could not have been the whole book, it was too thin. But it had some frightening pictures. I recall in particular a most vivid impression of the valley of the shadow of death. I thought a lot about death in those days.

John Bunyan was not the only author on hand to gratify this taste for the macabre. Achebe adds that there

> was another little book which frightened and fascinated me. It had drawings of different parts of the human body. But I was primarily interested in what my elder sister told me was the human heart. Since there is a slight confusion in Igbo between heart and soul I took it that that strange thing looking almost like my mother's iron cooking pot turned upside down was the very thing that flew out when a man died and perched on the head of the coffin on the way to the cemetery.

A part of what he read could be transformed by his own vivid, if inappropriate expectations; the rest he had to swallow whole.

> The kind of taste I acquired from the chaotic literature in my father's house can well be imagined. For instance, I became very fond of those aspects of ecclesiastical history as could be garnered from *The West African Churchman's Pamphlet* – a little terror of a booklet prescribing interminable Bible readings morning and night. It had the date

of consecration for practically every Anglican bishop who ever served in West Africa; and even more intriguing, the dates of their deaths. Many of them didn't last very long. I remember one pathetic case (I forget his name) who arrived in Lagos straight from his consecration at St Paul's Cathedral and was dead within days, and his wife a week or two after him. Those were the days when West Africa was truly the white man's grave, when those great lines were written of which I was at that time unaware: 'Bight of Benin! Bight of Benin! Where few come out though many go in!' But the most fascinating information I got from *Pamphlet,* as we called it, was the cryptic entry: *Augustine, Bishop of Hippo, died 430.* It had that elusive and tantalizing unfamiliarity that I always found moving.[17]

For some books in the house Chinua found uses that went beyond literary interpretation. 'There was one Arithmetic book I smuggled out and sold for half-a-penny which I needed to buy the tasty *mai-mai* some temptress of a woman sold in the little market outside the school.' Such little markets usually spring up in the vicinity of schools and Chinua was by no means the first nor the last child to be tempted, to fall, and to face the consequences.

> I was found out and my mother who had never had cause till then to doubt my honesty – laziness, yes, but not theft – received a huge shock. Of course she redeemed the book. I was so ashamed when she brought it home![18]

Fortunately, this kind of incident did not occur again. It would have been against the principles of headmaster Okongwu, who insisted on honesty, and it would also have affected the subsequent behaviour and attitude of the young Chinua Achebe. The Headmaster and his teachers were ever vigilant for misdemeanours concerning either moral or academic issues at the Central School. The deputy headmaster of the school, Walter Anionwu, was another strict teacher. He flogged the pupils excessively; it was said that he had even flogged masquerades. There was the band master, Akudo Bosah, who was an excellent cornet player. But there was also one teacher, a native of Achi named David Ike, who had the reputation of a jester. Sometimes he would play a prank that caused consternation, and then feign innocence.

The characters that flitted across the horizon of Chinua Achebe in those days included both teachers and prominent villagers, among whom he noticed especially those considered to be social deviants. At that time there was a woman in Ogidi known as Ifesoluonye who acted in a masculine manner, dressing like and associating with men. She had built a house and even married some other women. There was also a madman known as Umejiofu Achebe, though he was not related to the Achebes of Ikenga, hailing instead from Obodokwe village. Tall, slim and dark, Umejiofu was a good teacher whose last teaching post before his madness became apparent had been at Orlu. He was not violent, which made people regard him as a victim of *Oke Agwu* – possession by spirits. He had a mania for tidying things up and sometimes he took upon himself the task of tidying the stream. If anyone was unlucky enough to meet him there, that person would be flogged. Umejiofu attended church regularly, and Achebe recalls that when there was a passage to read he would be the first to find it. A priest named Anyaegbunam once gave him a cast-off shirt as a present but Umejiofu returned it with the comment: 'I have told you that I do not wear any shirt that someone else has used.' Once in a while, Umejiofu would go to the Central School, Akpakaogwe and insist on teaching the pupils. He once gathered the pupils in Chinua Achebe's class to talk to them about the geography of Ogidi. He talked about the villages of Ogidi and the pupils were amused, because geography in those days was about England, America and Asia. Then there was Jolly Ben, the madman who spoke English. Sometimes, when he was tired, he would shout: 'It is no longer the type of madness visited on Jolly Ben that is disturbing him.'[19] Chinua Achebe used the name in one of his short stories. There was also Mekao, who promised not to insult anyone who gave him presents and popularized the saying 'Madness is sweet but the constant walking is troublesome.' These sane and insane characters, these male and female participants in the affairs of the community, each with his or her own peculiarities, flitted across the scene as Chinua was growing.

In these years his academic work in the primary school was consistently excellent, and he participated in most village activities – though not in masquerading, for he was not initiated into the cult as a result of his religious background. At the beginning of his Standard Four year, several changes took place at the Central School, Akpakaogwe, Ogidi. S. N. C. Okonkwo could not continue teaching him in the upper class, while Headmaster Okongwu was transferred to Aba and replaced by Mr Anyiwo. It was not long before Headmaster Anyiwo noticed the brilliant Albert Chinua Achebe. He sought audience with Isaiah Achebe and told him: 'That son of yours is very brilliant. You should carry money with a wheelbarrow in order to train him because his education will not end in this country.' It was not the first time that Chinua's father had heard such comments, nor was it to be the last.

It was becoming quite difficult for retired catechist Isaiah Achebe to educate the children, although clearly he was convinced that education was essential and relevant. Fortunately the older children had completed their education at the higher institutions available in Nigeria at that time. Frank, who had qualified as an engineer, commenced work with the Post and Telecommunications. John, the second son, before continuing his education in England, was trained at Awka, the same teacher training college his father attended, then posted to Nekede near Owerri as a pivotal (not fully certified) teacher. It was at that stage that John first offered to take Chinua Achebe to live with him. Surprisingly, the greatest opposition came from Headmaster Anyiwo, who objected that Chinua was the type of student who made him proud of the school. The father did not overrule Anyiwo, for he too was reluctant and it was clear that he had a soft spot for his last son. Perhaps it was this love that gave one of Chinua Achebe's contemporaries, Akunwata Ugoka, the notion that he was pampered. All the older boys had been allowed to live with family friends at various times. Frank had lived with Rev. Onubuogu, John had lived with Mr Ikeogu from Obosi, while Augustine lived with Frank soon after he started work. It was perhaps through the presentation of these facts that John in the end persuaded his father to allow Chinua to live with him at Nekede.

Thus Chinua Achebe proceeded in late 1942 to the town of Nekede, about four kilometres from Owerri, to live with John Achebe, a teacher at the Central School serving the towns of Nekede and Ihiagwa. He helped his brother with the cooking, a skill he had learned at home and which suggests that he was not all that pampered. Nekede in those days was also a centre of conflicting cultures and Chinua was able to observe shades of difference between Igbo cultures and to learn more about landmark events of the early twentieth century in that part of Igboland. There was the chieftaincy tussle in Nekede at the death of Chief

Nkwazema in 1928, which led to what the historian Felix Ekechi calls 'the home rule movement'[20] with its insistence on the appointment of chiefs by each village or even by each kin group. In effect the son of Chief Nkwazema, later known as Chief Oke, literally became one chief among the many chiefs who sat at Oja court. These conflicts, which occurred not only in Nekede but also in many of the other towns of Igboland, clearly impinged on the more focused formative experiences of Chinua Achebe at this time.

The notoriety of the former district commissioner H. M. Douglas at Owerri, who was noted for road building and dictatorial administration, must also have filtered into the awareness of the young new pupil at Nekede Central School. Although clearly the intentions of H. M. Douglas were reasonable in terms of road construction – the major road in Owerri town still bears his name – the brutal manner in which he implemented the programme created alienation bordering on hostility. Douglas possessed a violent temper and demonstrated his overbearing approach in the seizure and deportation of chiefs like Njemanze who were unwilling to send men for road construction. Njemanze later returned, becoming so pliant to the wishes of the District Commissioner that he almost alienated himself from his people. The dictatorial and oppressive administration of Douglas is said to have led to the killing of Dr Stewart, mistaken for the disliked man, at Mbaise. Thus the train of events that culminated in the devastation of Ahiara, Mbaise by a colonial military expedition had its roots in the high degree of hostility towards European imperialism epitomized by Douglas. These events were still fresh at the time that Chinua Achebe attended the Nekede Central School.

But major public controversies were not the only aspect of life that affected the young boy at Nekede. A neighbour of John Achebe's, and the teacher of his younger brother at Nekede at this time, was Mr Obiakonwa from Nneobi. 'Obi Nekede' recollects that the town was a good place, well stocked with yams and wine, for the young male teachers of Central School.[21] It was at Nekede that Chinua became aware of the fascinating *Mbari* art. Ihiagwa town, which has a common boundary with Nekede, was a well-known centre of *Mbari*, which is the formal creation of art works as sacrifices to the gods. Thus Chinua Achebe was able to learn about the conditions of *Mbari* production, which commences at the instigation of the priest of the earth goddess, *Ala,* or the priest of *Amadioha,* the god of thunder. *Mbari* art is aimed at either appeasing the gods or seeking their protection. The participants are assembled through the democratic process of inviting one male and one female member of each kindred family. The gathered group commences work communally, first erecting the building and then proceeding to fill it with all types of sculptures. Chinua Achebe aptly describes it thus:

> Architecturally, it was a simple structure, a stage formed by three high walls supporting a peaked roof; but in place of a flat door you had a deck of steps running from one side wall to the other and rising almost to the roof at the back wall. This auditorium was then filled to the brim with sculptures in moulded earth and clay, and the walls with murals in white, black, yellow and green. The sculptures were arranged carefully on the steps. At the centre of the front row sat the earth goddess herself, a child on her left knee and a raised sword in her right hand. She is mother and judge. To her right and left, other deities took their places. Human figures, animals (perhaps a leopard dragging along the carcass of a goat), figures from folklore, history, or pure

imagination; forest scenes, scenes of village and domestic life, everyday events, abnormal scandals; set pieces from past displays of *Mbari*, new images that had never been depicted before – everything jostled together for space in that extraordinary convocation of the entire kingdom of human experience and imagination.

When the task is complete all the villagers assemble for celebration and merriment as they admire or criticize the works produced. Each of these sculptures possesses either social, religious or cultural values, extolling or condemning reality. According to Achebe,

> when Europe made its appearance in Igbo society out of travellers' tales into the concrete and alarming shape of the District Officer, the artists immediately gave him a seat among the moulded figures of *Mbari*, complete with his peaked helmet and pipe. Sometimes, they even made room for his bicycle and his native police orderly.[22]

Interestingly, all new phenomena – colonial officers, animals, motor-cars and abnormal acts – are depicted in the *Mbari* house, and thus the art is used to provide outlets not only for aesthetics but also for emotions. The idea is that anything new and powerful which appears on the horizon is brought in and domesticated in the *Mbari* house. We have noted the case of the local man whose brief career as a policeman at the beginning of the century had left a powerful enough legend for him to be represented in his uniform in a distant *Mbari* house and called simply Ogidi.[23]

Thus it was not only academic work that made an impression on Albert Chinua Achebe – but Obiakonwa remembers him as quiet and unobtrusive at this stage; he was developing like a stream which in its quiet meander down the hill murmurs to the conscience, dances round the rocks and pushes the pebbles gently down the slope.

3

The Ogidi Boy
Government College
1944–7

E A C H individual absorbs from the environment those social and cultural features that suit his nature as he grows and these elements are reflected in various ways in later life. Albert Chinua Achebe's responsiveness to the pulse of life as he passed through the primary schools at Ogidi and Nekede near Owerri is demonstrated in the many incidents and characters he recalls from that period, among them

> a half-mad minstrel called Okoli Ukpor whom I remember with the memory of childhood. If you went to Onitsha in those days and did not run into Okoli your visit was somehow incomplete. He played for money on his flute, whistling and blowing his instrument alternately: 'Man and woman, whoever holds money, let him bring!' Clearly not much of a lyric, but how appropriate to his day!

Achebe adds that

> occasionally he would raise an additional laugh and an additional half-penny by blowing each nostril in turn into the open drain – in time with his beat. Rumour had it that Okoli was as sober as the next man, that he had two wives and a barn full of yams in his hinterland home and only came down to Onitsha during the slack moments on the farm to raise quick cash from amused charity by pretending to be light-headed.[1]

It was only natural that characters like Okoli Ukpor could be seen at Onitsha, within its complex web of the mundane, the religious and the mysterious.

On his way to St Philip's Central School, Akpakaogwe, and on his travels from Ogidi to Nekede Central School, Chinua became familiar with the passenger lorries and mammy-wagons that ply the roads:

> Anyone who is familiar with Nigeria knows about the passenger Lorries or *Mammy-wagons,* and of the legends for which they are famed. Sometimes the inscriptions are self-explanatory, for example: They say, let them say; Salutation is not love; No Telephone to Heaven, etc. But once in a while you do come across a truly esoteric legend. On my way to and from school at the end of the Second World War, I used to see a Lorry with such a name; just one word: WAHEHE. Had it anything to do with laughter, I wondered. But its inscrutable name notwithstanding, WAHEHE was a most popular Lorry on the Enugu–Onitsha road. Whenever it came along children greeted it with loud cries of WAHEHE! WAHEHE![2]

Twenty years later Achebe found an explanation of that cryptic legend when he visited East Africa and discovered that Wahehe is the name of an ethnic group, but to the boy Chinua it was enough that the word was exotic and thrillingly alliterative.

A third memory concerns the strangers from another part of Igboland who came for the first time

> to our village during the planting season to work for the villagers for so much money and three meals a day. One day one of these strangers came to plant my mother's coco-yams. At the end of the day he received his pay, ate his last meal, and left. About two or three weeks later the coco-yams began to sprout and the whole village saw what this man had done. When he had got tired of planting he had simply dug a big hole in the ground and buried a whole basket of coco-yams there. Of course by the time his crime was discovered he had left the village and was not likely to come back.[3]

There is no doubt that this disgraceful deception had a wider dimension for Achebe, who recounted it to illustrate the argument that such crimes became possible when societies that were once strangers began to mix. All these incidents reveal, along with aspects of his nature and temperament, his powers of observation and critical response to social and cultural events as he prepared to enter secondary school.

He took entrance examinations to both the Dennis Memorial Grammar School, Onitsha and Government College, Umuahia. Unsurprisingly, he gained entrance to both prestigious schools, which made him a celebrity in Ogidi. Senior teachers came to Isaiah Achebe's house to offer congratulations. The problem then arose as to which school he should attend. The principal of the Dennis Memorial Grammar School (DMGS), Onitsha, a Mr Clarke, was keen that Chinua should attend his school because of his academic abilities and because his older brothers had also attended that school: the brilliant performance of Frank Okwuofu at DMGS was still fresh in Clarke's mind. The controversy was laid to rest when John Achebe told Clarke that Chinua would go to Umuahia, leaving the man to feel offended that the boy would be the only son of Isaiah and Janet Achebe to go to a different school. It is to the credit of John Achebe that he pointed out the benefits of attending a school that was free of missionary control and also destined to establish a reputation as one of the best colleges in Eastern Nigeria.

Other fundamental decisions in the Isaiah Achebe family were taken at this time. Frank and John Achebe, the older brothers, decided to help their father formally with the education of the younger children. Frank undertook the training of Augustine, while John took over the training of Chinua, officially becoming his guardian as he proceeded to Government College, Umuahia in early 1944. The college had come into existence through the enterprise of Robert Fisher, an Englishman. Fisher was transferred to the Education Department in Nigeria and posted to establish the Government College, Umuahia in 1928. Achebe confirms that 'the crest Fisher brought to Umuahia was a pair of torches, one black and one white, shining together silently. It was a generation later that the Australian teacher Charles Low added the words: *In Unum Lucent* as the motto of the college.' Fisher committed both vision and passion to creating the new college for 'when he was offered a bishopric in the course of his labour he turned it down'. Achebe said that 'he made efforts to make light of that decision' in later years by saying that 'he would not have made a good bishop',[4] but clearly

22

his dedication to duty and his pioneering role elicited that selfless decision. Fisher obviously utilized his own experience of an educational background that encompassed Marlborough College, Pembroke College at Cambridge University and Wells Theological College to introduce those traditions that transformed the college at Umuahia into one of the best institutions of its time in Nigeria. He cleared acres of jungle to build the school and established enduring traditions: many of the students he taught in the early years obtained higher qualifications and later became significant educationists in various parts of the country. At the time that Chinua Achebe sat and passed the entrance examination Robert Fisher had ceased to be the principal, but the spirit with which he endowed the institution was still alive.

The principal who carried on the tradition of Robert Fisher in 1944 was named Hicks; he was said to have fought in Burma or India, but was a gentle and kindly soul with halting speech. He continued Fisher's emphasis on careful selection of qualified boys for admission and academic excellence. About 3,000 boys usually applied for the 30 places available and sat the entrance examination at centres throughout Nigeria and the Western Cameroons, then a British protectorate. The entire staff worked diligently to produce a short-list of about 200 boys, of whom 130 were invited for an interview at the expense of the college. The interview also enabled the school authorities to check that they were the boys who had sat for the examination. There was no doubt that Government College was élitist in those days, but Achebe assures us that it was 'élitism based on the foundation of academic excellence' which did not take into consideration the material possessions of the parents of the boys who were offered admission. Many of the boys were brilliant as well as being the children of peasants and petty traders. There was the classic case of a boy from the Cameroons 'who walked all the way from Bamenda to Umuahia in order to take up his place in the college'.

Chinua Achebe's entrance into Government College, Umuahia was thus a considerable achievement. The letter of invitation from the principal asked him to please acknowledge receipt', which he took to be no more than 'a fancy way of ending letters'. When he got there the principal's welcome was: 'Oh yes, Achebe. Why did you not reply?' When Achebe answered that he did not know that he was expected to send a reply, the man brought out a copy of the letter. 'Please acknowledge receipt – what does it mean?'[5] The new recruit had no idea what it meant, but that initial confusion was soon overcome. The influence of the college environment became obvious the moment he set foot on the path close to the exquisitely trimmed quadrangle and the immaculate black-and-white administration building. The rows of red-roofed dormitories, the beautiful green lawns and the magnificent buildings were an intoxicating sight for new students like Chike Momah, who was admitted in 1944 along with Chinua Achebe.

Chike Momah had also benefited from the discipline and inspiration of Headmaster Okongwu, who had left Chinua Achebe's Central School, Akpakaogwe Ogidi and proceeded to St Michael's School, Aba, establishing there too the reputation of a strict and dedicated teacher. A week after he took over the school, Okongwu caned all the pupils. Chike Momah said that he had told them on the opening day: 'The first law in heaven is obedience and order; that is how it is going to be in St Michael's School, Aba!' Okongwu exhibited many of the characteristics he had displayed at Ogidi and he was even stricter with those pupils who were close to him, especially his relatives, which made it hard for Chike Momah who was from Okongwu's home town of Nnewi. If the headmaster was caning the pupils in the school and he encountered anybody he knew well, he would increase the number of strokes. In addition, he usually caned any pupil whose mother had made a report concerning a misdemeanour at home after calling out the pupil publicly and condemning their behaviour. Momah said that 'if the tears refused to come out in the process of punishing the offender, Okongwu would continue caning until they appeared'.

Headmaster Okongwu was as inspiring as he was severe, however, and attached great importance to his pupils passing entrance examinations into the famous secondary schools. Chike Momah recalls that in the year 1942 not one of the Standard Six boys at St Michael's School, Aba was successful in the entrance examination into Government College, Umuahia. Bitterly disappointed, Okongwu caned the whole class, girls as well as boys, and Momah adds that 'it did not bother the headmaster that the school had done well in all other entrance examinations. He regarded it as a matter of the school's prestige because the College at Umuahia was unique then.' This dramatic reaction made the next class determined to impress the headmaster and they did well enough, with three passes, to please Okongwu.

There was no doubt that Headmaster Okongwu was a remarkable man and his legend took on a life of its own at his death. Before the 1943 class at St Michael's School, Aba, sat that significant entrance examination, he told them of a boy at Ogidi whom he had left in Standard Three, three years earlier. He declared that any of the St Michael's boys who had the luck to pass the examination would meet that boy in Umuahia, where the boy would 'make the rain that would drench them'. This aphorism, which originated from the Igbo philosophy that rain could be instigated, was familiar to the boys: it meant that the 'Ogidi boy' would perform so brilliantly that his success would 'drench them with shame'.[6] On the day that Okongwu brought Chike Momah a cablegram informing him that he had gained a scholarship pass in the entrance examination, he also informed Chike that the Ogidi boy, Chinua Achebe, had passed too. The prediction of Okongwu was fulfilled, for Achebe was promoted from Class One to Class Two in his first year at Government College, Umuahia, which meant that he had double promotion and spent only four years in secondary school, not the usual five. Achebe's achievement had begun to fulfil the expectations of his primary school teacher at Ogidi, S. N. C. Okonkwo, and the prophecy of Headmaster Anyiwo.

When Chinua Achebe was in the second-year class at Umuahia – though the year was still 1944 – the government in Britain decided that a university should be established in West Africa. Achebe recalls that 'a high-powered Commission under Walter Elliot was sent to survey the territory and the situation on the ground'. At this time the reputation of Government College had grown so fast that the commission paid the college a visit and spent a weekend there. Most of the commission's members, according to Achebe, came to the chapel service on Sunday morning, 'but one of its members, the famous Julian Huxley, the biologist, roamed the extensive grounds of the college watching birds with binoculars'.[7] It was this Elliot Commission Report that led to the establishment in 1948 of Nigeria's first university institution at Ibadan, which was not autonomous but functioned as a university college in a special relationship with the

University of London. Chinua Achebe did not know then that he would be one of its pioneer students.

Meanwhile in the new Class Two, where he found himself in the company of five other boys who had also earned double promotion, Achebe performed brilliantly to take the first position. 'I thought my brother was good,' is Chike Momah's emphatic verdict, 'until he entered Achebe's class!' That elder brother was Godwin Momah, who had spent a year in Government College before the entrance of Chike Momah and Chinua Achebe in 1944. Achebe's immediate success was the result both of natural intelligence and of his willingness to respond to the organized college life. The boys thrived in an improved quality of physical environment, with essential academic resources at their disposal. They enjoyed good food and were supplied on the first day of every term with at least one shirt and one pair of shorts. Chike Momah asserted that

> returning to the school meant for many of us a return to a more agreeable physical environment and to a vastly improved diet. This is not in any way to suggest that mother's cooking was not, then as now, the best in the world. Rather it is an indication that at Umuahia we had a more balanced diet than most parents could have given us.

This awareness of the value of food was reflected in the principal's idea of grouping boys in the dining hall according to their eating ability, in order to reduce food wastage. Thus good eaters like Christopher Okigbo, who entered Class One in Achebe's second year (by which time the latter was in Class Three as a result of the double promotion), were given more food than their neighbours. Okigbo, in spite of his slim build and small stature, had a great appetite for beans and rice, but Chike Momah insists that 'the food hardly improved his wiry nature'.[8] This experiment in graded eating was discarded after a while, but the organized life of the college remained constant and the rhythm of life had a military tempo. The students were usually woken up at 6 a.m. and they followed the daily programme of morning bath, breakfast, morning assembly, classes, lunch, a period of compulsory rest in the dormitory, an hour of supervised study and homework, housework consisting in most cases of grass cutting, sports and games, evening bath, evening meal, and finally a period of recreation in which the boys engaged in whatever took their fancy until bedtime. This room for self-directed recreation led to the establishment of various clubs for the students. The daily order of activities never varied but it included elements that helped the boys to achieve a measure of self-fulfilment.

This regime was altered by the arrival of William Simpson, the principal who replaced Hicks in late 1944. Simpson was a Cambridge graduate who spent about 26 years in the colonial service in Nigeria and eight of those years as principal of Government College, Umuahia. His mere appearance was momentous: he was a man of considerable bulk and it was not long before he was given the nickname 'Dewar', after a large flask that was popular in those days and resembled the shape of Simpson's belly. Chukwuemeka Ike, who entered Government College in 1945, remembers that boys 'often found one excuse or another to make Simpson pronounce *amabunt* during the Latin class for the fun of watching his pot belly nod as he laid the stress on *bunt*!' But Simpson was a dedicated and committed principal who improved the already high standards and traditions of the Umuahia Government College. He thought highly enough of his charges to know the name of every boy, yet his sense of propriety, Ike tells us, made him rebuke a boy who had spoken contemptuously of one of the nightsoilmen who worked in the school: 'Everybody has his job. And that pail carrier is as important here as I am.'[9] The importance that Simpson attached to the affairs of the school, and his willingness to lead by example, was reflected in a fetish for punctuality. On some days members of staff and students would see him running to class, a practical exhibition that made a great impression on them. Chike Momah recalls that he thoroughly disapproved of ostentation and loud colours, restricting the boys 'to the simplest clothes and shoes, morning or night!'

Simpson managed to synthesize sports and academic work. His stress on the spirit of sportsmanship made him sanction only sports competitions between Umuahia and schools that had demonstrated a true regard for this spirit. Not everyone coped equally well with this emphasis on games. A boy named Gregory is said to have 'played football but … in his six years he never seemed to come to terms with the direction of play, and was as likely to score a goal against his own side as against his opponents'. Chike Momah teasingly recollects that he was never sure if his friend Chinua Achebe knew the right end of a cricket bat: Achebe, he reports, was not very good at games.[10] Fortunately, William Simpson was interested in brilliant academic performances as well as in the social and sporting life of his students. It was this social concern that led him, in about 1949, to arrange several meetings between the final-year students of Government College and the nearby Women's Training College at Old Umuahia, in the hope that they would get used to female company – as was recommended by the old boys of the college who had gone 'into the world'. According to Chukwuemeka Ike, one old boy who gained admission to the University College, Ibadan, 'was so bewildered when a girl called to see him in his campus room that he handed her his book of mathematical tables and fled from the room!'[11] It was a mark of his dedication that Simpson made practical efforts to prepare his students for every challenge they would meet after leaving school.

It was the introduction of what became known as the Simpson Text-book Act that made the most indelible mark on his students. The Act stated simply: 'During games times, that is, from five to six o'clock, nobody may be under a roof, nobody may read a text-book. If you are not put down for games, go on a stroll with a friend, chat, discuss. Or make your companion read a good book – a novel, a book of poems or essays. Sit in the shade and pass a pleasant hour.'[12] Furthermore, on three days of the week the reading of any text-book after classes was prohibited. Achebe recollects that 'under this draconian law we could read fiction or biographies or magazines like the *Illustrated London News* or write letters or play ping-pong or just sit about, but not open a text-book, on pain of detention. And we had a wonderful library from Robert Fisher's days to support Mr Simpson's Text-book Act.'[13] The impact of the Simpson method is best illustrated by the statistics provided by Chukwuemeka Ike: throughout his tenure of office as principal, only one boy failed the school certificate examination, passing it at the second attempt, while at the same time the college shone in the area of sports.[14]

There is no doubt that Chinua Achebe benefited from the Simpson method, although he was not noted for sports. He certainly played cricket, but he also utilized the Text-book Act to get acquainted with the numerous books in the impressive college library, 'walking into a long room with incredibly neat book shelves' and reflecting that he had never seen 'so many books in my life'.[15] It was there that he found and read his first book by an American, Booker T. Washington's *Up From Slavery*. He found it sad, but it showed him another dimension of reality; other books also aroused his imagination. His excitement at this world of books was not surprising: the signs that his imagination responded to stories and that he was becoming interested in books had been clear in the primary school. Chinua Achebe's world of stories widened at the Government College, Umuahia where he now read by the dozen books such as *Treasure Island, Gulliver's Travels, The Prisoner of Zenda, Oliver Twist, David Copperfield* and *Tom Brown's Schooldays*. At the same time he encountered classics of colonialism such as H. Rider Haggard's *She* and *Alan Quatermain*, and John Buchan's *Prester John*. At this time Achebe was still uncritical in his reading and he 'often took sides with the white characters against the savages'. He explains it thus:

> I did not see myself as an African to begin with. I took sides with the whitemen against the savages. In other words I went through my first level of schooling thinking I was of the party of the white man in his hair-raising adventures and narrow escapes. The white man was good and reasonable and intelligent and courageous. The savages arrayed against him were sinister and stupid or, at the most, cunning. I hated their guts.[16]

Achebe looks back on his encounter with literary works in this period of his schooling as innocent, although they 'can be used to put you in the wrong crowd, in the party of the man who has come to dispossess you'. But as he confesses, 'it all added up to a wonderful preparation for the day we would be old enough to read between the lines and ask questions'.

It was not long before William Simpson singled out Chinua Achebe as one of his most promising students. He wrote a letter to Chinua's guardian, John Achebe, who was still teaching at Nekede, inviting him to Government College. John was surprised to receive the invitation: when principals wrote letters it invariably meant that one's ward or child had been involved in an infringement of the school's regulations, and that there was need for drastic action. When he arrived, however, Simpson greeted him with more welcome news: 'I have watched your ward Albert Chinua Achebe and I am impressed by him, not only by his learning but also by his character. There is a scholarship for Owerri Division and since you live at Owerri and pay your taxes there, I see no reason why you cannot benefit from the scholarship. I am putting his name forward as one of the candidates to be considered.'[17] It was that decision by Simpson which led to the award of a scholarship to Chinua Achebe, who thus set an enviable record of not only passing through Classes One and Two in the course of 1944, but also getting a scholarship in the same year.

Achebe's pleasing performance was the result of his personal efforts, but many of his teachers at the college made significant contributions. There was Adrian P. L. Slater, who taught a course in logic by emphasizing the scientific methods of observation, recording, making hypotheses and experimentation. Although Slater would complain that he was 'sick and tired of African stupidity' and make derisive references to the idea of 'renascent Africa', he managed to inculcate in his students the habits of writing correct English and developing the power of analysis. He never made any concessions to their level of proficiency in standard English and often insisted: 'That isn't right; I'm not going to allow you write it!' He also wrote on the blackboard phrases that the students must not use, such as 'I voiced out', and 'I witnessed a football match'.[18] Slater was very strict, instilling discipline by the harsh use of a wooden ruler on the knuckles, a form of chastisement he called the 'love tap'. Chike Momah describes Slater's extremely severe marking system of 'deducting one point for any grammatical or spelling error. The result was that a boy might score 30 marks out of 50 for an essay' which Slater considered excellent, but then 'lose 35 points for specific errors in the text. The outcome: minus five out of 50 marks!' Slater's harsh marking system achieved the status of myth: he was said to have been involved in the marking of the Cambridge School Certificate examination and the boys had nothing but pity for any school whose English papers were marked by him. 'Failure in English meant automatic failure in the whole examination', as Momah recalls, 'but the Umuahia boys were consoled by the fact that since Slater was a teacher in their school he would never be required to mark their papers.'[19] Slater added to this myth by telling the boys that he would not like to mark the scripts of Government College, Umuahia. When one school registered zero per cent, remembers Momah, they blamed it on Slater. Despite being such a stickler, A. P. L. Slater laid great emphasis on the reading and analysis of novels. Every week he would read one chapter of the novel *Pinocchio* and declare: 'Tonight, summarize the part I read.'[20] The resulting essay he marked as ruthlessly as ever. He also asked students to read about a dozen novels on their own every term.

Slater was not the only one who taught Chinua Achebe English. He was also taught by Charles Low, an Australian who was not only a keen sportsman (he taught cricket) but also a poet and playwright. Charles Low had read Latin and Greek at Melbourne and Oxford universities, and he also possessed a prodigious memory. Chinua was impressed that this man knew *Paradise Lost* practically by heart. The remarkable Charles Low amazed students who observed the speed with which he read books. Whenever it was his turn to supervise 'prep', Momah and the other boys would 'watch him leaf rapidly through whatever book had taken his fancy from the library's shelves'. It was incredible to the boys that he was actually reading those books and not just 'flipping the pages idly because the speed at which he did so excited their wonder'.[21] Part of this man's legend, as Chike Momah tells it, was that he read novels like *The Prisoner of Zenda* in a single hour-long 'prep' period. In class, Chinua Achebe found Charles Low an inspiring as well as eccentric man:

> Low was totally unstructured. He would come into the class without any ideas as to what you were going to do that day. He would start something and then he would wander off and talk for about forty minutes. And he would say, 'That's an important digression!' Now most of what he did was a digression, but it was fantastic.[22]

There was no doubt that Achebe found Low an effective teacher as well as an an 'inspirer' who edited the school magazine with the Ogidi boy as his assistant. Chukwuemeka Ike, who was in Christopher Okigbo's class, confirms that Charles Low inspired many of the boys. At the time he came to Umuahia, Low was writing a play about the Cameroons, where he had worked before coming to Nigeria. He would come into the class and assign the students the task of 'moving the play on which he was working a little further'.[23] Sometimes the students would discuss Low's work with him. Low also encouraged them to write poetry and to read and appreciate other poets. One of Low's best-remembered works was a poem about the social gathering Simpson organized between the senior boys of Government College and the students of the Women's Training College. Ike reports that the 'teachers laboured gallantly to prepare the students for this first official encounter with the female sex' on the evening that inspired Charles Low's poem, 'The WTC Are Here'. With due apology to his classmate and friend C. W. Egbuchulam, Ike quotes the few lines that stuck in his memory:

> Alone in the corner Egbuchulam glowers
> Regretting how Oliphant's wasted his hours.
> You don't learn from Durrell how to say it with flowers
> The WTC are here![24]

The presentation of this poem to the students the next day was like a miracle, especially as they were seeing their experience of the previous day emerging in the form of a poem. In addition to writing poetry, Charles Low produced Gilbert and Sullivan's *The Mikado* and other plays.

Although Charles Low was unequalled in terms of individual characteristics that bordered on the extraordinary, there were other teachers who contributed immensely in refining the talents of the boys brought together at Government College, Umuahia. The history teacher was Mr Ogle, who enthralled the students with his fascinating narratives of the ancient world. Chike Momah says that he 'even had a map of the world put on a wall on which he marked the advance of the allied powers on Germany as they bore down on her, for he was principally responsible for keeping the school informed on [the war's] progress'.[25]

S. O. Bisiriyu, later the well-known academic S. O. Biobaku, also taught Chinua Achebe and once remarked that he was one of his best students. The science teacher was W. E. Alagoa, who had been a student at the Government College in the time of Robert Fisher and then returned to teach there. Alagoa possessed the rare dedication of a teacher who not only opens the doors of knowledge but is also a gentle guide. He was resourceful, making extensive use of the rural environment for biology fieldwork. There were frequent excursions; the school maintained gardens and even kept fish and crocodile ponds. Alagoa was very popular: Ralph Opara, who entered Government College in 1947, remembers him as The Master.[26] His versatility, a quality shared by many other teachers in the college, was evidenced in the fact that he even taught Bible knowledge. At that time religion was free of the hypocritical emphasis which it was later accorded in Nigeria. On Sundays both the Roman Catholic and the Anglican priests would come for church services. But the college was emphasizing high academic and social standards with an embedded moral consciousness, which produced the same results as religion under normal circumstances. This moral concern was stressed by a tough and uncompromising housemaster, Mr Jumbo, who had known the school from its inception in 1929. Jumbo never punished the boys without first giving them the opportunity to explain why they should be forgiven, and Chike Momah has praise for his refreshing directness of approach, whether in anger or good humour. He once accused the boys in the college netball team of 'catching breasts instead of the ball'. The occasion was a netball match against Women's Teacher Training College and Momah recalls that 'some of the boys were rather carried away by the occasion, and did not always keep their eyes on the ball'.[27] Jumbo's influence was reflected in his creation of three school houses as the population grew; Chinua Achebe became a member of Niger House.

Other dedicated teachers included I. D. Erekosima, an outstanding mathematician in Achebe's view and, like Jumbo, a foundation student who had come back to teach. J. C. Menakaya was known as Menaks, and the boys regarded him as perfect proof that 'one does not need to have a degree in order to be the master of one's subject'. Menakaya was one of the best geography teachers around then and had the reputation of being an expert. When he finally left Umuahia for England to take a degree in geography, Momah says, the students were convinced that 'in England he might improve his knowledge of English but not geography!' G. J. Efon, who taught physics, was another popular science master, fond of mixing 'seriousness with humour in a way that was sarcastic'.[28]

Many of the teachers stressed the importance of reading and writing well and it was important for the boys to learn the English language not only for academic purposes, but also to communicate with each other. There were a large number of boys who did not speak the Igbo language of Chinua Achebe and they were 'not foreigners' as he said, but his 'fellow Nigerian youth'. He lived 'in the same dormitory with them, attended the same morning assembly and classes and in the evenings gathered in the same playing fields'. To be able to participate in all those activities together, the boys had to 'put away their different mother tongues and communicate in the language of their colonizers'.[29] This emphasis on the compulsory use of English in the college is humourously narrated by Chike Momah, whose elder brother Godwin Momah was Achebe's classmate. When they were chatting one day, Chike became aware that Godwin was not responding as he should have been; instead 'he had his arms akimbo with a very disapproving expression on his face'. He stopped talking, and only then did Godwin announce: 'I don't understand what you're saying.' Chike was puzzled. 'You don't understand?' His brother retorted: 'I don't, and as long as you continue to talk in Igbo, I won't understand you.' He was confused, but then the suspicion of what the elder brother meant dawned on him and he asked: 'You mean we're not allowed to speak Igbo here?' Certainly it was 'a dramatic way of impressing a school rule on a new student',[30] as Chike felt, but it also reflected the encompassing influence of the college regulation that could not be circumvented by the closeness of brotherhood. Achebe himself recalls that the first punishment he received at the college was for lapsing into Igbo when asking another boy to pass him the soap.

Another influence which encouraged the boys not only to speak good English but also to write well was exerted by the house magazines of the college. Each house had its magazine, which was published more often than the school magazine. It was filled with creative efforts like jokes, very short stories, letters and short essays. The students wrote it out and then had the pages cyclostyled. The school magazine, however, was printed. Ralph Opara, who was also in Niger House, confirms that Chinua Achebe was the editor of his house magazine and also of the school magazine under the guidance of Charles Low. Achebe not only edited these ephemeral publications but also contributed poems, essays and short stories. It is certain that these magazines encouraged the boys to develop their creative potential and must have played some part in the emergence of well-known Nigerian writers like Gabriel Okara, who was in the college many years before the generation of Chinua Achebe, Chukwuemeka Ike, Christopher Okigbo, I. N. C. Aniebo, Elechi Amadi and Ken Saro-Wiwa. There were equally good writers who specialized in other disciplines like Bede

Okigbo, a cousin of Christopher Okigbo who became a notable agronomist, Chu Okongwu the economist and Alexander Madiebo, an army general who wrote one of the most thrilling and captivating books on the Nigerian civil war. Creativity was flowering at the college and even embraced the football field. Chike Momah can remember the two concluding lines of a panegyric by one Oboli on the victory of the college team: 'Thanks to Onwurah our goalie/The writer of this poem is Oboli'.[31]

Although Chinua Achebe cannot recollect the circumstances under which he won a poetry prize at Government College, Umuahia, as Agnes Achebe (wife of Frank Achebe) recalls, his brilliant academic performance was unmistakable. This pleased his father, though sadly Chinua was not a regular writer of letters. John Achebe wrote to him once telling him to write more often to their father Isaiah at Ogidi, and this request reflects an astute assessment of the relationship between father and son. Chinua himself notes that on some occasions when he came home on holiday it seemed to make his father particularly happy. His holidays were not all spent at Ogidi, however, for he passed some of them with Frank Achebe and his family in Kano. Agnes Achebe says that he used to read most of the time, often holding a book in one hand while he played with the children with the other hand.

The holidays he spent at Ogidi were full of varied and exciting activities. Nearly everyone came home at Christmas and the secondary school students who were on holiday organized a number of events: football matches for the boys, netball games for the girls and town-cleaning exercises for everybody. There were also a number of church-related activities: singing with the choir, variety concerts and performances with the school band. Students usually met at four o'clock every day at St Philip's Central School, Akpakaogwe for these holiday activities. The football matches were often between Ogidi and other towns like Obosi and Ugwuoba, or between students and teachers. Chinua did not participate in these matches: he was more interested in singing and recitations. He also took part in several church activities, especially in the usual Sunday exercise of counting the number of people who attended the service. These activities inclined the elders to the view that the Umuahia College and the small number of other reputable secondary schools in existence were producing good effects on the young people of Ogidi.

These effects were primarily a result of the discipline which the schools, and particularly Government College, Umuahia, had made intrinsic to student life. Achebe also tells us that one of the masters at Government College who 'had been a Captain during the World War started a little military training for the interested students and this group provided one of the first batches of Commissioned Officers in the Nigerian Army'.[32] The recruits who were later to play significant roles in the Nigerian army included General Alexander Madiebo and Brigadier Onwuatuegwu. The dreaded Umuahia two-kilometre 'run' introduced by William Simpson was part of this emphasis on instilling discipline. This punishment was executed at a fast pace and uphill, too. If the erring student failed to do the run in the allotted time, it meant another run. Boxing was another element in the college regime. Chike Momah explains that 'any boys caught in a private fight were summoned before the housemaster, made to put on proper boxing gloves, and asked to conclude their fisticuffs in a more public arena'. He recalls one such fight between two boys, one of whom had grown up in Lagos and the other in Enugu. As they were being helped into their boxing gloves, the 'Lagos' boy was heard to say over and over again that he would show the other boy that he came from Lagos, 'the centre of boxing'. When they joined action the tables were very surprisingly turned, and it was the boy from Enugu who administered the more telling punches. The Lagos boy found himself at the receiving end of so many straight lefts, left and right crosses and devastating uppercuts that he was reduced to clinging to his adversary as often as he could.

Momah adds that eventually the Lagos boy

grew a little taller than had seemed likely in his early days in the college, and there were some cranks who expressed the thought that the numerous uppercuts he received in that fight must have been largely responsible for his upward growth![33]

Chike Momah assures us that this kind of fight happened two or three times in his first year and that he could not recollect that there were other such public settlements of private disputes. That these sanctioned fights were rare demonstrates that the college was successful in instilling disciplined behaviour.

The slightest display of petulance or defiance meant a Saturday matchet parade or the famous Umuahia run. Chike Momah notes that 'a very brilliant boy who displayed petulance was threatened with expulsion' while another boy who was 'one of the best footballers was expelled because his general conduct had been unsatisfactory'. The expulsion of this boy occurred in Class Four and despite the fact that he had achieved a reasonably satisfactory academic year. Chike Momah himself was once given 'six of the best' because he had dared to say to a prefect: 'I don't care!'[34] The prefects possessed the power to punish even their own classmates and the boys were all taught to answer 'Yes please' and 'No please'. The college authorities exercised care in the appointment of prefects, however, recognizing they had wide powers in maintaining order and discipline. Inevitably there were some prefects who wielded their powers recklessly. Chinua Achebe was made a college prefect, though Chike Momah insists that he was restrained in the exercise of his powers and did not throw his weight about like some other prefects. His gentle approach led some of those who were under his authority to think that he may have been embarrassed by being made a prefect.

Although the prefects maintained order, there were still rebels within the college who deviated from the norm, especially in the reading of newspapers like the *West African Pilot* and the *Nigerian Spokesman* instead of the approved *Daily Times*. A. K. Sam Epelle was one such deviant and he formed the habit of summarizing the war news from the radio set in his own fashion. Such activities did not militate against the academic work of the rebels or, for that matter, of 'Chinua Achebe who wrote the best English in his class apart from Onwuka and Etuk'[35] in Chike Momah's account.

In spite of the brilliance of the students of Government College, Umuahia, however, getting an 'A' in English in the School Certificate examination was perceived as very difficult, which led S. O. Bisiriyu to write to the authorities at Cambridge giving a detailed criticism of their Ordinary Level General Certificate of Education questions. The authorities at Cambridge set a paper and sent it to Bisiriyu to try out on the students, but even his best student, Chinua Achebe, did not get an 'A' because the paper was too difficult. Bisiriyu then set a paper and sent it to Cambridge as a model. It was an appropriate response from an individual who was keenly interested and practically involved in the establishment of reasonable academic standards.

The final examination taken by Chinua Achebe's class at Government College became the apex of Chinua's brilliant secondary school career, fulfilling all the hopes of his teachers. His results were impressive: 'A's in history, physics/chemistry, biology, geography, Bible knowledge, and mathematics; 'C's in English language and English literature. The two subjects in which he had credits rather than 'A's were actually high 'C's. Achebe reveals that one of his classmates, Ekpo Etim Inyang, who became a physician, had an 'A' in English language.[36] Soon after, an examination was conducted for entry into the new University College, Ibadan which was expected to take off in late 1948. In that examination Chinua Achebe was said to have written as much as he believed was necessary and stopped well before time to hand in his answer paper.[37] That decision caused some consternation, since the Ibadan University College was going to admit a limited number of students.

In those days the fashionable courses at the university were engineering and medicine and John Achebe, his official guardian, took the decision that Chinua was to study medicine. He had been an all-round student and this choice did not seem outrageous. Chinua was not only one of the few students who passed the entrance examination to the University College and were selected, but he also earned a 'Major' scholarship with its associated privileges. Achebe confirms that there were only two Major scholars in any year, and about eight 'Minor' scholars, while the rest of the students paid fees.[38] His entrance into the University College, Ibadan marked a turning point in his life in more ways than one: it increased his social and academic horizon, and at the same time produced insights that were to affect his views of life and of his Nigerian society.

4

The Young Man in Our Hall
At University College, Ibadan
1948–53

T H E relationship between the University College, Ibadan and the University of London enhanced the reputation of the University College when it was established, and its foundation students felt a sense of fulfilment simply because they had secured admission. The University College opened its doors to them thanks to the pioneering efforts of Professor Kenneth Mellanby, who was appointed the first principal and offered, as his campus, an abandoned military hospital and army barracks at Eleiyele, Ibadan. Mellanby assumed office in 1947 but it was not until 1948, after modest renovations at Eleiyele, that the University College commenced activities. It was obvious right from the beginning that the principal was determined to establish a first-rate institution, in spite of the uncertainty of future funding.

Among his most daunting tasks was the provision of capable teaching staff. Having the power to make appointments, Mellanby made sure that those he appointed deserved their positions. He enticed not only professors in British institutions who expressed a desire to teach in Africa, but also younger academics with promise who were in line for senior academic positions in Britain. The result was the gathering of a group of dedicated academics whose serious purpose was to mould the University College into one of the best higher education institutions on the continent of Africa. Several of his senior appointments were younger academics who had demonstrated great potential and the capacity to run a department.

In those early days his wife, Jean Mellanby, was one of the younger academics and she taught history. In the English Department, Professor Paul Christophersen became the first head of department: his special interest was phonetics, which he considered to be of primary importance to an understanding of English literature. Among the other lecturers who joined the Department of English were Alex Rodgers who taught literature in a cultural context, Leila Parsons, a Miss Stein and Joyce Green, a graduate fresh from an English university who found that she needed to make certain cultural adjustments in order to teach the literature of the Victorian period. Professor Geoffrey Parrinder later joined the Department of Religious Studies where he brought to fruition the teaching experience he had garnered in Dahomey and Ivory Coast. His influence was complemented by that of Professor Welch, who also taught philosophy. Other notable members of staff in those early days included Ulli Beier, who was compelled to teach phonetics at that time, and Professor Fletcher who gave a series of lectures to the Students' Union on history and philosophy. Many of these members of staff were sympathetic to the tribulations of the pioneer undergraduates, for they recognized the ferment of ideas and the effects of their colonial heritage, including an unenthusiastic response to African Studies which arose from an unwillingness to be portrayed as possessing an inferior cultural status. While many members of staff were aware of these academic and cultural conflicts, there were others who exhibited contempt based on the bigoted view that some of the Nigerians they encountered were inadequate.

Ulli Beier recollects the attitudes of some members of staff in those days in describing a dinner invitation to the home of Professor Christophersen:

> The obligatory dinner invitation came from my boss. It turned out that I was totally unprepared for what was to follow. After the dozen or so guests had indulged in the foolish ritual of small talk over drinks it was announced that the ladies were going to powder their nose. As they disappeared giggling girlishly the men were invited to 'visit darkest Africa', which meant going out into the garden, standing in a line and peeing.

There was worse to come. The meal over,

> liqueurs were served in the sitting room and as an after-dinner entertainment Professor Christophersen passed round his latest acquisition – a magnificent *Ogboni* brass figure some 30 cm long. I had never seen anything like it, had no idea what it meant or where it came from but was overwhelmed by a feeling of awe as I held in my hand the heavy object, emanating so much power and ancient wisdom. My stomach turned as I heard yet another silly comment from the man to whom I had handed the figure.

This was a moment of truth for Ulli Beier:

> Suddenly I understood what colonialism meant: arrogance based on ignorance, sniggering condescension towards people one had come to 'help', an arrogance which reduced whole cultures to the level of curios. Even those members of staff who openly despised Nigerians had the obligatory *Ibeji* figures on their mantleshelf.

This attitude was also reflected in the interaction between some members of staff and the citizens of Ibadan, which created problems in certain areas. Such was the case of Lasisi, the son of the *Alafin* (a traditional ruler of Oyo), who according to Ulli Beier 'was given to ransacking his father's shrine. Everybody on campus knew he was a thief and a dealer in antiquities, although their export was forbidden, yet he was indulgently referred to as a "charming rogue".'[1] It was Lasisi who stole and supplied those *Ibeji* figures on the mantleshelves of the expatriate staff.

To an extent this problematic relationship emanated from the fact that both staff and students were pioneers who both needed to adjust to the cultural milieu. Thus the apparent success of some members of staff in taking into consideration the cultural context was helpful, in spite of the fact that several others did not make this adjustment. Such matters were not made easier by the two sets of students who found themselves at the University College as pioneers. In February 1948 a set of students from the Yaba Higher College, Lagos were transferred to form part of the nucleus of the new university. They were joined later in the year by the first set of regular students who went through the process of an entrance examination. Among that batch of students was Chinua Achebe, who was admitted as one of the recipients of a major scholarship to study medicine, which meant that he was to take both the general and specific science courses in the following academic session. The facilities available to these students were certainly not fashioned to reflect gradations of privilege, but as one of only two distinguished major scholars, Chinua Achebe was given a room to himself while the rest of the students shared. The value of this privacy, however, was questionable. The old barracks at Eleiyele consisted of some dilapidated buildings in a rustic environment; it was possible, according to Chukwuemeka Ike, to overhear what one's neighbour was doing with a girl in the next mat-partitioned room.[2]

Student life in that early period was certainly experimental. No one knew quite what to expect from university life. To add to the confusion, the students who had come from Yaba Higher College were accustomed to government control and regulations fashioned on the civil service model, while the University College was established with the idea of providing academic freedom. The students could not agree on what type of student body to form and this conflict led to the dismissal of the student executive after only a few weeks in office. The eventual establishment of a viable Students' Union owed much to the help of Dr Wright of the English Department in preparing a draft constitution that provided guidance for the operation of the union. On the basis of this constitution a Students' Union executive was able to stay in office for one year. It was this executive that in 1949 invited Professor Fletcher to give the students a series of lectures on History and Philosophy in an attempt to illustrate significant systems of thought in their settings down the ages.

There was certainly a desire on the part of the students to widen their intellectual horizons, for they also formed the United Nations Students' Association, inaugurated by the delegates to the United Nations from the old Cameroons. Several prominent nationalists like the celebrated Dr Nnamdi Azikiwe, whose *West African Pilot* was then a vibrant anti-colonial newspaper, and rising politicians like Chief Obafemi Awolowo and Alhaji Tafawa Balewa were invited to the university campus to address the students. Apart from these political activities, spurred by the imminent elections of the early 1950s in Nigeria, there was a conscious attempt by the students to educate themselves through internal seminars and discussions covering the various ideologies in vogue. In addition, distinguished members of the university staff gave lectures on the nature of social and academic activities in the European and American universities they attended. These lectures on the expected responsibilities of undergraduates increased the tempo of Students' Union activities, especially for those students interested in holding office who had to campaign vigorously on carefully constructed manifestos.

The uncertainties associated with these political activities were an important ingredient of the initial experimentation with ideas and forms of organization; at this stage it was unclear to the university authorities whether to appoint an academic or a non-academic as hall warden to regulate the conduct of the students and avoid disturbances. There was also the question of the form of discipline that the hall wardens should enforce. The evolving rules and regulations took varied forms, like the moral tutors appointed from among the staff who were each responsible for a group of about ten students. The moral tutor invited the students to his home for drinks and dinner and such occasions were used for discussions concerning the feelings of the students towards the various aspects of the university administration, and for the promotion of mutual understanding. These smaller meetings between staff and students were reinforced by the hall dinners, held once every month, during which all the members of staff attached to a particular hall dined with the students.

Experimentation in social arrangements was not an isolated case: academic standards, too, had yet to be firmly established. Thus first-year academic work in the university did not adhere to any rigid pattern, although the lecturers were strict in terms of the assessment and grading of examination scripts. Professor Mellanby, anxious that Ibadan should avoid the fate of being regarded as a degenerate version of its British counterparts, insisted on academic excellence and encouraged his staff to adhere ruthlessly to very high standards, in spite of the need for adjustment by both lecturers and students in the midst of a great ferment of ideas and cultural conflict. The effect was to place great pressure on students like the Major scholar Chinua Achebe. Major scholars paid no fees and were given free books, while most of their other needs were provided by the university. Mellanby, who established this system for rewarding excellence, was clearly someone who appreciated merit. Even in academic processions, the scholars were given the privilege of taking precedence over the lecturers. John Munonye, who became a well-known Nigerian novelist, was one of those early Major scholars and he comments that it became a joke in the university to state that the university scholars were paid by the college to read the library books in order to prevent the ants from devouring them.[3] Of course, much was expected from these students to whom so much was given. Chinua Achebe was aware of this burden of expectation even at an early age but the transition from secondary school to university proceeded at such a pace that he had no time to contemplate what the pursuit of education in a university required of the individual. In the secondary school independent research and resourcefulness were encouraged only to the extent that they enabled the students to mature under careful guidance; at university, in spite of the establishment of moral tutors, it was not possible to give undivided attention to the students, who were admitted as adults and were expected to behave as such. Moreover, there were no older students to help these foundation students in thinking out solutions to their academic difficulties. Chinua Achebe's workload was intense, and it became clear to him in that first year that the grinding work in physics and ultimately in medicine necessitated a different interest in these forms of knowledge than he had brought with him from secondary school. Achebe was not alone in harbouring such feelings, for John Munonye, who eventually graduated with a first-class Honours degree, only managed to scrape through with a marginal grade in the first term, after which he dropped English and took Greek. That first year reflected the experimental dimensions of academic work in the English Department, for the students were subjected to intensive courses in phonetics and linguistics in a process that paralleled the system in force at the University of London. Chinua Achebe, for his part, passed without performing very well: the consequence was that he lost interest in the sciences and medicine.

That first year was disastrous for many of the students. Achebe recollects that getting through the one year was quite traumatic. A large number of students were destroyed in that first year, thrown out of the university on the basis of the first year exams. It was a big thing, in the newspapers; there was an outcry from the *West African Pilot*. They had a cartoon of the principal, Dr Mellanby, with a basketful of young undergraduates, he's throwing them out of the window of a tall building.

The cartoon was more successful in finding admittedly dark humour in the situation than were many of the students involved. Some of them later sought admission into universities in other countries, including Britain, and later returned with excellent degrees. But there were others who could not rise from what they perceived as an academic defeat: Achebe remembers 'one young man who never recovered from that year, who went out of his mind'. It was that serious. Achebe now took a decision for the first time concerning his career and academic interests. He went to the Dean of Sciences towards the end of that first year and informed him of his intention to change his course of study. The dean was amazed, since the request came not only from a student admitted to study what was then perceived as a prestigious course, but also from a privileged Major scholar. 'How do you know that you can study English and history? You know, you came here on a scholarship because of your academic performance.' Then the dean brought out the results Achebe had obtained in the entrance examination and became a shade more responsive: 'Well, go and talk to the Dean of Arts and if they will take you, we will see.'⁴ Achebe proceeded to the Dean of Arts and, on the basis of his record, he was accepted into the Faculty of Arts. Unfortunately he lost his scholarship, since the basis on which it had been granted no longer existed.

Losing his scholarship was definitely a major setback. Education in those days required not only intellectual competence but also adequate financial capability. Chinua's presentation of the issue to his brother John, who was not only responsible for the decision that he study medicine but also for providing the extra money his younger brother needed, fortunately elicited sympathy. Chinua said that John Achebe 'had absolutely no doubt that I should go back, and then apply for a government bursary, which I got in the second year'. The other brothers then contributed money for Chinua's fees, but it was the selfless act of Augustine Achebe which was most touching.

> My immediate older brother was a junior civil servant. He had gone through secondary school, but had not gone to university, and was working. He was in Ibadan, and was about to come home on leave. The civil servants were given money for transport when they went on leave by the government. He decided he would cancel his leave and give me the money to help me with my fees.⁵

Fortunately the award of a bursary reduced the financial constraints in the next year. Achebe became a member of the Faculty of Arts and selected English, geography and history as his subjects.

Thus his studies at the University College, Ibadan commenced in earnest in the second year of his time there, while Professor Christophersen was still the head of department. Christophersen's phonetics course was not popular, and in spite of his stammer and lack of charm he managed to improve the spoken English of several students. He also taught Old English literature, which was his area of specialization. Later Achebe was also taught phonetics by Ulli Beier, who described it as a 'silly subject'. (Beier later moved to the Department of

Extra-Mural Studies.) Beier's rapport with the students survived the unpopularity of his subject:

> In spite of this disadvantage many of them developed a habit of dropping in casually and Chinua was one of them. We talked about other things rather than Phonetics. Chinua was one of the twenty students I knew personally. That was my first contact with him. By that time he had not published anything and one could not predict the future.

Ulli Beier was convinced, however, that

> he was an exceptional student. He was always serious. He wasn't casual in his remarks. He took life seriously, showing a kind of responsible attitude. That was a quality he had then and he was also quiet and very considerate. There was nothing flippant about him. Even then this was my first impression and of all the students we had then I remembered him extremely well.[6]

Other lecturers in their different ways impressed Achebe, like Eric Robinson, an English lecturer who had the reputation of being crazy. In the Department of Geography Achebe was taught by Professor Buchanan, who attracted many students 'because he was a fantastic lecturer', so that even 'Physics people would come'. In history, Jean Mellanby was an equally captivating teacher and included Chinua Achebe among her favourite students. She invited him several times to the principal's house for lunch when they had visiting dignitaries from abroad. Achebe was also assigned a moral tutor, and he recollects that

> they tried to institute the Cambridge/Oxford thing about having a tutor, a 'moral tutor', I think he was called. The moral tutor had about five students assigned to him. My moral tutor was John Potter, who was a very eccentric person. He was an Anglican priest who lost his faith and became an agnostic – and a very good teacher of history. He invited us to lunch a couple of times.[7]

The students had tutorials and Mr Lambert, who was also a warden, took Achebe's group.

By 1950 Chinua Achebe had settled down sufficiently as a student in the Faculty of Arts to express himself as a writer. There was a magazine sponsored by the university but controlled by the students which was known as the *University Herald*. He submitted a piece entitled 'Polar Undergraduate', partly an essay and partly a story, which was published in Volume 3, No. 3 of 1950. It begins in the form of a discussion among a group of undergraduates notorious for their reluctance to obey the regulations stipulating the periods for rest and relaxation. The work is full of humour and irony: they are known as 'polar undergraduates' since their concept of the length of a day is 22 hours and the idea of sleep is repugnant to them. The essay singles out one polar student to illustrate the typical features of his kind: noisy, uncultured (there is an attempt to mob the president of the Students' Union), poor home training, irresponsibility during lectures, dullness, aggression and gluttony. Part of Achebe's conclusion captures his style and budding creative talent:

> But to come back to our friends of the league. They are dull but aggressive and have a strong bias for *amala* and thermos flasks. Their only distinguishing feature during the day is their inactivity which diminishes as darkness sets in. It has not been possible, with our limited experimental facilities, to investigate thoroughly their behaviour after midnight. A student has recently reported that in the small hours of a certain day,

his neighbour fell off his chair, breaking his arm and his fountain-pen in the process. But an isolated and single observation has no statistical significance.[8]

'Polar Undergraduate' demonstrates Chinua Achebe's capacity for insightful observation in a manner already tending towards what would become a characteristically ironic style.

By 1951 Achebe had learned how to separate the cerebral essay from purely creative work and showed this capability in 'Philosophy', a short essay fashioned in the form of a letter to the editor and published in *The Bug,* a campus magazine, and also in 'Argument Against the Existence of Faculties', an essay published in the *University Herald.* In the short piece on 'Philosophy' Achebe, who was still using the name Albert at that stage, was responding to criticism levelled at a series of lectures on that subject:

> An article was published about lectures in Philosophy in the last issue of *The Bug.* It was written by Holy Devil. He said, *inter alia,* 'these (lectures in Philosophy) have progressed enough for us to be able to read a purpose into them'. He then told us that we have been 'swallowing without proper mastication these ideas which are in MY OPINION [capitals are mine] utterly unprogressive, for certainly to philosophize in the absence of adequate knowledge … will produce … worthless philosophy'. This argument is, to say the least, muddled and illogical. Philosophy, says the Holy Devil, is unprogressive because our knowledge (I suppose he means his knowledge) is inadequate. This, to my mind, is the height of absurd reasoning. A lecture does not become 'unprogressive' because a devil in the audience has not enough knowledge to follow it. It will be 'caviare to the general' as far as he is concerned, but certainly not unprogressive. His warning against 'swallowing without proper mastication' is unnecessary. He ought to credit us with a critical faculty. I strongly doubt whether we require a devil 'come from hell' to make us think – philosophy implies thinking. What Holy Devil wants us to do is not really to *think* but to *suspect* – 'to read a purpose into them'. Dear Holy Devil, don't you think we can do without so much suspicion in this place? Of course, when you said 'in my opinion', you made it clear that your statements were couched in the language of devils. We mortals must undergo a mental somersault before we can understand 'knowledge', 'unprogressive' and such other terms used in your article. This is an unfortunate and inevitable circumstance arising from the difference in ideas and values as understood by men and by devils. You are entitled to your views, Mr Holy Devil, but please do not translate them into print in a community with such an overwhelming majority of human beings.[9]

There appears to be no doubt, judging by this essay, that at the University College stage of Chinua Achebe's development as a writer he was strongly in support of freedom of speech, freedom of intellectual reasoning and the freedom of academic pursuit, the core of his argument being that the student who had written under the pseudonym of 'Holy Devil' should not foist his biases on other students.

It is also that concept of unhampered academic freedom that Achebe propounds in the interesting essay, 'An Argument Against the Existence of Faculties'. It displays several characteristics that became prominent in the later writings of the novelist. He starts with the ironic statement that

> it is not yet realized by many people that the usual practice of cramping up students into water-tight compartments known as faculties is a reproach on civilization. We hear so much today about freedom of this, that and the other, but never about freedom of academic pursuit.

The author adds two illustrations and then asks:

> Why should one not obtain a degree in Religious Studies, Applied Mathematics and Gynaecology if one wishes to do so? The reason is simple. We live in an age that is in love with tags and labels. We call History Arts and call Chemistry Science, and then sit back lazily thinking that we have fully accounted for these subjects. I have long suspected that even though we all talk so glibly about Arts and Science, nobody can really differentiate between them.

The essay then points to the incongruity of allowing the head of the Department of Mathematics to represent the Arts Faculty on the library committee. Achebe argues that the view that a faculty is a combination of related subjects is not tenable and he illustrates that history and botany are related through the juxtaposition of a botanical diagram on 'True Fruit' and the family tree of the Dukes of Lorraine. It is clear that the examples Achebe provides are not meant to be taken seriously for he writes that

> this restless desire for academic freedom may be seen in the way students discuss subjects outside their faculties with ease. A famous Arts student is reputed to have said that some plants were photographic while others suffered from photophobia. Another one was overheard explaining that it was dangerous to wear shorts at night because one might easily catch pneumonia of the legs. At about the same time a science student remarked that *The Doctor's Dilemma* was one of Shakespeare's famous novels.

The essay's conclusion reinforces its entertainment value:

> The second argument may be illustrated by a short story. The different departments in a certain University were asked to send in their requisitions for the year. One of them demanded an apparatus costing £3,000. Another one thought a bit and filled in 'a box of chalk'. Now, since the 'chalk box' departments seem to be concentrated in one Faculty, it means that very little is spent on a student in that Faculty. Naturally, he will resent it. We are told that the instinct of self-preservation is the strongest in man. This was perhaps true before money was invented. But certainly man's strongest instinct today is to get more than his money's worth. He is always striving to maintain a balance in his favour. If he is properly educated, he may learn to relinquish this balance; but that is as far as he can go. It means then that unless the 'chalk-box' student is allowed to study at least one 'expensive' subject we may well expect a real crisis in the Universities.[10]

The strong element of humour in the essay is interestingly fashioned to blunt the edges of the criticism, but the conclusion nevertheless emphasizes the author's desire to magnify some of the absurdities in the way university education is structured. The essays also betray the writer's growing awareness of the intricacies of human nature and human responses.

It is in the short story 'In a Village Church', published in the *University Herald*, that Achebe indicates most clearly the extent to which he is already capable of observing, assessing and narrating. The early signs of his effortless turn of phrase, the close fit between words and emotions, and the necessary distancing from the subject of the story are all there. The story possesses its own peculiar history: apparently it was written when the Department of English announced a short story competition with a prize for the winner. Achebe relies on an incident drawn from the life of his local community and the scene he sets provides the story's title. The narrator takes the reader to the church where the first character encountered is 'an old woman who suddenly cries out piteously:

I forgot to wear my shoes'. The narrator does not present this woman as a curiosity: her presence is our introduction to the peculiarities of the village church where the sitting arrangement 'influenced very strongly the procedure of worship' for the singing 'followed very closely the sitting pattern' and 'everybody seemed to agree that the organ was invented for the choir and such other young people as yet inexperienced in the service of God'. At the centre of the scene is the

> old man whose spectacles, resting so far below the usual place of contact, served probably to correct a defective sense of smell. They did not, in any way, interfere with his reading which he performed very simply by bending his head forward like a charging ram and peeping right over the spectacles at an antediluvian Bible held at arm's length.

This bible had 'undergone reorganization as well since it left the publishers' with the result that 'one saw portions of St Mathew's gospel peeping out, rather uneasily, from that region of the Bible usually assigned to the Prophets'. The old man falls asleep while the sermon is going on and, on being woken by the church warden, exclaims, 'Five and sixpence!' which the narrator perceives as 'a financial statement carried from dreamland'. After the service the narrator 'saw this man apparently quite satisfied with the part he had played in the worship'. On further consideration the writer compares the old man who sleeps during the church service to undergraduates 'who go to the library for their siesta'. And on that philosophical note Achebe concludes, with the satirical reflection that 'a village church is the best place on earth to learn philosophy'.[11]

This story indicates that quite early Achebe had learnt to localize his imagery, as with the old man bent 'like a charging ram'. The reaction of the staff in the English Department to the short story took a different form, however, as Chinua Achebe explains:

> I had never written a short story before, so I wrote one. No prize was given, although they said there was some 'interesting effort'. I was mentioned as one of the 'interesting' ones. Miss Green said something to the effect that the problem with mine was that it lacked the form of a short story. I said, 'What is the form of a short story?' She said, 'We'll talk about it', that she would find some time and explain. I reminded her in the course of the term. At the end of the term I reminded her again, and she said, 'I read your short story again, and I don't think there's anything wrong with the form.'[12]

That explanation did not clarify issues for the young undergraduate but it certainly made him much more adventurous in continuing with his creative work. Nevertheless, there were other inspiring teachers at the university, even if Joyce Green had been a disappointment. We have seen that Geoffrey Parrinder joined the University College after he had done some teaching in other parts of West Africa. Achebe welcomed his arrival:

> Comparative religion was a late comer to the campus, and there was this Dr Parrinder who had spent about twelve years as a Methodist missionary in French-speaking West Africa, in Dahomey, and had written a book called *West African Religion*. I heard from other students the kinds of things they were doing. It wasn't theology at all; they were comparing religions – all the way from Akan (in Ghana) to the Cameroons. I dropped geography and picked up this new thing, to see what it was, this religion. There was a bit of Christian religion, yes, but not much. Parrinder was a very enthusiastic and knowledgeable teacher. I don't know if Parrinder turned me toward the study of the

religion, but he certainly enlightened me. I already had the interest, even if I didn't know it. I certainly had an interest in our gods and religious systems.[13]

After he started attending Parrinder's lectures Achebe 'began to see that all the things' he took as 'the gospel's truth were being interpreted academically'. That was when he began to reflect that 'you can be a Christian and yet be able to worship your ancestors'. That Achebe had dropped geography, a subject in which he had scored an alpha in the General Certificate of Education examination (a rare achievement in those days) in order to take up religious studies reflected his own enthusiasm and deep interest. Geoffrey Parrinder was both an exciting lecturer and an exciting man. Ulli Beier remembers that

> he was a very kind man and I shall never forget that he took me on a trip round Ibadan and showed me three Yoruba shrines, one of them the famous *Shango* shrine at Agbeni which had been reproduced by Frobenius. I was both bewildered and excited by the experience but didn't know what to make of it.... Geoffrey Parrinder inspired me, however, with his love of Ibadan. Unlike most of the staff, who considered this city a huge slum, he was fascinated by the colourful life that throbbed behind a chaotic facade.[14]

Parrinder also extended his interest to his students. It was through him that Achebe read *Niger Ibos* by G. T. Basden, the man who had officiated at the wedding ceremony of Isaiah and Janet Achebe, and he also read *Law and Authority in a Nigerian Tribe* by C. K. Meek. Achebe turned out to be one of Parrinder's brightest students, as the former University College professor acknowledged in later years.[15] Achebe the student was motivated by his teacher to assess the strength and weakness of both the Christian and his traditional religions. The popularity of Parrinder extended beyond the students that he had to teach, as happens when a lecturer has the reputation of being an exciting teacher.

Soon after Achebe enrolled for religious studies, another popular lecturer joined the department; while Parrinder taught West African religions, the new man, Professor James Welch, taught the Christian segment. Welch was another missionary who had worked for some time outside England but had gone back to be the chaplain to the King. In addition he had been the head of the British Broadcasting Corporation's religious service. Ulli Beier describes Welch as a rather

> awesome figure. With a huge skull and a towering forehead he looked disconcertingly like Goethe. He suffered from back trouble and had to sit in a specially constructed straight-backed chair almost a foot higher than the standard armchairs supplied by the Works Department of Nigeria. As a result he towered above his guests like a true patriarch.

Beier recalls that this patriarch also had a slightly subversive side:

> James Welch was a few steps ahead of the rest of the staff. He wrote a provocative article on the role of Europeans in Nigeria entitled 'Needed and Resented' and his presence generally stimulated discussion. He set up a 'Town and Gown Group' which met once a week in his house. There I came into contact for the first time with Nigerian teachers, churchmen, doctors and dignitaries. Every week someone read a paper on a subject of topical relevance to Nigeria which was then discussed by the group.

Beier 'found the evenings somewhat stiff and self-consciously intellectual', but he was 'grateful for the contacts and the insights, however tenuous, which they provided'.[16] Welch identified Achebe as one of his bright students and the ensuing good relationship between them was to extend even after his graduation.

At the time that Welch and Parrinder were making religious studies so stimulating, something similar was happening in the Department of English, where Eric Robinson was teaching literature in his own peculiar way. One of the books that he taught was Joyce Cary's *Mister Johnson*. Although Robinson was a competent teacher who made the students see the world from an entirely different angle, his attitude was not necessarily the best to adopt in teaching such works. Robinson's discussion of Johnson did not challenge the recollections of an older Africa incorporated into the novel by Joyce Cary, who could not rely on first-hand experience. Robinson was unwittingly accepting the prejudices and myths about Africa circulated in Europe by travel books.

Meanwhile, Chinua Achebe and several of his colleagues were beginning to show signs of discrimination in their reading, at first instinctive but increasingly conscious and self-directed. It was becoming clear to them that there were different possibilities in the representation of characters that depended on the perspective of the writer. Achebe was one of the students who realized that there could be misjudgement and even straightforward discrimination and distortion. The European authors they read presented their works in such a way, according to Achebe, that the reader's sympathies were controlled: 'We should have immediately identified with the Africans but this was impossible because the dice was loaded against them, the way the story was told, the way the author took sides.' Achebe began to detect the distinct positions taken in the stories he read and this realization began to erase his secondary school innocence, when he had read stories as mere adventures. He recalls 'one of the brightest students in my class, Olumide, saying something to the effect that the only moment he enjoyed in Joyce Cary's *Mister Johnson* was the moment when Johnson was shot! This horrified our English teacher.'[17] Clearly Achebe and many other students at the University College were beginning to grow out intellectually from the constraints of a colonial perception of reality. It was at about that time, says John Munonye, that he was told by Chinua Achebe, who saw him reading Edgar Wallace's *Sanders of the River,* that he was 'reading bad books'.[18]

Intellectual struggles and the growing awareness of literary power did not hamper the social activities of Chinua Achebe and his contemporaries at the University College. He interacted with many of the people who were later to shape the destiny of his country, like Akin Mabogunje who was his colleague in the Department of Geography; James Ezeilo, who later became a professor of mathematics and university vice-chancellor; Grace Alele, who also became a professor and the first Nigerian female vice-chancellor; and Bola Ige, who later became a state governor and was associated with Obafemi Awolowo, a major Nigerian politician even in those days (Bola Ige regarded Achebe and Mabel Segun as the best writers of the English language among his fellow-students at Ibadan). The forum in which Achebe got to know several of these contemporaries was the Dancing Club, one of the numerous associations formed by the students. These associations added vibrancy to student social life, catering for their diverse interests: the Christian Students' Movement; Musical Society; Dancing Club; Thinker's Movement; Photographic Club; Football Club and Cricket Club. Those students considered as radicals embraced the Thinker's Club, but the Dancing Club was the most popular, even though there were few female students at the university then. Members depended on female patronage from the nearby trade and nursing schools, partly because of a campus prejudice that every one of the University College female students thought she was something special. It was perhaps the same notion that originated the wicked rumour that the female students had not passed the entrance examination and that the administrators had offered them admission to create a sense of balance. This view did not enhance relationships, and probably accounted for various mischievous lampoons that appeared in *The Bug*. Chinua Achebe and Mabel Segun (then Imoukhuede), who were friends, were cartooned at one stage. Some of these attacks were far from gentle, and it was said that one of the female victims nearly committed suicide. In another attack male students lampooned the few girls who had the courage to contest Students' Union elections.

This last incident annoyed several other students, including Chinua Achebe, C. C. Ifemesia, Clement Amobi and Elisha Aziekwe Etudo, who decided to stage a psycho-dramatic retaliation. They went to the notice board, removed the offending comments, and then, procuring an axe from the kitchen, made as if to smash the glass screen of the notice board – at which point everybody ran away. The gallant band, including Chinua Achebe, were reported to the authorities, who frowned on the threatened use of physical violence to eliminate literary violence. Achebe and his colleagues were fined no more than a token amount, however, for the university officials sympathized with them after hearing their explanations. Professor Welch, who had become the Vice-principal and who was on the disciplinary committee, regarded that token amount as a serious disciplinary measure. He later called Achebe into his office and told him:

> I am an Englishman, you see. You are African, you know. Very soon you will run your own independence. We cannot teach you how to manage your affairs. We are not experts in African religion or anything. We may not be able to teach you what you want or even what you need. We can only teach you what we know. After that you can do what you like with it.[19]

That remark was not forgotten by Achebe when the incident which originated it had receded in his mind.

Meanwhile, he carried on with the activities of the Dancing Club, where he had become an official. If Achebe was one of its leading lights, other Dancing Club members, like James Ezeilo, were good dancers too. The club did all kinds of dances: whirl, foxtrot, rumba, tango and even the Scottish reel. It attracted many people, and inevitably a diversity of opinions. Thus a dispute arose concerning a musical band that was invited to entertain the students. The rest of the members were against the officials, who regarded the attitude of the members as demonstrating a lack of understanding. Thus Achebe and the other officials decided to leave the Dancing Club and form the Social Circle, which became very active and virtually eclipsed the Dancing Club, drawing all the best dancers. The Social Circle became rather exclusive and through Jean Mellanby, Achebe's history teacher, it even attracted the powerful support of Kenneth Mellanby, who became a trustee. As Achebe recalls, 'Mellanby was very fond of [the Social Circle]. And he brought the Governor of Nigeria, Sir John McPherson, who was visiting the campus, to come and join us in the Scottish reel.' Patronage by the governor and the approval of Mellanby thus assured the Social Circle of both fame and popularity.

The support of Mellanby was not easy to acquire, even for members of staff, for Ulli Beier confirms that he 'was reputed to have a sharp tongue and the ability to demolish pompous academics, quite savagely at meetings'. One such incident occurred after he had chaired a lecture by Professor Webb on the theme 'Some Aspects in the Evolution of Lice', a subject within Mellanby's area of specialization.

> As soon as the lecture was over, Dr Mellanby got up and went to sit on the lecturer's table, dangling his legs. With the best mischievous schoolboy grin he could muster he went on to say: 'Chairing a lecture is usually a pretty boring affair; one has to sit and listen politely to somebody else talking about matters one knows nothing about. However on this occasion I do happen to know a little about the subject. In fact, I am even in the position of being able to correct the lecturer on one or two little points!' And then, as Professor Webb went purple all the way down to the neck, he proceeded to demolish him, smiling benignly the while.[20]

Achebe did not spend all his time dancing. Chike Momah, who usually accompanied him to classes, reports the standard comment of all the lecturers who took them that 'Chinua was the only person who wrote in English.'[21] His distinctive style was becoming obvious. As Eric Robinson once exclaimed, 'Even when he wrote rubbish, he wrote it like an angel!'[22] Towards the end of his career at Ibadan, Achebe was much influenced by the lectures that Alex Rodgers gave on Thomas Hardy's *Far From the Madding Crowd*:

> What appealed to me was his sense of reality, which is tragic; it's very close to mine. I think for the same reason I took to A. E. Housman.There are a lot of funny things, a lot of comic things that happen in the world, and they are important. But I think that the things that really make the world, the human world, are the serious, the tragic....This is, roughly, what Hardy says to me; this is what Housman says to me. It is, you know, the man who fails who has a more interesting story than the successful person.... Simplicity is part of the success of Hardy and Housman because the tragic situation is very simple; it's not 'convoluted' at all. I mean, the man who strives – there is no reason he should not be happy, why he should not reap some reward, achieve some success. That's not a complex thing at all. And Hardy knew that, and Housman knew it.[23]

The deep and original insights that Achebe was now bringing to bear in his critical responses to English authors must have attracted attention, because after being recruited as a member of the editorial board of the *University Herald,* which had published some of his work, he was elected its editor in his third year of study in the English Department (1951/2). Some of his talents were now being recognized and he was also beginning another aspect of the apprenticeship that would lead to his maturation as a writer and editor.

The first issue of the *University Herald* which Achebe edited carried one of his early surviving verse efforts, a limerick:

> There was a young man in our Hall
> Who said that because he was small
> His fees should be less
> Because he ate less
> Than anyone else in the Hall.[24]

This limerick caught the attention of Sir Eugene Millington-Drake, a visiting Englishman.

We were visited by an eccentric Englishman, a retired ambassador, who was travelling the world reading poetry. His lively performance infused excitement into the different kinds of English poetry which he presented. But he did something quite extraordinary for those days. To everyone's surprise he read three or four poems from our student magazine – a compliment that would not have occurred to our English teachers. One of the poems was a rather silly limerick I had written about a young man in my hall who argued that because he was small he ate less than others and should be granted a reduction in fees! When I heard my name and nonsense poem recited by the tall and gaunt Sir Eugene Millington-Drake you could have knocked me over with a feather. As if reading it in Ibadan were not enough, Sir Eugene was heard several months later on the powerful Radio Brazzaville in Central Africa reading it again. On that second occasion he added a description of me as a smallish person myself![25]

The next creative work that Achebe published in the *University Herald* was a short story, 'The Old Order in Conflict with the New', which explores the cultural implications of contemporary marriages in the urban centres of a developing Nigeria. This theme would also feature in his second novel eight years later, but the short story provides a happier resolution of the dilemmas posed than the novel does. The major character in the story, Nnaemeka, finds his marriage to Nene Atang opposed by his father because she comes from a different tribe. The main issue is presented in the authorial statement that Nnaemeka's father is convinced that 'never in the history of his people had a man married a woman who spoke a different tongue' and also in the comment that in Lagos prejudice among those of Nnaemeka's people who work there 'showed itself in different ways'. When word eventually gets back to the village that Nnaemeka and his wife are a happy couple, however, and when Nnaemeka's father receives a letter from Nene with the picture of their two sons enclosed, his heart is touched and the author concludes that 'that night he hardly slept, from remorse – and a vague fear that he might die without making it up to them'.[26] Achebe's growing interest in the dynamics of culture emerges clearly and some deft ironic touches point the way forward from this work of his apprenticeship to the style of his maturity.

Achebe did not publish only creative work at this time. He submitted critical work to *The Bug,* which in 1952 published 'Mr Okafor versus Arts Students' and 'Hiawatha', two articles which appeared on the same page.

MR OKAFOR VERSUS ARTS STUDENTS

The time has passed when a man can take the whole field of knowledge for his province. On the other hand, too much departmentalization of University education can be a real danger. Mr. Ezelu Okafor is therefore right when he warns Arts students against being 'unscientific'. Unfortunately Mr Okafor's warning carries with it that absolute lack of humility with which a certain vocal group of science students is afflicted. These science students believe that they are as good as, if not better than, arts students, even in their own subjects. This belief is very often based on no more solid merit than a superficial acquaintance with literature of the Peter Cheyney type. Mr Okafor who, one would have thought, should be above intermediate standard in English concludes his article thus: 'it shall be of interest to know ...' (a peculiar use of shall). People like Mr Okafor think that the greater their stock of technical terms, the better educated they are. He expects every arts student to know what a FEMUR is. An English student might as well expect him to be able to account for the loss in English of inflexional endings in the middle English period. Perhaps he knows about it.

47

Perhaps Achebe as an all-round student took particular exception to Okafor's comments, but his article is also an indication of his impatience with ignorance and conceit. The tone of the second essay is similar.

HIAWATHA

The behaviour of students during the performance of *Hiawatha* last Sunday was, quite frankly, disgraceful. Unintelligent and rude laughter, clapping and similar 'pit' reactions are out of place in a University. They exasperate the few who are prepared to appreciate great works of art in a sober manner. Those who cannot show proper response to art need not be blamed. But they should not disturb those who can. If a Shakespeare play is 'caviare to the general' to them they should keep away from it. Fortunately, film companies provide 'slapstick' for their boisterous taste.

NB: I understand that *King Kong* will be shown next week.[27]

It is interesting that Achebe used *The Bug* to disseminate his views, in spite of the fact that he had access to the *University Herald*. This sense of propriety is of a piece with the central argument in the articles: that human beings, especially in a university environment, should exhibit intelligence, reason and understanding.

This appeal to reason was particularly pertinent for Achebe at that time because of a crisis over the future of the *University Herald*. Some members of the Students' Union insisted that the journal should be controlled entirely by the students, which would mean that members of the editorial committee and the editor would be elected by the general student body, like the president and the secretary of the Students' Union. The policy of the *University Herald*, by contrast, was that the members of the editorial committee were appointed on the basis of competence, and that the committee elected the editor; Professor Kenneth Mellanby acted as a trustee, ensuring that this policy was maintained. When the university authorities turned down the new policy, its supporters in the Students' Union persuaded the union executive to establish a rival journal, the *University Voice*. On this occasion Etudo, who had joined Chinua Achebe and others in protesting against the lampoon attacks on girls who wanted to participate in students politics, was on the side of the Students' Union. The *University Herald*, meanwhile, continued publication, and Achebe's term as editor came to an end as the crisis subsided.

This crisis illustrated the political turbulence of the University College, especially when nationalist politics generated strong student interest. In 1949 the students had protested over the shooting of striking coal miners at Colliery Enugu. In the years that followed the students maintained a keen interest in the ideological positions, pronouncements and progress of the country's politicians, while on the campus Students' Union elections were organized on the basis of two parties, the Dynamic Party and the Progressive Party. We have seen that prominent politicians who operated on the national scene like Dr Nnamdi Azikiwe and Chief Obafemi Awolowo were invited to talk to the students; their visits aroused much interest, especially in the lead-up to the 1951 elections. There were some divisions of students support along the lines of the National Council of Nigeria and the Cameroons (NCNC) and the Action Group. But the students, in spite of their vociferous support for rival leaders or parties, often interacted amicably after the event.

One incident left a lasting impression on Chinua Achebe: Obafemi Awolowo's use of the Action Group, founded as a political party to introduce ethnic politics and destroy the aspirations of an overarching nationalism. Almost thirty years later, on the eve of another election in Nigeria, Achebe recalled that event:

> As a student in Ibadan I was an eye-witness to that momentous occasion when Chief Obafemi Awolowo 'stole' the leadership of Western Nigeria from Dr Nnamdi Azikiwe in broad daylight on the floor of the Western House of Assembly and sent the great Zik scampering back to the Niger whence he came. Someday when we shall have outgrown tribal politics, or when our children shall have done so, sober historians of the Nigerian nation will see that event as the abolition of a pan-Nigerian vision which, however ineptly, the NCNC tried to have and to hold. No matter how anyone attempts to explain away that event in retrospect it was the death of a dream-Nigeria in which a citizen could live and work in a place of his choice anywhere, and pursue any legitimate goal open to his fellows; a Nigeria in which an Easterner might aspire to be premier in the West and a Northener become Mayor of Enugu. That dream-Nigeria suffered a death-blow from Awolowo's 'success' in the Western House of Assembly in 1951.[28]

It was a great disillusionment for Achebe and many of his sensitive colleagues at the university. At that time, too, he perceived the signs that the departing British colonialists were reluctant to secure the political situation in Nigeria, an error that was to cost the nation dearly less than two decades later.

These political issues were jostling in Chinua Achebe's mind as he entered the last lap of his academic programme in the 1952/3 session. He managed, nevertheless, to publish an untitled short story in the *University Herald*. This story, reprinted in later years as 'Dead Men's Path', explores the experience of an enthusiastic primary school headmaster who insists, against all remonstrance, on closing a footpath that cuts through his school premises. Some nights later the villagers destroy the hedges, the flowers and the fence blocking the path. Earlier the village priest of Ani has called on Headmaster Obi to explain that 'the whole life of this village depends on it. Our dead relatives depart by it and our ancestors visit us by it. But most important, it is the path of children coming in to be born.' Obi's argument that 'dead men do not require footpaths' is a response to what he perceives as mere superstition. He had wanted to show his firmness in dismissing such superstition by closing the footpath. A few days later the white supervisor visits the school and, after observing the destroyed hedges, makes a damaging report.[29] This story highlights once more Achebe's preoccupation in the early 1950s with dialogue, understanding and some form of compromise and common sense in the organization of human affairs. He is stressing the need for humility in people who have benefited from Western education, a recognition relevant to his personal life at that time. Akunwata Ugoka recalls that Achebe would come home to Ogidi on holidays during his university days and still associate without superior airs with his former primary school colleagues and friends, joining them in their various social activities. Zinobia Ikpeze (née Achebe) recollects that during one of those holidays Chinua was cutting grass when a visitor arrived. The visitor enquired of him if Chinua Achebe was at home, and on getting an affirmative answer asked the man cutting grass to call him. Chinua went into the house to put on a shirt and when he emerged the man was surprised, wondering if this was not the person he had seen cutting grass. Then he saw the joke and they both burst into laughter, but it was this modesty that Achebe expected from his contemporaries and others who were in positions of political authority in the 1950s. These views were to become pronounced after his degree examinations and entrance into public service.[30]

The degree examinations of 1953 reflected the strict and rigid desire of the university administration to set enviable standards. But while it was easy to insist on excellence in principle, it was extremely difficult to set a realistic level for that excellence since the students were pioneers. Each department insisted on the best and Chinua Achebe, taking degree examinations in English, history and religious studies, had to battle with high academic standards on three fronts. The two students who subsequently obtained what was labelled First Class were helped by the fact that they had chosen precise subjects like Latin and Greek. The examination had its own drama: Chukwuemeka Ike tells the story of a student who had prepared an answer on the 'Biblical Kings', only to discover when the paper came that the question was on the 'Biblical Prophets'. The man prefaced his answer with the remark: 'Who am I to write on these holy men of Israel? I write about the Kings!'[31] Legend has it that the man passed and was awarded a First Class. It was also said that Bola Ige, who had made his mark as a student poet and politician on campus, was so terrified by the degree examination that he appeared with cold towels wrapped round his head that morning, saying that his brains were boiling. He had to wait another year before he graduated. Achebe took his examination without such dramatics or histrionics and whatever facts he knew he put down to the best of his ability. Geoffrey Parrinder's view was that 'the internal examiner, at London, was too conservative'.[32] Be that as it may, Chinua Achebe passed and was awarded a second-class degree.

Graduation marked the stage in Achebe's life when all the seeds had been planted and some of them had even produced fruits in the creative and critical work published in student magazines in the secondary school and at the university. His intellectual horizon and his social vision had widened through his encounters with a variety of Nigerians and foreigners. In addition, residence in various parts of Nigeria had made him sensitive to other cultures in his society as he stepped into the waiting world.

5

Stepping into the World
Teaching & Broadcasting
1954–7

T H E socio-political scene in Nigeria in the early 1950s was full of possibilities, especially for those who had acquired a Western education.
Impending independence made the future even brighter for many
young male and female graduates. But Chinua Achebe did not think in terms of
settling down immediately, for he felt that there was still much knowledge that
he had not acquired. Thus he did not, like some of his fellow graduates, con-
ceive immediate plans for cashing in on the vacancies available. For the first
time in his academic career he had not achieved the best result. Although the
second-class degree which he had was treasured by many others who felt lucky
to have survived the trauma of degree examinations at the University College,
Ibadan, Achebe was convinced that he merited and deserved, by virtue of his
academic record, something close to the best if not the best result. Now he was
unsure of his future plans. Towards the end of his undergraduate courses some
of the books he had studied, especially the novels, had aroused in him a deeper
level of interest, making his thoughts revolve around the idea of further studies.

> I had no idea of what work I wanted to do. In my time getting a job was no problem,
> people were looking for you. I just didn't think of work or how I was going to go on.
> Things looked a bit nebulous to me; I thought there was still so much I wanted to
> know, but just where to find it I wasn't so sure. Professor Welch came in at this point.
> He was very fond of me, thought very highly of me, and he said: 'I'm going to write to
> my college, Trinity College, to give you an exhibition'. And he did.[1]

It was not surprising that Welch took that decision, for he had come to know
Achebe well after the controversial protest against the harassment of female
undergraduates. In addition, the enthusiasm and intelligence demonstrated by
Achebe in his academic work reinforced Welch's high opinion. Unfortunately,
however, nothing came of his letter to Trinity College. It may be that the 'conservative' external examiner at the University of London had something to do
with this further disappointment, but Achebe felt no bitterness, accepting the
outcome as perhaps part of his destiny. He was to make a joke out of it forty
years later when he was invited by the University of Cambridge to deliver the
annual Ashby Lecture at Clare Hall in 1993. Achebe in his introductory remarks
commented that on a second reading he felt that the invitation from Clare Hall

seemed to suggest that it was going to be a scholarly event. I must say I wondered for a while, but then I said to myself: look, you have not campaigned in any way for the invitation. The fellows in Cambridge must know what they are doing. If they think you are a scholar, it must mean you are a scholar, of sorts.

In his characteristic manner Achebe added that his reason for that remark was

to establish quite early and quite clearly where the fault must be sought if somehow a mistake has been made. Though I would much rather have a successful performance than the satisfaction of being exonerated in failure, I cannot help adding that failure, sad as it would be, must also reveal the workings of poetic justice, because I missed the opportunity of becoming a scholar forty years ago when Trinity College, Cambridge, turned down my application to study there after my first degree at the new University College, Ibadan.... Anyhow, I stayed home then, and became a novelist.[2]

More immediately, Achebe accepted the rejection by Trinity College and returned to his home town, Ogidi, to contemplate the future. Professor James Welch did not forget or lose confidence in the young graduate, as later events revealed.

At Ogidi there was not much activity to sustain Achebe's interest. He read some of the books he had acquired and continued to turn over in his mind some of the literary questions that had become important to him. It was also an opportunity for him to re-examine theories derived from the books he had read by juxtaposing them with the intricate patterns of village life. Once more he absorbed consciously and unconsciously those patterns of life with their human characters, their interactions and distractions, as well as the evolving norms and mores of the society. It was in the midst of these meditative activities that James Ezeilo, who had also graduated from the University College, paid him a visit. Chinua had associated with Ezeilo in the Dancing Club and their friendship had progressed, although Ezeilo was in the Science Faculty with mathematics as one of his major subjects. Ezeilo was aware that Chinua Achebe had not thought out clearly what career he wanted to pursue, but he was sure that graduates in English were in high demand in the Ministry of Education, the communication media, the civil service and the private secondary schools. Many secondary school proprietors at that time were known to boast about the number of graduate teachers in their institutions. It was both a desire to entice this young graduate to a fledgling secondary school and also a desire to have in the same institution a colleague who was a friend that led James Ezeilo to ask: 'What are you doing? Come to the Merchants of Light Secondary School, Oba. They are looking for a teacher of English. They will pay you anything you want to earn.'[3]

It was not so much the promise that he would be paid handsomely that made Achebe follow James Ezeilo to Oba; he wanted to keep himself engaged while he pondered fully on his next line of action. An idle stay at Ogidi would have elicited the inevitable gossip that perhaps the young man had run into an academic obstacle; in those days there were few undergraduates and fewer graduates, with the result that the villagers there were aware of whose daughter or son was making progress even in obscure parts of the world. Anyway, Achebe accompanied Ezeilo to the Merchants of Light Secondary School at Oba, which even in 1954 was not considered too far from Ogidi. It was sufficiently distant, however, to reveal some cultural variations, in spite of the fact that it was the same ethnic group that inhabited those areas.

At the Merchants of Light School in 1954, the principal was A. E. D. Mgbemena, who later became a reverend canon, and he was pleased to employ Chinua Achebe in the school. The proprietor of the school, who had laboured to establish it, was Mr Oli, but he had become involved in political activities and in that year had been made a regional minister at Enugu, the capital city of Eastern Nigeria. The regular members of staff in the school included Ofili, Ugwuegede, F. U. Mbakaogu, Ifejika, Anaeto from Ozubulu, Njubuigbo and Obi, a native of Oba. These teachers were inadequate for the population of students, but they were supplemented by several part-time teachers who were coming from the University College, Ibadan during the long vacation, especially for those subjects in which graduates were scarce. One of the boys Chinua Achebe taught English in Class Three during the four months in which he was a member of staff was B. N. Igwilo, who survived the difficult days of the Merchants of Light School and later became a lecturer in the Department of Fine and Applied Arts at the University of Nigeria, Nsukka. Most of their tutors at that time were either High Elementary or Senior tutors, Igwilo remembers, and whenever graduate teachers were employed the students looked upon them as models and sources of inspiration.[4]

There was no doubt that the Merchants of Light School, Oba was still in its infancy at the time that Achebe accepted a teaching appointment. Quarters for both staff and students were insufficient. In addition, the buildings of the school were erected on a place known as 'bad bush' in Oba; not only had it been the dumping ground for several corpses, but several potent fetish objects had been deposited there. In *Things Fall Apart* Achebe describes such a forest thus:

> Every clan and village had its 'evil forest'. In it were buried all those who died of the really evil diseases like leprosy and smallpox. It was also the dumping ground for the potent fetishes of great medicine-men when they died. An 'evil forest' was therefore alive with sinister forces and powers of darkness.[5]

It was on such ground that Oli built his school. The dormitories were made of mud and coated with cement. In order to make sure that the students contributed positively to the development of the school, two types of punishment prevailed – uprooting stumps of trees and digging holes for the erection of new buildings. 'Once you dug a tiny hole,' Igwilo recalls, 'you unearthed bones. The students were using their buckets to collect the bones and throw them away. My father asked me not to come back home with the bucket which I used in the school.'[6] It was not surprising that soon the students had successfully constructed the football field, for every punishment stipulated working on it. At that time there was neither electricity nor piped water; the students trekked to fetch water from either the Ogba stream in Akwuzu village in Oba or the Ose stream. These expeditions also provided the water for cooking meals for those in the boarding houses. They woke at 4 a.m. in order to fetch water at least twice from the stream before the commencement of classes. 'The water Prefect possessed a large bucket', Igwilo adds,

> which he used to measure and make sure that the water fetched was up to a certain volume. If the water was not up to that volume the student would forfeit his food. Fetching water was also another source of punishment for the students.

The water problem was really acute at Merchants of Light in those days. Later on, however, the principal managed to build water tanks that were then controlled by the water prefects. Perhaps the hardship associated with life in the school explains why many of the students from the neighbouring towns of Ojoto, Ichi and Akwukwu did not live on the school premises as boarders, although some of them lived there if their parents had the wherewithal to provide them with essential comforts. The standard of ordinary school food was low because of strained financial resources. Igwilo insists that 'after preparing the soup, for instance, it would be diluted with water. One could even see one's reflection in that soup. However, the main menu was beans which consisted of more sand than beans.'[7] In order to subsidize food procurement the school had a piggery and the pigs were fed with the leftovers of meals from the dining hall. The students naturally expected that the resulting pork would supplement their meals, but whenever the pigs were slaughtered they were given only a token portion, while the rest was sent to market. The students did, however, obtain fish from the stream and they grew vegetables too.

Despite these basic failings the school had a practical approach to academic life; there was organization and discipline. Chinua Achebe was disappointed by the library, however: 'I discovered that the school "library" consisted of a dusty cupboard containing one copy of the Holy Bible, five pamphlets entitled *The Adventures of Tarzan* and one copy of a popular novel called *The Sorrows of Satan.*'[8] It was a shock to Achebe, who could only compare this level of provision with Government College, Umuahia, endowed lavishly with rows and rows of books. The set-up at Merchants of Light, Oba, was not helped by the fact that it was situated in a rural community. The nearest town was Onitsha but it was not easy for the students to go there since the only means of transport was the Uzodinma bus that plied the Onitsha–Nnewi road. The rural nature of the school was reflected in several ways, especially in the provision of bamboo beds. Few students could afford portable plank beds and the rest depended on the bamboo beds made by a local carpenter, many of which were crawling with bed bugs. Furthermore, the fact that the students were not protected by a school wall made it possible for the villagers to infiltrate the school premises. Even the *Ayaka* masquerades came to bother them, especially the two troublesome types – those that appear in the day on *Eke Mgba* days and those that appear at night. In one incident some of the boys confronted the *Ayaka* masqueraders and beat one of them up. This action, considered sacrilegious, was treated with leniency since the boys were obviously provoked. Thus the villagers did not exact a terrible revenge on the students, who were referred to as *Umu Oli* – the children of Oli, the school's proprietor.

Discipline in the school was good and was exercised in a way that took into account the presence of some girls in the student population, though girls were not admitted after 1953. They were all day students and came from either Oba or Ojoto. One of them was Oli's daughter, another was her cousin, and the others were also girls known to him. The presence of these girls did not affect the boys negatively; indeed, it encouraged them to cultivate polite manners. House competitions embracing football, athletics, hygiene and even traditional dances helped to nurture healthy attitudes to life. The school houses were named after major cities such as Enugu, Port Harcourt, Lagos and Kaduna, and the activities and competitions were organized accordingly. B. N. Igwilo led a team from Lagos House which won a shield for traditional dances. That competition was not a rare event, since the students often participated in moonlight displays on the school premises. On such occasions they would prepare some dances and even masquerades for entertainment. There is no doubt that the principal encouraged such activities in order to create a sense of belonging in the students and also to help them come to terms with their harsh environment. On Sundays he would purchase for the students two pots of a special palm wine that Oba was noted for, a wine that gave rise to the popular traditional song *Ihe di n'Oba* – 'There is Something at Oba'. In spite of this liberal attitude the students were not free to leave the school premises; when they had to go, exeat cards had to be obtained and signed.

Chinua Achebe was now plunged into the midst of these activities as one of the teachers at Merchants of Light, Oba, remaining only too aware of his own secondary school background at Government College, Umuahia, where students did not have to battle against bedbugs or the excesses of villagers. He quickly understood the odds stacked against the students in these unpleasant surroundings, in spite of their willingness to use the academic opportunities they were offered. Accordingly he made efforts to eliminate impediments to the academic life of the students, while at the same time trying to establish the standards he had imbibed at Umuahia. Although he taught history as well, he was in greater demand as an English teacher: the English language had become an essential medium of communication in the Nigeria of the 1950s. The school's shortage of teachers was such that he might well have taught physics, chemistry, biology or mathematics, which were all liable to be taught by people with minimal qualifications. There were few graduate teachers, and some of these were external candidates of London University who studied and passed their examinations at home because of the University College of Ibadan's limited intake.

It was not long before the students perceived the unusual but relevant nature of their new teacher. Igwilo acknowledges that they saw him 'as a model and he was very particular about grammar'. This insistence on grammatical rules and the construction of correct sentences in English obviously resulted from Achebe's own experience at both Government College and university, though he was not as ruthless as A. P. L. Slater who had taught him at Umuahia. Like Slater he encouraged the students to read since many of them had had a limited exposure to books. Igwilo claims that not many students were keen on reading the few newspapers available, contrary to the Umuahia experience where students were provided with foreign and local newspapers. Thus Achebe made his own private reading materials, including newspapers, available to interested students. In his classes, Igwilo says, Achebe stressed originality, especially in the writing of essays from 'local' rather than 'foreign' sources of information. Thus the traditional context of his teaching helped to arouse the interest of the students. He also helped in preparing students for public performances like school debates. Achebe gave them tips on how to combat stage fright. B. N. Igwilo concludes that he had 'the right manner of approach for he presented things not in their abstract sense'.[9]

Chinua Achebe was not destined to be at the Merchants of Light Secondary School for long. He had been there about four months when he received a letter from the Controller of the Nigerian Broadcasting Service (NBS), a Mr Elphik. The Controller's letter stated that his name had been forwarded to the organization as a qualified candidate for a vacancy in the Broadcasting Service. Elphik asked him if he would be interested in an interview: would Achebe come to

Lagos, or would he prefer that they (the interview team) come to Onitsha? Achebe promptly asked the Controller to come to Onitsha, which he did. This was not an unusual procedure: the NBS was in need of suitable employees, despite the number of Nigerians anxious to secure employment in promising organizations at the time. The interview was held and the Nigerian Broadcasting Service was pleased to offer Chinua Achebe employment from the middle of 1954; it invited him to Lagos to assume duties.[10]

At the interview Achebe found out how his name had been forwarded to the Broadcasting Service. The Director of the NBS in Lagos, Tom Chalmers, who had been seconded from the British Broadcasting Corporation (BBC), had made inquiries of James Welch at the University College, Ibadan. Chalmers wanted Welch to recommend somebody who would become their senior broadcasting officer in the Eastern Region. It was necessary to make such plans, in the opinion of the authorities at the NBS, since impending political independence held the implication that expatriates would make their exits soon after that event. It did not take James Welch long to come up with the name of the young Ogidi graduate he had earlier recommended to the University of Cambridge. This second recommendation launched his former student on a career that Welch himself had found fulfilling at the time of his association with the religious programmes of the BBC.

At that time, and to a great extent in later times, Lagos was the centre of social and political activity in Nigeria. Achebe's residence there, and his employment at the NBS as a senior broadcasting officer enabled him to perceive political, social and economic events in the country from close quarters. Achebe was deployed to the Talks Department which was then headed by Angela Beattie, whose assistant he became. Mrs Beattie inducted him into 'what to do and what to look for' in the productions of the Talks Department, enabling Achebe to conceptualize the spoken word as different from the written. Ralph Opara, who joined the Talks Department four years later on the encouragement of Chinua Achebe, insists that

> the Talks Department was important, because the basis of broadcasting was the spoken word. The Talks Department was responsible for all programmes, especially the informative and educative ones like 'Radio Lawyer' for instance. Anyone who joined Broadcasting House as a graduate was sent to the Talks Department. It was important that the distinction between what one heard and what one read be made.[11]

In later years when Chinua Achebe became head of the Talks Department he introduced a programme known as 'Sunday Night Spot' which Ralph Opara regarded particularly highly: it involved participants with valuable ideas which could range from a plan for improving education to a series of talks on historical topics by leading scholars in Nigeria. The staff of the Talks Department also looked after all the 'Grade One' talks like the ministerial broadcasts or addresses by the head of state. There is no doubt that in the mid-1950s the Talks Department played a key role in collating and disseminating information concerning political developments in Nigeria.

When Achebe started work in Lagos he was practically the only Nigerian working in the department and depended on the competent Angela Beattie for advice. But it did not take long for him to acquire a knowledge of the intricate process of production, becoming the first Nigerian to do the job. In his third week in the department Mrs Beattie gave him a story to produce and later she passed the script on to other Europeans in the Broadcasting Service and there was much whispering over it. Soon it became clear that she was very impressed by Chinua Achebe's performance, and after that handed over an increasing volume of work to him. What really helped Achebe in mastering the technique quickly was that he had an ear for dialogue and instinctively knew what was appropriate and what was not.

> Broadcasting at that point was a very exciting thing to do. And I learnt a lot by handling scripts. I was involved with the spoken word programme, although I was never an announcer but a producer. So I learnt a lot. We did short stories, short fifteen-minute talks, debates, current affairs and so on. But the short story was really my special interest and I encountered a lot of ideas just handling that, converting what is written on paper to what you can speak.

He was preoccupied with what makes speech memorable and cultivated an awareness of the difference between a 'literary style' and a 'spoken style'. For Achebe the spoken style

> is pretty close to dialogue in the novel. But there are things you don't think about until you put somebody on the air – things like 'tongue twisters'. I remember one day, I think it was the man in charge of the Nigerian Ports Authority, he wrote a very fine script and when we started recording him, he got to a point where he just stopped! He just couldn't go on and the whole thing was ruined!

Achebe explains that what was down on the script was something like

> six-storied shed, you know, a lot of 's' sounds piled up, and this was a thing which, when you read with the eye you can't see it, but in reading aloud you are tied in knots, you can't say the word. So the profession of a producer in radio was very useful to me.[12]

Achebe's editorial responsibilities meant that he had to point out the difficulties and help writers whose work he was producing to make the transition to the spoken word; this meant that he was acquiring an education in the writing of dialogue. There were nevertheless signs that he was still serving his apprenticeship in the work he handed over to Angela Beattie. His position in the Talks Department as the highest-ranking Nigerian meant that he was being groomed for a leadership position, although ultimately that depended on his demonstration of competence. It was not hard for Achebe to fulfil this requirement since he was more than ready to justify the expectations of his employers, who made his life easier by giving him accommodation in a low-density area of Lagos. As a graduate he automatically joined what was known then as the 'senior service', with its benefits and privileges of interest-free loans, car allowances and good accommodation designed by the Europeans for themselves.

Achebe nevertheless found opportunities to absorb the sights and sounds of Lagos as he traversed its length in the course of his duties. Some of the scenes captured in *No Longer at Ease* (1960) are clearly informed by his experiences in Lagos in the 1950s. There were the various expatriate clubs with their tennis courts, swimming pools and bars. By the time Achebe went to live in Lagos those clubs had relaxed their rules somewhat and were admitting a few token Nigerians. Achebe also became aware of the increasingly effective Ogidi Town Union, made up of Ogidi indigenes in Lagos. It served as a forum for social and financial interactions while providing help for members in financial need and scholarships for their deserving sons and daughters. Achebe also experienced the excitement of Saturday nights in Lagos, although he was not a night owl. There were the film shows in the cinema houses and the Highlife dances in the hotels like the one Achebe describes in *No Longer at Ease:*

> There were as many ways of dancing the Highlife as there were people on the floor. But broadly speaking, three main patterns could be discerned. There were four or five Europeans whose dancing reminded one of the early motion pictures. They moved in triangles in an alien dance that was ordained for circles. There were others who made very little movement. They held their women close, breast to breast and groin to groin, so that the dance could flow uninterrupted from one to the other and back again. The last group were the ecstatic ones. They danced apart, spinning, swaying or doing intricate syncopations with their feet and waist. They were the good servants who had found perfect freedom.

Highlife music was not only inspiring in terms of rhythm; the lyrics were also spiced with relevant aphorisms. The song in the novel, entitled 'Gentleman Bobby', in which a musician is kissed by a woman carried away by his music, reflects something of the legend associated with Highlife musicians who are insightful observers of the society as well as very sexy.[13]

In *No Longer at Ease* Achebe depicted the two sides of Lagos in the 1950s:

> Going from Lagos mainland to Ikoyi on a Saturday night was like going from a bazaar to a funeral. And the vast Lagos cemetery which separated the two places helped to deepen the feelings; for all its luxurious bungalows and flats and its extensive greenery, Ikoyi was like a graveyard, it had no corporate life – at any rate for those Africans who lived there. They had not always lived there of course. It was once a European reserve. But things had changed, and some Africans in 'European posts' had been given houses in Ikoyi.

Ikoyi is one side. Lagos mainland comes into focus when Achebe describes Obi Okonkwo standing 'beside his car [one] night in one of the less formidable of Lagos slum areas waiting for Clara to take yards of material to her seamstress'. We wait with him as Obi's 'mind went over his earlier impressions of the city. He had not thought places like this stood side by side with the cars, electric lights and brightly dressed girls.' Obi's car is

> parked close to a wide-open storm drain from which came a very strong smell of rotting flesh. It was the remains of a dog which had no doubt been run over by a taxi. Beyond the storm drain there was a meat stall. It was quite empty of meat or meat sellers. But a man was working a little machine on one of the tables. It looked like a sewing machine except that it ground maize. A woman stood by watching the man turn the machine to grind her maize.

Achebe's mastery of such scenes is shown in the ease with which he sets them in motion, as when he tells us that

> on the other side of the road a little boy wrapped in a cloth was selling bean cakes and he seemed half asleep. But he really wasn't, for as soon as the night-soil-man passed swinging his broom and hurricane lamp and trailing clouds of putrefaction the boy quickly sprang to his feet and began calling him names. The man made for him with his broom but the boy was already in flight, his bowl of *akara* on his head. The man grinding maize burst into laughter, and the woman joined in. The night-soil-man smiled and went his way, having said something very rude about the boy's mother.[14]

Passages like this one reflect the variety of the writer's interactions with the people of Lagos as he cultivated new friendships and met new faces in the conduct of both his public and private affairs. Meanwhile his best friend at university, Chike Momah, had secured employment as a librarian at the University of Ibadan, while Chukwuemeka Ike, who graduated in 1955, and Christopher Okigbo, another product of Umuahia Government College, became closer friends. When Ike graduated in 1955 he teased his friend: 'I made the same degree that you made, so you should not swank.' And Achebe replied in the same playful spirit: 'There are many stars in the firmament but some shine brighter than others.'[15] That playful tone notwithstanding, Achebe's prediction was to be fulfilled in more ways than one.

A young man of about 24 years in a senior staff position with a promising career is liable to be perceived as good husband material by many young women. Even in those days Lagos girls had acquired the reputation of being able to get the men they desired. There is no doubt that Achebe encountered these Lagos girls. He was interested in dancing and his friend Christopher Okigbo was noted for attracting all kinds of female companions and encouraging others to copy his liberal attitudes. But Achebe was not the type of young man to flaunt his sexual escapades and critics of his novels were later to point out that in his first novel he had been particularly restrained in depicting sexual behaviour: 'Even in those days he was not a man of many words. He just carried her into his bed and in the darkness began to feel around her waist for the loose end of her cloth.'[16] His other novels, however, hardly suggest that he was a novice in romance.

> I saw Elsie standing in a group with other student nurses and made straight for her. She turned out to be a most vivacious girl newly come to the nursing school. We danced twice, then I suggested we took a walk away from the noisy band and she readily agreed. If I had been left to my own devices nothing might have happened that day. But, no doubt without meaning to, Elsie took a hand in the matter. She said she was thirsty and I took her to my room for a drink of water.[17]

Odili Samalu's first encounter with Elsie in *A Man of the People* does not end with the glass of water:

> She was one of those girls who send out loud cries in the heat of the thing. It happened again each time. But that first day it was rather funny because she kept calling: 'Ralph darling'. I remember wondering why Ralph. It was not until weeks later that I got to know that she was engaged to some fellow called Ralph, a medical student in Edinburgh.

The female companions Achebe attracted in real life at that time cannot be assumed to be of the 'Elsie type' only, because then as now there were many women – responsible and irresponsible, natural and artificial – residing in the city of Lagos.

The responsibilities and duties of a senior broadcasting officer occupied much of Achebe's attention in 1955. In the January 1955 issue of the *Radio Times* it was reported that 'the Talks section in Lagos carries a big responsibility for imparting information, as distinct from news. In this way the Nigerian Broadcasting Service tries to fulfil one of its functions, that of educating the listener.' The report added that Angela Beattie had garnered many years of varied experience both at the BBC and in the field of weekly journalism, while the other member was Chinua Achebe.

> It was originally intended that he should work in the Eastern Regional Headquarters of

the NBS at Enugu. Such, however, was his flair for literary work that it was decided to specialize him in talks production rather than in the more routine aspects of programme work.

The writer went on to explain that

a very real creative effort is required in producing talks. The producer has to bring out of the speaker what he or she really wants to say, which is by no means what the speaker always writes. Then too there is a vast difference between writing for the eye (newspapers, books) and for the ear (radio). Add to this that the producers are responsible for seeing that the talks are balanced, and do not contain any tendencies or mischievous material, and you can see that their job is a very exacting one![18]

In spite of those exacting responsibilities, Achebe found time to play host to several friends, former colleagues and former teachers, like Ulli Beier:

When he started working in Lagos I did see him then. The capital was not an overcrowded, violent megacity into which it has deteriorated now. It was an attractive little town with many quarters built entirely in the beautiful 'Brazilian' style architecture. These visits to Lagos gave me a chance to see Chinua occasionally. I dropped by his office to chat on literature and politics.[19]

Such conversations no doubt provided social and political insights for Achebe, who had started work on a novel which would reflect some of his reactions to the social and political issues confronted by his culture. This cultural consciousness was enriched by the fact that productions in the Talks Department incorporated various aspects of the climate of change in culture, religion, education, the economy and the art of governance. There was no model that Achebe could emulate since modern African fiction written in English was minimal, with Amos Tutuola's *Palm-Wine Drinkard* and Cyprian Ekwensi's *People of the City* among the precursors. The pamphlets sold at Onitsha market were in vogue but they elicited a certain degree of disdain from educated Nigerians who considered their contents trivial. The novel Achebe was writing, therefore, was in the nature of what a literary explorer at the frontier of creativity would produce. He conceived it as the story of three generations of people; a man whose life commences before the advent of colonialism, his son who is converted to Christianity and acquires some Western education, and the grandson living on the verge of independence after the turmoil of past events. In concept it was an ambitious novel with three segments reflecting those three characters: by late 1955 it was gradually taking shape, both in the mind of the writer and on paper.

It was while Achebe was working on his novel that Queen Elizabeth visited Nigeria early in 1956. Achebe recalled: 'We had a Royal visit to Nigeria. As a broadcaster I was very busy during the day working and very busy at night with this novel. So it sticks to my mind.'[20] The queen's visit certainly illuminated many issues: it highlighted for Achebe the ideas intrinsic to his status as a colonial subject and an African citizen. It also brought into prominence the grand idea behind the European civilizing mission in Africa in the areas of politics, religion and economics. This idea is one that Achebe started to question in his novel. By the end of March 1956 he had virtually completed the first draft of a novel to which he gave the tentative title *Things Fall Apart*. It was a title that alluded not only to the fast pace of political events but also to the endemic internal pressures that were emerging, with the Eastern and Western regions in

Nigeria asking for independence and the Northern region reluctant to take it. In the Broadcasting Service, meanwhile, the expatriate employees in authority were getting ready to relinquish posts to the indigenes, and they encouraged those Nigerians considered competent to embark on relevant courses.

In early 1956 Chinua Achebe and Bisi Onabanjo, editor of the *Radio Times*, were nominated by the NBS, Lagos to attend the BBC Staff School in London organized for participants from Africa, Australia, New Zealand, Canada and Asia, and especially for those from countries in which there were British interests and English was the language of communication. The broad criteria for selecting trainees were competence and relevance. The first segment of the course was in basic radio techniques, followed by a tour around the BBC regional stations. Finally, a series of attachments were arranged around the trainee's expertise; the total period for the course and attachments could be up to five months. Achebe was scheduled to attend a general Radio Production course for overseas broadcasters from 3 April to 11 May, to be followed by attachment to a BBC department from 12 May to 31 August. It was his first opportunity to travel out of Nigeria. 'For the first time, I needed and obtained a passport, and saw myself defined therein as a British Protected Person. Somehow the matter had never come up before.'[21] This was the colonial reality, although self-government had commenced in the Eastern and Western regions of Nigeria. Achebe took the manuscript of the novel he had written and flew to London where he shared an apartment – for it was a non-residential programme – with Bisi Onabanjo.

The Radio Production course was

> designed to develop high standards of programme-making, editorial judgement and performance at the microphone. It covers all the main areas of radio production and presentation – programme research, planning, script writing, interviewing, editing, studio and OB [Outside Broadcasting] recording techniques, commentary, music selection and presentation, magazine and feature making, introduction to radio drama and so on.

The training was meant to improve the expertise of the participants, placing

> emphasis on practical work so that each trainee gains as much 'hands-on' experience as possible. Trainees visit BBC network radio and world service and see something of the BBC's regional and local radio stations to study the various ways in which pro-grammes are made and to talk to their opposite numbers in UK Broadcasting. This exchange of ideas is intended to expand the trainees' horizons, to refresh their pro-gramme thinking, and is particularly suitable for programme makers, who after a few years in the profession are about to take on added responsibilities.[22]

That he would be offered additional responsibility on successful completion of the course and his return to Nigeria was by no means certain to Achebe as he absorbed the various aspects of his professional training in London. The course timetable indicated a gradual introduction to the elements of broadcasting through workshop exercises. The studio exercises involved drills in dialogue sessions of *Real People Talking* and radio plays. The technical aspects of the course, concerning the use of microphones and acoustics for drama, were demon-strated and emphasis was laid on the important processes of selecting scripts, producing radio plays, editing tapes, making sound effects and translating and adapting drama. The course offered valuable experience in using music in drama, dubbing and editing in the transformation of a script into broadcast material. The participants attended recording exercises that afforded them an opportunity for analysis and criticism as well as visits to the sound effects and play libraries of the BBC. The nature of this course was not really different from what Chinua Achebe had learnt on the job, either instinctively or through Angela Beattie. Nevertheless, the sessions broadened his outlook and provided him with fresh perspectives. Part of what the course reiterated, though it highlighted the importance of basic radiophonics, was the essential ingredient of creativity in the writing of the scripts.

It must have been after one of the writing sessions that Chinua Achebe's colleague Bisi Onabanjo became aware that Achebe had written a novel which he had brought to London. One of the lecturers at the BBC school was Gilbert Phelps, and Achebe and Onabanjo gathered from the other students that he was a novelist. Onabanjo urged Achebe to show his novel to Phelps: 'Show him what you're doing!' Achebe recalls that 'Onabanjo said it to me a number of times. And in the end I agreed and went forward timidly and said to him, "Would you look at something I've done?" And he accepted rather politely.'[23] Phelps agreed to look at the novel without evincing much enthusiasm, which did not buoy the spirits of the young Nigerian broadcaster. It was at the end of the course and the participants were on a trip around the country which took them to several towns. When after some days the touring party stopped at the city of York, Gilbert Phelps telephoned their hotel but they were all out. He had read the manuscript within days and he left a message that Achebe should call him as soon as he came back to the hotel. When Achebe returned and acknowledged the telephone message he was invited to dinner by Phelps. The dinner took place at Phelps's home some days later when the group returned to London, and it was then that he delivered his enthusiastic verdict, telling Achebe he had written a very good novel. In fact, Phelps wanted to show it to his own editor and publishers immediately, but Achebe asked for more time: 'It isn't quite what I wanted yet.'[24]

Phelps's enthusiasm was nevertheless the break that the young writer needed. That first draft still linked the stories of Okonkwo, his son Nwoye (also known as Isaac) and grandson Obi Okonkwo. Achebe did not want to submit the manuscript to the publishers immediately because he 'wanted to make some corrections, especially the latter part which was *No Longer at Ease*. It was actually two novels in one.' Meanwhile the enthusiasm of Phelps made some of the other instructors at the BBC school aware that a Nigerian broadcaster had written a novel. One of them said to Achebe, 'I heard you are writing a novel, is it going to be like Cyprian Ekwensi's?' Achebe remembers how 'without meaning to be rude, I said "I hope not". And then, you know the British, he said, "I hope not too!"' Achebe explains that

> everybody has his own idea. I mean, Cyprian had developed one style and kind of writing and I had no intention to imitate or repeat what he had done. Tutuola was a total world of his own too. But that was one different style and approach and everything, and Cyprian was another. I wanted something of my own style.[25]

The BBC programme drew to a close at the end of August and Achebe prepared to return to Nigeria. He chose to travel by ship this time, having flown to London earlier in the year. Obi Okonkwo's experience in *No Longer at Ease* thus draws on his own, although this section was not added until Achebe had restructured the first draft of *Things Fall Apart*. In *No Longer at Ease* Obi had joined 'a small cargo boat carrying twelve passengers and a crew of fifty'. On the first day the protagonist/Achebe

> kept to himself viewing the sea or reading in his cabin. It was his first sea voyage and he had already decided that it was infinitely better than flying. He woke up the following morning without any sign of the much talked about sea-sickness. He had a warm bath before any of the other passengers were up, and went to the rails to look at the sea [which had become] an endless waste of restless, jaggy hillocks topped with white.

That voyage back to Nigeria passed through Madeira and Funchal, and close to Freetown, Sierra Leone. In Funchal the boat anchored, enabling the passengers to stretch their legs, watch the coin-divers and walk along the 'cobbled streets past quaint cars in the taxi-rank', past two oxen pulling a cart which was just a flat board on wheels with a man and a sack of something in it, and the little gardens and parks. Achebe finally succumbed to sea-sickness, which kept him awake for a few nights as he lay on his cabin bed and 'rolled from one edge of the bed to the other groaning and creaking in the darkness'.[26] He recovered quickly, though, and was able to enjoy the pleasures of the remainder of the voyage to Lagos.

Achebe was assigned to his former duties in the Talks Department at NBS which he commenced with renewed zeal. He also found time, however, to start revising his manuscript, pruning what he considered to be the loose ends of the story. He excised the second and third parts of the novel, leaving only the story of Okonkwo. This story he restructured, adding fresh chapters, and paragraphs and generally turning it into what he considered a reasonably substantial novel. The revision kept him quite busy until early in 1957. He then saw an advertisement in the *Spectator*, copies of which were sent to various offices and institutions in Nigeria, which stated: 'Authors' manuscripts typed'. He sent the only copy of the handwritten manuscript he had prepared to this typing agency by ordinary mail. In their acknowledgement the agency requested a fee of £22, which Achebe sent by British postal order. That was the beginning of his anxiety, for he heard nothing from the agency for many months. Achebe wrote some reminders but there was no response, by which time he had become quite worried. Fortunately, as the year was drawing to a close Angela Beattie, about to relinquish her post as head of Talks, was going to London for her annual leave. Achebe asked her to ascertain the fate of the manuscript he had sent to the typing agency. She was furious when she arrived in London and confronted the people at the agency. They retrieved the manuscript gathering dust in a corner of the office. Her intervention eventually forced them to type it and send it back to Achebe in Lagos, supplying only one typed copy.[27]

Angela Beattie's intervention probably ensured that events in Achebe's life took their present course, for the loss of the manuscript would have been disastrous for his writing career. Mike Awoyinfa records Achebe's response when asked what his reaction would have been if the manuscript had been stolen: he said 'that he would have died'.[28] Alan Hill says that Achebe answered: 'I would have been so discouraged that I would probably have given up altogether. Even if I had forced myself to write the book again, it would have been a different book.'[29] In spite of the anxiety concerning his manuscript, 1957 was a good year for Achebe's career in broadcasting: he was promoted to head of Talks, succeeding Angela Beattie.

6

On the Path of Life
Controller of the Eastern Region
1958–60

T H E new responsibilities of Chinua Achebe at the Nigerian Broadcasting Service in 1957 coincided with new political realities, not only in Lagos, but also in the regional capitals of Enugu, Ibadan and Kaduna. This meant that he was in a position where he could monitor the speeches, assess their worth and generally observe the political trends in the country. The tribal politics which had materialized in the Western House of Assembly when he was a student about six years before had become increasingly disconcerting. But his optimism that the future would turn out well, reflected in the general high expectations of independence, was not really dampened. It was in this mood of hope that he sent the typescript of *Things Fall Apart* to the literary agent of Gilbert Phelps in 1958, in search of an interested publisher.

Early in 1958, too, the career of Chinua Achebe at the NBS received another boost when the colonial administrators started a policy of indigenization in the ministries and parastatals. Achebe was promoted as controller of the Broadcasting Service for the Eastern Region at the age of 28, while Victor Badejo became controller of the Western Region and Umaru Ladan controller for the Northern Region. The promotion meant that Achebe had to proceed to Enugu where he would be in charge of the Enugu, Onitsha and Port Harcourt stations, taking over from T. B. Radley, an Englishman. Before he arrived, the Eastern zone of the service had developed a more forward-looking policy than the other zones. Ejike Obumneme Aghanya, who joined the NBS at Enugu in 1954 after his school certificate examination, remembers the Mangol salary revision exercise in that year.

> Mr Mangol recommended more money for the programme staff of the NBS than he recommended for the engineering staff who have the same qualification. This gave rise to agitations among the Engineering staff and it led to the formation of the Engineering Workers' Association whose aim was to correct the anomalies generated by Mangol's review panel.

Aghanya, as the president of that association, could see that the mandate of the union was not universal enough, and convinced the members of the association to work for the entire staff of the NBS so that they would not only achieve their aims but also win broader support. His first act as president was to persuade the

members to start a staff canteen. This association of NBS staff was still in its formative stage when Chinua Achebe was appointed controller of the NBS at
Enugu.

Aghanya recalls that the new controller immediately supported the association morally and financially by buying some shares in the canteen. Other members of the senior staff like Egbuna Obidike and Sam Nwaneri, who was head of
programmes, also bought shares. The money generated was used to operate the
canteen which was built by the direct labour of the members. After the canteen
had operated for a while, it was profitable enough for the members of the association to buy a refrigerator. The canteen enabled the workers to eat regularly
despite the nature of their duties that required shift work. Within a short time
enough money was made to compensate all shareholders and allow the canteen
to operate on the profits generated. Aghanya emphasizes that as controller
Achebe was thoroughly impressed by the way the association handled the canteen business. He also took a keen interest in the Engineering Workers' Association, and with his help their financial aims were achieved. Achebe also used
the example of the Enugu Association to convince the director-general of the
NBS at Lagos that a staff canteen at the national level was necessary. It was that
recommendation that led to the establishment of canteens at the other regional
headquarters. As Aghanya concludes,

> Achebe was unassuming and humble as the controller. He was a big part of the success
> of the association at Enugu. His manner of approach in handling matters affecting his
> subordinates helped in a tremendous way to make the administration easy.[1]

As Achebe settled down to administering the Eastern zone of the NBS, his
manuscript was doing the rounds of the London publishing houses. Several
rejected it on the grounds that fiction by African writers did not possess good
financial prospects. Finally the manuscript reached the office of William
Heinemann, where it was presented to James Michie and through him came to
the attention of Alan Hill, a publishing innovator. Alan Hill has described that
moment:

> Heinemann's normal fiction reader read it and did a long report but the firm was still
> hesitating whether to accept it. Would anyone possibly buy a novel by an African?
> There are no precedents. So the rather doubting bunch at the top of Heinemann's
> thought of the educational department, who after all sold books to Africa and were
> supposed to know about Africans. So they showed it to one of our educational advis-
> ers, Professor Donald MacRae, who was just back from West Africa. He read it in the
> office and ended the debate with an eleven word report: 'This is the best novel I have
> read since the war.'[2]

Thus *Things Fall Apart* was published in hardback on 17 June 1958 with a print
run of 2,000 copies. The publishers did not 'touch a word of it' in order to correct
it and it achieved instant acclaim in the British national press, with enthusiastic
reviews by such critics as Walter Allen and Angus Wilson'.[3] It changed the
direction of Alan Hill's publishing life and added a new dimension to the list of
books published by Heinemann. On 20 June 1958, three days after the publication of the novel, the *Times Literary Supplement* wrote that the novel 'gen-
uinely succeeds in presenting tribal life from the inside', while 'patterns of feeling and attitudes of mind appear clothed in a distinctive African imagery,
written neither up nor down' and the literary method of the author 'is appar-

ently simple, but a vivid imagination illuminates every page, and his style is a model of clarity'. The novel displays Achebe's powers of observation and memory, for no detail eludes him as he blends the various elements of the story. He captures and enshrines the whole ethos of his people. The reviews emphasized both the importance of the novel and the talent of the author. *Time and Tide* called it a 'fascinating story' and considered that 'Mr. Achebe's style is a model for aspirants'. Echoing this view, *The Observer* praised it as an 'excellent novel' which is 'well worth reading' while *The Listener,* in a judgement flavoured with the prejudice of the period, thought that 'the author possesses literary gifts of a high order, writing a clear and meaty style free of the dandyism often affected by Negro authors'.[4] These praises in the British press were free of condescension: it was Achebe's competence that interested them.

Chinua Achebe's first novel[5] is based on the life of Okonkwo, a prominent member of the Igbo society. He achieves success as a wrestler, farmer and elder in the tradition and customs of his people. However, the incursion of Western civilization disrupts the cultural ethos of his people, plunging him into tragedy as he resists the effects of such alien ways of life. Achebe chronicles both the positive and negative aspects of his development, particularly the disintegration of a viable socio-cultural order. In addition Achebe depicts the state of affairs before the European arrives as well as the consequences of that arrival. It is a story that captures the tension and passion of the colonial encounter.

The use of language is distinctive, drawing on a rich oral tradition. Achebe, writing some years later, argues that 'the prose tradition of non-literate people is often presumed to consist of folktales, legends, proverbs and riddles', but that 'they represent the least important part. If one takes the Igbo society, which I know best, it seems quite clear that the finest examples of prose occur not only in those forms but in oratory and even in the art of good conversation.' His argument is that 'serious conversation and oratory' call for 'an original and individual talent and at best belong to a higher order. Unfortunately there is no way of preserving them in a non-literate society. One catches glimpses of the glory of the Igbo oratory by listening to the few people remaining in the villages who can deploy the full resources of the language.' He adds:

> Some of the finest examples of oratory I have heard have been performed from the village pulpit by Christian converts of my father's generation. The good orator calls to his aid the legends, folklore, proverbs etc. of his people; they are some of the raw material with which he works.'[6]

It was this awareness of cultural resources that was to change the literary scene in many parts of Africa after the frontier-clearing role of Chinua Achebe.

At Enugu, however, where Achebe was gradually getting used to the daily responsibilities of administering the Eastern zone of the NBS, the publication of the novel enhanced his reputation only in the circle of the élite. Ralph Opara, who had been sending stories to him at the Talks Department in Lagos, joined the Broadcasting Service in September 1958 under Frances Ademola as head of Talks and Sunday Young-Harry as senior producer. Opara became the programme assistant in charge of Talks. At Enugu, meanwhile, it was the practice to offer vacation jobs to students from the few higher education institutions in the country. The idea was to attract as many qualified people as possible after their graduation. In 1958 three young women – Christie Chinwe Okoli from

Umuokpu, Awka, a Miss Okwor and a Mrs Aboyade – were among those offered vacation jobs at the NBS, Enugu. Christie Okoli was in Enugu because her parents lived there and she normally spent her holidays with them. She had been born in Port Harcourt and grown up at Calabar and Enugu as the sixth and last child in a family of five girls and one boy. She was preceded by her sisters Uzoamaka, Onejinuno, Amaogenu and Enuma, and her brother Umeadim. Christie Okoli was interested in drama and singing which made her vacation work in radio helpful. In addition she also had a column, 'Little Things That Interest Me', which she wrote for the *Nigerian Outlook,* then managed by M. C. K. Ajuluchukwu and Sam Epelle. Comparing notes as they settled in their vacation jobs, Christie and Miss Okwor discovered that Mrs Aboyade was rated higher and her remuneration calculated accordingly. The two women were surprised and Miss Okwor urged Christie Okoli to do something about it immediately.

Miss Okwor insisted so much that Christie went to see the controller, Chinua Achebe, in order to argue that they should be given an increment. That was the first day that Christie met Chinua Achebe – hardly a romantic occasion, she recalls, although she did feel instinctively that 'this man's wife is very lucky'. That day they discussed business and it did not occur to the young woman that she was going to develop romantic feelings. The case which she presented was that she considered it unfair that someone who was employed some days later was placed on a higher scale of pay. Chinua Achebe carefully explained to her that Mrs Aboyade had worked somewhere else before securing the vacation job at the NBS. Christie felt that 'it was an objective, dispassionate discussion'. But Achebe must have ascertained from a general introduction that the woman was from the same Awka town, though a different village, from which his mother hailed. That element of familiar context in the discussion must have enhanced the feeling of relaxation as the discussion progressed and even in future interactions after the initial meeting. But as Christie confessed in later years:

> There was nothing at all to suggest I will even end up with him. I had a medical student boyfriend before meeting him. But there is something about Chinua; this simplicity he appears to have. He is full of inner strength which gives you as a person interacting with him a lot of security. You know he is somebody you can fall back on. From so many angles he is somebody you can rely on. It is important to have somebody who will not let you down. It is a strong anchor to have in life.[7]

When Christie started the vacation job nobody thought that she would be dislodged from her boyfriend. He was a lot of fun, although she did not feel comfortable about the uncertainty of his place of origin. Her relationship with him had progressed positively to the extent that one of his relatives once called on Christie to thank her for the manner in which she had managed to control his habits – making him better behaved, encouraging him to reduce his desire for alcohol and generally contributing to his refinement and polished appearance. But after a while it became apparent to Christie that the young man had not told her the whole truth about himself, for he did not even know the identity of his father, a cultural feature that was regarded as essential in her society. She started developing mixed feelings about the relationship; as she talked to her friends, it dawned on her that she might become the mother of the man's children yet she was not really certain of his identity. Christie expressed her misgivings sincerely but the young man did not take kindly to her change of heart. Some time later, when he learnt of her relationship with Achebe, he wrote to her father telling him about 'a tree he was planning to cut which some other person had cut down'.[8] Many years later the young man revealed to Christie that he had accepted her challenge and managed to establish his identity, which made him a native of Rivers State.

It was when Christie's relationship with the medical student started to deteriorate that Chinua Achebe stepped into her life. At just this time she had an appendectomy: her appendix had almost ruptured, but fortunately the operation was carried out in time. At the NBS offices where she worked, she had not shared her problems with her colleagues; she was therefore surprised when the controller, Chinua Achebe, paid her a visit while she was convalescing. She was touched by the attention of this man who would come to the hospital with gifts and magazines. When she recovered Christie went to express her thanks and found Achebe even more helpful, but she still felt restrained in responding to his generosity, although her friend Miss Okwor would prod her to ask for things like soft drinks. Certainly Achebe was becoming attracted to this young woman from Umuokpu, Awka. It was thus that the relationship developed and started growing, even as Christie ended her vacation job and resumed her studies at the university.

Achebe, on the other hand, was engaged in many activities at Enugu, especially in connection with impending independence. Meanwhile, he was pleased to learn that the publication of his novel had generated notice outside Africa, though by contrast recognition was slow to come in Nigeria. Alan Hill, who visited Nigeria in January 1959, said that he 'felt there must be other potential authors among the new university-educated generation in Nigeria'. So he went to West Africa and took Achebe's book around with him:

> Everywhere I was greeted with total scepticism that a recent student from the University of Ibadan should have written a novel of any significance at all. At the University of Ibadan they didn't take me seriously when I told them that one of their alumni had written a great novel. 'What, Chinua Achebe write a novel! How ridiculous!' they exclaimed.[9]

One of the professors, Molly Mahood, made her students laugh when she said: 'That will be the day when English literature is taught from Chaucer to Achebe.'[10] Ironically, she would be teaching *Things Fall Apart* at a location much closer to where Chaucer lived before the passage of many years. There were more enterprising teachers, however, like Ulli Beier who had joined the Department of Extra-Mural Studies under Dr Robert Gardiner.

> The Extra-Mural department allowed me to use Chinua's book in my classes and the university could not control what I taught. Actually what I taught depended on what the students requested provided a teacher could be found to teach it. It would be the duty of the regional tutor to find a teacher and arrange the fees. If I persuaded my students that it might be more interesting to read Chinua Achebe and they accepted, then the books were recommended. At that time the Department of English would not teach African Literature. When I started to run the Extra-Mural Programme in 1953 I had to rely heavily on francophone authors: I translated poetry by Senghor, Césaire, Diop and Rabéarivelo. My Extra-Mural students had some difficulties with Tutuola's *Palm-Wine Drinkard*. They couldn't accept the fact that Tutuola wrote 'wrong' English and they argued that these were mere children's tales which they had heard from their grandfathers. It was the appearance of *Things Fall Apart* that finally made everything fall into place. Although my students were almost entirely Yoruba speakers, they

could identify with this book. For the first time the extra-mural classes on African literature really came alive.[11]

Such classroom discussions made the value of the novel clearer to its Nigerian readers.

Perceptive Nigerian readers included Pius Okigbo, the elder brother of Christopher Okigbo, who had qualified and had a reputation for brilliance as an economist. Pius Okigbo perceived the potential of the new novelist and also the fact that the novel had cleared a frontier: this made him both pleased and worried.

> I recall sending for Chinua soon after reading the book and lamenting to him that that book had finished him as a novelist. It had seemed to me so original, fresh and path-breaking that it would be impossible to pass that route more than once.

Pius Okigbo was pleased to be proved wrong by subsequent events which 'goes to show you what a poor literary judge Pius Okigbo will always remain'.[12] Other reviewers in Nigeria acclaimed the novel. Diana Speed wrote in *Black Orpheus* that

> not since *Mister Johnson* has a novel about West Africa written in English shown such love and warmth for his subject as this first novel by a young Nigerian author.... The book as a whole creates for the reader such a vivid picture of Ibo life that the plot and characters are little more than symbols representing a way of life lost irrevocably within living memory. The quiet unpretentious prose, deceptively simple, lends credence to the activities of an agrarian community whose unquestioning acceptance of age-old moral values, customs, beliefs and fears make the society the entity it is.... This is a piece of history; the reader feels the calamity on every purposeful and organized society in which the individual personality is not an end in itself but a contribution to the whole.[13]

Similarly G. Adali-Mortty, in another issue of *Black Orpheus,* concludes that

> when comments on the content and the style of the book have been exhausted, its intangible beauty remains. Some may call it magic; others the halo, the aroma, the charm, or the unanalyzable quintessence which binds everything together in harmony and unity.[14]

Soon after this was written, *Things Fall Apart* was awarded the Margaret Wrong Memorial Prize, named after an English missionary who promoted literary activities and whose vision contributed to the establishment of the East African Literature Bureau in Nairobi and the Northern Rhodesia and Nyasaland Publications Bureau. Margaret Wrong had died of a stroke in 1948 while travelling as the Secretary of the International Committee on Christian Literature in Africa. After her death a Memorial Prize for Literature in Africa was organized as part of a Trust Fund to stimulate African Literature. A call for manuscripts by the Trust Fund had inspired Amos Tutuola to write *Palm-Wine Drinkard* in three days.

The Margaret Wrong Memorial Prize confirmed Achebe's achievement but he did not rest on his laurels. His next publication was a short story, 'The Sacrificial Egg'.[15] It is a story about Julius Obi, a clerk in Umuru who visits his fiancée Janet and her mother one evening in the midst of a smallpox epidemic which is described as a 'decorating artist'. In it Achebe explores another aspect of his culture. Julius Obi, in his haste to escape the night masks, accidentally breaks an egg which is part of the sacrifice by an individual striving to overcome the effects of smallpox. Barely one week later Janet and her mother become victims and the story ends with the sorrow of Julius Obi whose 'emptiness deepened with every passing day' because he stands 'on this side of life' while on 'the other side' are 'Ma and Janet whom the dread artist decorated'. The manner in which Achebe contrives to make the setting and the cultural atmosphere part of the story, and the evocation of life in Umuru with its associated legends and myths, combine to make it an interesting story woven around the tensions between religious beliefs and social relationships. Thus the story further illustrates the creative qualities that had attracted his publishers, Heinemann, and earned the African novelist his first laurels. Achebe's interest in culture, tradition and especially the mores and norms of society had not flagged and it was this interest that drew his attention to a programme produced at the NBS, Enugu at this time.

In those days the presentation of programmes was followed by a post-mortem in order to improve the efficiency of the producers and make the contents more relevant. In one of these post-production assessment sessions which Chinua Achebe as the controller hosted at home, he overheard something which attracted him.

> There was a programme which had been done by one of our best producers in those days called Chijioke Abagwe, in which someone was being interviewed about his village, and the story of this Chief Priest who was imprisoned by the District Officer came out in the interview.

Chijioke Abagwe was the head of Igbo programmes and he had a special interview programme in which he presented stories illustrating various aspects of the New Yam Festival in many places. In that particular programme a community was presented as holding its own festival in February, unlike other Igbo communities which had theirs in November. That community was Umuchu and the man who had featured in the interview was a retired policeman known as Alagbogu Nnolim. His story was the seed which eventually germinated as *Arrow of God*. It tells how the chief priest in Umuchu, who had been imprisoned, succeeded in winning the support of his people, and of their decision to celebrate the New Yam Festival three months late. Achebe explains:

> I was so fascinated by this story that I got Abagwe to locate this man again and we went to his place and he told me a lot more about the incident. Not only that, we even went to his village in order to have a feel of this place.[16]

The features of that story were documented in Achebe's mind although the events were skeletal: the incident illustrates well how the young controller was able to integrate fascination with his culture and his administrative duties – something also illustrated, in that year of 1959, by the series of short essays ('Listening in the East') that Achebe wrote for the Lagos-based monthly, *Radio Times*.

In the January issue he informs readers of the opening of a medium-wave transmitter at Onitsha and of the various programmes available: jazz presented by Ben Osuagwu, Brian Atkinson's classical music programme and a new series of talks on Nigerian wild life by A. B. Couzens which, Achebe insists, would be 'an opportunity to gain an insight into the sometimes fascinating life and behaviour of Nigerian animals' although he acknowledged that it 'is said that most Nigerians are only interested in animals when they can eat them or sell them'. He also reminds listeners of the programme 'It's Your Money They

Are After', aimed at 'exposing the way swindlers get hold of your money'. The most interesting programmes highlighted by Achebe in those essays, however, relate to the oral tradition: he mentions the story of the cat and the rat who were great friends but who quarrelled, and also asks the audience to 'listen to the wonderful story of the sheltered life of an Ozo man's wife'. He stresses the importance of vernacular programmes like *Ndi Beanyi Kedunu* in Igbo, *Ekombo* in Efik and *Kon Otu Ifie* in Ijaw. In the February essay Achebe mentions again some of the programmes highlighted in the January essay in addition to a review of the industrial magazine and religious programmes. He concludes with a reminder of an Igbo play, *Azege na Ogene,* which tells how a woman native doctor 'sought to marry the son of a Chief as her reward for curing the chief of his ailment'.[17]

In March Achebe praises the songs of Harcourt Whyte of the Leper School at Uzuakoli. He described the songs as possessing a tense and 'sometimes disquieting mood' which was like 'the good wine that needs no bush'. One programme which Achebe mentions in that essay must have fascinated him particularly:

> this month we are contributing to the National programme a thought-provoking feature on the caste system in Eastern Nigeria, with particular reference to the *Osu* and the *Oru* systems. Egbuna Obidike, who will write and produce this programme, says that the *Oru* are slaves bought and sold like ordinary household goods. But the *Osu,* in addition to being bought and sold, are dedicated to the gods. You might think that an *Osu* would be in a happier position than an *Oru.* But you would be wrong; whereas an *Oru* could buy his freedom, an *Osu* is always an *Osu* as are his descendants after him.

In the April essay Achebe again stresses the value of the information to be derived from the programmes, mentioning Bob Ogbuagu's 'Eastern Note-Book' and W. W. Echezona's weekly illustrated talks on the musical instruments of Eastern Nigeria.

The May essay reminds listeners of the regular programmes in addition to new ones like 'Our School Sings', 'Radio Gardener', 'Books in General' and children's programmes with their various highlights. In June he describes the Women's Programmes, and cites the Igbo and Efik plays as innovative additions to the broadcast from the Eastern Region. The July essay mentions two 'new five-minute talks': the first series by Brian Atkinson is intended for 'students going to England' and 'will tell them all they need to know'; the second, 'To Talk of Many Things', will range 'from cabbages to kings' with Cecil Greatorix the first speaker in the series.[18]

There is no doubt that many of the programmes mentioned in these essays must have exerted an influence on Achebe's creativity. The stories also made him recognize the competence of those working within his sphere of influence, like Okokon Ndem. The most interesting aspect of Ndem was his voice, which he modulated expertly to suit what he read; eight years later, during the Nigerian civil war, Okokon Ndem was to become a significant voice on Radio Biafra.

Meanwhile Achebe had started work on his second novel, based on part of what he had written in 1957.

> I thought of *Things Fall Apart* as spanning a period of two or three generations of the first people who confronted the white man, say Okonkwo, his son and his grandson, as a continous story covering those three generations. This was the way I thought of

the story to begin with; so in a way the chronology of the crucial period was already in my mind when I was thinking of writing *Things Fall Apart.*

But he discarded that plot because it did not seem satisfactory and

decided to concentrate on Okonkwo's story and after to deal with Nwoye and then Obi. That's how I solved the problem. I didn't find enough for Nwoye, so I put it aside and did the third story, Obi. That middle story is still waiting to be written.[19]

The story of Obi, which turned out to be *No Longer At Ease,* kept him busy in 1959 as he reworked some of the chapters he had written already and added details drawn from his experience in London when he attended the BBC course in 1956. More importantly, he turned the story into an interrogative study of the effects of the new dispensation on that generation that had acquired university education and was also on the verge of acquiring political authority.

Achebe was therefore engaged in the combined tasks of putting the strands of the novel together and administering the NBS at Enugu. It was at this time that he was visited by Christopher Okigbo in the company of Alex Ajayi, the principal of Fiditi Grammar School. That visit was part of a journey that had taken Okigbo and Ajayi to the towns of Onitsha, Ojoto, Ogidi, Enugu, Orlu, Mgbidi, Owerri, Aba and Port Harcourt, meeting many of Okigbo's relations and friends. As Ajayi recalls,

During the Easter holidays of 1959, I requested Okigbo to accompany me on a grand tour of Eastern Nigeria to enable me to know my country more and to meet Chinua Achebe, who was at the Nigerian Broadcasting Service, Enugu, writing his second novel, *No Longer At Ease,* the draft of which he showed us. I was at the time doing a write-up on 'The Beginning of Novel Writing in West Africa' for the University of Durham, with the guidance of Professor M. Mahood, the Head of English Department, University College, Ibadan.[20]

Such visits were becoming normal for Achebe as many local and foreign people sought to know him. Janheinz Jahn, the German scholar who had conducted research in Nigeria and other parts of Africa, had passed through Enugu many months earlier and had lunch with Achebe at his home. That visit by Jahn was part of a tour he had undertaken and culminated in a book he published years later as *Through African Doors,* an account of his experience of African food, modes of travel, cultural perceptions, popular attitudes and social life in both the rural and urban areas.

Achebe welcomed these visitors who came with a genuine desire to meet him as a writer and was courteous to others who came with grievances. The latter included a group from the National Council of Nigeria and the Cameroons, a political party which became the National Council of Nigerian Citizens (NCNC) in 1960 when Southern Cameroon broke off to join the Cameroon Republic. This party was in power in the Eastern Region, and its visit may not have been totally unconnected with the political campaigns for the 1959 Federal elections. It was crucial for the political parties – NCNC, the Northern People's Congress (NPC), and the Action Group Party (AG) – to win the 1959 elections in order to control the seat of government in Lagos. The public servants in control of the media for communication and dissemination of information like the broadcasting stations were made to feel the political pressures as the various candidates sought substantial allocations of air time and extensive coverage of their political campaigns. The premier of the Eastern Region was Dr Nnamdi

Azikiwe, a foremost nationalist who had been forced to abandon the Western House of Assembly, where his NCNC party had won a majority in the 1951–2 elections, after Chief Awolowo convinced the Yoruba members of his party to cross over to his Action Group Party. We have seen that Achebe had been an eyewitness to that incident which had contributed to the magnification of tribal politics in the early 1950s. The Action Group used its majority, acquired through tribal pressure, to make it impossible for Azikiwe to be elected, and the elected officials Olorun-Nimbe and Adeleke Adedoyin did not step down for their leader. Azikiwe thus found himself in the unattractive position of opposition leader in the Western Region. Achebe was also aware that Azikiwe's eventual return to the Eastern Region – contesting and winning a seat in the reconstituted Eastern Legislature to become the leader of the government there – had meant the unwise alienation of former leaders like Eyo Ita whose expulsion from the party led to his formation of the National Independence Party in association with other expelled members. Another leadership quarrel led to Kingsley Mbadiwe breaking away from the NCNC and forming his Democratic Party of Nigeria and the Cameroons (DPNC).

Those facts were known to Chinua Achebe when a group of ministers that included Attorney-General Ajaegbo, the Minister of Information Basil Okwu and A. K. Disu paid him a visit in his office as the controller of NBS. Their visit, however, was made at the time that Kingsley Mbadiwe had started his 'Zik Must Go' campaign following the formation of his political party. The ministers gradually came to the reason for their visit. They complained about the way that the NBS was handling the election campaigns, arguing that it was giving undue air space to Mbadiwe and his group by sending a reporter to cover its functions. They also stated that at the convention of the NCNC the matter had been taken quite seriously which made their visit necessary. Although it was becoming increasingly clear that the politicians who were getting into positions of authority possessed the power to enhance or destroy the career of anybody in an administrative government position Achebe was not afraid to confront them logically. It was also clear to him that his promotion to the position of regional controller had not been due to influence from any of the contending parties. He explained to the group of ministers that the duty of the staff at the Broadcasting Service was to get as many of the contending views as possible and reflect them. He argued that Kingsley Mbadiwe was well known which 'is news and what he says in challenging the NCNC is also news' . He added that

> Mbadiwe has started his political campaign, and whenever the NCNC starts its own campaign too we will give it coverage. As for our sending a reporter it is quite in order. We will probably send two reporters when the NCNC starts its own campaign since it is a bigger party with more newsworthy personalities.

But that argument did not convince the ministers who continued to press: 'Why did you send an Aro man to cover the Mbadiwe campaign? You know he will believe whatever Mbadiwe says like a kinsman and report him without criticism.' Mbadiwe's hometown was Arondizuogu, a town that was founded by citizens from Arochukwu which means that the town has Aro ancestry. Achebe found this new dimension to their argument somewhat amusing, although he explained courteously that: 'We do not send out people on such duties according to their ethnic zone.' Then he asked, 'By the way, who is the man you are talking about, is it not the fellow named Okereke? He comes from Nsukka.'

But that only made the ministers laugh. 'That is what you do not know. That man Okereke comes from Nsukka but he is of Aro extraction. He is still an Aro man.'

'I did not know that', Achebe replied, 'but if there is any specific incident which you want us to correct we will do so. I have explained to you the nature of our responsibilities.'[21] There was really no specific incident except the displeasure of the regional ministers that the Broadcasting Service should extend coverage to their political opponents. Achebe courteously maintained his stand and the ministers took their leave. Soon after this Achebe learned that at the NCNC convention the party had decided to start its own radio station, although it did not do so immediately. Chief Obafemi Awolowo, meanwhile, established a regional radio station in his stronghold, the Western Region. The Northern Region also established a regional station with a transmitter powerful enough to command greater attention in the Eastern Region than the Western Region's station. His proximity could not but increase Achebe's awareness of these political developments, although he perceived them largely as the consequence of political ineptitude which would vanish as soon as the politicians garnered enough experience. He expected that after gaining that experience they would behave with maturity and learn to utilize both literary and cultural opposition, learning from unfavourable views in the manner of the British Governor of Eastern Nigeria, Sir Robert Stapledon de Stapledon, whose wide sweep of reading included *Things Fall Apart.*

> He would always invite me whenever he had important people visiting and there was a dinner or luncheon. I was a kind of celebrity. He would wave me almost around to those people as something happening in his territory. On each occasion he would bring a copy of *Things Fall Apart* and show it to the group of visitors, usually from abroad. I remember that he said a number of interesting things about the book.

But Achebe adds that the fact that this colonial officer read

> does not mean that we do not have leaders who read. Somebody like Azikiwe read a lot. But as you come down from that generation you have a category of leaders who have little regard for Literature, for creative writing. Most times they fail to realize that there is something to be gained from writing.[22]

Stapledon was a perceptive man, especially in terms of giving encouragement to writers, anthropologists and archaeologists. It was at one of his dinners that Achebe met Thurstan Shaw for the first time, and became aware of another aspect of the history of his society which also inspired him to write *Arrow of God.* Thurstan Shaw had worked at Igbo-Ukwu where archaeological discoveries had been made in 1959. He was encouraged and given practical assistance including the loan 'of the tarpaulin off the verandah roof of Government House' by Sir Robert Stapledon de Stapledon and his aide-de-camp, Jonathan Coode. When Shaw completed the first stage of his excavations he decided to make the first display of the Igbo-Ukwu artifacts at a dinner party which the governor gave and to which Chinua Achebe was, as usual, invited. Thurstan Shaw described the sites of the excavation as consisting of 'a store house or shrine for keeping of sacred vessels and regalia', the 'burial chamber of some dignitary' and 'a disposal pit in which pottery and bronzes, animal bones and burnt material had been intentionally deposited'. He asserted that the

74

most remarkable manifestations of this culture are in the form of copper and bronze objects of considerable artistic virtuosity, accompanied by highly decorated pottery and accumulated riches in the form of ivory tusks and thousands of imported beads.[23]

Shaw excavated at Igbo-Ukwu between 8 November 1959 and 15 February 1960. The assembled objects he displayed included ornaments, chains, knife hilts, a knotted wristlet, an anklet with twisted loop, a calabash handle, a scabbard support, hooks, brackets, a fan-holder, bowls, pendants, medallions, a conical bell, an ornate staff-head, a belt plaque, a roped pot-on-stand and a leopard's skull. It was a fascinating collection of items through which Igbo history, or the history of the Igbo at Igbo-Ukwu in particular, could be reconstructed. Achebe gazed at these objects and the inspiration for *Arrow of God,* which had already absorbed the story of the chief priest whose detention led to a three-month delay in the celebration of his people's New Yam festival, began to take shape in his mind. 'I was quite impressed by the display', Achebe recollects, 'especially by the fact that something like that would come out of the Igbo land.'[24] The items showed that the culture of his people had enabled them to produce numerous aesthetic objects and utilitarian gadgets. These images of Igbo culture and history coalesced with contemporary events and stories in Igboland in Achebe's imaginative synthesis.

Sir Robert Stapledon de Stapledon added a catalyst when he made some documents associated with colonial officers and their activities available to Achebe. Sir Robert must have noted the reference at the end of *Things Fall Apart* to the district commissioner who was working on a fictitious work entitled *The Pacification of the Primitive Tribes of the Lower Niger.* He invited Achebe to review his own reports which he had written and compiled as a field officer. Those reports were placed in the government archives at Enugu and Achebe read several of them. He did not adopt any particular pattern but it was clear that some of these reports gradually became woven into the novel *Arrow of God* which was gestating in his mind. Thus when Achebe sat down about two years later to begin work on his third novel the inspiration he had derived from those field reports clearly informed his portrayal of Captain T. K. Winterbottom and the presentation of the memorandum of the lieutenant governor which the district officer in that novel read.

Meanwhile Achebe submitted the manuscript of his second novel, *No Longer at Ease,* to his publishers in London. At the same time the young novelist was preparing to make some major changes in his life, for he had become close to Christie Chinwe Okoli. Christie started seeing Achebe regularly and their respective families met in the traditional manner in order to organize the cultural aspect of the marriage. Christie said that 'Chinua would come for a meeting at Ibadan and he would break it off to see me.'[25] Although they had undergone a slightly different education process, for Christie had attended a college of technology before entering the University College, Ibadan, while Chinua had entered university directly from the secondary school, the young man and woman clearly possessed some characteristics in common that still needed time to blend and perhaps blossom into a harmonious union. Marriages in their society are expected to unite the individuals involved as well as their relatives.

Achebe continued his creative activities while that relationship was proceeding. In 1960 he wrote two short stories. 'Chike's School Days' appeared in the

Rotarian of April 1960 and in it he described the life of Chike, the last child and only son of Amos and Sarah whose marriage had broken a taboo.

> Chike's father was not originally an *Osu*, but had gone and married an *Osu* woman in the name of Christianity. It was unheard of for a man to make himself *Osu* in that way, with his eyes wide open.

In spite of the opposition of old Elizabeth, the mother of Amos, the marriage is made. Thus when Chike refuses 'heathen food at the tender age of four years or maybe five', the slighted neighbour 'muttered under her breath that even an *Osu* was full of pride nowadays, thanks to the white man'. Chike never feels the full effects of his cultural dilemma for he is still young. He starts his education at the village school where he 'developed a strong hatred for Arithmetic' and 'liked particularly the sound of English words even when they conveyed no meaning at all'. His school days over the short period which the story depicts are in effect full of interesting events, songs and strange words from a teacher 'fond of long words'.[26] The short story concludes with a description of Chike's fascination with education. Achebe manages to convey his deeper concern with cultural and religious conflicts, although he portrays Chike's father as exhibiting courage. The authorial perspective of the narrative effectively juxtaposes tradition and modernity and the ironic implications of the story point to the conflicts that emerge more fully in *No Longer at Ease*. It is also significant that when Achebe himself was thinking of marriage these issues relating to cultural and matrimonial realities occupied his creative attention.

The story 'Akueke' was published in the anthology *Reflections* edited by Frances Ademola, who was working at the NBS in Lagos as head of Talks. Achebe uses the village setting of the fictitious Umuofia, made famous in his first novel, and he also uses the name Matefi which is to appear in his third novel. Akueke is stricken by the disease of the 'swollen stomach', which defies cure in spite of the diviners and medicine men consulted by her six brothers. As the only female child the appearance of her sickness shortly after her sensational performance at her age-grade's public dance, and the subsequent visits of suitors anxious to marry her, add to the poignancy of the story. Akueke's maternal grandfather 'was very fond of his granddaughter', who, they said, was the image of his own mother. He rarely called Akueke by her name: 'It was always *Mother*. She was in fact the older woman returned in the cycle of the life. This relationship grew stronger' after the death of Akueke's parents, 'thus when her brothers deposited her at the "evil forest" in order to prevent her death in the home which would have incurred the wrath of the Earth goddess Ani as an abomination', the old man intervenes. He rescues her and carefully tends Akueke into good health. Her brothers, who had thought her dead, respond to the grandfather's invitation to visit him where they are shocked to see the sister they had presumed dead and for whom they were about to perform purification rites. The old man makes his decision definite: 'As for your purification rites you may carry on because Akueke is truly dead in Umuofia.'[27] Achebe synthesizes mundane and mythical elements in this story to caution against hasty judgements. It is a lesson that was relevant to the Nigeria of 1960, with its excessive optimism associated with impending independence from colonial rule.

The general notion among the people was that independence would transform social and economic activities in the country, thereby opening opportunities for self fulfilment and development. In songs, in newspaper articles and in various political speeches expectations were indeed high. That optimism was reflected in the emergence of a community of Nigerian writers and critics, many of them graduates of the University College, Ibadan.

> I think what was happening then was an indication that there was a certain ferment in the society. It was not just one person or two people, but something general, something in the air. Something that has to do with the fact that we were about to become independent.

Certainly there was hope, there was determination and there was a reasonable sense of patriotism. 'We were rediscovering ourselves', Achebe continues,

> We were about to take our lives into our hands again. You see, we were going on the initiative again in our history, because this is what colonialism and all that meant, a loss of initiative and you just have no say in who you were, your own self-development and all that. There was that feeling that at long last all this was coming to an end and one was intoxicated and it produced this feeling of euphoria. We had a story to tell, we were a different people, we must tell this story and we insist on being heard.[28]

Part of that story Achebe had told in *Things Fall Apart* where he literally highlights where the rain, according to an Igbo proverb, began drenching the Nigerian specifically and the African generally. He was also convinced that the story he personally had to tell formed a chain and when the manuscript he had given to Heinemann was published in 1960 as *No Longer at Ease*[29] it became clear that the chain of stories had been strengthened. This novel was dedicated to Christie, the young woman he had come to love with a deep love that had made him commence the traditional rites of marriage.

No Longer at Ease opened a new vista in Achebe's creativity, for it illustrated the ability of the writer to move in time and space in fiction writing. It portrays the élite class gradually coming into leadership positions. Obi Okonkwo, the major character who is also the grandson of Okonkwo in *Things Fall Apart,* returns from studies in England to secure employment in Lagos. His educational career in the village and England confirm his brilliance and intelligence which unsurprisingly secures a civil service job for him. But his promising career and social life as the fiancé of Clara are jolted when he is entangled in the corruption in Lagos. The subsequent tragedy of Obi Okonkwo epitomizes the various elements that confronted the generation he represents and how they fared in the changing world of a nation on the verge of independence.

The pressure that beset Obi clearly foreshadowed some of the forces that would contribute to the disintegration of the new Nigerian society. Obi's problems revolve around conflicting expectations held by the family, the clan, the village, the ethnic group and even the society. His eventual imprisonment for bribery, which astounds the people, is rooted in the cumulative effect of those pressures. In an early review published in *Black Orpheus,* Omidiji Aragbalu writes that 'Chinua Achebe's second novel has been expected with anxiety. His first novel had undoubtedly created a considerable impression' and questions now centred on whether 'the author could be equally convincing when he deals with contemporary Nigerian life', but 'my own fears have certainly been allayed'. For this reviewer, the hero of this novel is not an unusual type. We all know dozens like him. He is not an unforgettable character as [was] his grandfather the warrior Okonkwo, the hero of *Things Fall Apart* [but then] this new novel is about the new Nigerian middle class, as like most bourgeoisies in the world the Nigerian one does not produce particularly powerful and memorable characters.

His conclusion is that 'Achebe has gained a new confidence'.[30]

This new confidence coincided with the formal granting of independence to Nigeria on 1 October 1960. Abubakar Tafawa Balewa became prime minister, for his party (the Northern People's Congress) had won the election. It was a political act that was hailed as an example worthy of emulation, especially since it was conducted, as far as the colonial government was concerned, with decorum in a free and fair election. Unfortunately, the interests of the colonial administrators in Northern Nigeria had made them set up certain political structures associated with indirect rule that were to demand a terrible price. That was still in the future as the songs celebrating independence were chanted; school children were feasted and given souvenirs; the politicians surveyed their respective regions and made their political plans; the civil servants anticipated appointments and promotions; and commercially inclined Nigerians rubbed their hands over their profit forecasts. That month of October 1960 brought pleasant tidings of a different kind to Chinua Achebe. He was awarded a Rockefeller Fellowship 'to travel for six months anywhere', and chose Africa and America.[31] His African destinations would take him to East, Central and Southern Africa.

7

Striding to the Frontier
The 'Voice of Nigeria', Marriage,
& the 'African Writers Series' 1960–2

T H E Rockefeller Fellowship which entitled Chinua Achebe to six months of travel was rightly perceived by him as 'the first important perk of my writing career'.[1] It meant an opportunity to assess developments in other parts of the continent as well as an avenue for the acquisition of knowledge and experience. Its award in the month of Nigerian independence also provided a much-needed distance from the whirl of activities related to politics, so that Achebe was able to contemplate and reflect on these events. Thus one month after independence, in November 1960, Achebe set out on a visit to Kenya, Uganda, Tanganyika, Zanzibar and Southern and Northern Rhodesia (to be known later as Zimbabwe and Zambia respectively). The young novelist 'set forth with one month's worth of ex-colonial confidence' and also 'with high hopes and very little knowledge of real Africa', although he had visited Ghana which 'had been independent for a few years and was justly the pride of emergent Africa'.

Achebe set out with an open mind, but

> The first shock came when we were about to land in Nairobi, Kenya and we were handed immigration forms to fill out. After your name you had to define yourself more fully by filling in one of four boxes: European, Asiatic, Arab, Other! At the airport there were more of the same forms and I took one as a souvenir. I was finding the experience almost funny.[2]

But that experience was to become deeply disconcerting as he continued his travels in East Africa while meeting a variety of people. He observed the phenomenal spread of Swahili:

> A European scholar told me it was more momentous than the rise of nationalism in Africa. An unbalanced assessment, I thought, showing a forgivable partiality for a subject very dear to his heart. But the importance is indeed enormous. That is why every foreign power, great or small, engaged in the new scramble for Africa is daily pouring out radio programmes in that language.

Yet in a discussion of literature with a group of intellectuals in Nairobi 'one or two of them admitted quite frankly that they would not care to read a work written in Swahili'.[3] Such comments made Achebe thoughtful as he evaluated prevalent notions about African literature at that time. 'If you change the names of this book [*Things Fall Apart*] to Kikuyu names,' somebody also told him, 'this would be our story.'[4] He was aware that 'obviously the differences are not as startling, but they are there, and it would be foolish to ignore real differences where they exist'.

Some of those differences he perceived with unease when he proceeded to Tanganyika and Zanzibar on the second leg of his journey. The interesting incidents included the debate in 'a European Club in Dar es Salaam' whether 'it ought to amend its rules so that Julius Nyerere, Chief Minister, might be able to drink there on the invitation of a member', and his visit to 'the home of a rich and good-natured Asian (with children in expensive public schools in England) who complained bitterly that in spite of the large sums of money he had contributed to African charity he was neither appreciated nor trusted' although he was born there and he had 'no other home'. Other incidents were irritating for the Nigerian traveller, who found himself patronized more than once by the colonial rearguard. He encountered a 'nice matronly British receptionist in the second-class hotel' he had checked into in Dar es Salaam who told him that 'she didn't mind having Africans in her hotel and remembered a young West African woman who had stayed there a year or so ago and had "behaved perfectly" all the time she was there and spoke such beautiful English'. His experience in Tanganyika and Zanzibar, later to be renamed Tanzania, struck Achebe in other ways too. He listened to a Legislative Council debate on school integration in which a contributor said: 'We tell the world that we live in a happy multi-racial society; it's all lies, nothing but lies', which made him observe that

> Tanganyika may well become a happy multi-racial country in future. Today it is three racial societies living in one country. And it will probably remain so as long as racial differences tend to coincide with educational, economic and other opportunities.[5]

The implications of that statement were clearly disturbing. Achebe had also witnessed a mass meeting of the Tanganyika African National Union (TANU) 'one hot afternoon in Dar es Salaam'. It was a mass meeting where it was anticipated that a popular minister and secretary of TANU whose public wedding had taken place at St Paul's Cathedral, London, would make his first public appearance, and also that Julius Nyerere would react to the murmurs of dissatisfaction in the party. First 'a number of people spoke from the platform, but the crowd sat unmoved, apparently unimpressed', and it occurred to him 'how totally different all this was from the irrepressible ebullience of a Nigerian political crowd. For one thing a Nigerian gathering would not sit – let alone placidly.' Some time later Achebe noticed that things began to warm up and look a little more familiar as Madam Bibi Titi took the stage 'for she was the leader of the women's wing of TANU and one of Tanganyika's most formidable politicians'. Nevertheless, the most interesting aspect of that rally was Julius Nyerere himself, a man whose simplicity shrouded a highly perceptive mind.

> While his lieutenants spoke Nyerere appeared completely indifferent, smoking or merely toying with his cigarette in apparent boredom. He looked frail and out of place in that robust company. I had never seen a politician appear so unconcerned about his crowd. And yet when he finally rose to his feet and began to speak he was brilliantly effective. From beginning to end the crowd never ceased to cheer and clap and laugh.[6]

The contrast between the ebullience and grandiloquence of Nigerian politicians and the effective and brilliant simplicity of Nyerere was educative. It revealed to the observer that quite often the public accoutrements of Nigerian politicians in the early 1960s were unnecessary; certainly they were not indicative of levels of political commitment. Achebe experienced that commitment in another form when he met Sheikh Shaaban Robert, 'the leading Swahili poet', who was 'greatly depressed by the apathy of his people to Swahili literature'. He told Achebe of 'the difficulty he had publishing new works and how a South African university published one of his books and paid him nothing until he wrote them a letter of protest, whereupon they sent him £40'. The positive dimension to the sad story, according to Achebe, was that

> with very little capital Sheikh Robert has now set up as a publisher and has brought out two books of poetry; one of them, *Masomo Yeme Adili*, I understand is particularly good. Robert plans ultimately to publish not only his own works but those of other African writers as well.[7]

It was a unique literary encounter, for though Achebe and Shabaan Robert spent some time talking about writing, there was no real contact. Robert spoke Swahili and Achebe responded in English, and the real nature of each writer's works was not known to the other. However, Robert gave his visitor two books of his poems in Swahili which Achebe could not read although he treasured them. That encounter was probably one of the factors that convinced Achebe of the viability of setting up a publishing house six years later. Much more importantly, he never forgot the Swahili writer and was instrumental in introducing him, many years later, to James Ngugi, now better known as Ngugi wa Thiong'o.

In addition to the events and literary trends in East Africa, Achebe also became acquainted with the land, the people and their cultures. One of the most interesting sights was Mount Kibo, the highest peak in the Kilimanjaro range.

> It is at first somewhat disappointing. It simply does not look high enough to be the highest mountain in Africa. It lacks the spiritual majesty of Mount Kenya. But it grows on one. There is something of a ritual at sunset when it reveals itself from the thick mantle of cloud which hides it in the day. As night falls the white dome is lit up by the last rays of light while the foothills and the rest of the world sink into darkness. At that hour, if at none other, Mount Kibo is truly magnificent.

Achebe's traveller's tale does not stop at the admiration of beautiful sunsets. There were the Wachagga, 'a very progressive people who inhabit the slopes of the Kilimanjaro'. Achebe was told that 'the Wachagga used not to be very popular with the British administration, especially with one particular Governor who had strong views on natives in lounge suits'. Achebe's judgement is that while 'the Masai took one look at Western civilization and turned their back on it, the Wachagga took a plunge without looking back. They are always trying out new things'. Achebe reports that 'Nyerere praised their go-ahead spirit, but suggested obliquely that there was also virtue in giving a system time to prove itself before embarking on a new one.' It was that spirit and desire to master new ideas and new things that elicited the Nigerian traveller's observation that 'in the end life will favour those who come to terms with it, not those who run away', and he was neither 'surprised to find that although the Wachagga had no tradition of art they have produced East Africa's best-known painter Sam Ntiro, and one of its best sculptors', nor was he surprised 'to meet a Chagga in Moshi who was working with devotion on a script written from the bottom of the page to the top!'

On the other hand the warlike Wahehe, a name Achebe had encountered inscribed on a Nigerian passenger lorry in his primary school days, presented an aspect of colonial history that made him thoughtful. The Wahehe, he was told, 'were great warriors with an astonishing record which included [not only] the defeat of the much celebrated Masai but also of the colonizing Germans, more ruthless in battle than even the Masai'. The eventual defeat of the Wahehe after their initial terrible losses was the culmination of a three-year plan by the Germans with 'their immensely superior armament at a time Sultan Mkwawa who was in power had not completed building a stone wall round his capital'.

That defeat, however, did not fulfil the expectations of the invading army.

> They discovered that they had practically to subdue every hut separately and yet were unable to capture Mkwawa on whose head a large reward had been placed. For three long years more he eluded them. Then one day a young officer going into the forest to investigate a shot that had been heard found the Sultan's body. He had shot himself rather than surrender and be taken prisoner. The young officer cut off the head and took it to headquarters in Iringa and a reward of 5,000 rupees was paid over to him.

Achebe adds that 'the Germans, who seemed to have a curious taste in these matters, dried the head and sent it to a museum in the fatherland'. Many years later the skull of Sultan Mkwawa was identified from among '2,000 others in a museum in Bremen and returned to Chief Adam Sapi, Sultan Mkwawa's grandson, at a solemn ceremony watched in silence by thousands of Wahehe people'. Chief Adam Sapi invited Chinua Achebe to tea and he found the chief 'quiet and totally unassuming, wearing a smart lounge suit'. But there was a poignant touch to that meeting for Achebe:

> The next morning as I was packing my bag to return to Dar es Salaam someone knocked on my hotel door. It was Chief Sapi come to make me a present of a miniature Wahehe spear. I was greatly moved and flattered by such attention from the grandson of the great Sultan Mkwawa.[8]

Such meetings enlivened the travels of Achebe in East Africa, from where he journeyed on to Rhodesia in January 1961. Another country introduced another aspect of the African experience, succinctly captured in Achebe's recollection:

> I was met at Salisbury Airport by two young white academics and a black post-graduate student from the new University of Rhodesia. The Rockefeller Foundation apparently knowing the terrain better than I did had taken the precaution of enlisting the assistance of these literature teachers to meet me and generally keep an eye on my programme. The first item on the agenda was to check into my hotel. It turned out to be the new five star Jameson Hotel which had just opened to avoid such international incidents as the refusal of hotel accommodation to the distinguished countryman of mine Sir Francis Ibiam, Governor of Eastern Nigeria, President of the World Council of Churches. But I was a poor, unknown writer, travelling on the generosity of an enlightened American Foundation. This generosity did not, however, stretch so far as to accommodate the kind of bills Jameson Hotel would present. But that was another story which would unfold to me later. For the moment my three escorts took me to my hotel where I checked in and then blithely offered them a drink. It was the longest order I had or have ever made. The waiter kept going and then returning with an empty tray and more questions, the long and short of which was that the two bwanas

could have their beer and so could I because I was staying in the hotel but the other black fellow could only have coffee. So I called the entire thing off. Southern Rhodesia was simply awful.[9]

His journey entailed an overnight stop in Livingstone, Northern Rhodesia. In the hotel where he stayed the manager spotted him at dinner and came over, introduced himself and sat down for a chat. Achebe said he thought he was coming to eject him but it transpired that the man had been the manager of the Ambassador Hotel in Accra, Ghana. In the course of the chat he 'learnt that Victoria Falls was only twenty odd miles away and a bus went there regularly from the hotel'. He decided to visit that tourist attraction.

So the next morning I boarded the bus. From where I sat – next to the driver's seat – I missed what was going on in the vehicle. When finally I turned round, probably because of a certain unnatural silence around me, I saw with horror that everyone around me was white! As I had turned round they had averted their stony gazes whose hostility I had felt so palpably at the back of my head. What had become of all the black people at the bus stop? Did they have a separate bus? Why had no one told me? I looked back again and only then took in the detail of a partition and a door. I have often asked myself what I might have done if I had noticed the separate entrances before I boarded; and I am not sure. Anyhow, there I was sitting next to the driver's seat in a Jim Crow bus in Her Majesty's Colony of Northern Rhodesia, later to be known as Zambia. The driver (black) came aboard, looked at me with great surprise but said nothing. The ticket collector appeared as soon as the journey got under way. I did not have to look back any more: my ears were now like two antennae on each side of my head. I heard a bolt move and the man stood before me. Our conversation went something like this:

TC : What are you doing here?
CA: I am travelling to Victoria Falls.
TC: Why are you sitting here?
CA: Why not?
TC: Where do you come from?
CA: I don't see what that has to do with it. But if you must know I come from Nigeria, and there we sit where we like in the bus.

He fled from me as from a man with the plague. My European co-travellers remained silent as the grave. The journey continued without further incident until we got to the Falls. Then a strange thing happened. The black travellers in the back rushed out in one huge stampede to wait for me at the door and to cheer and sing my praises. I was not elated. A monumental sadness descended on me. I could be a hero because I was in transit and these unfortunate people, more brave by far than I, had formed a guard of honour for me! The awesome waterfall did not revive my spirit. I walked about wrapped in my raincoat and saw the legendary sight and went back to the terminal and deliberately walked into the front of another bus. And such is the speed of hopeful news in oppressed places that nobody challenged me. And I paid my fare.[10]

That experience was unnerving. But then so many things were happening that were unnerving to the black race, and Achebe after that encounter found himself in a better position to understand the situation in South Africa, where apartheid had become a state policy. In fact, his travel plans had been organized to cover South Africa but the experience in Northern and Southern Rhodesia contributed to making him change his mind.

Thus he returned to Nigeria in January 1961 sadder but definitely wiser. He published an essay entitled 'Can There Be a Multi-Racial Society ... Not in

Tanganyika' in the Lagos newspaper *Daily Express*. The essay centred on his observations and impressions of racial problems in that country; the whole journey he aptly summarized as 'scenically wonderful but politically depressing'.[11]

Political developments in his own country were exhibiting depressing signs even as he was recalled to Lagos from Enugu and appointed the Acting Director of Programmes at the NBS, which became the Nigerian Broadcasting Corporation (NBC) at about the same time. His return to Lagos in 1961 was preceded, however, by the completion of traditional marriage rites making Christie Chinwe Okoli his wife. His residence at Enugu had yielded both social and literary opportunities, but Lagos was the national capital city and the centre of activities; he would also be closer to several of his friends and to other young intellectuals there and at Ibadan.

It was at this time that he discussed with Ulli Beier, who had started *Black Orpheus,* the idea of a literary club. As Ulli Beier recollects:

> At the planning stage discussions took place between Ibadan and Lagos. For some time we were pondering over the name we should give the club. We were toying with Ori Olokun, a good name with a suitable meaning – but somehow the name wasn't short and snappy enough. I remember sitting down with Wole [Soyinka] in his office in Ibadan, when the phone rang. 'It's Chinua,' he said, 'he has come up with another suggestion: *Mbari.'* Immediately I knew that this was it: *Mbari* suggests creativity in its purest, most vital form. Creativity as a ritual act, rather than a commercial activity for the production of marketable objects. Creativity as a communal activity, as a revitalizing force.[12]

Beier accepted the name but he explains that

> having given the club its name, Chinua could not be as active in the running of it as we would all have wished. He could not come to Ibadan very often. And although we conferred with him over the phone, in all major issues, we missed his presence.

Achebe was often taken to Lagos by the activities of writers and artists like John Pepper Clark, Demas Nwoko and Wole Soyinka. Soyinka participated in some of the radio programmes at the NBC, including one programme in a Sunday night series in July 1961 entitled 'The African Novel': he spoke on the novelists William Conton, Amos Tutuola and D. O. Fagunwa after an introduction by Chinua Achebe. Some months earlier Yemi Lijadu had adapted Achebe's *Things Fall Apart* as *Okonkwo*; it was produced on 7 April 1961 with Wole Soyinka reading a part in the radio production.

Achebe's growing reputation as a novelist did not blind him to the usefulness of using other media of communication such as journals in expressing his views. He had noted the enterprise of Ulli Beier in *Black Orpheus* and also the diligence of the Ghanaian academics who had started publishing *Okyeame.* He wrote a review of the two periodicals in an essay entitled 'Two West African Library Journals' published in *Service.*[13] Neither did Achebe's reputation as a novelist obstruct his interactions on an individual basis with other writers like Christopher Okigbo, T. M. Aluko, Cyprian Ekwensi, D. O. Fagunwa and those others who were still to emerge like John Munonye and Chukwuemeka Ike. Thus his circle of friends widened.

Chukwuemeka Ike, who had become deputy registrar at the new University of Nigeria, Nsukka after working as an assistant registrar at the University of Ibadan, was influential in this process. Ike attended a meeting in Lagos where he met Hugh Vernon-Jackson, the principal of a teacher training college in the Cameroons. In the course of discussion, Achebe's name was mentioned. Vernon-Jackson expressed a great longing to meet the Nigerian novelist.

> I said that I could take him to Achebe and he could not believe it. We drove to Achebe's house at Milverton Street, Ikoyi. But before we got there the man asked me to inform him as soon as we were near the house. When I told him we were close to Achebe's house, he brought out his comb to straighten his hair and he also put on his tie. However, we arrived and met Achebe in a pair of shorts. Dr Vernon-Jackson was surprised to see such a simple man.[14]

Christie Okoli had noted the same simplicity in spite of Achebe's rise in his career at the NBC; it was one reason why she had decided to marry him. The wedding service took place at the Chapel of Resurrection on the campus of the University of Ibadan. The couple felt that there was 'no point going to wed at any other place'. Although one of Chinua Achebe's close friends, Chike Momah, was a librarian at Ibadan, it was a mark of his 'detribalized' outlook on life and sense of belonging to a new, united nation that he and Christie decided to wed on 10 September 1961 at Ibadan rather than in Igboland. The best man was Chike Momah while the chairman at the reception was Sam Nwoye. An unsolicited but welcome wedding present was the award of the Nigerian National Trophy for Literature by the Governor General to Chinua Achebe on 1 October 1961, as part of the activities marking the anniversary of Nigerian independence.

The wedding fulfilled an aspect of Igbo tradition that regards marriage as part of a young man's achievements, but the new husband was not unaware of the attached responsibilities. About 30 years later he was to write:

> the Igbo are not starry-eyed about the world. Their poetry does not celebrate romantic love. They have a proverb, which my wife detests, in which a woman is supposed to say that she does not ask to be loved by her husband as long as he puts out yams for lunch every afternoon. What a drab outlook for the woman! But how does the man fare? An old villager once told me (not in a proverb but in real life): my favourite soup is *egusi,* so I order my wife never to give me *egusi* soup in this house. And so she makes *egusi* every evening! This then is the picture. The woman forgoes love for lunch; the man tells a lie for his supper! Marriage is tough; it is bigger than any man or woman. So the Igbo do not ask you to meet it head-on with a placard, nor do they ask you to turn around and run away. They ask you to find a way to cope. Cowardice? You don't know the Igbo.[15]

Of course that insightful observation was not the result of a few days of marriage experience, for there were 'periods of adjustment' for Chinua and Christie.

Fame added new dimensions to that need for adjustment, in addition to the responsibilities associated with a life of writing which made certain forms of compromise imperative. Chinua Achebe was working at the NBC; Christie found employment at the Ministry of Information, discovered that her duties there were not demanding enough, and so switched to teaching at St Gregory's College, Lagos. When Chinua started working on a novel which took much of his time, Christie felt that 'he spent a lot more time on the book than on me' but the feeling of resentment did not last as husband and wife adjusted to the situation.[16] There was one other instance when the marriage was faced with this issue of resentment. Christie Achebe says that the only time we had a disagreement was during the earlier period of our marriage. As a new wife I had to pack his clothes in a bag whenever he had to travel. There was a time I saw a little note accompanying a new pair of socks.[17]

The note expressed the feelings of the sender who had been attracted to Chinua Achebe. But Christie adds that apart from this incident

there is basically trust. There was never a time that I confronted a woman because I saw her with my husband. I did not bother to ransack his belongings if he returned from a trip.

Thus the harmony of the marriage was not destroyed as sacrifices were made and trust blended the relationship. Christie notes that even in those days Chinua thought deeply on most questions.

He ought to be listened to when he says something. He thinks a lot. He doesn't talk very much. As a matter of fact that's one of the problems in the home, he is not the chatty type.

Increasing success affected neither Chinua nor the members of his immediate family. Christie reveals that

even in the home, Chinua does not exhibit any outward emotion in terms of success. He would simply give me a letter and it is only when I have read the contents that I would exclaim with surprise at the good news.

That reticence was to serve as a subject for constant teasing when the children started arriving and the oldest daughter would occasionally urge: 'Daddy, I know you like it, so smile! You are waiting to tell it to your darling wife.'[18]

That was still in the future. Meanwhile the fresh husband, Chinua Achebe, was made Director of External Broadcasting and mandated to establish the 'Voice of Nigeria'. Achebe recalls:

We were independent and we wanted to set up our own international external broadcasting service, and the three Controllers, Badejo in Ibadan, Umaru Ladan in the North who was the most junior and myself in the East were considered. Badejo was already moving to become Director-General, so I was made Director of External Broadcasting.[19]

The acceptance of that appointment entailed sacrifice from Chinua Achebe, who was to have completed the second part of the Rockefeller travel scholarship in December, 1961 but decided not to take it up. In those days the chance of a foreign tour was highly prized. His decision not to embark on the trip first, and then return to take up his job later, typified his attitude: 'I wanted to be in on it from the very beginning; not to take over someone's work.' It was a very busy period, especially in the later part of 1961 as Achebe set about supervising the erection of the physical and technical structure of administration for the external broadcasting service. A report in the journal *West Africa* on the commencement of that service early in 1962 indicates that

The programme is still experimental – one hour a day of news, music and a talk. Apart from Achebe there are two French-speaking broadcasters – a Negro American who learnt his French-speaking at school and a man from Senegal. English and French are the only languages as yet. There are two transmitters of 10KW each, carrying Achebe's programme throughout tropical Africa, even as far as Southern Morocco and Algeria, but excluding the North African Coast.

At that stage, it was still a matter of test transmission, as Achebe reported in early 1962: 'We are at the stage of testing reception – the engineers send out letters to Nigerians living in every country and ask for reactions.' Some of these reports were favourable and they enabled Achebe to cross another frontier – this time in broadcasting – by establishing a firm 'Voice of Nigeria' which would represent the country to the outside world. His aim was to make the service objective for, as he stressed at that time: 'Telling the truth is the only way, in the long run, that you get listened to.' The report quoted above adds that 'from next August [1962], Achebe plans to have three 100KW transmitters with which he will be able to reach Europe and the United Kingdom.' The report also indicates that he proposed to add Arabic, Hausa and Swahili as languages of broadcast and that when he 'is organized and has a deputy, he hopes to be able to travel and compare notes with other stations, especially that of the UAR in Cairo,which appears to have taken a leading position in the organization of external news'.[20]

It was not only their techniques that interested Achebe: this is clear from the broad sweep of his own account of the origin of the external service in 1962. In a broadcast in the series 'Nigeria Today', later published in the *Voice of Nigeria* magazine, Achebe records that the 'new service took the air on New Year's Day 1962' and also that 'some people have doubted the wisdom of spending large sums of money to put one more voice on the already overcrowded air when Nigeria is so short of money for her six-year development plan'. He assures his listeners that 'Nigeria occupies a very important position in contemporary Africa, and what she says or does is of enormous significance, and ought to be known and understood.' Achebe quotes the Federal Minister of Information, T. O. S. Benson, who said at the inauguration of 'Voice of Nigeria' that its 'main function will be to project Nigerian news, activities and culture abroad, and to ensure that the country's policies and views are better understood by her neighbours'. In performing this function, Achebe stresses, the service will

> never presume to teach others how to live or how to manage their affairs. It is not the voice of the schoolmaster but the voice of a friend. Our news broadcasts will strive to be accurate and our commentaries to be objective. We shall attempt to portray our country as truly as we can so that anybody who wishes to know about her may have a true guide. In all we do we shall try to avoid hysteria and all types of posturing.

Apart from information, the listeners would be offered entertainment and the cultural diversity of Nigeria would be portrayed in music programmes, although attempts would also be made 'to broadcast material from all parts of the continent' – indeed, Achebe concludes, 'we have already taken the first steps in this direction and we are grateful for the response we have so far had from many broadcasting organizations in Africa'.[21] Anyone listening to this broadcast would have recognized the voice of an individual with a vision who had applied that vision to a complex public task.

The realization of that vision exacted a busy schedule with sacrifices of time and energy that would make no concession to the young director's recent marriage. *West Africa* magazine, obviously aware of the vision that Achebe had, reiterated those expectations and hopes:

> To see facts as they are, unclouded by sentimentality, fear and cultural insecurity, requires a very special effort in West Africa today. The politicians, in particular, in their struggle for independence have created, almost naturally, a fog of myths and

prejudices by which now they only deceive themselves. Fortunately, Achebe is not alone in Nigeria in seeing the need to look honestly at the world, his country and his people. Such an attitude does not exclude sympathy or love, but it is love for what the young men know to be important and real, and not a synthetic emotion about an imaginary past or contemporary achievement. By standing up and honestly facing the world these men give a real dignity to Nigeria and the whole African continent.[22]

That observation was not an understatement and the fears were not unfounded, either. Political events were assuming frightening shapes soon after independence. Achebe watched the situation keenly while striving to maintain the broadcasting standards he had outlined. Amid this uncertainty, news came to him from Ogidi in January 1962 of the death of his father, Isaiah Okafor Achebe, at the age of 85. It was the death of a man full of years, but it occurred at a time when the children were beginning to reap the rewards of the old man's vision that education was essential in the present dispensation of Nigeria. It was equally sad that, apart from the first daughter Zinobia who had married and was now Mrs Ikpeze, the other children were not around him when he died. Chinua Achebe was in Lagos; the eldest son Frank was in Yola with his family; the other sons, John and Augustine, were in England. Considering his life as they performed his funeral rites, the inhabitants of Ikenga would judge that Isaiah had fulfilled himself by producing reasonable and successful children who had struck out worthy paths in life.

Achebe came back to Lagos after the burial to continue his task of administering the external service of the Broadcasting Corporation. The political situation was degenerating. A split in Chief Obafemi Awolowo's Action Group Party between the leader and Chief S. L. Akintola came to a head in February 1962 at the party's convention. The members of the party at the convention supported Awolowo and declared Chief Akintola, his former deputy and premier of the Western Region, guilty of maladministration. The governor of the region dismissed Akintola as premier and appointed Chief Adegbenro to form a new government. The conflict led to a fracas in the Western House of Assembly which empowered Prime Minister Balewa to declare a state of emergency in the region. The conflict worsened and the threatening clouds of political violence darkened the sky. An inquiry by the Coker Commission into allegations of corruption unearthed the fact that public money was channelled into party funds and thereafter utilized by individuals. Events gathered momentum as Awolowo and his lieutenants were arrested and charged with treasonable felony later in the year. The case was to last for eight months as the names of Awolowo, Anthony Enahoro and Sam Ikoku became prominent in the proceedings.

These political events were disconcerting, especially in a country that was barely two years independent. The politicians were exhibiting signs of excessive greed, parochialism and devotion to selfish interests. Achebe was one of those who expressed anxiety as the initial confidence in the progress of the country diminished. 'Now there is a lack of something – there is no national point of view,' he said in an interview.

> Before, justice may have been fierce but it could not be bought or sold. People had vitality and they had a feeling for beauty. They used to go for miles to get Iroko wood for carved decorations for their houses: now cement will do. There were titles and distinctions but they were gained by hard work; it was the strength of your arm that counted. Now all that is changed.[23]

The blatant desire to profit through political appointments and the obduracy of the politicians in suppressing opposition worried not only the novelist and Director of External Broadcasting but also many of his more sensitive country-men. In the midst of these debilitating developments, Achebe persevered at his new frontier, external broadcasting. It is worth noting that the position he held was the kind that many in public life would have used illegally to amass wealth, since it involved the award of contracts and recruitment of staff. But he clearly performed his duties with great honesty and in the best interests of Nigeria. It could be argued that he had achieved fame at that point and that any malpractice would have exposed him immediately to ridicule and sanction. It was equally true, however, that the politicians and civil servants who abused their offices were also famous and even popular, which did not deter them from implementing their dishonest plans.

Achebe also found time to continue his creative activities through the publication of *The Sacrificial Egg and Other Short Stories* in April 1962. The work was printed and published by Etudo Limited of Onitsha. It collected the stories published in the *University Herald* when Achebe was an undergraduate and others that had appeared in magazines in 1959 and 1960. The publication of 'The Sacrificial Egg', 'Dead Men's Path' (originally published without a title), 'Chike's School Days', 'Beginning of the End' and 'Akueke' in a 32-page booklet made them available to a wider audience and, more importantly, to the enor-mous Onitsha market readership. In an insightful introduction to the collec-tion, M. J. C. Echeruo, a member of staff at the University of Nigeria, Nsukka whose reputation was beginning to grow, writes that 'Chinua Achebe is today an important Nigerian writer, almost certainly the most important writer of fiction', and that the collection

> has the advantage of including two stories written before the novels, and three written after. The collection thus gives the reader both an indication of the past out of which the novels have emerged [and] a glimpse of the future towards which Achebe is probably heading.

Echeruo's concluding remarks clearly foreshadow the creative vision in *Arrow of God,* the third novel Achebe had started writing:

> These stories tell of mysteries without presuming to know the explanations to them. If it is in the direction of stories like 'Akueke' and 'The Sacrificial Egg' that Achebe plans to move in his future fiction, and if he can sustain that independent sympathy, this 'credulousness' which rightly belongs – or used to belong – to the folktale, he would have chosen a form which could enable him to bridge the gulf between the innocence of Amos Tutuola and Ekwensi's sophistication.[24]

Achebe's observations after a second visit to East Africa also threw light on the issue of his future path in fiction. That second visit was prompted by the organization of a conference of African writers in English in June 1962 at the Makerere University College in Kampala, Uganda. It was convened by the Mbari Writers' and Artists' Club, Ibadan in collaboration with the Department of Extra-Mural Studies, Makerere College and sponsored by the Congress for Cultural Freedom. There were 39 participants from Nigeria, Ghana, Britain, Cameroon, the United States of America, Dahomey (later Benin Republic), Kenya, Uganda, South Africa, the West Indies and Senegal. It was a gathering of emerging figures in African literature and criticism that included Achebe,

Samba Amadou, G. Awoonor-Williams (later to be known as Kofi Awoonor) John Pepper Clark, Arthur Drayton, Dennis Duerden, Cameron Duodu, Bernard Fonlon, Langston Hughes, Paulin Joachim, Jonathan Kariara, B. L. Leshoai, Yemi Lijadu, Arthur Maimane, Bloke Modisane, Gerald Moore, Ezekiel Mphahlele, John Nagenda, Rajat Neogy, James Ngugi, Lewis Nkosi, Rebecca Njau, Donatus Nwoga, Grace Ogot, Gabriel Okara, Christopher Okigbo, Okot p'Bitek, Segun Olusola, Barry Reckord and Wole Soyinka. The centre of interest was Africa and the non-Africans present were virtually guests of honour or special observers. It was a lively conference in which Christopher Okigbo made the comment about not reading his poems on the ground that he never read to non-poets and Soyinka, while criticizing Negritude, made the remark which has haunted him, that the tiger does not proclaim its tigritude.[25] There was also a heated argument over the definition of African literature which caused the delegates great anguish as they tried to decide whether it meant literature by Africans of disparate backgrounds or whether it entailed certain characteristics.

Achebe contributed to the debate by insisting:

> I don't think this is a very significant question. One should wait till there is a body of writing large and varied enough to constitute a tradition or a number of minor traditions, which will show natural lines of division and order.[26]

His conclusion was that it was still early to define what constituted African literature and that legislation was anathema to the literary artist. But there were also other areas of controversy like the comparison between works written by English-speaking and French-speaking Africans; a contrast between South and West African writing; and the relationship between African writers and their publishers. Bloke Modisane reported that 'at the conference the writers tore at each other, pointing out the bad from the good. A writer's best loved passages were described as "stock".' Ezekiel Mphahlele, on the other hand, felt that constructive practical proposals had been made, including the recommendations to establish writers' workshops, encouragement for Mbari publications, and the exhortation of literary journals to be more enterprising. Chinua Achebe reported on the merits of the conference in an essay published as 'Writers' Conference: A Milestone in Africa's Progress' in the *Daily News,* and republished as 'Conference of African Writers' in the *Radio Times.* He notes that 'the writers' Conference was an important milestone in Africa's progress from comparative obscurity to the centre of world affairs' and on a lighter note describes how

> Mr Clark's new play *The Song of a Goat* was performed by a Kampala amateur dramatic group in honour of the Conference. It was a fine gesture even if the actual performance was not of a high standard. An unkind critic said after the play that the only actor who knew his part was the Goat. But for all that, there was something moving in the spectacle of these inexperienced actors in Uganda grappling with a Nigerian tragedy. This, if you ask me, is Pan-Africanism at its best, that is without the noise.

In proffering a reason for the conference, Achebe feels that 'the most important reason was the need for us writers to get acquainted with one another. At present African writers work in isolation and even ignorance of one another.' He concedes that 'conferences of this nature could very easily degenerate into back-slapping complacency. But this one was nothing of the sort'; instead, the participants 'settled down to a rigorous examination of what we have produced so far'. In that assessment 'the self-pity of much of South African writing was severely criticized' and 'as one of the critics put it, the South African writer must now begin to see beyond the point of the white man's boot'. Nevertheless, 'West African Writing had its own share of criticism. But it was all done in great good humour and in the best of taste'.[27]

Some, like Lewis Nkosi in the *Manchester Guardian,* report moments of drama at the Kampala Conference:

> The writers were mostly young, impatient, sardonic, talking endlessly about the problems of creations, and looking, while doing so, as though they were amazed that fate had entrusted them with the task of interpreting a continent to the world. The older writers like the South African, Ezekiel Mphahlele and the Nigerian, Chinua Achebe, looked by far the calmest, most disciplined and trustworthy, in what appeared to be a company of literary cutthroats, out to get one another at the slightest provocation.... Mocking, irreverent, they read one another's poetry loudly in a kind of mortifying parody. The young Nigerian playwright, Wole Soyinka, went so far as to invent a 'negritude' poem on the spot, while addressing the conference, in a sudden astringent parody of Senghor's poetry and its preoccupations with the African personality, an act of creation which succeeded only too well for it enraged the delegates from French West Africa.[28]

But the writers did not spend all the time arguing or criticizing, for John Nagenda reports a 'general relaxation at the *Top Life and Dive* and various other night spots' and also that at the end of the conference 'all but one [participant] was still sampling the joys of this beautiful town of ours'.[29]

A significant meeting occurred in Kampala between a student known as James Ngugi, who was at the Makerere University College, and Chinua Achebe. Ngugi attended the conference, he confesses, to 'see Ezekiel Mphahlele' and to

> meet Chinua Achebe, the young Nigerian novelist whose two novels seem to herald the birth of a new society in which writers, freed from the burden of political protests and jibes at a disintegrating colonialism, can cast an unsentimental eye at human relationship in all its delicate and sometimes harsh intricacies.

He would feel that the discussions reflected 'the immense political changes that have taken place' and that 'with the death of colonialism, a new society is being born. And with it a new literature.'[30] That birth of a new literature which Ngugi notes took on a new but positive dimension for him before the end of the conference.

One morning, about mid-way through the conference, Achebe heard a knock on his door. He opened it and welcomed a young man who timidly claimed to be a student at Makerere. Courteously Achebe bade him welcome and a few minutes later it transpired that the young man had written a novel which he wanted Achebe to read. In spite of the hectic activities and conference events, Achebe promised to read the novel which turned out to be *Weep Not, Child.* When the young man called again Achebe informed him that it was a very good novel. He also recommended certain structural changes and told Ngugi that he was handing it over to Van Milne, the representative of his own publishers, Heinemann. To Milne, Achebe added the weight of his own recommendation in favour of publication.

Alan Hill of Heinemann, who was in London, captures the drama succinctly:

I was sitting in a Board meeting at Kingswood one Wednesday morning in June 1962 when I was called out to take a telephone call from Kampala. Van Milne was at the other end very excited. He was attending a conference on African writing, and had picked up what he believed to be an outstanding MS by a young Kenyan student at the Makerere University College. Could he have my authority to accept it, sight-unseen? Without hesitation I said yes, and returned to the Board meeting. The Makerere student had shown his half-finished MS to Achebe, who liked it, made some practical comments and passed it to Van Milne, who at once saw its potential.[31]

Two years later *Weep Not, Child* was published. Achebe had cleared a frontier, by his example as a writer and his keen perception as a critic, for the emergence of Ngugi wa Thiong'o, whose distinguished career would parallel his own.

It was also in 1962 that Heinemann Educational Books decided to make available to a wider African audience a cheap paperback series of books by African writers. It was the pioneering idea of Alan Hill and Van Milne, and they published four books in the series in 1962: Achebe's *Things Fall Apart* and *No Longer at Ease*, Cyprian Ekwensi's *Burning Grass* and Kenneth Kaunda's *Zambia Shall Be Free*. Part of Alan Hill's motivation was to rectify an unfair situation in which British publishers 'regarded West Africa only as a place where you sold books'. He was also outraged that 'they were taking their profits out of West Africa and putting nothing back in the way of investment in local publishing and encouragement of local authors'. Thus he determined

> to make an entirely new start – to show that on the basis of our African school book business we could provide a publishing service for African authors. The time was ripe. There must be other writers comparable to Achebe, awaiting a publisher with the confidence and resources to launch them on a world-wide market.[32]

It was not only as a pioneering writer that Achebe occupied a central place in Hill's vision:

> I felt the need for a General Editor 'on the ground' to develop the series. So in November 1962 I sent out my number two, Tony Beal, to Nigeria to meet Chinua Achebe to invite him to be General Editor. The two met in Lagos, in the Bristol Hotel, and Chinua at once said 'Yes'. He accepted and we were in business. His role was crucial. Not only did he read every MS, in some cases undertaking editorial work, but he would identify good new authors for the series. His very presence was a magnet for would-be writers during the ten years of his editorship.[33]

It was a fruitful decade for Heinemann Educational Books but taxing for Chinua Achebe, who continued to roll back the frontiers of African literature, until soon he had the reputation – at the age of 32 – of a father figure in African literature.

In his own family, he also had to play the role of a father with the birth of a daughter, Chinelo, on 11 July 1962. The arrival of the baby a month after his return from the Kampala conference and three months before he became the general editor of the African Writers Series meant that he was quite busy in 1962. In addition, his friendships with several writers and other Nigerian citizens added to the demands on his time. Christopher Okigbo, for instance, who had become the representative of Cambridge University Press, became a regular visitor and through him Achebe had established a relationship with John Pepper Clark, then working for a newspaper in Lagos. The well-known newspaper columnist Sam Amuka, whose pen name 'Sad Sam' became popular as a result of his incisive articles, was also a close friend. In these relationships it was obvious that even when his acquaintances exhibited libertine tendencies they hardly affected Achebe. Christopher Okigbo, well known for his amorous relationships, would arrive unannounced and quite often accompanied by a lady and Achebe would welcome him. On one occasion Christie Achebe was woken up by raised voices quite early in the morning.[34] When she came out to investigate, she discovered that Okigbo had arrived with a girl some time earlier. He had made himself at home and the voices that had woken Christie were those of Okigbo and his girl in an argument. Chinua Achebe was to write some years later:

> Christopher Okigbo could not enter or leave a room unremarked; yet he was not extravagant in manner or appearance. There was something about him not easy to define, a certain inevitability of drama and event. His vibrancy and heightened sense of life touched every one he came into contact with. [He] had a gift for fellowship surpassing anything I had ever seen or thought possible. He had friends, admirers, fans, cronies of both sexes, from all ages, all social classes, all professions, all ethnic groups, in Nigeria and everywhere. He was greedy for friendship as indeed he was for all experience, for risk and danger.[35]

That greed for friendship and danger was to lead Okigbo into new adventures and new acquaintances later in the decade.

Meanwhile Achebe settled down as Director of External Broadcasting after establishing the 'Voice of Nigeria', which by the end of the year had made an appreciable technical advance. He also settled down to edit the new African Writers Series for Heinemann Educational Books. It was not an easy combination of responsibilities but Achebe soon found his feet. 'You are talking of a heavy burden,' Achebe confesses.

> It really is a heavy burden for a writer to begin to plough through acres and acres of other people's manuscripts and so on and to select or discuss with the publishers what ought to be published and what ought not to be published.[36]

That burden notwithstanding, his decisions often turned out well and he learned to treat even the unsuitable manuscripts and their authors with tolerance as he made recommendations. Alan Hill confirms:

> We decided in the end to be guided by literary quality – to publish anything of real merit which came our way, irrespective of its 'category'. In point of fact, the great majority of the first titles were new fiction, interspersed with poetry and drama. The fact that some of the titles were set for school and University examinations was an incidental if a very welcome bonus.

The success of the series had much to do with Achebe who, Hill says,

> did all this work for nothing. He did it for the good of African literature [and made an] enormous contribution to the African Writers Series. His name was the magnet that brought everything on and his critical judgement was the decisive factor in what we published.[37]

Thus it was that a young Nigerian woman, Flora Nwapa, sent her manuscript to Chinua Achebe in Lagos. Nwapa says:

> I started to write *Efuru* in 1962, completed it that year, sent it to Chinua Achebe who liked it and sent it to Heinemann.... I felt encouraged to go on writing because as soon as I knew it had been accepted for publication I started thinking about my second novel which was *Idu* and I had even started writing it before *Efuru* was published. I

can say that I was lucky in that I knew Chinua Achebe who read my manuscript in three weeks, even gave it a title, and sent it to Heinemann and the next thing that I heard was that it had been accepted.[38]

Achebe's role lay not only in discovering writers, or in clearing the frontier for a pioneering female writer like Flora Nwapa. Alan Hill also tells us that 'The fantastic sales of his own books, selling by the million, provided the economic basis for the rest of the series.'

It might be imagined that Achebe's dedication to writing would show in his social behaviour and style of life. But Hill emphasizes that

> in those early days I used to go out to see Achebe in Nigeria, in Lagos. He was the very image of a modern Nigerian 'yuppie' in those days. He had a very handsome British colonial-type house, he used to wear a sharp suit, dark glasses, and had a Jaguar car..., But of course, once one started to talk to him, one realized that there was something very different below the surface.

Hill clearly valued this agreeable relationship with Achebe who 'was a very understanding and accommodating author'.[39]

That understanding and tolerance did not prevent Achebe from airing his views, even when they were not popular. In December 1962 he wrote a review of Christopher Okigbo's *Heavensgate* for *Spear* magazine in which he extolled the good qualities of the poetry collection as well as pointing out its flaws.[40] More importantly, he published an article entitled 'Where Angels Fear to Tread' in the December 1962 issue of *Nigeria Magazine* in which he states that Nigerian writers 'are not opposed to criticism but we are getting a little weary of all the special types of criticism which have been designed for us by people whose knowledge of us is very limited'. The burden of the article is what kind of criticism is relevant. Achebe distinguishes three types: the hostile critic, the amazed critic and the conscious critic who restores a sense of balance. His final comment that 'no man can understand another whose language he does not speak (and "language" here does not mean simply words, but a man's entire world view)' was perhaps too insistent. He questions: 'How many Europeans and Americans have our language? I do not know of any, certainly not among our writers and critics.'[41] That remark aroused resentment, but Achebe's argument centred on the cultivation of a sense of critical humility. Unfortunately, the essay was to generate angry responses from critics like Austin Shelton. In a way it was a fitting end to a year in which the arguments had been warm and engaging and it also indicated that the broadcaster, editor and novelist was aware of the various dimensions that now made up the reality of African literature.

8

Walking under a Gathering Storm
From *Arrow of God* to *A Man of the People*
1963–6

I N the year 1963 Chinua Achebe was engaged in various editorial, critical and creative enterprises. He published a review of Jean-Joseph Rabéarivelo's *Twenty-Four Poems* in *Spear* magazine.[1] In late January he completed work on the final draft of *Arrow of God*. The incident of the delayed New Yam festival, the records of the colonial officers in Enugu and Thurstan Shaw's archaeological research had provided essential material. But then Achebe blew life into the major character he had created and into the story as a whole.

The writing of the novel at a time when he had begun building a family required the cooperation of his wife, who had started teaching at the Methodist Boys' High School as well as tending the young Chinelo. It was Christie Achebe's first extended close contact with Chinua's creative writing sessions in the home. 'His pattern as a creative artist is peculiar', she says.

> There is this sense that ideas for him are just like power. If he has an idea that he wants to nurture until it blooms, he does not go telling about it. There is this sense that if he talks about it, it loses power. Contrarily what happens to me is that I have lots and lots of ideas which I like sharing with friends and colleagues. Often I may not go on to realize them. However, while Chinua is working and there is something that has not crystallized, he may want to try it out on somebody very close. Generally when he has completed a work, before it goes out to the publishers, he may give it to a very close friend or to me. Then one can comment on it but not before then.[2]

That may have accounted for the publication of one chapter of *Arrow of God* in *Transition* in June 1963. It was the chapter in which Captain T. K. Winterbottom ruminates over his duties in the colonial service. That chapter may have been made available to *Transition* by Christopher Okigbo, who was the journal's editor for West Africa. In an earlier issue of *Transition,* in March 1963, Achebe had published a letter in which he criticized Janheinz Jahn's *Through African Doors* for making general and misleading statements about the monotony of African food and Ezekiel Mphahlele for insisting that 'our writing can only be valid if it interprets contemporary society in a mode of expression that hits on the intellectual, emotional and physical planes of meaning'. Achebe's main contention was that

> we are all anxious that more and better writing should come out of Africa. But

experience and instinct would suggest that the way to achieve this is not to enthrone pontiffs with power to announce on what shall be valid but to leave writers free to experiment in their different ways.... Only thus can we ensure the growth of each individual talent and a rich and healthy harvest for Africa.[3]

This comment made by Achebe in 1963 and the essay on 'Where Angels Fear to Tread' published the previous year earned two replies as 1963 progressed. Anthony M. Astrachan, in an essay entitled 'Does it Take One to Know One?', in *Nigeria Magazine,* took exception to some of the views Achebe had expressed in 'Where Angels Fear to Tread', although he also made some concessions.[4] It was Ezekiel Mphahlele's response in *Transition,* however, that led to a sustained and engaging argument. Mphahlele argued that he had 'expected Achebe to see my intention straightaway from the whole context of the quotation, which does not seem to differ from his own opinion' and that he had 'wanted also to make [that] guiding remark [which Achebe criticized] as general as possible, not like a pair of rails on which one runs a toy, not to pontificate, as I am being charged with'. Mphahlele agreed that a 'great writer follows his own disposition and succeeds in moving the reader at the same time' and that 'Achebe does it'. He was sure, however, that 'Achebe does not mean that writers should follow their own temperament even when they become unintelligible or obscure or cheaply sentimental for the reader?' Perhaps in retaliation to the jibe that Achebe had labelled him 'a very important personality' (VIP) in African literature, Mphahlele concluded:

> Let writers follow their own temperament, by all means. But they should not start squealing when they are being told that some of their tam-tam poetry or some of their verbal violence is just so much gas, or that some of their sedate prose is mouldy and stinks, or that people have their every day concerns even while they are acting out the conflict of generations. Otherwise if writers want to please themselves and themselves only, the peak of Mount Kilimanjaro is very near or they can charter a space ship.[5]

The argument was not pursued further since the views highlighted by Achebe and Mphahlele did not seem much different. Achebe's next critical foray was an essay, 'A Look at West African Writing' in *Spear* of June 1963 in which he stresses the variety of the works in terms of subject matter and even techniques, contrary to the prevalent opinion then that West African literature was only sedate and leisurely.[6]

While these literary exchanges were in progress, the political situation in Nigeria continued to deteriorate. The census results of 1962 had been condemned and finally cancelled on 19 February 1963, but the new census conducted in 1963 was also rejected on the grounds that preposterous population figures were tabulated. The main factor that influenced the inflation of population figures was the desire for political advantage, especially through a new delimitation of federal constituencies and allocation of resources. Thus the favoured Nigerian People's Congress (NPC) welcomed it while it was criticized justifiably by the National Council of Nigerian Citizens (NCNC) and the Action Group (AG). The controversy raged as the treason trial of Chief Obafemi Awolowo and his lieutenants progressed. The trial was concluded on 13 June 1963 but judgement was delivered by Mr Justice Sowemimo only on 11 September 1963. It took him almost eight hours to review the proceedings, conclude that there was a plot to overthrow the federal government by force, and sentence Awolowo to a jail term of ten years. Some of Awolowo's colleagues, like S.G. Ikoku and Anthony Enahoro, were also jailed. The judgement exacerbated political events in the Western Region which gathered momentum as the time for the federal elections approached. In Lagos Achebe watched the developments with dismay for, as a writer recognized internationally and also as Director of External Broadcasting, he felt compelled to inform the wider world honestly how the events occurred. He did not obscure the facts and at the same time he tried to make sure that the information disseminated was objective.

Intellectual circles in Lagos, generally committed to the corporate existence of the independent nation, were disconcerted by the politicians who seemed bent on acting in negative ways that would bring division. That observation made Achebe start outlining a new novel in his mind although the one he had submitted to his publishers most recently had not yet been published. The publishers were still working on it and Keith Sambrook at Heinemann Educational Books pointed out that a particular sequence in the manuscript did not seem appropriate. Achebe found the suggestion valid 'and swapped chapters'. He explained that 'the issue had to do with the flashback technique' and 'not much revision really'.⁷ Meanwhile Achebe's reputation continued to grow like a forest fire, with *Things Fall Apart* and *No Longer at Ease* listed as best sellers in Uganda in February 1963. That success brought further recognition as UNESCO awarded him a Fellowship for Creative Artists. 'They came along and asked where I would like to go. Without hesitation I said: USA and Brazil. And so I came to the Americas for the first time in 1963.' It was the time of the Civil Rights Movement and Achebe was prepared intellectually and psychologically for his trip.

> Before I came to America, I had discovered and read *Go Tell It on the Mountain* by James Baldwin and [I was] instantly captivated. For me it combined the strange and familiar in a way that was entirely new. I went to the United States Information Service Library in Lagos to see what other material there might be by or on this man. There was absolutely nothing. So I offered a couple of suggestions and such was the persuasiveness of newly independent Africans in those days that when next I looked in at the library they had not only Baldwin but Richard Wright as well.

On that visit to America Achebe interacted with several writers and extended his acquaintance with literary works by Americans, too.

> My intention which was somewhat nebulous to begin with was to find out how the Africans of the diaspora were faring in the two largest countries in the New World. In UNESCO files, however, it was stated with greater precision. I was given a Fellowship to enable me to study literary trends and to meet and exchange ideas with writers.

He did meet several writers:

> John O. Killens, Langston Hughes, Ralph Ellison, Paule Marshall, Leroy Jones and so on; and for good measure Arthur Miller. They were all wonderful to me. And yet there was no way I could hide from myself or my sponsors my sense of disappointment that one particular meeting could not happen because the man concerned was away in France. And that was the year of *The Fire Next Time!*⁸

That man was James Baldwin, whose works had come to epitomize the intrinsic African-American challenge to the racial establishment.

Achebe met other prominent figures and appeared on television to question Robert Kennedy with a number of other journalists. 'One got the feeling that, at last, something was going to happen.' He also listened to a spell-binding black

American leader addressing an audience in New York. 'Our roots are not in the past', he said, 'but in the future.'

> Quite nonsensical, I thought at first, then I wondered whether this man spoke from a common mystical view of history which refuses to yield to despair and which incidentally is not to be confused with the mechanistic belief in progress, nor the improvident man's delusion that tomorrow will somehow produce its own goodies.[9]

Similarly Achebe's visit to Brazil was also replete with insightful reflections and meetings with writers. 'A number of writers I spoke to were concerned about the restrictions imposed on them by their use of the Portuguese language. I remember a woman poet saying she had given serious thought to writing in French!' That remark was not a complete surprise to Achebe, for at that time he had read Jorge Amado's *Gabriella* and glimpsed something of that 'exciting Afro-Latin culture which is the pride of Brazil and is quite unlike any other culture,' and was aware that the works of the vast majority 'will be closed to the rest of the world for ever'[10] if they are not translated into a world language. That worry emanated from attending the Brazilian National Writers' Festival where he saw hundreds of writers.

When Achebe returned to Nigeria the political turbulence there had increased. The experience he gained in the Americas enabled him to reassess the reality of his own society and he published in *Spear* the essay 'Are We Men of Two Worlds?'[11] He shows how the classification of the African as a 'man of two worlds' invariably leads to the view that Western education will never really affect him. In many of the essays that Achebe wrote at this time he was interested, like a good frontiersman, in eliminating untruthful but prevalent notions. A searching interrogation of political as well as cultural activities was necessary as 1964 was ushered in with a rejection of the latest census, this one conducted in December 1963, by a majority of the politicians who all felt that the figures failed to favour their localities. In spite of the controversial census figures, 1964 was an election year: the political tension could only increase.

Early that year Heinemann Educational Books published Achebe's *Arrow of God*. Its appearance coincided with the publication of an article entitled 'The Offended *Chi* in Achebe's Novels' by Austin J. Shelton in *Transition*. Shelton felt that he had studied the Igbo language well enough to contradict Achebe's interpretation of *Chi* as 'personal god'. His article insists that 'the *Chi* of a man is not his personal god but the emanated spirit of Chukwu by which the individual participates in the spiritual Godhead'. On that misleading premise Shelton interprets the characters Unoka, Okonkwo, Nwoye and Obi as expressive of Achebe's heresy. But it is really in his conclusion that the origin of his displeasure becomes apparent:

> Achebe makes a vainglorious attempt in these two books – and I suspect he will continue so in *The Arrow of God* [sic] – to ascribe all the evils which occurred in Ibo society to the coming of the White man. But he stacks the cards in the novels, hinting here and there at the truth, yet not explaining fully the substratum of divine forces working to influence the characters.

Shelton adds that Achebe's

> motives perhaps are linked with his patent desire to indicate that outsiders can never understand the works of Igbo-speaking writers (whose novels are in English) although one must properly leave the subject of authors' motivations to psychologists.

With that remark Shelton had proceeded from the literary to the personal, thereby stepping beyond the boundaries of literary criticism. The central thrust of the article, however, was that

> what caused 'things to fall apart' and what made the Ibo man 'no longer at ease' in the case of Achebe's works, were the evil actions of Okonkwo who brought the wrath of Chukwu, the *alusi* and the *Ndichie* upon his own lineage.[12]

Achebe felt that the essay was too preposterous to deserve a reply. But Donatus Nwoga, who was later to enjoy a reputation as a prominent, pioneering and distinguished critic, responded in another *Transition* article, 'The *Chi* Offended'. Nwoga begins with the remark that Shelton's 'studies of Ibo *Weltan-schauungen* (whatever that may be) appear to have confused him thoroughly in his treatment of Achebe's novels in his essay'. He disputes Shelton's claims, pointing instead to the artistic balance in Achebe's presentation of 'the popular reaction to Okonkwo's achievements and his extravagances'. An essential aspect of Nwoga's case is his testimony that: 'from my childhood I had been made to think that one's *chi* was his personal god, within or without the individual and with distinct personality.' He concludes that if 'Achebe does not explain the substratum of divine forces working to influence the characters, it is only when these forces are not important'.[13] Nwoga's rejoinder made more cogent Achebe's observation concerning misleading and uninformed criticism in the essay, 'Where Angels Fear to Tread', which had elicited Shelton's displeasure.

The critical skirmish set the scene for the publication of *Arrow of God*,[14] a novel that synthesized the mythic, religious, cultural, economic and social traditions of the Igbo in a bid to explore the African condition. This third novel also possessed a scope that exceeded the incidents that inspired it as well as the social milieu which it depicted. Achebe dedicated *Arrow of God* to his late father, Isaiah Okafor Achebe. He uses its protagonist, an old dignified Chief Priest of Ulu known as Ezeulu, to tell a story of war and peace in the midst of cultural, religious and economic upheavals. Setting his scene in the Igbo village of Umuaro in the early twentieth century – when the intervention of a British District Officer, Captain Winterbottom, prevents a war between Umuaro and Okperi – Achebe depicts the initial attempts to create warrant chiefs and indirect rule in the area. The first encounter between the white man and Umuaro convinces Ezeulu to send his son to learn both the secret of the white man's strength and his Christian ways, but this triggers another conflict when the overzealous son tries to kill a sacred royal python, undermining Ezeulu's opposition to the white man. This opposition must also contend with the rabble-rousing antagonism of Nwaka. As all these strands are gathered, events move inexorably towards a poignant tragedy that engulfs Ezeulu and his people.

Many of the reviewers in London pronounced *Arrow of God* an accomplished novel. Tom Stacey in the *Sunday Times* thought that 'the telling is polished; images effortlessly light up the pages, the style is faultless' and 'there is a poignant melody echoing deeply that should not be lost' while for the *Times Literary Supplement* reviewer 'Mr Achebe's evocation of atmosphere and his presentation of the way Africans speak and of their often utterly alien thought processes are both fascinating and convincing.'[15] Benedict Nightingale in the *Guardian* argued that 'what makes *Arrow of God* so attractive is its unsentimental evocation of a rich, vital way of life that really satisfies those lucky enough to be born in it'. John Coleman in *The Observer* affirmed that 'Chinua Achebe is surely the most interesting of those young African writers who are enlarging our horizons by documenting unknown territory, spiritual as well as geographical, from the inside'.[16] Although these reviews praise the competence of Achebe, it is equally obvious that the reviewers were examining the novel from their own Western cultural perspectives.

Many of the reviews that appeared in Nigeria were also authored by Western critics. In *Transition* Gerald Moore acknowledges that 'Achebe emerges as a novelist of considerable originality and power' and also that the novelist 'tells his moral tragedy with his usual economy and strong sense of design'. He ends, however, with the reservation that

> Once again the white characters are not much more than parodies, though perfectly fair ones. Certainly, dull and conventional Europeans abounded in the colonies. This is not necessarily a reason for writing about them. Some day Chinua Achebe must give us a white man whom he takes as seriously as he does his Ibos, rather than a series of *dei ex machina*. But *Arrow of God* takes these weaknesses in its stride and adds greatly to the achievement of the earlier books.'[17]

Moore's reaction is particularly interesting when considered as a mirror image of the displeasure Achebe had felt on encountering the fictional African characters of Joyce Cary and Joseph Conrad. John Ginger, reviewing the novel in *Black Orpheus*, has a different assessment of the author's intention and creative focus:

> The ambitious scope of Achebe's novel can be gauged by his own distance from the two characters on whom its events hang: an Englishman and a priest. Winterbottom, of course, can remain an outsider without detracting much from the novel's achievement, he is more important in his function than in himself. The writer does not intend more than a sympathetic sketch here.[18]

Alan Hill and Keith Sambrook of Heinemann Educational Books went to Nigeria to arrange the launching of the novel on 4 April 1964 at the Bristol Hotel in Lagos. That visit also coincided with the death of Daniel Fagunwa, an author who wrote in Yoruba and was also in charge of the business affairs of Heinemann in Nigeria. Alan Hill recalls that 'it was the first publishers' reception ever to be held in Lagos to launch a Nigerian novel', and that the '300 guests ranged from Government Ministers to leading figures in every walk of Nigerian life'.[19] This latest outbreak of fame and general appreciation did not deflect the even course of Achebe's creative and professional life, one strand of which continued to be his work as general editor of the African Writers Series. It was at this time that he had a visit from other African writers like the East African poet Joseph Kariuki, whose much anthologized poem 'Come Away My Love' Achebe has described as capturing 'in so few words the trials and tensions of an African in love with a white girl in Britain'.[20] Such visits also helped Achebe to reflect on the perplexing issues raised by modern African literature, and to add to his critical output. His essay on 'The African Writer and the English Language' was first presented at the University of Ghana and afterwards published in *Spear* magazine in July 1964 and also in *Transition*. The essay was taken erroneously to be solely a response to Obi Wali's trenchant *Transition* essay, 'The Dead End of African Literature'. Wali criticizes the 1962

Conference of African Writers by asserting that its most important disclosure was 'that African Literature as now defined and understood, leads nowhere'. Wali is careful to note that the purpose of his article

> is not to discredit those writers who have achieved much in their individual rights within an extremely difficult and illogical situation. It is to point out that the whole uncritical acceptance of English and French as the inevitable medium for educated African writing, is misdirected.

In Wali's view

> until these writers and their western midwives accept the fact that true African literature must be written in African languages, they would be merely pursuing a dead end, which can only lead to sterility, uncreativity, and frustration.[21]

Wali was certainly controversial and writers and critics like Barry Reckord, Ezekiel Mphahlele, Wole Soyinka, Gerald Moore, Denis Williams, John Clare and Austin Shelton responded with varying degrees of antagonism to his argument.[22] Austin Shelton satirically reviewed an imaginary novel *Ekene Dili Chukwu* mischievously credited to Obi Wali, for he had never written a book with such a title.

Although Achebe's essay was not occasioned by this controversy, in many ways it answered the basic contentions of Wali's argument. Achebe begins from the premise that

> you cannot cram African literature in a small, neat definition. I do not see African literature as one unit but as associated units – in fact the sum total of all the *national* and *ethnic* literatures of Africa.

He proceeds to predict the rise to prominence of national literatures following the 'rise of individual nation states'. Achebe the critic does not overlook or gloss over issues. He stresses that the factors 'which have conspired to place English in the position of national language in many parts of Africa' were owing to the fact that 'these nations were created in the first place by the intervention of the British', which he hastened to add was not saying that 'the peoples comprising these nations were invented by the British'. Thus his argument is that African writers who have chosen to write in English or French are 'by-products of the same process that made the new nations states of Africa'. He draws illustrations from the poetry of Christopher Okigbo and J. P. Clark to illustrate the available exciting possibilities in the use of a foreign language. One of the basic questions Achebe examines, however, is: 'Can an African ever learn English well enough to be able to use it effectively in creative writing?' His answer is 'yes' but he adds, 'If on the other hand you ask can he ever learn to use it like a native speaker, I should say, I hope not.' In his subsequent illustrations, using Tutuola whom he calls a natural artist juxtaposed with himself as a conscious artist, Achebe reproduces a passage from *Arrow of God* which indicates it could have been written differently. At the end Achebe reiterates: 'I feel that the English language will be able to carry the weight of my African experience. But it will have to be a new English, still in full communion with its ancestral home but altered to suit its new African surroundings.'[23] The essay answered Obi Wali insightfully and comprehensively; part of it was published in *Spear* as 'Handicaps of Writing in a Second Language',[24] in which Achebe acknowledges that the use of a second language poses difficulties of competence.

101

Another essay which highlighted Achebe's views in 1964, 'The Role of the Writer in a New Nation', was presented as a lecture to the Nigerian Library Association and later published in *Nigeria Magazine*. He writes of the great 'challenge which the African writer must counteract', identifying it as 'the one that calls his full humanity in question'. To meet this challenge requires the firm understanding that 'African people did not hear of culture for the first time from Europeans; that their societies were not mindless but frequently had a philosophy of great depth and value and beauty, that they had poetry and above all, they had dignity'. At the same time, 'we cannot pretend', he cautions, 'that our past was one long, technicolour idyll. We have to admit that like other peoples' pasts ours had its bad as well as its good sides.' It is in this essay that the novelist explains:

> What I have said must not be understood to mean that I do not accept the present-day as a proper subject for the novelist. Far from it. My last but one novel is about the present day and the next one will again come up to date. But what I do mean is that owing to the peculiar nature of our situation it would be futile to try and take off before we have repaired our foundations.

Achebe points to the issue of the confusion of values in the new nations and he laments that 'today we have kept the materialism and thrown away the spirituality which should keep it in check'. He touches on the linguistic question, submitting that 'those who can do the work of extending the frontiers of English so as to accommodate African thought patterns must do it through their mastery of English and not out of innocence.' Achebe ends by calling on 'artists and writers of today, to take up the good work and by doing it to enrich not only our own lives but the life of the world.'[25] As usual the essay argues persuasively and the illustrations are both apt and informative; thereby emphasizing the concern of the novelist with the relevance of creativity. It also emerges that Achebe is working on a fourth novel exploring the contemporary Nigerian reality.

Although these two essays by Achebe did not end the controversies over an appropriate language or subject matter for African literature they contributed to the clarification of issues. Another kind of responsibility was declaring itself to the Nigerian novelist. He had received several letters from readers expressing their appreciation of his novels but one of them drew his attention. It was from Northern Nigeria and it stated:

> Dear C. Achebe,
> I do not usually write to authors, no matter how interesting their work is, but I feel I must tell you how much I enjoyed your editions of *Things Fall Apart* and *No Longer at Ease*. I look forward to reading your new edition *Arrow Of God*. Your novels serve as advice to us young. I trust that you will continue to produce as many of this type of books. With friendly greetings and best wishes.
>
> Yours sincerely
> I. Buba Yero Mafindi [26]

This letter from the Northern Region, usually regarded as not harbouring many Western-educated citizens, made it clear to Achebe that many of his readers regarded him as a teacher. Achebe also received his own share of 'Help me succeed in my exams' letters from students who had to read his books for the General School Certificate examinations. The troubling experience of Christie

Achebe, who was teaching at St Gregory's College, Lagos, having transferred from Methodist Boys High School, also had a bearing on the writer's responsibility as a teacher. Chinua Achebe was told by Christie in August 1964 of the boy in her class 'who said he couldn't write about the harmattan because it was *bush*' and that he would 'rather write about winter'. Achebe's reaction was that

> things like this show one that the writer has the responsibility to teach his audience that there is nothing shameful about the harmattan, that it is not only daffodils that can make a fit subject for poetry but the palm tree and so on.[27]

Such issues were occupying his mind when Achebe received an invitation to participate in the first Commonwealth Literature Conference to be held at the University of Leeds under the direction of Professor Norman Jeffares. Thus in September of 1964 Achebe travelled to Leeds to present a paper on 'The Novelist as Teacher': it was to become one of his most-quoted and misquoted essays, depending on the temperament, purpose or mischievous inclination of the quoter.

In that lecture at Leeds, published in the *New Statesman* the following year, Achebe begins by citing several responses received from his readers. In particular he cites the Ghanaian female teacher who 'took him to task for not making the hero [of *No Longer at Ease*] marry the girl he is in love with'. Achebe feels that 'this young woman spoke with so much feeling' that he could not 'help being a little uneasy' at the accusation that he 'had squandered a rare opportunity for education on a whimsical and frivolous exercise'. After that introductory but relevant remark Achebe stated his basic contention:

> Here then is an adequate revolution for me to espouse – to help my society regain belief in itself and put away the complexes of the years of denigration and self-abasement. And it is essentially education, in the best sense of that word. Here, I think, my aims and the deepest aspirations of my society meet.

Thus he confirms that 'the writer cannot expect to be excused from the task of re-education and re-generation that must be done. In fact, he should march right in front.' The novelist acknowledges that he would not wish to be exempted from rendering genuine services to Africa as a writer. And he restates his case: 'I would be quite satisfied if my novels (especially the ones I set in the past) did no more than teach my readers that their past – with all its imperfections – was not one long night of savagery from which the first Europeans acting on God's behalf delivered them.'[28]

Although it was a short lecture, Achebe as always contrived to make it succinct and relevant. Its importance was to be confirmed by the varied references to it, some by commentators who mischievously perceived it as Achebe's only manifesto as a writer. Even before the end of that Leeds Conference, Achebe had explained to Donatus Nwoga in an interview that he

> was using teacher there, not in the narrow sense of teaching a scale or teaching to pass an examination. I was thinking primarily more of a deeper meaning of teaching and what I had in mind, what I think a novelist can teach is something very fundamental, namely to indicate to his readers, to put it crudely, that we in Africa did not hear of culture for the first time from Europeans.[29]

Achebe's presentation of those ideas and their effect on his audience made him an attractive keynote speaker sought by various organizations.

In the evening of the day he delivered his lecture at Leeds, Professor Norman Jeffares held a reception at his home where Achebe was one of the prominent personalities. It was at that reception that Douglas Killam met him for the first time. Also present were critics and scholars from the European countries whose interest in African literature was aroused at that conference. Achebe helped these scholars to feel the intrinsic pulse of African literature, drawing attention to its qualities at a key moment when the Association for Commonwealth Literature and Language Studies was being established.

After that frontiersman role in England, Achebe went back to Nigeria to tackle both his public and private responsibilities: Christie was expecting a baby; the Voice of Nigeria, now fully established, required administrative pruning and refinement; political activities were increasing in tempo, obviously in anticipation of the December elections, and he had also become involved in the setting up of structures to encourage creative interaction between writers. About two months after Achebe's return from Leeds his wife gave birth to a baby boy on 3 December 1964. He was christened Ikechukwu, 'Through the might of God', a name that seemed to indicate an appreciation of God's blessings in producing a daughter and a son without any attendant anxieties.

The December elections made up for the absence of anxiety in Achebe's personal life. The new political alliances which virtually reduced the contending political parties into two did not alleviate political tension. The election would have been a contest between the United Progressive Grand Alliance (UPGA), made up of the NCNC and Action Group parties, and the Nigerian National Alliance (NNA), made up of the NPC and some breakaway former NCNC and the Action Group members. The delimitation of the federal constituencies on the basis of the disputed 1964 census, and the allocation of more seats to the Northern Region, contributed to the general political acrimony. In addition, the prime minister, Sir Abubakar Tafawa Balewa, rejected President Nnamdi Azikiwe's suggestion, based on an appeal to the president by aggrieved politicians, to invite United Nations experts to supervise the elections since it became difficult for the UPGA candidates to campaign in the North where they were subjected to arbitrary arrests. Instead, Balewa announced on 28 December that the election would be held on 30 December 1964 as scheduled. On the same day three members of the Federal Electoral Commission representing the East, Mid-West and Lagos resigned. The election was held in the North and some parts of the Western Region but boycotted in the East, Mid-West and Lagos. The result declared showed that Balewa had been elected as prime minister. President Azikiwe expressed dissatisfaction and initially refused to call on Balewa to form a new government. It was a period of political uncertainty; after a while Azikiwe asked Balewa to form a new government on the understanding that it would be a broad-based one after elections were finally held in the East, Mid-West and Lagos in February 1965.

Political controversies raged on into 1965, however, with signs of further deterioration. Achebe was following the events closely, of course, since he worked in an establishment that was a primary source for the dissemination of information. At the same time he was performing his role as the father of two children. The first child, Chinelo, had begun attending a nursery school in Lagos. Achebe found it necessary to make time to discuss with the child some of the new words and perceptions of reality she had imbibed. That was how he and Christie discovered that their daughter 'was developing very strange notions about race and colour'. Achebe was convinced that

> she couldn't have picked up any of that from home, so my wife and I tracked it down to the racially mixed school that she attended, and I immediately wrote in protest to the headmistress, a white lady. Most of the teachers were white. And we found that it wasn't just that, but the entire educational system, including the books they read. So even if the teachers did nothing at all the books would have done it.

Those books had been written with a built-in social prejudice which Achebe's daughter absorbed; it was only when she reflected those views at home that the parents became worried. Chinua Achebe describes the issue thus:

> I never read those books myself when I was growing so I didn't know what was in them. This was in Nigeria not in Europe or America. To give you a very quick run down of the kind of story I saw, it is a story of a kite. There is a little boy, a white boy in Europe; you know, it's a glossy book, a lot of illustrations. You see the idea of Europe, town, big city, and this boy is flying a kite; and then the kite goes right up and gets caught in the tail of an aeroplane that is passing. And this aeroplane carries it and on and on and on, and somewhere far away this kite dislodges itself and begins to fall and it falls into a coconut tree. And then you see the huts, the round huts, and a lot of luscious background; and then you see a little black boy, naked, climbing the coconut tree, and then half way up he sees this kite, and so he is frightened, and he jumps down and calls his father who comes out with a spear and looks up and sees this kite; and he's scared and there's a big bustle in the village. They send for the witch doctor, naturally. So the witch doctor comes with his group and a lot of drumming, and they dance around the tree seven times, and then the witch doctor's attendant climbs up and brings down this strange being with great reverence, and there is a big procession and they take it to the village shrine where it is worshipped to this day. This is a very dangerous story. I don't think any one has the right to tell children that kind of story about other people. Even if they had the right I would not want my children to be brought up with that kind of story.[30]

One aspect of that discovery was that Achebe started considering the type of books he procured for his daughter. That desire to buy the right books led him to the discovery that there was a paucity of books for children in Nigeria. His worry deepened even as he put the finishing touches to the novel he had completed in 1964, *A Man of the People*, written as a social, political and cultural satire.

The completion of that novel and the inevitable period of creative rest in which the novelist reflected on what he had written while contemplating new works for the future found him considering the kind of books available for children to read in Nigeria. There was a certain sense in which the novelist felt like a missionary in the area of African literature as he considered new areas likely to prove receptive to his creative vision. Meanwhile the obvious signs of accomplishment in his writing career continued to flow. In 1965 *Arrow of God* was awarded the first-ever Jock Campbell-New Statesman Award of £1,000. It was a deserved prize for a frontier novel and a frontier writer. The accomplishment in *Arrow of God* had not gone unnoticed by novelists working in other cultures. The American novelist John Updike had written Achebe a letter commenting on his impression that a great character like Ezeulu was destroyed in a few pages at the end. 'The final development of *Arrow of God*', Updike wrote,

> proved unexpected and, as I think about them, beautifully resonant, tragic and

theological. That Ezeulu, whom we had seen stand up so invincibly to both Nwaka and Clarke, should be so suddenly vanquished by his own god Ulu and by something harsh and vengeful within himself, and his defeat in a page or two be the fulcrum of a Christian lever upon his people, is an ending few Western novelists would have contrived.

The American novelist clarified that 'having created a hero, Western novelists would not let him crumble, nor are they, by and large, as truthful as you in their witness to the cruel reality of process'. It was an illuminating comment and Achebe confessed that as he 'thought about the peculiarity' Updike had observed 'in the handling of' the character a 'number of matters' were clarified for him. A central point was that the non-Westerner does not have the obligation of creating the individual hero, 'the very paragon of creation' because the individual is subordinate to the community and 'is subject to non-human forces in the universe'.[31] That kind of dialogue enabled Achebe to understand the dynamics of the creative enterprise. Meanwhile Valerie Wilmer was writing, in *Flamingo* of August 1965, that Achebe 'has a profound gift of observation and tells his story with an adept touch. He is probably the best African novelist of today.' Wilmer also notes the 'acute gift for building up tragedy' in his three published novels.[32] These dialogues with writers and critics clearly provided Achebe with opportunities to refine his thoughts and creative focus, especially on political issues.

That contemplation of political events resulted in a short story that used some of the material that had inspired his fourth novel, *A Man of the People*, already submitted to his publishers. In 'The Voter', published in *Black Orpheus*, Achebe weaves the story around politics as the protagonist, Rufus Okeke, in the midst of his machinations as chief campaigner for the election of chief the Honourable Marcus Ibe, is visited by the leader of the opposing campaign team.[33] He is offered five pounds, subsequently made to take an oath with 'an object covered with a red cloth' which was 'a fearsome little affair contained in a clay pot with feathers stuck into it'. The construction of this story, centring on money politics, reveals the contagious nature of an immoral attitude as the villagers, who feel they 'have climbed the Iroko tree today and would be foolish not to take down all the fire wood needed' blatantly ask for bribes. The fall of Rufus Okeke demonstrates the deepening level of corruption and the dimming of noble principles. Although Rufus overcomes his personal dilemma on election day by tearing his card in two – one piece for Maduka, the opponent, and one for Chief Marcus Ibe, his own employer – that act illustrates the basic unreliability and political dishonesty Achebe is satirizing. The plot of the story, hinging on this man who is bribing the electorate and who is bribed in turn, drives home the deviant tendency of the political scene.

Such deviance would become magnified in Nigerian public life before the end of 1965. Meanwhile Achebe managed to encourage submissions, offer editorial help and make essential contributions towards the publication of many new titles for Heinemann Educational Books. Within three years it had been possible for the public to find in the African Writers Series works by Cyprian Ekwensi, Peter Abrahams, Ngugi, Richard Rive, T. M. Aluko, Olaudah Equiano, William Conton, Mongo Beti, Mugo Gatheru and John Munonye. In the case of Munonye he benefited distinctly from the trail-blazing role of Achebe as he confessed to Bernth Lindfors several years later:

First of all I read Chinua Achebe's *Things Fall Apart*. Chinua happened to be a very good friend of mine; we had been at the university together, had spent holidays together, had cracked jokes together, and we thought alike on many issues. We also came from roughly the same community; he is from Ogidi and I am from Akokwa, and those two towns are not far from one another. So when Chinua got away with writing a novel, I said to myself, 'why not try?' And I did.[34]

Thus Munonye explains how he 'began to write' around 1963–4. That confession does not detract from his own achievement, but certainly highlights the benefits to other writers of Achebe's pioneering role. Even Chukwuemeka Ike, who was published by Fontana, claimed that *Things Fall Apart* was a great inspiration, and that when he wrote *Toads for Supper* he sent the novel to Achebe who made some helpful suggestions.[35] Achebe had already sent Flora Nwapa's novel *Efuru* to Heinemann Educational Books after making some editorial suggestions; it was then awaiting publication.

Other Nigerian writers like Elechi Amadi were published, too; Amadi's novel *The Concubine* became No. 25 in the African Writers Series. Wole Soyinka, who was making a name as a playwright, wrote his impressive novel *The Interpreters,* which was reprinted as No. 43. Achebe was not parochial in his editorial work, however; Heinemann also published the Ghanaian writer Francis Selormey's *The Narrow Path.* S. A. Konadu's *A Woman in Her Prime* and Amu Djoleto's *The Strange Man*; the Cameroonian Ferdinand Oyono's *Houseboy,* the Zimbabwean Stanlake Samkange's *On Trial for My Country,* and a number of books (nearly all banned in their own country) by South Africans: Cosmo Pieterse's *Ten One-Act Plays,* Alex la Guma's *A Walk in the Night and Other Stories,* Aubrey Kachingwe's *No Easy Task* and Dennis Brutus's *Letters to Martha and Other Poems.*

That close association with writers from other parts of Africa made Achebe realize the importance of having an association of writers in Nigeria. Thus he became involved in the establishment of the Society of Nigerian Authors in 1965: its members included J. P. Clark, Flora Nwapa, Cyprian Ekwensi, T. M. Aluko and many others. It was a forum for formal interactions between writers resident in Lagos. Achebe continued to enjoy informal contact with writers who had also become his friends. Christopher Okigbo, still working for Cambridge University Press, visited Achebe on several occasions and on one of those visits, in 1965, said to Achebe in his irrepressible manner: 'Chinua, you must write for us. We want a children's book from you.'[36] That request coincided with Achebe's own inclination at that time, especially with his uneasiness at the kind of books available for his growing children to read. He accepted the offer after some discussion with Okigbo and commenced work on an adventure story, situated in a recognizable cultural milieu, in which an enterprising boy named Chike becomes involved in several escapades. It was something he wrote quickly, and also rewrote according to the specifications of Cambridge University Press. Writing a children's book, Achebe discovered, 'was not easy [although it] was fun'. He was discovering several new strings to his creative bow as writer and editor. In addition, he was tackling his ongoing administrative responsibilities as the founder of the Voice of Nigeria. It was in the course of these duties that Achebe hired Mike Enahoro as an announcer with Voice of Nigeria after Enahoro had worked as a part-time news reader and producer of programmes.

Meanwhile the serenity of Achebe's Lagos environment was being steadily eroded. The political controversies in the Western Region were assuming alarming proportions. In October 1965 the government of Chief Akintola scheduled elections to the Western House of Assembly. In that election on 11 October there were various instances of election malpractices in which contestants were beaten and detained, and ballot papers destroyed. It was a desperate situation, for Awolowo's Action Group wanted to utilize the opportunity to demonstrate the popularity of the party in the region, while Akintola's NDP government wanted to establish a secure political foundation. To the amazement of the Action Group, the results announced victory to Akintola's party. It was at the height of this crisis that Wole Soyinka was said to have held up an announcer at the Western Radio Station, an incident in which the governor's speech was changed and a different, damaging speech read. Soyinka was subsequently arrested, was tried in court, discharged and acquitted. Enraged by the 'results' of the election, angry Action Group members called on the Prime Minister, Balewa, to annul the election and declare a state of emergency as he had in 1962, but they were ignored and told to seek redress in the law courts. It was a costly mistake, for the people had lost confidence in the rule of law and took the law into their own hands in what became known as the terrible *Operation Wetie* ('wet it'). In Ibadan and Lagos many people were subjected to violence; houses were burnt and hundreds of people fled their homes. That state of anarchy continued into the new year of 1966 with barricades erected by opposing factions and many commuters killed or spared according to the answers they gave to the roving political thugs. The prime minister pretended publicly that the situation was under control, even when the Commonwealth Premiers' Conference was held in Lagos. Meanwhile, the real power behind the throne, the Northern premier Sir Ahmadu Bello, held consultations with Chief Akintola on 14 January at a secret meeting also attended by a high-ranking army officer, Brigadier Ademulegun. It was later said that discussion at the meeting centred on a coup that would change the political structure of the country. Events during that month of January were assuming forms that would confirm the notion of a plan between Ahmadu Bello and Akintola. The army commander, Major-General Ironsi, was ordered by the defence minister to take his accumulated leave and Louis Edet, the inspector general of Police, was also ordered to proceed on leave, while Alhaji Kam Salem was appointed his deputy.

It was also on that evening of Friday 14 January that the Society of Nigerian Authors met at the Exhibition Centre in Lagos. Chinua Achebe, the president, had a copy of *A Man of the People* at that meeting; the novel was scheduled for general publication on Monday, 17 January. Heinemann Educational Books were billing this fourth novel by Achebe as a fascinating departure from his previous work:

> It is a hilarious yet disturbing satire on corrupt government and the 'cult of personality' in an unnamed newly independent African state. The chief 'personality' under attack is Nanga, the semi-literate Minister of Culture, who at the opening of the novel pays a ceremonial visit to the school at which the narrator, Odili Samalu, is teaching. He recognises Odili, a former pupil of his, and invites him to stay at his house in the capital, Bori. There Odili is introduced to the manipulation of power and the practice of corrupt and, for some, highly profitable government. But there is another reason

why Odili comes to Bori: Elsie, a delightful and startling personality, who is to be the immediate cause of Odili's clash with his host. Odili in turn becomes involved with Edna, Nanga's intended 'parlour-wife' or supplement to Mrs Nanga (whom her husband considers too 'bush' for important entertaining). Combining political conviction with private vengeance, Odili decides to stand as Nanga's opponent for election to the Parliament. The story of his ventures comes to a head in a general election, which turns out to be the height of corruption and chaos.[37]

Achebe's ending – a military coup – reflects a creative purge of the rotten political system. In this novel he also utilizes a first-person narrator, which taxed his talent in the creation of an ironic tone, a satiric focus and an analytic perspective. The advance copy of *A Man of the People* that Achebe had at the meeting had just been returned to him by John Pepper Clark. Achebe and Clark had become good friends since Clark had come to live in Lagos. They also had mutual friends like Christopher Okigbo and Sam Amuka. Circumstance also brought the Achebe and Clark families even closer for they had one set of children who were born at about the same time: Achebe's son Ikechukwu and Clark's first daughter. It was a reflection of this closeness that when Achebe had read his advance copy of his new novel, he should pass it on to his friend. J. P. Clark's response was enthusiastic: 'Chinua, I *know* you are a prophet. Everything in this book has happened except a military coup!'

The writers' meeting ended by confirming plans for future activities that increased the responsibilities of Chinua Achebe, who had also been made a member of the governing council of the University of Lagos that January, an appointment which brought him closer to the administrative intricacies of a Nigerian university. Achebe went to bed that evening having paid little attention to the words of J. P. Clark; the next morning, Saturday, he went to his office at Broadcasting House.

> I found the place surrounded by soldiers. I had no ideas what was going on. They looked at my pass and saw that I worked there. They said, 'There's been a coup. Nobody knows where the Prime Minister is!'

Achebe was still wondering about what had really occurred when his attention was drawn to an altercation at the gate of the building:

> J. P. Clark who was by this time teaching in Lagos University, dashed over to come to tell me that there had been a coup. When he got to the gate he was nearly shot by these soldiers because he had no business there.[38]

The last 'prophecy' in Achebe's novel, completed about a year before the coup, had been fulfilled.

As the full story of the coup emerged Achebe learned that its leader, Major Chukwuma Kaduna Nzeogwu, had taken control of the Northern Region. Nzeogwu's subsequent announcement on the radio from Kaduna presented his vision clearly:

> Our enemies are the political profiteers, swindlers, men in high and low places that seek bribes and demand ten per cent, those that seek to keep the country permanently divided so that they can remain in office as Ministers and VIPs of waste, the tribalists, the nepotists, those that make the country look big for nothing before international circles.

The high-minded vision of Nzeogwu never materialized, for his fellow coup plotters in Lagos and the Eastern Zone, led by Major Emmanuel Ifeajuna, did not accomplish their tasks. They failed to arrest Major General Aguiyi Ironsi, the army commander, although they eliminated some of the corrupt politicians including the governor of Western Region, the prime minister and the finance minister whose ostentatious lifestyle symbolized the waste Nzeogwu had deplored. The bungling of the affair in Lagos made it possible for Ironsi to assert his authority in a dramatic manner and he eventually crushed the coup plot. Nzeogwu was later enticed to Lagos, where he was arrested and detained, while some of his collaborators like Ifeajuna, who had fled to Ghana, were also brought back, arrested and detained.

Initially the coup, including the deaths of some prominent politicians, was welcomed enthusiastically. The military casualties included three Northern army officers, two Westerners and two Easterners (an Igbo Major and Colonel Arthur Unegbe who was in charge of the armoury). In the Northern region the home of the autocrat, Sir Ahmadu Bello, was ransacked by jubilant Hausa citizens. But all that was to change. The politicians were granted their freedom by General Ironsi who became head of state and did all he could to soothe the injured feelings of the powerful men against whom the coup had been aimed. Ironsi's inordinate desire to deal leniently with the former political leaders would almost cost Chinua Achebe his life when events took a different turn.

9

Retreat to the Citadel
Genocide, War & the Leopard's Claws
1966–7

THE emergence of the military leadership provided temporary respite as Nigerians assessed and evaluated the events. But the error of the military in not curtailing the activities of the politicians soon became apparent as the latter deliberately misinterpreted the pattern of killings. It was convenient for them to centre their argument on those politicians who had been killed, but not on the soldiers who also lost their lives. If the controversy had raged around the death of the soldiers it would have been possible for the public to know that three Northern, two Western and two Eastern senior army officers had died. In addition, it would have been clear to the public that Major-General Aguiyi Ironsi, who reluctantly assumed the leadership position, had never contemplated participating in the intricacies of political administration. He had even sought formal permission from the members of the senate before he assumed the position of head of state. However, some of his honest decisions were mischievously misconstrued by the politicians and presented to the gullible public as possessing ethnic motives. The consequence was that members of his ethnic group started experiencing alienation from other ethnic groups, particularly in the Northern part of the country, as they were suspected of involvement in a plan to entrench themselves in leadership positions. Chinua Achebe, working in the Broadcasting House as the Director of External Broadcasting, was largely beyond the influence of the ethnic factor, but he noted such developments with sadness.

He was considering a change of career at about that time, having risen to one of the pinnacles of his profession. He had written four successful novels, some insightful essays and several short stories – one of which appeared in *Black Orpheus* in March 1966. 'Uncle Ben's Choice' demonstrates a new dimension of Achebe's creativity, for he makes abundant use of humour. The major character, known as Jolly Ben, is reminiscing over an adventure in his youth when he was a popular clerk in the Niger Company at Umuru. In those days he had epicurean tastes and engaged in amorous escapades. Jolly Ben's idiosyncratic monologue narrates how he had gone to the African Club one New Year's Eve and after a lot of merriment proceeded home to sleep. He got home but without bothering to put on any light he removed his clothes and fell on the bed. The touch of a naked female body makes him assume that one of his acquaintances, a local girl known as Margaret, has paid him an unannounced visit but a greater surprise is in store:

> When I touched the hair and it was soft like the hair of a European my laughter was quenched by force. I touched the hair on her head and it was the same.

Then when the woman speaks in Igbo he is emboldened to strike a match and in panic runs to the home of his kinsman Matthew. It is there that Matthew tells him: 'It depends on what you want in life. If it is wealth you want then you made a great mistake today, but if you are a true son of your father then take my hand.'[1] Thus it dawns on Ben that he has been visited by Mami Wota, the lady of the River Niger. The parable of this story was relevant in 1966, a year of conflicting desires, for Ben's experience enables him come to terms with his real objectives in life. The posing of a choice in terms of acquiring either financial or human possessions reflects the kind of choice Nigeria was making, for the country found itself in a situation where it had to choose either peace or war.

Events were proceeding as if the choice of war had been made, with the politicians gradually asserting their influence in the Northern Region. It was while these turbulent events were occurring that the First World Festival of Negro Arts was held in Dakar, Senegal in April 1966. Several prizes were awarded in the areas of drama, poetry and fiction. Chinua Achebe did not attend but, as John Povey reported,

> the English novel prize went to James Ngugi for *Weep Not, Child*. This is a tender and accurate record of Ngugi's early life in Kenya and it does not belittle Ngugi's achievement if one mentions that Chinua Achebe, by electing to be a member of the jury, had eliminated his own work from consideration.[2]

At home, the political tension had taken new directions, especially with the spread of the rumour in Northern Nigeria of impending domination of the nation by Southern Nigerians. It was a dangerous rumour, conceived and propagated with the intention of discrediting the Ironsi regime.

In the month of the Dakar Festival, Chinua Achebe moved into a new house built for the Director of External Broadcasting on Turnbull Road, and one Philip Ume-Ezeoke moved into his old house in Milverton Street, which was also an official residence owned by the Nigerian Broadcasting Corporation. Shortly after that change of residence, *Chike and the River,* the children's novel Achebe had written on request, was published. The story follows Chike's adventures as he leaves his village environment to live with an uncle at Onitsha. At Onitsha Chike discovers new friends and a new urban culture, which invariably leads to comparisons in terms of cleanliness and attitudes of honesty. In that new environment Chike encounters Ezekiel, a spoilt dishonest child, and he also finds himself in a group of pupils sent to the village of Okikpe. The journey to Okikpe provides him with an opportunity to demonstrate his bravery. The story is obviously fashioned to interest young readers and a major aspect of Achebe's fictive purpose is moral and didactic. When the pupils consume fake 'brain pills' with the idea that the tablets will make them successful in their examination, their lack of wisdom is clearly pointed out. Chike's greatest desire is to travel in a boat across the River Niger, but when he picks up a coin on the street that will allow him to fulfill his dreams, he foolishly succumbs to the tricks of a magician who steals his money. Chike's perseverance pays off when he receives payment for washing cars: with the money he boards a ferry and travels to Asaba on the other side of the river. Unfortunately he misses the last boat home and spends a frightening night in a lorry used by some robbers. In the morning his identification of the nightwatchman as an accomplice enables the police to arrest the robbers. The conclusion of the adventure is that his 'photograph appeared in the local newspaper and his name was mentioned on the radio'. Later Chike 'got a letter from the manager of the shop. He announced that the company which owned the shop had decided to award a scholarship to Chike which would take him right through secondary school.'[3] That conclusion to the story clearly stresses the importance of honesty and the value of resourcefulness and intelligence.

The publication of two books and a short story in 1966 did not distract Achebe's attention from the political scene, with the country now plunged into social violence. The politicians had once more taken the initiative in galvanizing public opinion against the military establishment, especially in the Northern Region. The Unification Decree which was unanimously accepted by the Supreme Military Council gave those politicians an excuse for insinuating that it was designed to make it possible for one ethnic group to dominate the country. In the volatile situation in which General Ironsi found himself his only weapon of defence was his honest intentions, which he hoped would be convincing to the entire nation. Ironsi was convinced that his lack of political ambition was obvious since he had made it clear as far back as 28 February 1965, in an interview granted to the *Sunday Times* after his appointment as the first Nigerian commander of the Nigerian Army on 15 February. In that interview he was asked sensitive questions on the possibility of military intervention in Nigeria but he replied that 'what we should get clear is that the crisis was a political crisis' which 'did not require military action'. When the interviewer wanted his reaction on a possible internal war Ironsi had answered bluntly: "I don't know what you're trying to get at ... whatever you might have in mind, the Army supports the Government that is!'[4] It was clear that Major-General Ironsi was a loyal soldier who found himself in the cockpit of events; unfortunately the discredited politicians, particularly from the Northern Region, who were unhappy to be isolated and ignored, had succeeded in infecting with ideas of mutiny the Northern Officer Corps, which included many soldiers recruited by those politicians when they were in power. The same politicians also succeeded in spreading rumours that there was discrimination against the Northern Region in the policies of the federal military government, while an organized process of indoctrination commenced in the Northern civil service. The culmination was what was labelled officially as 'riots' but which actually meant a systematic massacre of Eastern Nigerians living in the North. That massacre in May, with the deaths of Easterners of mainly Igbo origin, was estimated at three thousand and it led to a further marked rise of tension in the country.

News of the violence filtered into Lagos at about the time that Chinua Achebe had started work on a fifth novel, a work in which he hoped to achieve a kind of summary of the major themes in his earlier novels. But the increased political tension, the uncertainties of life and a sense of disillusionment eventually led him to feel that the novel was irrelevant. That was after the escalation of violence and the disturbing news that citizens of Eastern Nigeria and of Igbo origin had been the victims of 'organized riots'. The night before the news broke in Lagos, Chinua and Christie Achebe had attended a party in J. P. Clark's house. Next day, when Chinua Achebe heard the news of the massacre, he drove from his office to Clark's house on the University of Lagos Campus in order to discuss this perplexing event. He was surprised to find Clark's house padlocked which meant that the owner had no intention of returning soon. Achebe drove back to his office at the NBC from where he telephoned one of their mutual friends, Sam Amuka. It was Amuka who informed him that J. P. Clark had gone to his village. The news was a shock to Achebe, who felt that his friend should have given him prior information. All in all, social life in Lagos was beginning to lose its excitement and interest for him.

There was no doubt that General Ironsi was battling against many political odds but he did not entertain doubts for his safety and did not pause to reflect on the wisdom of selecting his guards and assistants from the Northern Region. It was not an astute decision because that region of the country had exhibited significant resentment of the political dispensation at that time, but Ironsi apparently felt that his sincerity in crushing the coup of 15 January and his eventual appointment of regional governors – Lieutenant Colonel Hassan Usman Katsina as governor of the North, Lieutenant Colonel Adekunle Fajuyi in the West, Lieutenant Colonel David Ejoor in the Mid-West and Lieutenant Colonel Chukwuemeka Odumegwu Ojukwu in the East – would appease the people. He also embarked on a tour of the country in a bid to make personal appeals. It was because of his nationalist outlook and his desire to play the role of objective military statesman that he ignored his region of origin, the East, in his scheme of activities. He visited the Northern Region and was completing a tour of the Western Region when the Northern army officers, whom he trusted but who had cashed in on his absence from Lagos to complete plans for their coup, struck on 29 July 1966. It was the culmination of the plans of the Northern politicians, who finally succeeded in using soldiers of Northern origin to achieve what the ballot box had failed to accomplish. The coup was also used as an opportunity to attempt to wipe out all the military officers from Eastern Nigeria. It was a merciless, devastating and comprehensive slaughter. The officers were killed in their homes; they were shot at the airport or the railway station or as they were fleeing; some of them were even enticed from hiding with an announcement that the situation had been brought under control and brutally murdered. It was relatively easy for the Northern soldiers to kill General Ironsi, since his guards were of Northern origin and the soldiers he trusted like Lieutenant Danjuma and Lieutenant Walbe were the ones who made sure that he was murdered. In the process, his host and friend Lieutenant Colonel Fajuyi, the governor of the Western Region who was entertaining Ironsi that evening and who honoured the value of friendship, was also murdered after refusing the offer of the soldiers to spare him if he deserted his guest.

The details of the coup night's activities were to become clearer later when Lieutenant Colonel Yakubu Gowon assumed the position of head of state on 1 August 1966. Before then, on 30 July, Achebe had attended a meeting of the governing council of the University of Lagos, unaware of what had happened. He had heard that there was unrest in the army, but that was all. On his way to the meeting at the University of Lagos, he called on Christie, who as usual was teaching at the high school. The meeting of the governing council was brief and when Chinua returned home he informed Christie that the military member of the council was in battledress. The soldier had told them only that there had been a mutiny by a section of the army. Initially Achebe regarded the problem as a purely military affair; but after some days, and especially after the assumption of the position of head of state by Yakubu Gowon with the confirmation of some of the stories concerning the atrocities committed, he began to perceive the matter from a different angle. He was shocked into awareness that a large-scale massacre of citizens of Eastern Nigeria living in other parts of the country had ensued. The Eastern Nigerian army officers were slaughtered (among them was Achebe's cousin); then ordinary soldiers from the same part of the country were killed; the massacre then extended to senior civil servants, ordinary workers, teachers, business people, technicians, traders, medical personnel and students. The tales ranged from pregnant women with stomachs cut open, to men, women and children locked inside houses that were subsequently set on fire. It was a mad August. Gowon did nothing, the traditional rulers in the Northern Region maintained silence, and the rest of the country apart from the Eastern Region acted as if the violence was not their business. The events caused Chinua and Christie extreme anguish because they had conducted their lives on the basis that the nation was more important than the individual. In their home they had a steward who was from Maiduguri in Northern Nigeria, the region that was hostile to Easterners. This Hausa-speaking young man had felt so much at home with the Achebes that he was treated as a member of the family. But that harmonious relationship was soon to be overtaken by events as citizens of Eastern Nigeria were hunted down and killed.

Somebody on Achebe's staff telephoned him on Sunday, at the height of the violence against Easterners, and gave him information that a group of soldiers had come to Broadcasting House looking for him. If those soldiers had gone to that office the previous day, or if they had waited till the next day which was a Monday, they would have caught and killed their quarry. The telephone message from that worried staff member was succinct: 'If I were you, I should leave your house.' When Achebe asked for the reason, the man answered: 'The troops are looking for you.' Achebe felt that he had done nothing and that he was not a criminal either, so he telephoned Victor Badejo, director-general of the NBC, to ask why soldiers should be looking for him. 'Where are you calling from?', inquired Badejo anxiously. 'From my house of course', answered Achebe, 'from Turnbull Road'. 'You better leave immediately,' advised Badejo, 'You better take Christie and leave.'[5]

That advice from Victor Badejo, whose high rank placed him in a position where he could receive authentic information, made it clear to Achebe that the armed soldiers searching for him were not interested in inviting him to a picnic. It also turned out that his hunters had not ended the search at the NBC offices but had gone on to the former residence of Achebe in Milverton Street. Philip Ume-Ezeoke, who was occupying the house, managed to escape attention; he was an Easterner, too, and would have been killed if they had found him. It transpired that the soldiers were looking for Achebe. The sheer coincidence that *A Man of the People* ended with a military coup, and had been published in January 1966, had convinced them that he must have been privy to the coup of the Nigerian majors. It illustrated the kind of stupid logic that had taken root, along with desperation and violent inclinations. Chinua and Christie thus had to consider, and quickly, where they could hide until the situation returned to normal. The best place Chinua could think of was the house of Frank Cawson, the British Council representative in Lagos. Fortunately he had come to know Cawson well; it was this British Council man who had extended the invitation to him to visit Ghana the previous year in order to deliver his lecture on 'The African Writer and the English Language'. Chinua Achebe took his family and went there. He did not leave Lagos right away because he still hoped that the whole question of killing the Igbos was a huge mistake and that somebody would stop it.

Two weeks later things were getting worse, with visible signs of official support for the killings and the extension of hostilities to Easterners living in other regions. Peter Enahoro, from the Mid-Western Region, then resident in Lagos and the editor of the *Daily Times*, describes the atrocities thus:

> Two friends drove up to the house and gave me a first-hand account of the Northern revolt in progress. Ibos were being abducted from offices and taken away to 3rd Battalion Barracks. There was a road-block between us and Lagos. There were road-blocks on the two routes out of Lagos. They had seen Ibo policemen being marched off by Northern troops and they were scared.... A woman ran into my house. She was hysterical. She had been among a group of people walking past a road-block; suddenly one of the soldiers called to them to line up. They obeyed. They were asked what part of Nigeria they came from. Those who said, 'East', were separated from the others. Then right before their eyes, the 'Easterners' were gunned down.... Abductions were being carried out by marauding soldiers and executions were going on all the time.... A burst of machine gunfire exploded so loud it seemed to have come from the sitting room downstairs. The fighting was literally at my door step. My house was situated in an isolated area and my only neighbours – white employees of a Dutch Firm – had evacuated their complex of bungalows the previous day. Some fleeing Ibo soldiers had hidden in the garage of one of these bungalows. The Northerners, conducting a search-and-destroy operation, found the Ibos and calmly fed ammunition into their bodies.[6]

It was organized mayhem and some of the Igbos who escaped returned on foot; the lucky ones had tattered clothes and there was hardly a man, woman or child who did not bear either a knife or a gun wound. Many of them were maimed, with eyes gouged out, limbs cut off or broken and lacerated heads. They were like the victims of a devastating, bitter war. The news of these atrocities that Frank Cawson regularly received made Achebe decide to send his wife Christie and the children to his home town. He was worried about Christie's physical state, however: she was pregnant and required rest and physical comfort. The journey to the East could not be undertaken in a car because of the numerous roadblocks mounted by soldiers intent on searching, identifying and executing the Easterners. The alternative that appealed to him was the use of a boat which would ply the relatively unwatched creeks until it got to Port Harcourt, escaping the attentions of the rampaging soldiers and policemen. He took Christie, Chinelo and Ikechukwu to one of those little ships that was about to proceed to Port Harcourt. Achebe recalls that the most disconcerting part of the experience, as his wife and children boarded the ship, was hearing the laughter of those he had lived with in Lagos for almost ten years when they 'looked around the deck of the ship at all the refugees preparing to leave and said: let them go, food will be cheaper in Lagos'.[7] It was a chilling experience for an individual who had worked for the progress of his country, who had been married in the Western Region at Ibadan as a matter of choice, and whose contemporaries and friends were drawn from several parts of the country.

Christie and the children departed on the ship and Chinua went back to the home of Frank Cawson. The ship was carrying palm kernels which added to the general dirt and unhygienic conditions as the pregnant Christie soon noticed. Many of the passengers were not in the best of health after their desperate existence for some days and weeks hiding from marauding and rampaging bands seeking not only to kill but also to rape the women and young girls. There was much spewing, spitting, vomiting and sea-sickness. The murk of sea life was unmitigated and Christie's condition visibly deteriorated as she struggled to care for the children as well as taking steps to ensure her own good health. That was almost impossible; they slept, when they could, on planks which made their bodies ache; they all suffered from upset stomachs. The food offered to passengers was cooked in a drum of doubtful cleanliness and stirred with a big stick of equally nauseating appearance. The famished occupants of the ship were only interested in survival, however, and hoped that the consumption of such unpleasant food would be temporary. Yet in subsequent months such food was to be a luxury and the sight of food cooked for a large number of people in big drums was to become commonplace, too. The little ship crawled through the creeks, hugging the shore even though the Nigerian Navy was still inactive and unable to conduct patrols along the coast. Fortunately the vessel arrived in Port Harcourt safely, where Christie Achebe and her children were welcomed by her brother Dr Okoli, a medical officer who had left Lagos earlier. The journey took its toll, however: Christie had a miscarriage and lost the baby she had carried in the womb for several months.

Chinua Achebe was still in Lagos waiting, wondering and worrying as he mulled over what had happened. Although life had become so cheap he stubbornly clung to his view that the current events were part of the pains of nationhood. A week after the departure of his family he took a walk in the evening in a bid to feel the pulse of the people and decipher the true nature of events. It was in the course of that walk that he met Victor Badejo, who was also taking an evening stroll. Badejo, shocked that Achebe was still in Lagos, exclaimed: 'Life has no duplicate! You must go away immediately.'[8] Back in Cawson's home Achebe started considering his next move. Some days later he went out again to find out what was happening and when he came back Frank Cawson asked him if he had given anybody the phone number of his (Cawson's) house. Achebe replied that he would not have done that, considering the fact that he was in danger and in hiding. Cawson then informed him that someone had phoned asking if Chinua Achebe was staying there. Fortunately Cawson had answered, and his reply was deliberately fashioned to deflect suspicion. It was this incident that finally persuaded Achebe to return to the Eastern Region. The telephone inquiry indicated clearly to him that it was only a question of time before the armed soldiers came calling; in that event Frank Cawson, though a British Council representative, would be unable to protect him. He quickly made arrangements to travel in a convoy with Philip Ume-Ezeoke, the man who had moved into his old house. The next morning Achebe discovered that Uma-Ezeoke had left and he had to travel back to the East alone. His journey was a race against time for there was a lull in the killings and the soldiers and civilians involved in the massacre were beginning to feel that all available Easterners had either been accounted for or had fled home through the bush. Achebe managed to avoid the trouble spots, which made the journey longer, but he finally got to Benin. At that point it was impossible for him to avoid contact with the soldiers and anti-riot policemen on the road who were from the Mid-Western Region. He joined a long convoy of people waiting to be cleared. When it got to his turn they asked for his identity and he calmly presented his papers. After a cursory glance the policemen cheerfully waved him on, for he was close to his home region and they had recognized him as the popular novelist. It was an incident that revealed the dichotomy in the Nigeria of August 1966; the novelist was a wanted man in one part of the country, while in another segment of the same country he was hailed as a writer. Achebe finally arrived at Ogidi to the joy of his mother, wife, children and relatives.

Such arrivals were occasions for celebration because some families had been wiped out entirely, while in other cases only the children managed to return to the East, their parents having been killed. A process of identification and registration commenced at Enugu in the attempt to create some sort of order. It was through that process that the 30,000 people who had lost their lives were computed by the Eastern Regional government. The events were traumatic for Easterners, including Chinua Achebe as he told Harvey Swados later:

> These massacres happened at the same time of day throughout an area as large as Western Europe. This was not chance. The only reason that more than 30,000 people were not killed is that there were not enough people to do the killing, which was produced by a combination of envy and the tradition of the *jihad*, the holy war. Colin Legum, the British correspondent who witnessed some of the worst of the slaughter, may have changed his position on the Nigeria–Biafra conflict, but it was he who applied the word 'pogrom' to what he had seen, and he told me himself that he considered the journalism that he had done from Northern Nigeria to be the most important thing he had ever done in his life.[9]

It was the comprehensive nature of that massacre that confirmed it as an act of genocide, a fact not lost on Achebe, who only managed to escape alive because a member of his staff had warned him in time and because he had recently moved into a new house.

Achebe did not go to Enugu as soon as he returned. He stayed in his Ikenga village in Ogidi, ruminating on these events. 'I did not go to Enugu. I did not ask for any job,' he said later.

> I did not want anything. I just stayed in the village. And it was clear to me that Nigeria did not intend that this thing should cease. It was very clear. So we were pushed out. And Awolowo said so. He used that word in a statement, 'if the Ibos were pushed out of Nigeria'. So when I finally decided to throw in my support with these people, the Eastern Nigerians, it was not really a matter of having an option. There were no options.[10]

Meanwhile, at Ogidi, Achebe managed to read the newspapers that were still circulating in some parts of the country in order to keep abreast of events and public opinion. It was thus that he read Tai Solarin's essay in his weekly *Daily Times* column on 20 October 1966 in which he advocated the use of Hausa as Nigeria's *lingua franca*. It was an unwise statement in the midst of the hostilities that had taken place within the year in Nigeria. In the course of his argument Solarin attacks Achebe:

> It is sickening reading Chinua Achebe defending English as our *Lingua franca*. I do not blame Achebe or any other Nigerian novelist, taking the same stand. Their books are, commercially speaking, necessarily written in English.

The essay that Solarin refers to is Achebe's 'The African Writer and the English Language' published more than a year before as a statement of fact about the reality of English in the affairs of African people. Achebe found the attack 'unwarranted' and he regarded Solarin's statements as made up of 'potent words worthy of close attention'. His reaction, 'In Defence of English? An Open Letter to Mr Tai Solarin', was published in the *Daily Times* of 7 November 1966. Achebe commences by remarking that

> it is unlikely that many of your readers will have seen my article to which you referred. So I should begin by explaining to them what I did say since you were obviously too sickened to comprehend it.

In a partly sarcastic and partly ironic tone the novelist explains that his aim was not to defend the English language which 'seems more than able to defend itself' but to indicate the historical reasons for the ascendancy of English and to suggest ways in which our imaginative writers who choose to write in it might enrich their idiom and imagery by drawing from their own traditional sources'. Achebe then proceeds to examine the two sentences that had been an attack on him.

The novelist states that he has no financial interest in defending English because by then his novels had been translated into sixteen major languages around the world and if Nigeria chose Hausa as the national language his books would 'immediately be translated into it'. He adds, 'So you see, I need not fear such an event. Financially I might even be the better off for it.' Then he asks why Solarin's essays, his newspaper column and his pamphlets were not written in Hausa or Yoruba or Igbo. Solarin, he points out, has written much in English and yet is 'sickened by' his 'defence' of it. Achebe wonders if Solarin has 'acquired the dog's facility for being sick, throwing up and then returning to eat the vomit?' In making his analysis Achebe insists on realism:

> Now let us take a quick look at your defence of Hausa. Isn't it incredible that anybody outside a mental asylum should choose a time such as this to urge 'the Nigerian Army' (which one? by the way) to impose Hausa on the country? It is unlikely that any one will take any notice of your proposal, but making it has portrayed you as an unfeeling, dry-as-dust logic chopper with no capacity at all for respecting human anguish.

Part of the insensitivity of Solarin which Achebe deplores is his suggestion that the massacres would not have occurred if Nigerians had been taught Hausa rather than English. Achebe reminds him that the reason was that the 'makers and rulers of Nigeria were not Hausa but English' and that many of those people who were killed 'did speak excellent Hausa and little English'. That open letter indicates that Achebe blamed the tragic events on political irresponsibility and the inability to respond sensitively to the tribulations of other people. In his final argument he cautions Solarin: 'In your grand designs for Nigeria do not discount human beings; it will get us nowhere.'[11] That caution was also aimed at the rest of the country, but it was not heeded.

The lull that occurred in the last months of the year was not the result of consideration for human lives. It was a period that was used to fill the numerous vacancies created by the killed or departing Easterners. In the universities as well as in the civil service, in the broadcasting, railways, electricity and water corporations as well as business firms, and in the private as well as public sectors, there were efforts to fill those vacancies with less qualified people. It was a bad decision. In later years that large-scale attempt to recruit and deploy people with inadequate qualifications led to a disdain for merit and the enthronement of mediocrity. As the lull continued Christie Achebe took the decision to travel to Lagos and retrieve some of their property, for the activities of the murdering gangs had diminished. It was a brave act by Christie and a painful decision for Chinua, whose safety could not be guaranteed outside the Eastern Region if he embarked on such a mission. Thus Christie, in disguise, made her way into the Mid-Western Region and finally to Lagos. The NBC staff she met in Lagos responded favourably and helpfully, and under cover of darkness she packed some of the items that she could conveniently carry and returned to the East. Thus Chinua Achebe secured some of his books and prized manuscripts, but they were not destined to survive.

The year ended on that note of extreme anguish in the Eastern Region, a sense of jubilation in the Northern Region, and a feeling of ambivalence in the Western Region, although many individuals had benefited selfishly from the events. In 1967 it was obvious that the large number of people who had escaped and returned safely to the East must be absorbed into the system. It was a difficult process but the mass of talented individuals and the large population that had just been increased made it imperative that a solution be found. Lieutenant Colonel Odumegwu Ojukwu, the military governor, had his hands full as he battled with the events. The Aburi Accord (signed at Aburi, Ghana) that sought to settle the political contentions collapsed when Gowon returned to Lagos and was advised to ignore it. Altercation now raged within the military establishment and the nation tottered towards collapse as Chinua Achebe finally went to live and work in the Eastern Region capital city of Enugu.

In early 1967 Achebe decided to get involved in the affairs of the Eastern Region. The events had made it inevitable for him to consider another career. While he thought of setting up as a full-time writer, his friend Chukwuemeka Ike, a registrar at the University of Nigeria, Nsukka, wanted him to help in setting up the Institute of African Studies. The possibility of Achebe's presence in the Institute made some members of the academic staff uncomfortable, however, since it appeared to them that Ike was bringing Achebe to displace them. But the Registrar's only concern was the creation of a respectable Institute of African Studies and Achebe himself wanted a quiet place where he could get on with his literary work. Christopher Okigbo also wanted to join the Institute in 1966 but there were signs of resentment from some members of staff: ironically, Okigbo would be killed several months later while trying to defend Nsukka and the university. Part of the reason Achebe was in the end acceptable to the university, in spite of the discomfort he generated among those who felt threatened, was that he was perceived as a respectable man, unlike Okigbo who had a reputation for unconventional behaviour.[12] Nevertheless the Institute of African Studies took steps towards the creation of a Centre for Creative Writing and the aim was that Chinua Achebe and

Christopher Okigbo would staff this centre. Both writers were to be seconded to the institute by the military government of Eastern Nigeria, which also undertook to continue to pay them. Achebe was now living in Enugu with Okigbo as a neighbour and their friendship continued. The move to Enugu was welcomed by Christie, who had become pregnant again and needed an environment in which care was readily available.

Residence in Enugu in 1967 placed Achebe in a good position to evaluate events. He decided to abandon the novel which he had started writing but could not find a new creative direction. He was, however, able to travel outside the country in the months of January and February. He had been sent by the Eastern government to carry a letter to President Léopold Sédar Senghor of Senegal. The aim was to solicit the help of Senghor in averting a civil war in Nigeria.

> I did that as an individual, not as a member of the Foreign Service. They thought a writer would be received by Senghor and they were right. Senghor was very keen to talk with me about literature. In the end he wrote a letter. He didn't do anything about what the letter said.[13]

At one point Senghor took Achebe to a window overlooking three hills near the Presidential house. They were like women, he said, women reclining, sitting, leaning.

Achebe also travelled to London where he met his publishers, did some editorial work and also granted an interview to Robert Serumaga in the studio of the Transcription Centre in London. It was not a lengthy visit and he did not use the opportunity, as several of his contemporaries did, to escape from the Nigerian crisis. His visit to London brought Achebe into renewed contact with Ulli Beier, who had left Nigeria in December 1966, after accepting an appointment at the University of Papua New Guinea. Beier recalls their meeting:

> I was to spend, however, six months in London to complete a book before taking up the new appointment. Those months in London were times of great restlessness and anxiety. Tensions in Nigeria grew, the country was moving rapidly towards civil war but the British papers seemed to ignore the situation. One day Chinua Achebe rang us up. He had come to London on some sort of official mission. We went out to dinner together. I suggested that we might arrange an interview with Colin Legum of *The Observer*, who was then the most respected Africa Correspondent in Britain. I was present at this interview in which Chinua pleaded in his sober and rational way for the understanding of the position of Eastern Nigeria. 'We have had too many compromises,' he said. 'But we have become tired of compromises. We want clear cut decisions. There has been too much suffering'. Colin Legum then asked: 'Would you say, that compromise has become a dirty word amongst Igbos?' Chinua said quite emphatically: 'No, I haven't said that at all. I said that we want the issues to be resolved – not glossed over – in order to avert tragedy.' Later during the interview Colin Legum asked again whether compromise had become a dirty word in the East. Again Chinua said clearly that that was not what he had said. The following morning the interview appeared in *The Observer*. There was a photograph of Chinua and underneath it the caption: 'Compromise a dirty word.'[14]

It was an outrageous caption as Ulli Beier comments: 'I was deeply shocked. I had known of course that this is how journalism often works, but I had never expected a man of Colin Legum's expertise and understanding to resort to such cheap tricks.' His article takes the view that 'there seems to be no question of the Easterners launching an aggressive action. At the same time, there is no convincing evidence that the rest of the country is planning to invade the East.' Legum concludes that

> those who still believe in the ideal and practical value of Nigerian unity comfort themselves with the knowledge that the country has stood on the brink of the precipice on four equally dangerous occasions in the last three years; and each time it has drawn back at the last moment.

That view did not take into consideration even the remarks of Chinua Achebe which Legum quotes, for Achebe had explained that

> it is impossible to understand the depth of feelings in the East. The mood is very ugly. For a long time the Military Governor has had to work hard to keep these feelings from boiling over. There are feelings of revenge, and strong feelings of wishing to be left alone to build new lives in their own homeland, consistent with Ibo dignity.... The people demand that the future should be settled at once. They are unwilling to accept any sacrifice of principles for some idealistic sense of unity which they now realise never in fact existed in Nigeria.[15]

Achebe took the misrepresentations of Legum in his stride for he knew that he was talking to people with diverse motives and he corrected them whenever he could. He continued his journey from London to Nairobi, where he met many people worried by the developments in Nigeria. Moreover, many of those people were unaware of the root causes of the social and political upheavals. With them he discussed the implications of the political disasters in his country, explaining them in a full perspective. In an interview he granted to Tony Hall, published in the *Sunday Nation* newspaper, he comments:

> Right now my interest is in politics or rather my interest in the novel is politics. *A Man of the People* wasn't a flash in the pan. This is the beginning of a phase for me when I intend to take a hard look at what we in Africa are making of independence – but using Nigeria which I know best.[16]

That decision was informed by the disconcerting political scene across Africa as well as in the country to which he was returning without knowing how its torments would end.

He returned to Enugu then, to his pregnant wife and children. With Christopher Okigbo as a neighbour there was always something interesting happening at the Catering Rest House in which he lived. Achebe recollects one of those incidents:

> I remember very well one day that Christopher Okigbo had with him a traditional poet from Ikwerre. I don't know how he found him. One day he shouted across and said: 'Chinua! Come and see a genuine poet. We are all wasting our time!' So I went in and saw the genuine poet, and he was genuine.[17]

The proximity to Okigbo also meant that they had an opportunity to discuss a number of social, political, cultural and literary issues. After one of those discussions they decided to set up a publishing company known as Citadel Press. 'Okigbo suggested that we set up a press', explains Achebe.

> I said well, you set it up, you know about it, and I'll join. He said, You'll be chairman and I'll be Managing Director, so the Citadel Press was formed. The name came from the idea of the fortress – you flee from a foreign land, in danger, and return home to your citadel.[18]

122

The press was expected to benefit from the publishing experience of Okigbo who had been a representative of Cambridge University Press while Achebe's reputation, editorial experience and administrative expertise would synthesize everything. In addition, the uncertainties of the period had made the idea of developing the Creative Writing Centre at the University of Nigeria, Nsukka, unrealistic. Thus the Citadel Press was expected to provide a vehicle for fulfilling their literary interests while they waited for a normalization of the political situation. Thus Achebe embarked on another pioneering task, this time at the frontiers of publishing. The major aim was to publish relevant works by Africans for children, thereby encouraging the exploration of the oral traditions of the people.

The political situation was deteriorating further, however, and some foreign visitors confirmed it. Douglas Killam visited the Eastern Region in April 1967 and he said:

> Geoffrey Hill, the British poet, had come to Ibadan for a term on leave from Leeds. Desmond Maxwell, Dean of Arts at Ibadan at the time very kindly let us have the Peugeot 404 Faculty Wagon for our journey. We trekked to Benin and then to Nsukka on a two-day hop. On the West of the Niger it was easy enough; after Asaba/Onitsha one had a portent of things to come. We found Nsukka, then a wonder of a University, aglow with health and enquiry and forwardness, everything that should exist to serve the nation with disinterested enquiry [and make a] helpful comment on nationhood.

He observed, however, that

> the hospital grounds, in the outlying areas of Enugu, were literally littered with maimed and injured bodies of victims of the Northern Pogroms of the November/ December of 1966. Okigbo showed a photo book of horrible injuries sustained by Northern Igbos, photos on the verso, captions on the recto. Achebe said: I don't think the captions are necessary.[19]

After the abandonment of the Aburi Accord by Lieutenant Colonel Gowon, Governor Ojukwu published the recorded decisions and the slogan 'On Aburi We Stand' became popular. In Lagos, Yakubu Gowon made it clear that he was not interested in its implementation as he commenced an economic blockade of the Eastern Region. Gradually most of the links between the region and the rest of the country were severed. In Enugu the economic developments did not adversely affect Citadel Press and Achebe and Okigbo made an announcement soliciting manuscripts. Okigbo's active nature also helped in the publicity for Citadel Press as Achebe found himself engaged in activities emanating from the Ministry of Information to which he was also attached. Like a good neighbour Okigbo helped to play the role of a father to Achebe's children. Ikechukwu, Achebe's son, found him an interesting companion. It was a development that gave Christie much-needed breathing space as her pregnancy advanced. In the process of their fraternization Christopher Okigbo once aroused the little Ikechukwu's anger. The incident occurred when Christie had a craving for a 'goat-head' dish. The delicacy was prepared for her and kept in the refrigerator but Okigbo called in the morning and, since the Achebe house was like a second home to him, he found the dish of goat-head which he ate. In the evening when he called again the little Ikechukwu got hold of him with his puny hands and took him to task for eating the food that was reserved for his mother.[20] Okigbo managed to soothe his feelings and promised to compensate.

Okigbo's presence in the Achebe house was helpful in another way, since his Catering Rest House home had a telephone, unlike the Achebe chalet. Thus when Christie Achebe gave birth to her third child safely on 24 May 1967 she telephoned him first with the request that he should inform Chinua Achebe. But Okigbo, rather than give the message to Achebe, went first to the hospital to see Christie and the baby. According to him his aim was to ascertain all the particulars concerning the baby before informing the father. He later went to inform Achebe and told him that he had seen the baby who was fine and healthy.[21] That third child, a son, was given the name Chidi – There is God. It was an appropriate name, for the disasters that had dogged the Chinua Achebe family in Lagos had not ended in tragedy.

There was loss as well as renewal, however, for Chinua's mother, Janet Anenechi Achebe, died at this time. Although she had lived to see her children become successful, she had not lived as long as her husband. Perhaps she had foreseen that events would take a turn for the worse and she wanted a full traditional funeral. Her burial was perhaps one of the last partly Christian and partly traditional funerals to be witnessed by the Ikenga Ogidi Community. The church ceremony embraced the singing, dancing and wake keeping that had been associated with familial grief in the traditional community. It was a suitable farewell to a woman who had done her duty and who was handing over to a new generation of women expected to make the society a better place for human habitation.

It was an expectation which sadly would not be immediately realized in view of the tragic acceleration of political events. On 27 May 1967 Lieutenant Colonel Yakubu Gowon announced in Lagos the creation of twelve states in Nigeria, with the implication that the Eastern Region would be split into three states incorporating distinct ethnic groups, fuelling their rivalries. On that same day the Consultative Assembly and the Advisory Council of Chiefs and Elders of Eastern Nigeria met at Enugu and mandated

> His Excellency Lieutenant Colonel Chukwuemeka Odumegwu Ojukwu, Military Governor of Eastern Nigeria, to declare at the earliest practicable date Eastern Nigeria a free sovereign and independent State by the name and title of the REPUBLIC OF BIAFRA.[22]

It was a mandate that Ojukwu could not ignore in spite of the military unpreparedness of the region. That mandate made references to the atrocities against the Easterners, the confiscation of their property, and other acts of gross discrimination and injustice. On 30 May 1967, Ojukwu had no choice but to proclaim the Republic of Biafra. He commenced by stressing his consciousness of the supreme authority of God, an awareness of the lack of safety for Easterners in Nigeria, and his rejection of any association or authority that does not guarantee freedom. He declared:

> Having mandated me to proclaim on your behalf and in your name that Eastern Nigeria be a sovereign independent Republic, now Therefore I, Lieutenant Colonel Chukwuemeka Odumegwu Ojukwu, Military Governor of Eastern Nigeria, by virtue of the authority, and pursuant to the principles, recited above, do hereby solemnly proclaim that the territory and region known as and called Eastern Nigeria, together with her continental shelf and territorial waters shall henceforth be an independent sovereign State of the name and title 'THE REPUBLIC OF BIAFRA'.[23]

There was no doubt that it was a momentous occasion and a far-reaching announcement. The coming into existence of Biafra also meant that the inhabitants had to restructure their attitudes to life and the world. Achebe, like most of the people who felt the effects of the preceding acts of violence, accepted that decision as an inevitable course for the Eastern Region which, in the words of Obafemi Awolowo, was 'pushed out of Nigeria'. In spite of that fact and even in that season of chaos in the rest of Nigeria, Achebe was still conscious of his values. 'I don't think I could function effectively as a paid government propagandist', he declared.

> My commitment isn't to a government but to a cause. Fortunately, so far, although they've called on me for all kinds of services, the government has never asked me to do anything that I would balk at doing. If you like, you can take that as an example of the unity between intellectuals and government.[24]

That service which Achebe was called to perform was to stretch in several directions in the coming months because on 6 July 1967 the Nigerian army attacked the Republic of Biafra in a bid to crush what Nigeria labelled a rebellion. The Gowon regime perceived it as a 'police action' that would be over in days since there was the awareness that the young nation had not been able to acquire arms or muster much international sympathy.

Incredibly, even as the situation worsened there were responses to the call for manuscripts by the Citadel Press. A graduate of London University from Amachara, Umuahia, John Onyekwere Iroaganachi, sent in a story he called *How the Dog was Domesticated*. It was a children's story and Achebe promptly accepted it for publication but in the course of editing it the story was transformed. Achebe remarks:

> It just seized on my imagination and it went on changing and changing. It was almost like an obsession, and by the end of my involvement with it, it was a totally different story.

The story was actually a folktale about the dog, a 'charming, traditional-type story', in which the dog 'is the nice guy, a wonderful fellow who became a slave. But I don't like slaves, so this is why I turned the plot around 180 degrees.' He also asked Okigbo to write the lamentation of the deer, 'the song it sings when it's thrown out of the house by the dog'.[25] The transformation of the story was made to retain the essence of Igbo philosophy, while at the same time extending its wider implications. It was also shaped in terms of dialogues, narrative sinew, cultural notions and moral values in order to suit the envisaged readership – children – while maintaining an appeal to adults. The title was changed to *How the Leopard Got His Claws*, and it became a moral tale narrating how the animals lived together happily under the leadership of the leopard, who was kind and gentle and wise. At that time the animals did not fight each other because none of them, apart from the dog, had sharp teeth or claws, and the other animals teased the dog over his ugly teeth. The leopard persuades the other animals to construct a common shelter for relaxation and protection from rain after a request by the deer. The dog, who has never liked the leopard, and the duck, who enjoys water, refuse to participate but the other animals build the house, all making their various contributions. One day a heavy rain falls which drives the dog away from his cave, and he goes to the common house where he chases all the animals away. Meanwhile the leopard, who has been away on a visit, hears the lament of the deer, the first victim of the dog's brutality, and rushes home in response to the deer's cry that 'the worst has happened to us, because the common shelter we built, the cruel dog keeps us from it'.

The leopard returns to confront the dog but is attacked by the dog with its teeth and claws. The leopard beckons the other animals to join in attacking the dog as a group, but they are too cowardly to agree: instead they hail the dog as their new king. The toad makes a new song of praise calling the dog great and good. Sadly the leopard goes away. He travels to the home of a blacksmith and begs to be given 'the strongest teeth from iron' and the deadliest claws from bronze. His request is granted after a narration of his sad story. He also goes to the home of Thunder pleading for some of its sound in his voice, and his sad story also makes Thunder fulfil his request. Fortified, the leopard returns and easily defeats the dog. Then he orders that the house be pulled down, with each animal taking its original contribution in making the shelter. The leopard also announces that from that day he will 'rule the forest with terror' because 'he was a kind and gentle king' but the animals turn against him. The dog, who has run away, seeks protection in the home of a hunter and the narrator concludes the story with the statement: 'Today the animals are no longer friends, but enemies. The strong among them attack and kill the weak.'[26]

The transformation of the story possesses obvious symbolic implications: it reflects the divisive deeds that have led to the civil war, while the lament of the deer reiterates the violence and dispossession associated with those deeds. The development of the war was confirming the injustice of the deer's lament even as Achebe worked on that manuscript and received others. Christopher Okigbo was instrumental in procuring two of them.

One of the manuscripts was a story Okigbo solicited from Gabriel Okara, who was working at the Ministry of Information at Enugu. Okara recalls:

> Okigbo came one day. One of the first things he and Achebe wanted to publish was a short story written by me. They were hard up, but I said, 'Look, you can pay something.' He said, 'We haven't got anything, you know this is war time. You don't want anything.' Well, I liked him and I gave him the story.[27]

Okigbo also brought another manuscript to Citadel Press which was from Emmanuel Ifeajuna, one of the plotters of the 15 January 1966 coup. The manuscript was Ifeajuna's story of the coup and he gave it to Okigbo who enthusiastically passed it on to Achebe after reading it. It was a work that Achebe considered important so he also read it immediately. But he discovered that there were flaws in the story. He criticized it for two reasons:

> It seemed to me to be self-serving. Emmanuel was attempting a story in which he was a centre and everybody else was marginal. So he was the star of the thing. I did not know what they did or not but reading his account in the manuscript, I thought that the author was painting himself as a hero.

The other reason was quite serious, as Achebe explains: 'Secondly, within the story itself there were contradictions.' Achebe thus told Okigbo that it was not a reliable and honest account of what happened. As an example, he cited Ifeajuna's description of the coup plotters at their first meeting in a man's chalet in a catering guest house. The plotters are coming into the chalet late in the night and Ifeajuna describes the room as being in darkness since they are keen not to arouse suspicion. They all assemble and Ifeajuna claims that he stood up and addressed them while *watching* their faces and *noting* their reactions. Since it is supposed to be dark, Achebe regarded that description as dubious. Okigbo laughed and remarked that Ifeajuna was probably being lyrical. Some days after that conversation Okigbo came to Achebe and told him that Chukwuma Kaduna Nzeogwu had asked him: 'I hear you and Achebe are going to publish Emma's lies?'[28] That comment by Nzeogwu, a principal actor in the January coup, confirmed that the manuscript was unreliable.

Times were to turn disastrous for many of those actors before the end of 1967. In later years Achebe reflected that he might have made a different decision if he had known what lay ahead for Ifeajuna, Okigbo and Nzeogwu. He added, however, that even if the manuscript had been accepted by Citadel Press, it would not have been published, because the publishing house was destroyed at the same time as these three men when the war moved closer.

The war indeed moved closer to Achebe and his family in its second month. By that time Christopher Okigbo had joined the army and on his visits to Enugu regaled his friends with stories of his exploits. Gabriel Okara remembers that he once came from the war front and

> started describing how he blew up an armoured car, a Nigerian armoured car, of the Federal forces with a rocket. It was funny when he said, 'Look, when you fire those things you've got to stand very firm, or otherwise you go with the rocket'. So Okigbo said he stood there waiting and saw the cars coming gradually, until they were very close, then firing and hitting – the distance was so close that some of the fragments – little pieces of metal – penetrated his own skin, all over, like a powder. He was not asked to go again but he insisted on going.[29]

Achebe, on the other hand, worked with the Ministry of Information and at Citadel Press, and 'whenever Okigbo had some time, he came back and we discussed things'. It was in the midst of such a discussion during Okigbo's return on leave from the Nsukka front, where he was serving with the rank of a major, that a Nigerian war plane came to Enugu. There was a stampede with Achebe and Okigbo ducking under a table; the plane dropped several bombs and when it was over they dusted themselves off and continued their discussion. Achebe did not know the consequences of those bombs until later.

> After Chris left I went to the printer to check some details on the children's booklet, and the talk about the bombing made me think that the bombs might have fallen near my house. I hurried home and found that it was indeed my house which had been hit, and that my books and papers were gone. The whole town turned out, Chris himself came back, rather dazed, to commiserate with me, and we parted once again.[30]

It was fortunate for the Achebes that Christie had taken the new baby Chidi and the older Chinelo and Ikechukwu to Awka to see her mother, who was sick. It was that visit to Awka that saved the family. Such narrow escapes were to become commonplace as the war progressed.

10

The Idea of Biafra
Enugu, Aba, Umuahia
1967–9

DEATH, and narrow escapes from it, became commonplace; but this did not obliterate, in the struggling Biafrans, feelings of sorrow, pain, suffering or even joy as the war progressed. Such feelings were to be mixed and remixed in the following days even as it became clear, two months into the war, that it was not going to be a mere 'police action', as Hassan Katsina of the Nigerian army had imagined.[1] In Biafra the pressure intensified to recruit more people as soldiers, train them adequately and arm them effectively. The funds were not there to procure the arms, and old flint guns, machetes and bows and arrows could not counter the superior arms of the Nigerian forces. But hope was alive and with that hope was linked a feeling that their cause in Biafra was just. Many young men from diverse occupations volunteered to join the army, especially undergraduates and civil servants. Christopher Okigbo had been one of those volunteers and many other intellectuals were motivated to serve the nation in areas where their services would be helpful and their expertise appreciated.

The convergence of so many people with active minds meant that ideas beneficial to the society often emerged. Some creative artists even began to project their imaginations beyond the war and think in terms of the kind of activities that would enable the society to progress. Chinua Achebe, in the midst of the war and in spite of the fact that he had to change location after the bombing of his house, was thinking of the future:

> Among other things, we were planning a magazine. We called it *New Society*. A number of thinkers feel that in this new society we must make sure that certain evil practices and abuses about which we complained so much in Nigerian society are not allowed to take root, so we have got to start talking about them now. How do you organize this kind of society?[2]

Even in the midst of the devastation creeping closer to Enugu, Achebe never forsook the task of actively charting a course of progress for his society in the tradition of a frontiersman. That intellectual and creative engagement was not made in isolation, for other poets, playwrights, musicians, storytellers and artists found themselves converging and interacting in Biafran towns like Enugu.

128

Yet, even as they converged the war crept closer to their lives and those of their relatives, or friends and colleagues. Many of them had been associated with the University of Nigeria, Nsukka, renamed the University of Biafra. The Nigerian soldiers went on a spree of terrible destruction in the university town of Nsukka. Books that were collected from the university libraries, the homes of lecturers, and student hostels were set ablaze, and the soldiers danced around the fire in sheer joy at the destruction of those symbols of Biafran pride in their intellectual prowess. It was said that one soldier picked up a large book, opened it at the centre, and struck it with his forehead while repeatedly chanting: 'Book enter my head, if na Biafra man you go enter!'[3] The wanton destruction that took place at the university was itself to become a symbol, in later years after the war, of the propensity of the Nigerian soldiers to succumb to a bestial fury. The destruction at Nsukka touched many among the Biafran soldiers who appreciated the value of that institution and the value of knowledge. Many embarked on suicide missions to salvage some of those resources; their inevitable failure increased the anguish of the populace.

It was in the midst of that season of devastation that Chinua Achebe found death at close quarters, snatching one of his close associates only five days after his house was destroyed at Enugu.

One afternoon, I was driving from Enugu to my village, Ogidi, where I lived following the bombing of my house, with my car radio tuned to Lagos. Like all people caught in the mesh of modern war we soon became radio addicts. We wanted to hear the latest from the fronts; we wanted to hear what victories Nigeria was claiming next, not just from NBC Lagos, but even more extravagantly from Radio Kaduna. We needed to hear what the wider world had to say to all that – the BBC, the Voice of America, the French Radio, Cameroon Radio, Radio Ghana, Radio Anywhere. The Biafran forces had just suffered a major setback in the northern sector of the war by the loss of the University town of Nsukka. They had suffered an even greater morale-shattering blow in the death of that daring and enigmatic hero who had risen from Military anonymity to legendary heights in the short space of eighteen months, Major Chukwuma Kaduna Nzeogwu. Before his enlistment Okigbo had begun to talk more and more about Nzeogwu, but I had not listened very closely, the military didn't fascinate me as it did him. Now I was only half-listening to the radio when suddenly Christopher Okigbo's name stabbed my slack consciousness into panic life. Rebel troops wiped out by gallant federal forces. Among rebel officers killed: Major Christopher Okigbo. I pulled up at the roadside. The open park land around Nachi stretched away in all directions. Other cars came and passed. Had no one else heard the terrible news? When I finally got myself home and told my family, my three-year-old son screamed: Daddy, don't let him die! He and Christopher had been special pals. Whenever Chris had come to the house the boy would climb on his knees, seize hold of his fingers and strive with all his power to break them while Christopher would groan in pretended agony. 'Children are wicked little devils,' he would say to us over the fellow's head and let out more cries of pain.[4]

The people of Biafra certainly appreciated the sacrifice of Christopher Okigbo; like Nzeogwu's his name was added to the list of heroes in a popular song that literally drew tears: Okigbo, Nzeogwu and Ironsi, those three 'elephants' from Biafra who were no more.

Soon after that tragedy, Enugu itself was threatened and there was the introduction of the destabilizing element of sabotage with the arrest and execution of Emmanuel Ifeajuna, Victor Banjo, Sam Agbam and Philip Alale in September

1967. They were found guilty of plotting a coup and sabotaging the advance of the Biafran soldiers in the Western part of Nigeria. The combination of these events added to the sadness that had arisen from the unpleasant task of fighting a desperately uneven war. At the Ministry of Information where he was formally employed, Achebe had access to part of that information but he never wavered from his support for the young nation. Even the invitation he received from Gwendolen M. Carter of the Program of African Studies at North-western University, Illinois, did not change his determination to help his people. It was the kind of opportunity that many others quickly utilized to escape from the tragedy and horrors of the war. Instead, Achebe sent a message to his publishers through someone going to London. Heinemann Educational Books in turn would contact Professor Carter and offer Achebe's apologies for his inability to accept the position.

The message Achebe sent coincided with the loss of Enugu in October 1967 and he subsequently began a life of moving from town to town as the Biafran nation dwindled. Although his home town, Ogidi, was still safe, Achebe had to move to Aba, the new Biafran headquarters where the Ministry of Information was located. The influx of people into Aba again brought many of the creative writers in Biafra into contact. One participant in those wartime activities was Chukwuma Azuonye:

> After the fall of Enugu, we found ourselves converging at Ogbor Hill, Aba, the new location of the Biafran Information and Propaganda Complex. At our first poetry reading meeting at the Seagull Hotel, over chicken and beer, most of the poems presented smelt heavily of Okigbo. But, there in our midst in flesh and blood, was Gabriel Okara, an intensely introspective and lyrical poet with a kind of zen delight in the paradox of direct-pointing in the attempt at describing the indescribable. His first war poem, 'The Silent Voice' and the propaganda piece, 'Leave us Alone' which he read to us at Seagull changed all that.

That interraction made it possible for talents to emerge. Azuonye recollected that

> the Seagull Hotel poetry reading meetings produced many pleasant surprises. Rosemary Ezirim, an outgoing socialite (who no one would ever have associated with poetry) came up with intense lyrical pieces, notably, 'I saw them sleeping', a poem inspired by the death-sleep of bodies seen by the poetess at a refugee camp.[5]

The creative bug also bit Chinua Achebe in Aba, but he only found it possible to create short pieces like poems.

A Kenyan admirer of Achebe at this time purchased copies of *A Man of the People* and gave one copy to each government minister in Kenya for Christmas.[6] It was his way of pointing out to them the consequences of corruption which could result in a military coup d'état. But the situation in Nigeria had gone beyond the prophetic implications of the coup in that novel. It had degenerated into a war and the efforts to crush Biafra became steadily more intense. The Nigerian army was attempting to capture the main Biafran towns and the effects of such military pressure were becoming overwhelming, especially with the shortage of food and ammunition. But that did not deter the committed Biafrans from making invaluable sacrifices in the midst of extreme deprivation. Achebe acknowledged the dedication of the Biafrans when he remarked:

The Nigerians used to call us the Parker pen soldiers because we gravitated to the higher echelons and the desk jobs of the country's 8,000 man army. And it's true, the Ibo people were never warlike or aggressive. But I've seen them change before my eyes and it's been a tremendous experience for me.[7]

Part of Achebe's appreciation was extended to the suffering civilian population that was called upon to make incessant sacrifices. In a poem 'Refugee Mother and Child', he captures the effect of starvation through the images of a refugee mother and her child in the midst of 'odours of diarrhoea of unwashed children', 'washed-out ribs and dried-up bottoms' and 'rust-coloured hair'. The poignant nature of the poem emerges in the last segment through the poet's comparative presentation of the woman combing the hair of the child:

> In another life this
> would have been a little daily
> act of no consequence before his
> breakfast and school; now she
> did it like putting flowers
> on a tiny grave.[8]

The presentation of that maternal act as foreshadowing the death of the child indicated the extent to which such tragedies had become daily occurrences.

That preoccupation with death even in creative writing was not unrealistic, for as early as January 1968 many lives had been lost. Achebe had lost his friend Christopher Okigbo about five months before, and the sorrow of that loss generated the poem 'Mango Seedling' dedicated to Okigbo. Achebe perceives him in that poem as caught in

> Primordial quarrel of Earth
> And Sky striving bravely to sink roots
> Into objectivity, mid-air in stone.

The final image of the mango seedling which fails to grow as a result of lack of nourishment and which dies is linked to the death of Okigbo, as the writer laments:

> Today I see it still –
> Dry, wire-thin in sun and dust of the dry months –
> Headstone on tiny debris of passionate courage.[9]

The courage not only of Okigbo but of so many other Biafrans was coming to the attention of the world even as the devastation of battlefield and air raid became alarming. Achebe describes one of these air raids:

A friend of mine had his three children killed, just like that, they went out to buy books – five minutes later it was over, it does not take long – 10 seconds. It is quite frightening. It was right in the centre, in Biafra, the planes generally avoid anywhere they think they would have no protection, so they go into the centre of the population. On this occasion, it was right in the heart of the city, and they stayed in the sky – they could not have been aiming at anything in particular and sent a number of rockets right into the centre of the city, Aba. This happened right in the presence of twenty foreign journalists who had just arrived. This was actually the point where the protests in the press in Britain began. People had thought all we had said were lies, propaganda. I remember this occasion very well, because the journalists came the night before, in fact, and a few people told them about the bombing, they were not interested in what happened yesterday, and then they saw this happen.[10]

Although Achebe was saddened that such tragedies could occur in Biafra, he was glad that foreigners were present at one of those instances of devastation. His primary desire was to engage in acts that would ameliorate the suffering and pain in the nation and this was his motive in staying.

Thus when a second letter dated 9 January 1968 came from Professor Gwedolen Carter, Achebe did not waste time in stressing that his commitment to the war effort in Biafra made it impossible to accept her offer.

> c/o Ministry of Information
> Aba
> Biafra
> 28 February 1968

Dear Miss Carter,

Your letter of January 9 got to me today. I am disturbed to see from it that a message I tried to send to you in October through my London publishers obviously did not reach you. I suspect it may not have reached my publishers to begin with. I had asked them to get in touch with you and say with my profoundest regrets that it was very unlikely I should be able to take up my appointment with you next spring. The reason was the war between my country and Nigeria which at the time I sent the message had just entered its 4th month. In particular I had been completely disorganised by the bombing of my home in Enugu in which I lost most of my papers and books. As you know the war still rages. I cannot possibly leave Biafra while it goes on. I have to be here and do whatever little I can to help this terribly wronged country. I am really sorry to upset your plans. It is particularly distressing that you should be hearing about all this only now. I was looking forward very much to being at Northwestern University this Spring. I hope we can arrange something later.

Yours very sincerely,
[Chinua Achebe][11]

Ordinary Biafran soldiers like those on guard duty at checkpoints were aware of the kind of sacrifice Achebe was making. An incident that showed their appreciation, and the value of the novelist as a Biafran, is recalled by Agnes Achebe, the wife of Chinua's brother, Frank. Chinua was driving with Agnes from Port Harcourt to Aba and as usual they were stopped on the way by soldiers at a checkpoint. The soldiers, clearly devoted to their duties, were conducting the necessary searches with diligence. They pulled open the boot and the glove compartment, and in the course of that painstaking search one of them suddenly discovered the identity of the writer.

'Na you be Chinua Achebe!' exclaimed the soldier.

'Yes', answered the writer quietly.

'Come – o, A beg come!' called the soldier as he beckoned on his other colleagues, 'Come see Chinua Achebe.'

There was a mini-riot as some of the passers-by were also attracted to the scene in a bid to see and perhaps shake hands with the writer. It was then that one of the soldiers turned to Agnes and asked: 'Are you not proud that you are married to this man?'[12] He had mistaken Agnes for Christie, but the question was well taken as Agnes responded with an enigmatic smile. Clearly such encounters strengthened Chinua Achebe's belief that the career of writing on which he had embarked was useful, relevant and also a responsible one. It was this sense of responsibility that made him accept the assignment to travel to other countries in order to let the world know the enormity of the suffering in Biafra.

In early 1968 he travelled to London and other European cities as part of this effort to draw attention to his country's plight. In the course of his journey he called at the Heinemann offices. According to Alan Hill,

during the civil war he used to come over to London. He used to get into a clapped-out Super Constellation aircraft at the Uli-Ihiala airstrip and he'd fly to Lisbon; then he would transfer to an ordinary commercial aircraft and come to London. And he would come strolling into the office as cool and as humorous as if he'd just come from Chelsea or Kensington. We used to hold parties and receptions for him.[13]

James Currey, who was with Heinemann Educational Books then, confirms that

during the war, Chinua Achebe came to London from time to time. I do remember him occasionally coming through, and this was exciting because he had this tremendous enthusiasm and vision of the new Biafran state. This meant that he found it more and more difficult to have a regular dialogue with us on the African Writers Series, but nevertheless he was tremendously supportive and we, who were becoming more and more confident, would say: 'We've got this and this which looks interesting, and these are the reports.' And Chinua had more and more an overview and less and less reading of the individual manuscripts of that time. We would talk things through with him, and as a sympathetic ear he was very, very good.[14]

It was a time of intense pressure for Achebe since he was in Biafra one day confronting the destructive effects of enemy guns and the next day responding to the demands of editorial work at Heinemann Educational Books or addressing an international audience. In an interview in 1968 he gave a vivid account of the uncertainties in the life of a Biafran:

It depends on where you are. If you are very close to the war zone you hear the sound of war. My village, which is 6 miles from Onitsha, had this distinction for months. We had the Nigerians trying to come over from Asaba and from Enugu. You got used to sleeping with the sound of shelling and all other things. Far away from the immediate areas of war, life approaches something more normal, but in the last few months (March–July 1968), the intensive air attacks are introducing a completely new element everywhere. From morning about 7 a.m. to about 6 p.m. there is this tenseness. At any moment they might come. It does not take long – a few seconds – and 120 people are charred to ashes, charred black, and perhaps 20 buildings wrecked, and this is a very real thing. I only realized how nervous I had become when I got out to London about three weeks ago. The first sound of an aeroplane I heard and my first reaction was to take cover. This has become a way of life for everyone, children too. This is the atmosphere in which you live and you try to make life approach such normality as you can. Food is short, drugs are short. Thousands – no, millions by now – have been uprooted from their homes and brought into the safer areas where they really have no roots, no property, many of them live in school buildings, camps, and the committee does what it can. It is really quite amazing how much people are ready to give. In many camps arrangements exist for at least ensuring that these people get two meals a day. Meat is very short. On the other side you find a new spirit, a spirit you did not know existed, a determination, in fact.[15]

The new spirit which Achebe noticed was exhibited by a section of the Biafran population when he returned after those three weeks of travel. It was a new spirit fostered by the will to survive which complemented Achebe's efforts on the diplomatic circuit.

When I got back I found young girls had taken over the job of controlling traffic from the Police. They were really doing it by themselves – no one asked them to. This kind of spirit exists, and this makes it so tremendous and hopeful.[16]

Thus Achebe became convinced that whatever he achieved in London or any other city was relevant to those other people in Biafra, battling against odds. Although Heinemann Educational Books had a firm policy against taking sides in the war, they sympathized with writers on both sides of the conflict and helped them, if they could, to survive those odds.

The writers in Nigeria were Wole Soyinka, who was in detention, and J. P. Clark, while in Biafra, now that Okigbo was gone, there remained Achebe, Nwapa, Ekwensi, Okara, Ike and Munonye. Heinemann welcomed any of those writers whenever they came to London and that was how Chinua Achebe met John Pepper Clark at the Heinemann offices in London. It was an encounter that brought home to the publishers the extent of the political wedge that had been driven between Nigeria and Biafra. Clark described the quarrel that arose from that meeting and the exchange of harsh words as 'one of the most chilling experiences and that Achebe felt that I had betrayed him, and Chris'.[17] The collision course was inevitable for Achebe supported Biafra while Clark supported Nigeria. It was an equally painful experience for Achebe who had accepted Clark as a very close friend and had dedicated *A Man of the People* to him and Christopher Okigbo at a time when he had yet to dedicate a book to his mother, Janet Achebe. Clark recalls that Achebe felt so strongly over the issue that he instructed his publishers to withdraw that dedication from the novel. Time was to restore both that friendship and the dedication after the war, about ten years later, but that was in the womb of the future. In the burning present, Achebe returned to Biafra convinced of the rightness of the Biafran cause and the need to highlight the dimension of genocide in that war. Thus he published an article under the headline 'Darkness in Africa: Biafra' in the London *Sunday Times*.[18]

That idea of genocide was not imaginary: Biafrans had endured brutal and continuous bombings, shelling and gunfire, and it seemed to them that the world was only watching and waiting, like a clan of vultures. Although several countries and their leaders had spoken in sympathy for the beleaguered nation, their support stopped short of a clear indication of recognition for Biafra. Early in 1968, however, concerned academics like Stanley Diamond had written on the tragedy of the war. Diamond had argued that

> politically, economically, and socially, Biafra has the potential to become the first viable state in Black Africa and the crystallizing centre around which a modern Africa could build itself. The reasons lie in the history of the Ibos' relations with the British and with their African neighbours and above all in the character of the Ibos themselves.[19]

Such positive comments helped tremendously to influence world opinion and perhaps in the subsequent recognition which now came from some African countries. Tanzania under the leadership of the wise and sensitive Julius Nyerere recognized Biafra on 13 April 1968. It was the first country to do so and the reaction in Biafra was tumultuous. Achebe acknowledges that

> It was a fantastic day. I know. I was sitting in my home with my wife; we were feeling very depressed, I don't know why, then suddenly somebody ran in and told us, but we

said, 'Don't be silly', because we had heard such things before. And then we heard on the BBC, and my wife rushed up and said she was going to teach in Tanzania. Soon after that the streets were filled with people dancing and singing. For the first time in months you found dancing again, and the radio was playing Tanzanian music. People were reassured again that there was justice in the world, because we were already becoming quite cynical about the outside world, saying to ourselves, 'Don't imagine anyone would come to your rescue – they know you're right, but it doesn't pay so they won't do anything. We were more or less persuaded that we would have to fight on our own. The gesture meant nothing in military or material terms but it reassured us – the effect it had on us – was electric.[20]

President Nyerere in the statement explaining his decision insisted insightfully that the 'unity of a country can only be based on the general consent of the people involved'.[21]

It appeared as if some other countries had been waiting for Tanzania to take the lead because in the next month there were announcements from other African leaders. Gabon recognized Biafra on 8 May 1968 and Ivory Coast announced its recognition on 14 May. On 20 May, President Kenneth Kaunda of Zambia, a man of strong convictions, announced Zambia's recognition of Biafra. The news of those recognitions was dampened by the fall of Port Harcourt on 19 May, which left the Uli airstrip as virtually the only viable one in the country. The facilities there were improved and it became one of the busiest airports in Africa in 1968. The fall of Port Harcourt did not deter the commitment of the Biafrans to their survival as a nation; they marshalled all their human resources and fought on. Many undergraduates in both the sciences and the humanities were drafted to the research institutes or other appropriate centres. Obiora Udechukwu, studying fine and applied arts, remembers that

> By March 1968 a message was sent to me that I was needed in Aba. So I went to Aba and started working as a graphic designer in the Ministry of Information doing cartoons, posters, magazine design and so on.[22]

In addition there was the creation of an organization known as the Biafran Organization of Freedom Fighters (BOFF) under the command of Colonel Ejike Obumneme Aghanya.

Aghanya had been the president of the Nigerian Broadcasting Service Staff Union at Enugu when Chinua Achebe was controller for the Eastern zone. He had joined the Nigerian Army some time before the coup of 1966. As a trained engineer he quickly became a reliable and highly rated officer in the Biafran army. BOFF originated as a forum for involving civilians in the war. The idea was that since soldiers and civilians were working together there was the need to educate both groups so as to avoid conflict and to close the gap between them. According to Aghanya, the motivation to create BOFF

> came as a result of the fact that as the war continued it became clear that we were not only landlocked, but we also felt like prisoners because all the neighbouring countries to Biafra were not really with us. The only outlet for Biafra was the sea. In addition, the Biafrans did not have the fire-power that could match the fire-power of the other side, so it became necessary for us to plan and formulate our battles in terms of defence warfare. All the people who were thinking alike wanted to form an organiza-tion that would achieve these aims. The primary aim was to drive the enemy out of the land of Biafra and not to capture strange lands. The organization was to involve fellow Biafrans in captured areas to help in driving the enemy out. Since the regular army

was there, there was the need to demarcate areas of operation. The regular army operated in front while the BOFF operated behind enemy lines. The aim was that as the regular army became weaker then the Freedom Fighters would become stronger.[23]

Thus, in the end, everybody would become a freedom fighter. It was clearly a preparation for psychological warfare and the aim was to weaken the enemy from that angle.

The recruitment for BOFF was based initially on commitment. The organization, therefore, commenced by accepting people who had personal and convincing reasons to fight, especially those who had lost their dear ones before the war started, particularly during the May, July and September massacres of 1966. People who had painful memories of the pogrom were used because they had lived most of their lives outside Biafra and were thus familiar with the zones of war which lay in enemy territory. Colonel Aghanya explains that

> Most of those people wanted to avenge the death of their dear ones. They had to be organized to fight the enemy. Even traditional rulers like chiefs, civilian administrators and provincial secretaries were used. The supply of food and water to the regular army was also part of the duties of the BOFF.

Aghanya was given the title of chief of staff and key members of his staff included Dr Ukwu I. Ukwu, Dr Oyolu, Major Okoye and Chinua Achebe, who was invited by Aghanya to join them. Each of the members was expected to make contributions in their respective areas of expertise. Oyolu initiated a farming programme through the Land Army Scheme, for he was an agriculturalist. Civilians were taught not to depend on begging for food and the refugees were also encouraged to cultivate any available piece of land. Eventually even the army was taught how to farm.

There was also BOFF technology which produced wooden spoons, cups, forks and plates for the people generally. The organization taught people to produce items that would sustain their lives like basket weaving and other handicrafts. 'The main idea', according to Aghanya, 'was to keep life going through the use of the natural environment.'[24] Although BOFF emphasized those aspects of life necessary to human existence, it played a major role in the eventual recapture of Owerri in 1969. Without physical weapons, BOFF's members depended on their brains and verbal persuasion. That was how Chinua Achebe helped in nurturing the recruited members on how to operate in order to weaken the enemy. He was really a kind of theoretician to the organization but he also made practical contributions to one of the aims of BOFF, which was to ensure that the route of the enemy from the rear to the front line was full of obstacles:

> A BOFF man was expected to infiltrate enemy locations where civilians were in captivity or even help the farmer behind enemy lines to cultivate his land and in the process worm his way into the heart of the farmer. At the end the BOFF man would educate the farmer on the disadvantages of helping the enemy soldiers getting the help they needed from civilians.

Achebe did not work with the organization for long because Lieutenant Colonel Ojukwu, the head of state, invited him to operate on the international scene. Dr Okonjo took over from Achebe, and Aghanya said that

> Okonjo changed the style and laid more emphasis on the propaganda aspect rather

than on the education of the civilians. Chinua's style was to educate BOFF and even the Biafran soldiers on how to keep an area they have taken because it is easier to conquer an area than to keep it.[25]

The utilization of Achebe as a roving ambassador was also helpful since he had earned the respect of many foreign intellectuals. In the course of his international assignment he visited Uganda, where he presented the basic issues involved in the conflict to an audience there. He was also interviewed by Rajat Neogy, the editor of *Transition,* with the assistance of Raymond Apthorpe, Paul Theroux and Robert Serumaga. Achebe explains in that interview the nature of the suffering in Biafra, the courage of the people, the genocidal dimensions of the war and the position of the writer in the struggle. When he is asked 'to place [himself] in the Nigerian position at the present time and to argue out their case in terms of integration', he replies:

> I have no intention of being placed in a Nigerian situation at all. I find the Nigerian situation untenable. If I had been a Nigerian, I think I would have been in the same situation as Wole Soyinka is – in prison.

Achebe also has a view of the future, however:

> The kind of picture I see is of two peoples (Nigeria and Biafra) living side by side and developing over the years with more and more areas of cooperation. If, on the other hand, they pursue a military objective and succeed, then the question of what I would want, does not arise. Just now, and I think this is a fairly common view, the best you can get is two states living side by side. We cannot help being neighbours, so we might as well make what we can out of it.[26]

Achebe also read a paper on 'The African Writer and the Biafran Cause' to a political science seminar at Makerere University College, Kampala on 25 August 1968. He argues that the point his paper

> will be making really amounts to this: that the involvement of the Biafran writer today in the cause for which his people are fighting and dying is not different from the involvement of many African writers – past and present – in the big issues of Africa. The fact of war merely puts the matter in sharper focus.

He commences by reaffirming that the writer in Africa must be relevant, confronting social and political issues; he also points out that Africa 'has been the most insulted continent in the world'. The artist, on the other hand, 'is a human being with heightened sensitivities; he must be aware of the faintest nuances of injustice in human relations' and 'the African writer cannot therefore be unaware of, or indifferent to, the monumental injustice which his people suffer'. He quotes Equiano, David Diop, Léopold Senghor and Kwame Nkrumah to highlight the devious motives of the colonialist. Achebe perceives those dubious motives as linked to contemporary problems that have led to the political disintegration in Nigeria.

Achebe illustrates the insensitivity of the political leaders and characterizes them as corrupt:

> The point I want to make here is that the creative writer in independent Nigeria found himself with a new, terrifying problem on his hands. He found that the independence his country was supposed to have won was totally without content.... The old white master was still in power. He had got himself a bunch of black stooges to do his dirty work for a commission. As long as they did what was expected of them they would be praised for their sagacity and their country for its stability.[27]

In this view, the intervention of the military through a coup which was welcomed enthusiastically, was later manipulated with false interpretations by influential foreign countries with interests in Nigeria, thereby generating animosity that led to the massacre of 30,000 Easterners. He emphasizes that Biafra 'stands in opposition to the murder and rape of Africa by whites and blacks alike' and that it also 'stands for true independence in Africa'. He reiterates that the Biafran writers are committed to the revolutionary struggle of their people for justice and true independence', and that he 'believes [the] cause is right and just', concluding that 'this is what literature in Africa should be about today – right and just causes'. It was a powerful statement in a public forum and it made intellectuals in Tanzania, Kenya and Uganda understand the nature of the war. It was on that occasion that Achebe saw Alhaji Aminu Kano for the first time. He recalls:

> I remember very well seeing Aminu Kano of the Nigerian delegation sitting in front and looking so distressed. This is one of the strongest impressions the man made on me, compared to people like Chief Enahoro who was the leader of the delegation swaggering as conquerors, and even Asika. Aminu Kano seemed to be so different; in fact, he seemed to be looking out of the window. While his colleagues were speaking arrogantly and bent on our surrender, Aminu Kano was calm and in pain.[28]

Achebe did not end his journey in Uganda but visited London where Harold Wilson, the head of government, had become an antagonist to the Biafran cause. As an eye witness to the debate in the House of Commons on 27 August, Achebe recollected that

> if governments were largely unmoved by the tragedy, ordinary people were outraged. I witnessed from the visitors' gallery of the House of Commons what was described as unprecedented rowdiness during a private members' motion on Biafra. Harold Wilson, villain of the piece, sat as cool as a cucumber, leaving his foreign secretary, Michael Stewart, to sweat it out. It was hardly surprising that many remarkable people would want to visit the scene of such human tragedy.[29]

That scene of human tragedy in Biafra had worsened while Achebe was away as Aba fell to the Nigerian soldiers on 4 September 1968. Aba was a strategic town, one of the big towns in the nation and the temporary capital of Biafra which housed the Ministry of Information. In addition, Achebe's family had been living there before he left the country. The responsibility to evacuate the children, as well as Chinua's father-in-law who was living with them, fell on Christie. She salvaged as much of the property as she could. As she wryly comments:

> It seemed peculiar that whenever Chinua was sent to a foreign country on an errand, the town in which we lived would fall and the family would pack to another place before he came back.[30]

Chinua Achebe returned many days later and was reunited with his family. They now went to live at Umuahia, the new Biafran capital. Achebe stayed with his family for some time in the home of Chukwuemeka Ike, the novelist, who was the provincial refugee officer for Umuahia. Some time later Achebe was able to get accommodation in a house in the town.

Residence in Umuahia brought the horrors of war closer still. There was an air raid at Umudike, Umuahia, where Dr Onyechi was living. A demolition bomb was dropped and Achebe's sister-in-law who was living there was lucky to escape alive when a large part of the house was destroyed. Such war scenes, and even the implicit threat they carried of worse times to come, did not deter Achebe from carrying out his responsibilities, both local and international. One international duty arose in connection with a letter by Dame Margery Perham to *The Times* in which she asked the Biafrans to surrender. *The Times* sent a cable to Biafra asking Achebe if he cared to reply. His letter, entitled 'In Reply to Margery Perham', was published on 19 September 1968. Achebe begins by noting that

> Dame Margery Perham was until recently regarded as a powerful friend of the Biafrans. I particularly valued her support for the cause of my people, and now regret her withdrawal of it.

Next he presented his credentials in support of his right to reply:

> I was a Nigerian and a great believer in Nigerian unity. I was until 1966 Director of Nigeria's external broadcasting. I had lived most of my adult life in Nigeria outside the Eastern Region, now Biafra. I knew and loved Nigeria. Now I do no longer. The change was brought about by a terrible traumatic experience which we call genocide.

Reacting to the call to surrender and the 'great mass of Ibo documentation piled up in [Perham's] study', Achebe argues that

> despite her impressive credentials, [she] never really understood the Biafran case. This is why one short visit to one side in the conflict has so easily brought about a change in her thinking. One wishes she had visited Biafra as well. But presumably this was unnecessary because the Biafran case is a matter of papers which she already has in large quantities in her study.

Achebe's letter unfolds as a step-by-step counter to the assertions of Dame Margery Perham:

> The genocide we talk about is a fact which continues to this day. Only the other day Nigerian planes bombed and machine-gunned a crowded market in Aguleri. Latest figures show 510 dead and almost 1,000 maimed from the worst bombing and strafing since the war began. Two Russian made planes were involved.... Biafrans know the fact of this war. They know the depth of hatred and estrangement which sustains it. After their recent experience they choose to be judge of their own security. Dame Margery was surprised to see an Ibo Permanent Secretary living happily (and giving parties to foreign visitors) in Lagos. I don't know why this should have surprised her. Collaboration is neither a new phenomenon nor is it a monopoly of Europe. Dame Margery in her journey inspected 'a large structure near the road (and) found it full of Ibo women complete with beds busily cooking for their reasonably healthy children.' Did she ask what happened to their menfolk?
>
> Dame Margery is certain that if Biafra were to surrender the Nigerian authorities 'could not easily get away with a policy of brutal repression!' Who will stop them? 'Journalists and practical philanthropists of many nations', says Dame Margery. Biafrans must be forgiven if they are somewhat sceptical about this kind of guarantee. They do not doubt that the atrocities committed against them will be duly reported afterwards. For the moment they are concerned to fight their murderers to the bitter end. They see these murderers not only as Nigerians but the British and Russians who provide the weapons with which the crime is committed. It is strange that Margery Perham's criticism of British involvement in genocide is stated no more strongly than a 'hope that this whole business of our trade in arms will in the near future be reconsidered'. Her real criticism is reserved for the French and de Gaulle, who have

done no more than to state their belief in the principle of self-determination for Biafrans.

Lord Lugard would have approved such anti-French sentiments as Dame Margery expresses today. But in the circumstances of British crimes against a sovereign African people such sentiments are entirely frivolous.[31]

It is an angry letter but at the same time it clearly enunciates the case for Biafra. Achebe shows that Perham's argument is unrealistic and unreliable. There is no doubt that if he failed to convince Perham, at least he placed the British public in a better position to appreciate the Biafran reality.

At Umuahia that reality was clear to the people and their leaders, and there were attempts to articulate principles and ideas to address it. Thus in late 1968 letters came from the State House, signed by Odumegwu Ojukwu himself, to various Biafran citizens including Chinua Achebe. These letters announced the formation of a National Guidance Committee with Chinua Achebe as the chairman. Other members appointed included Dr Ifegwu Eke, Dr Nzimiro, Dr E. N. Obiechina, Justice Aniagolu, Dr C. C. Ifemesia and Professor Eyo Bassey Ndem. The chairman of the committee was given the mandate to coopt members of the public as he deemed fit, which was how Chukwuemeka Ike came to attend one of the meetings. The National Guidance Committee itself was mandated to discuss the future of Biafra in terms of the kind of society that should be established and also to articulate a relevant ideology. The members held their meetings every week at Etiti, on the premises of Madonna High School. The committee was subsequently structured in terms of units and those units contributed thoughts and opinions on various topics. C. C. Ifemesia reveals that

> everything about the community was discussed, with people making suggestions. Recommendations were also made which people took home to their units. The meeting of the committee was a two-way thing for the members also brought recommendations from their units. Ojukwu as the Patron always attended the meetings. There is scarcely any meeting he did not attend.[32]

However, the main task of organizing the committee rested on Chinua Achebe as the chairman, for he assembled the contributions and synthesized them in order to enable the committee to take appropriate decisions.

The ideas ranged widely, for the members were looking beyond the immediate needs and exigencies of Biafra to a new social order. The kind of society that would be built after the war was a major concern. It was this committee that Ojukwu formally asked to produce a document that would incorporate the political objectives, intellectual aims and human aspirations of Biafra. They started working on the document in late 1968 and it took them into the next year because there were so many ideas to refine, restructure and present to the public. The year 1969 thus started as another busy one for Chinua Achebe, Chairman of the National Guidance Committee at Umuahia. The devastation of the war made that task much more essential, and his own sensibilities sharpened. He responded creatively to desperate times, writing a poem in January 1969 entitled 'Air Raid', a brief requiem after a devastating aerial strike on Umuahia.

> It comes so quickly
> the bird of death
> from evil forests of Soviet technology

A man crossing the road
to greet a friend
is much too slow,
His friend cut in halves
has other worries now
than a friendly handshake
at noon.[33]

Death was becoming an ever-present companion, as the poem records: bringing with it a psychological brutalization which struck the children hardest. Death was losing some of its reverence. Achebe remarks in an interview at that time:

You don't find people tearing their hair. There is a lot of humour. I remember one occasion after an air raid – and these are really horrible things – somebody saw two vultures flying very high up and he said, 'That is a fighter and a bomber', and everybody burst into laughter. It is a very poor joke, I know, but you have to keep your sanity, surely, if you want to survive. You don't realize that you're living on a completely different level until you come out. That's when I noticed it. One day you're more sensitive than another, some days you're very nervous, but on the whole it creeps in on you. You don't wake up one day and feel you are different. It piles up and it's only when you come out – like being in Kew Gardens with a plane overhead – that you realize it.[34]

Achebe was right, but his engagement in creative activities in Biafra enabled the writer's sensitive mind to weather the storm.

The convivial group of Biafran intellectuals and artists had moved from Aba to Umuahia, as Azuonye remembers:

With the fall of Aba, we converged at New Town Tavern, Umuahia, where we held many fruitful poetry reading sessions over palm wine, chicken and *odudu*. Umuahia gave birth to some of the finest poetry of the civil war. The air raids had become menacingly more frequent and intense with gruesome bombing and strafing of Biafran towns. The Russian MIGS came in rapid relays over areas of civilian concentration.

He recounts with great vividness how one of their circle responded to the intensity of enemy fire in salvoes of verse:

In his apartment in an uncompleted building in one of the most vulnerable centres of Umuahia, I met Gabriel Okara one afternoon in one of the most unrepeatable acts of creation: between bouts of taking cover from the air-raids, he scribbled lines that eventually blossomed into one of his most dramatic war time pieces 'Suddenly the Air Cracks!' Achebe was too busy on the diplomatic front to share [fully] in these 'war time dishes'; but his 'Air Raid' poem somehow circulated at our meetings. The image of the man cut into two as he stretches his hand to greet a friend strikes a familiar ironical note in the poetry of this ubiquitous season of raids.

It was at Umuahia that several foreign visitors met that group of Biafran artists for the first time. Azuonye confirms that

Umuahia gave our community the first taste of an international audience. Ruth Bowert, of Pro-Afrika, recorded a discussion with our group which was later broadcast over West German radio. She also put together a selection of poems from some of us later published under the title *Gedichte aus Biafra* in 1969.[35]

There is no doubt that these creative interactions helped the artists to survive mentally and even physically, because 1969 was the high point of the war. It was also the year in which the Biafrans proved their intellectual as well as military resilience.

Chinua Achebe and the members of the National Guidance Committee were part of this strategy for the intellectual survival of a people. Achebe combined that responsibility with diplomatic duties, for he travelled to New York in 1969 to persuade the United Nations to discuss the issue of Biafra. Such trips were made over days rather than weeks, which meant that he did not miss National Guidance Committee meetings or the special receptions for numerous visitors who risked their lives to go to Biafra. Achebe remembers some of those visitors:

> Auberon Waugh came and afterwards wrote a devastating book on Britain's duplicitous policy. He also named his new-born child Biafra Waugh! Frederick Forsyth, a mere reporter then, was soon sacked by his employer, the BBC, for filing stories too favourable to Biafra. Count Carl Gustaf von Rosen, the Swedish nobleman who became a legend in the 1930s when he volunteered to fight for Haile Selassie against the Italians, came back to Africa to embrace Biafra's cause, and put Nigeria's air force of MIG and Ilyshin fighters into disarray and panic, with five tiny two-seater Minicon planes. There was an American Air Force Colonel (retired), whose name I cannot now recall, who came out of *his* retirement in Florida to fly food and medical supplies on behalf of Joint Church Aid from the Portuguese island of Sao Tome into Biafra. He flew many missions into Uli Airport – a strip of highway the Biafrans, with great ingenuity, had converted into a landing strip, camouflaged during the day with leaves and transformed into one of Africa's busiest airports at night. One stormy night the Colonel did not make it back; I called on his widow during a visit I made to Florida. It was a painful meeting. I didn't really know the man, and there was nothing I could say to this woman, who sat so calm and courteous, but remote. But before I took my leave she asked her question: 'Tell me honestly, did he do any good coming?' 'Yes', I said, 'Definitely. He saved a few children'. She smiled then, with tears in her eyes. There was a small group of American writers – Kurt Vonnegut, Herbert Gold, and Harvey Swados – who came to show solidarity with Biafra's beleaguered writers. Stanley Diamond came like all these others. But he also brought something additional – a long-standing scholarly interest and expertise in the territory.[36]

These visitors responded from humanitarian motives that also had an intellectual dimension. They provided elements of understanding, contrary to the insensitivity of the leaders of government in their respective countries. Achebe and his fellow Biafrans appreciated, valued and treasured them in that terrible year.

11

To Understand What Happened
Art in the Midst of War & in the Aftermath
1969–71

NO foreign visitor to Biafra departed without expressing amazement at the ability of the people to survive in spite of tremendous odds. In 1969 particularly, the scourge of *kwashiorkor* induced by protein deficiency had devastated a large number of the population. In addition the quantity of food available through the relief agencies was prized and inevitably its distribution through the priests and selected officials often introduced elements of acrimony. The soldiers were in need of food, the civilians were in need of food and in the effort to acquire that food quarrels often materialized. Those quarrels may not have resulted in deaths but hunger and the terrible bombing and strafing raids took their toll on the people. In 'Vultures' Achebe captures part of the horror of that period through the image of the vulture that had

> picked the eyes, of a swollen
> corpse in a water-logged
> trench and ate the
> things in its bowel.[1]

But such horrors did not deter the people from accomplishing whatever tasks were set before them, even as the geographical area of the nation dwindled.

The Biafran attitude to life was highlighted by Conor Cruise O'Brien, who visited Biafra in the company of Stanley Diamond at Easter, 1969. The two men were trustees of the American Biafra Relief Services Foundation. O'Brien was convinced that the 'survival of Biafra' would be 'a victory for African courage, endurance and skill, and an opportunity for the further development of African creativity'. In his report on that visit in *The New York Review of Books* he points out that of the 'two best-known writers of the old Nigeria – and perhaps of all Africa – one, Achebe is a convinced Biafran patriot and the other, the playwright Wole Soyinka (a Yoruba) is a prisoner in Northern Nigeria'. O'Brien insists that

> no one seriously interested in African literature, in its relation to African social and political life, can have failed to ponder the meaning of the choices and fates of these two men.[2]

143

Choices and fates in Biafra were compressed by the sheer physical fact that more people had to share a tinier area of the nation as its size was reduced. Many of the refugees were accommodated in the primary and secondary schools which most Biafran villages and towns had erected through communal effort. Such concentrations of human beings inevitably exposed deficiencies in the organization of human affairs. By 1969, however, the reorganization of society had progressed to such an extent that new buildings with thatched roofs and bamboo walls were erected and primary schools and a few secondary schools were reopened in Biafra for refugee children and children in areas still unaffected by the civil war. The idea, of course, was to prevent a situation in which those children would find themselves coming of age as illiterates if the war continued for many more years. The dedication exemplified by the re-opening of schools and the teaching of the pupils was visible in all areas of life in the nation. Among the many talented individuals who flourished in the midst of the devastation was Okokon Ndem who performed his duty as a Radio Biafra announcer and news reader with such flair that his voice became synonymous with the station. He had acquired the foundation of his impressive range of skills while serving under Chinua Achebe, then NBS controller in the Eastern zone.

Such instances of sincere dedication to duty helped foreign visitors to appreciate the Biafran ideal as worthy of support. An American novelist, Harvey Swados, was one of those visitors in 1969.

> I wanted to meet Achebe, since I hold to the notion that often more is to be learned from the idiosyncratic opinions of creative people than from the considered utterances of political or military figures.

Swados was not disappointed because

> within five minutes after [Achebe] had dropped in at the former agricultural experiment station where I was being put up, I felt that we were old friends; and we saw each other daily thereafter until my departure.

He described the Achebe he met in Biafra as

> an almost conventionally handsome Ibo in his late thirties, trimly built, with a receding hairline, a full moustache, a quick grin, and a rock-like handclasp. As we talked together, sometimes at table, sometimes with our feet up, sometimes bouncing around back roads in his little car, the pattern of his life since the ultimate break-up of the corrupt society he had been anatomizing in his novels gradually emerged.[3]

Harvey Swados not only observed but also experienced the unique pattern of life in Biafra. He attended a 'smouch and tramp session' in which the musical group, the Fractions, were presenting 'A Special Soul Dressed Weekend in Aid of the Refugees' in a high school in old Umuahia:

> it was a bit of a job finding the school – when you drive about at night in Biafra you are halted every few hundred yards at road blocks manned by soldiers who poke their rifles and flashlights into your darkened car – but it was worth it. I had anticipated beforehand what I had in fact been experiencing – the sea of misery in which countless thousands of refugees are slowly dying [but I] had not expected to attend a dance at which the Fractions, a hard-rock group dressed in army camouflage, would belt out James Brown and Aretha Franklin songs to the delight of sweaty fragging Biafran youngsters ranging from amputee veterans to girl civil servants in beehive hairdos and clinging satin dresses, nor had Chinua expected to bump into a nephew

he hadn't seen in a long time, a guitar-playing fourth of the Fractions. The sound was deafening and mixed-media effects were provided by the occasional failure of the power supply and the flickering of flashlights in the darkness.

It was an exhilarating experience for Swados as he encountered the soldiers, the leaders, the musicians, the civilians and the spirit of Biafra. That peculiar Biafran spirit obviously made him insist on meeting other Biafran writers, too, which Achebe arranged at the Information House of Umuahia Press Headquarters:

The power, as it is apt to do, had long since failed, and I found the group of half a dozen men gathered around a guttering kerosene lantern. On my right Chinua was sprawled across an iron cot. On my left the poet Gabriel Okara, older, gracious, sat upright and attentive. Beyond him Cyprian Ekwensi, the dour and rather grim-faced novelist, slouched sardonically in a chair. Facing me were Nkem Nwankwo, a younger novelist, and John Ekwere, a poet and actor. We talked of what Colonel Ojukwu, the Head of State, had referred to during an interview as the 'claustrophobic condition' of life under siege and blockade. It was particularly difficult for men like these, accustomed not only to reading the periodicals and new publications of the West, but to travelling freely. Okara had been Nigerian delegate to the International PEN Congress in New York a few years earlier, and we spoke of his meetings too with poets in Michigan and at the Writers Workshop of the University of Iowa, where I had once taught; Ekwensi reminisced of California – he had been a guest of Henry Miller at Big Sur. But while they missed the free flow of books and ideas which had been a normal part of their life before the advent of this particularly horrible war, they did not ask about specific books. Rather Nwankwo and Ekwere wanted to know something of the current social role of the American writer; which writers are taken seriously as public spokesmen? Which ones have genuine social weight, in the sense that they are listened to in Washington or quoted by the press when they speak out on public issues? All of these men were fully involved in one way or another with the grinding daily struggle for survival and like Achebe could manage nothing more than a very occasional poem.

'Tell me something', I asked, 'about your opposite numbers in Nigeria.'

'Well of course there's Wole Soyinka. And he's in prison.'

'If he is alive'. An argument broke out as to whether Soyinka was indeed still alive, or had been murdered by a regime afraid to confess the fate of the country's leading playwright.

'Let's face it,' Ekwensi said with quiet irony. 'The most important writers of Nigeria are sitting around you in this room right now.'

'It might be worthwhile pointing out to you', Gabriel Okara observed mildly, 'something that we ourselves tend to take for granted. That is, that not all of us are Ibos, as foreigners may tend to think. I myself am an Ijaw, and Ekwere there is an Ibibio. But today we are all Biafrans, and we are united as never before by a common bond.'

They wanted to know how they might best make themselves heard to the American public. As they spoke it occurred to me that their actual voices could be raised to far greater effect in America than in this closed-off room and I said so.

As soon as I suggested, 'Why don't you select a group of say three men to come over to the States and give a series of readings?', the discussion grew vivacious. They had already envisioned something of the sort, perhaps a dance company, or a travelling exhibit of Biafran art, and the talk immediately proceeded to specifics. By the end of the evening, I felt, certain firm decisions had been made.[4]

That visit by Harvey Swados was inspirational in many ways, for one of the firm decisions taken was to project Biafra through its writers, artists and musicians. It was a decision that involved many other talented citizens who now found it possible to express themselves creatively.

Achebe was one of the moving spirits behind that recognition and utilization of the arts in aid of Biafra. In the sessions of the National Guidance Committee he emphasized the role of the arts in the mix of ideas from various professionals that were absorbed, synthesized and produced in a suitable format for Biafran needs. One of the documents which the committee completed and submitted to General Ojukwu as head of state was *The Principles of the Biafran Revolution*. The final draft of the document had been made in Ojukwu's house by the Committee after intensive, elaborate and careful work. Ojukwu gratefully accepted it and sent it off to Mark Press of Geneva, Switzerland for printing and publishing. A decision was taken that the principles would be declared at Ahiara Village, but the citizens of Biafra were to know of the radical nature of that document several months later.

Unfortunately, soon after the completion of that document, the town of Umuahia fell to Nigerian soldiers, but the spirits of the people were revived by the triumph of the Biafran soldiers in recapturing Owerri soon after. The Biafran Organization of Freedom Fighters played a role, supplementing the expertise of the regular army which applied tactics of encirclement until the occupying Nigerian soldiers were flushed out. With the fall of Umuahia, however, the headquarters of Biafra changed location again, and the ministries and other important units were redistributed. The group of artists whose regular meetings at Umuahia had attracted attention moved to Alaenyi, Ogwa, near Owerri. Azuonye records that

> with the fall of Umuahia the community once again suffered a dispersion. But with the creation of the culture centre and its location at Alaenyi, Ogwa, a new forum for contact culminating in the formal baptism of the community emerged. The creative efforts of this phase bespeak of the deep sense of frustration and optimism not often backed by facts. Now nothing but pessimism prevailed. The most remarkable piece of the period is the play, *Veneration for Udo*, the first of the communally written and produced pieces by Odunke Artists. It was on the eve of the production of this ritual dramatic prayer for peace that the Odunke Community of Artists took its name [from] a traditional festival in Awka-Etiti which features all the arts of the community in a harmonious relationship.[5]

The formal recognition of this community of artists encouraged many civilians and soldiers to make their creative works public. Several of those works were published in foreign countries. The established writers like Achebe also published in foreign journals. The poem 'Mango Seedling' which Achebe dedicated to Okigbo was published in the *New York Review of Books* on 22 May 1969.

The play *Veneration for Udo*, written and produced by the Odunke Group, contains sharp criticism of the vices that had materialized in Biafra and the artists illustrated the danger posed by the traitors, cheats, defectors, profiteers and racketeers who materialize in every war. Such vices convinced General Ojukwu and Chinua Achebe's National Guidance Committee on the importance of their document on the Biafran revolution. Thus on 1 June 1969, Head of State Chukwuemeka Odumegwu Ojukwu, General of the People's Army, presented that document under the title, *The Ahiara Declaration: The Principles of the Biafran Revolution*. It was as comprehensive as it was radical, as insightful as it was informative. Ojukwu, an eloquent speaker, did justice to the labour of the committee, captivating the people who had gathered to listen to him. The document begins by praising the sacrifices of Biafrans in the struggle to assert their independence. It comments on the war situation and identifies the indifference of the world to the plight of Biafra as racist. It also analyses the myth of the negro, reiterating the racist dimension of the conflict and stressing the essential principle of self-determination, including a rejection of Arab-Muslim expansionism and the exploitation of Africa. In a world scarred by Russian imperialism and Anglo-Saxon genocide he identifies a negro renaissance, highlighting Nigerian corruption as an impediment to that renaissance, which is why it is important for independence to be rediscovered.

> Our Revolution is a historic opportunity given to us to establish a just society; to revive the dignity of our people at home and the dignity of the Black man in the world.

Thus Biafrans are exhorted to expunge Nigerianism and enthrone the power of the people.

> In Biafra the people are supreme; the people are master; the leader is servant. You see, you make a mistake when you greet me with shouts of 'Power, power!' I am not power – you are. My name is Emeka. I am your servant, that is all.[6]

Thus the basic principles of the Biafran revolution are declared to consist in belief in the sanctity of human life and the dignity of the human person; a rejection of genocide; the placing of a high premium on patriotism; the need for peaceful co-existence; the knowledge and reasonable demand for civic rights; the cultivation of humility by those who exercise power; and the importance of accountability. Those are truly egalitarian ideas, and in defining the task of a leader the declaration gives them substance. A leader is a servant, who must be just, should not perpetuate himself in office, erect memorials to himself in his lifetime or convert government into a family business. Social justice is one of the cornerstones of the revolution and property should be considered as belonging to the community. After setting out those principles, the declaration states that they need to be 'transformed into reality through the institutions of society'. It identifies the legislature, reformed politics, a restructured civil service, the judiciary, the police force and the armed services as avenues for that transformation. Public servants and citizens are to be trained and educated accordingly. The guarantees of the revolution include equal opportunities for employment, security for all workers and encouragement in the acquisition of knowledge. The *Ahiara Declaration* pronounces self-reliance as the key to putting the Biafran economic house in order. The qualities of the individual who constitutes the final irreducible unit of 'the people' are cited, among them patriotism, honour, good neighbourliness, truthfulness, responsibility, courage, respect for law, love of freedom, industry, resourcefulness and inventiveness. The declaration ends with the promise: 'Biafra will not betray the black man. No matter the odds, we will fight with all our might until black men everywhere can point with pride to this Republic, standing dignified and defiant, an example of African nationalism, triumphant over its many and age-old enemies.'[7]

It was an epic declaration which reflected the work of Achebe's team of intellectuals; at the same time it had Ojukwu's personal touch, for he had studied the document before that presentation. Some of the influential people who had benefited from the Nigerian tradition of corrupt public office holders

147

before 1966 were said to have expressed great reservations over the principles of the revolution. They squirmed, and some of them were also said to have defected to Nigeria in 1969 as a result of that powerful document. But such defections did not stop the war at that time, as ordinary Biafran citizens continued to dedicate themselves to their duties.

The horrors of the war continued, through narrow escapes or harrowing setbacks. The Achebe family experienced a near miss at Ezinihite where they were living. On that day there was a sudden air-raid and only the bunkers offered a doubtful safety. The planes were so low that the people could even see the crew pushing out the bombs. Christie Achebe had taken cover before she noticed Chidi, then about two years old, walking calmly in the open wearing his white napkin. She dashed out, screaming frantically, and rushed him to safety before the pilot could react. The bombs that the plane eventually dropped exploded in the distance, without injuring them.[8] Chinua and Christie knew that such dangers could not be avoided entirely as long as the war lasted. Thus they placed the experience in the compartment of their minds reserved for haunting, helpless memories.

The idea which Harvey Swados had planted bore fruit and in October and November of 1969 three writers, Chinua Achebe, Cyprian Ekwensi and Gabriel Okara, visited the United States on a speaking tour. The choice of Achebe as one of the writers to embark on that tour was inevitable, for he had become the most widely read African writer. The first two book-length studies of his work had appeared that year: Arthur Ravenscroft's *Chinua Achebe* had been published by Longman and the British Council, and G. D. Killam's *The Novels of Chinua Achebe* by Heinemann Educational Books in London and the Africana Publishing Corporation in New York. In addition Heinemann announced that same year that *Things Fall Apart* had sold more than 400,000 copies in the paperback imprint alone. Gabriel Okara, an Ijaw and easily the most interesting poet after Okigbo, was a good second choice and the prolific novelist Cyprian Ekwensi a worthy third choice. Achebe summarized the objectives of that intensive tour for Bernth Lindfors:

> I'm here on a program arranged by the Committee for Biafran Writers and Artists. This is an American Committee which is trying to bring over Biafran artists and writers to show that Biafra is all kinds of people and not only starving children, though that is a part of it. The Committee is also trying to send American writers into Biafra to see things for themselves.[9]

The same committee arranged for a travelling exhibition of Biafran art works under the supervision of Uche Okeke. The interest shown by the committee had also helped in the development and formalization of the Odunke Artists in Biafra. According to Obiora Udechukwu,

> the cultural workshops were established under the directorship of Gabriel Okara. Uche Okeke was in charge of the art workshops. Then Onuora Nzekwu was the Deputy Director to assist Gabriel Okara and Okogbule Wonodi ran the Writers Workshops. There was an Atilogwu Dance Group from Udi, and they went to perform in Gabon. Sonny Oti's theatre group was also attached to the cultural workshop: it became known as the Armed Forces Theatre. Finally there was the Armed Forces Entertainment Band, doing folk operas and that sort of thing. It was led by Meki Nzewi.[10]

It required sacrifice from the participants to gather, reflect, and create art works in the midst of a war and Azuonye insists that

> it was by no means a form of escapism; each and every one of us was deeply involved in one way or another with the nitty-gritty of the war effort [and] so important were the Odunke meetings that some of us who lived and worked outside Ogwa spared no risks to travel in rickety vehicles through thickets of road-blocks and past hordes of conscripting soldiers to keep every Odunke date.[11]

The achievements of those cultural workshops and the Odunke meetings were reflected in the confidence with which the three writers, Achebe, Ekwensi and Okara, presented their views, making many more Americans aware, on that tour, of both the creativity and tragedy in Biafra.

That tour was a 30-campus, two-week journey in North America during which the three writers lectured at various universities and talked to many people officially and unofficially. Catherine Lyn Innes was teaching English at the Tuskegee Institute, Alabama, a college of higher education for African-Americans, when Chinua Achebe arrived for one of those lectures in 1969 and she met him for the first time. She had become acquainted with Achebe's work through Professor Samuel Allen (also known as the poet Paul Vesey) who taught African literature at Tuskegee.

> *Things Fall Apart* was a favourite text among the students, who saw Okonkwo as a real 'Black Power' in those days when Black Power as a movement was at its height. Chinua was on a speaking tour of America on behalf of the Biafran cause, and the students were at first surprised by his diffident and quiet manner, for they were used to the powerful rhetoric and confident use of the media of such speakers as Malcolm X, Martin Luther King, Jesse Jackson and Stokeley Carmichael. Chinua avoided such rhetoric and such a style, but nevertheless proved a moving and eloquent spokesman for his cause, and left a strong impression on the students.[12]

The journey was predictably strenuous, and Bernth Lindfors comments that

> when Chinua Achebe visited the University of Texas at Austin in November 1969 on the final leg of a month-long American speaking tour, he was very tired but more than willing to undergo another hectic round of interviews, speeches and discussions. Within the space of twenty-four hours he gave a press conference, conducted two University classes, taped a half-hour television interview, delivered a public lecture and met with numerous students, faculty and townspeople at an informal reception held in his honour.[13]

Inevitably many of the things Achebe has to say to Lindfors concern Biafra, although he also answers questions concerning his novels. He acknowledges that for Africa the 'most meaningful job' at that time 'should be to determine what kind of society we want, how we are going to get there, what values we can take from the past, if we can, as we move along'. Achebe confesses that he cannot write novels under the uncertainties of the Biafran situation and he adds:

> I can write poetry – something short, intense, more in keeping with my mood. I can write essays. I can even lecture. All this is creating in the context of our struggle. At home I do a lot of writing, but not fiction, something more concrete, more directly related to what's going on.

His conviction is that 'there are forms of creativity which suit different moments' and he would not 'consider writing a poem on daffodils particularly creative' in 'his situation' at that time because 'it would be foolish'. All the same he is still optimistic that writing novels is 'always possible, if one survives. There's always time. But these are not normal times, not for me. These are not normal times at all.'[14]

Indeed, the times were not normal and some of the humorous incidents that occurred on that tour, like Gabriel Okara getting lost and losing his raincoat, generated only a little laughter from Okara and his companions. But at the same time Chinua Achebe found the tour illuminating in several ways, for it was in the course of it that he came upon the story of the three hundred Igbo slaves chained together, who decided not to accept that humiliation and committed suicide by jumping overboard together. That incident became known as 'the Igbo Landing' which is the name of the place in South Carolina where it occurred. Achebe recollects:

> That story of the Igbo slaves who walked into the sea was told at a meeting which I addressed in the south, in the United States, during the war. I was travelling there to explain what was going on; and at the end of my lectures this old man, this old black man, got up and told the story of the Igbo landing. It was a very strange feeling! Nobody knew what to say after that! He didn't say: 'Your people have done that before or anything like that!' He just told the story and sat down![15]

Achebe and his companions made efforts on that tour to increase awareness in America of the plight and importance of Biafra before returning to their country in November 1969. It was nevertheless clear to Achebe that theirs was a journey into despair because he found that 'world policy is absolutely ruthless and unfeeling' which was 'a bitter and enormous shock' for him. He explains to Michael Smith and Harry Cowen that it had become necessary for him to go out and 'try to explain what's going on and hopefully to influence the thinking in those areas where the power lies. This is the only reason for my coming out now.' Achebe is aware that power may not lie in the universities but he argues that

> a writer can only talk to those who respond to writers. If I went to the State Department to talk to officials at the Africa desk, they would not know what I was saying. There are other people in Biafra who can talk to them. I do not underrate the importance of the university groups, the intellectual groups and so on, in terms of final results. They are not likely to bring about a change immediately but they might help in bringing about a change in policy.[16]

It was with that bare hope that Achebe and his colleagues returned to Biafra where the war situation appeared fairly stable, with few signs of significant change. The Biafran soldiers were becoming increasingly tired under extreme pressure, however, and the civilians more pessimistic. The Nigerian soldiers were equally tired and disillusioned as the end of 1969 approached. And so Christmas Day dawned on Biafra's sorrow, watched by the world for almost thirty months while a group of people fought tenaciously and without respite against impossible human and technological odds. Chinua Achebe, who had spent many years of his life in radio work, tuned to some foreign stations on that Christmas Day. The idea for the poem 'Christmas in Biafra' came to him as he listened,

> out of the kind of desperation which you felt hearing carols on short-wave radio and being reminded that there were places in the world where people were singing about

the birth of the Prince of Peace and you were trapped in this incredible tragedy. Now it's a very powerful feeling indeed.[17]

The scene Achebe recreated was the setting up of a 'plaster-cast scene of Bethlehem' in which the figures of Jesus, the parents and other significant Biblical characters were placed. The poem describes a woman who comes to that Bethlehem scene:

> Poorer than the poor worshippers
> before her who had paid their homage
> with pitiful offerings of new aluminium
> coins that few traders would take and
> a frayed five-shilling note she only
> crossed herself and prayed open-eyed. Her
> infant son flat like a dead lizard
> on her shoulder his arms and legs
> cauterized by famine was a miracle
> of its own kind. Large sunken eyes
> stricken past boredom to a flat
> unrecognizing glueyiness moped far away
> motionless across her shoulder... [18]

The juxtaposition of the sadness of the woman with the intrinsic joy of the birth of Jesus Christ in Christian belief effectively evoked the suffering in Biafra. The obstacles the people had surmounted and the suffering they had overcome, reflected in that 'mother and child' image, were enormous. As the new year of 1970 began, they were not sure when the torment would end.

Many Biafran citizens – soldiers and civilians – were prepared to make more sacrifices. Internal problems in the 14th Division of the Biafran army had affected morale and organization, however, ultimately leading to its collapse. Nigerian generals are wont to claim credit for what was not achieved on the battlefield, but the sudden end of the war, which none of them anticipated, exposes the unreliability of such claims. The formal signing of some documents renouncing secession would be made to create the impression that there had been a defeat and a surrender. Before then, on the night of 9 January 1970, General Ojukwu, after due consultation, had left on the last flight out of Biafra. There was no doubt that he had played his role as a leader to the best of his ability. His last broadcast on the eve of his departure emphasized that role as he praised the people 'who have borne the brunt of the strains of this fight', thereby suffering 'unmentionable privations at the hands of an enemy that has used every conceivable weapon, particularly the weapon of starvation'. He reiterated that the sacrifices of the people had been made 'with the sole purpose of achieving security which was the main motive forcing our taking up arms to defend ourselves'. He pointed out that the 'task of a leader at war is to be responsive to the plight of his people, to determine what level of sacrifice can be accepted'. He enumerated the moves that Biafra had made for peace and added that

> once more, to show our honesty, and in accord with my own frequent affirmations that I would personally go anywhere to secure peace and security for my people, I am now travelling out of Biafra to explore with our friends all these proposals further and fully and to be at hand to settle these issues to the best of my ability, always serving the interests of my people.

He announced that Major General Philip Effiong had been mandated to 'administer the Government with the rest of the cabinet (and) to run the affairs of this Republic', then he ended by paying tribute to the Biafran armed forces and invoking God's blessings.[19]

Even if Ojukwu had known about the impending collapse of the Biafran Army's 14th Division, it was his absence that saved many of the people from massacre, because it created a strong element of uncertainty in the Nigerian army about whether the Biafran soldiers had other plans in mind. By the time the true facts were realized it was too late to embark on a massacre or brutal repression on a general scale. It was easy, however, for some of those in charge of the administration and other prominent people to blame General Ojukwu for the many difficulties faced by Biafra as the war ended and they as individuals sought to escape any form of maltreatment. Ojukwu became a convenient scapegoat but Major General Philip Effiong, who made the formal announcement of surrender on 12 January 1970, was courageous and diplomatic in his statement under the prevailing circumstances. Effiong reminded the people of his role as 'the officer administering the government of the republic' and declared that his broadcast had the 'mandate of the armed forces and the people of this country'. He noted that 'throughout history injured people have had to resort to arms in their self-defence where peaceful negotiations fail' and congratulated the armed forces on their gallantry, while also thanking the civil population. He insisted that the suffering must stop and that 'those elements of the old government regime who have made negotiations and reconciliation impossible have voluntarily removed themselves from our midst'. He announced that he had 'instructed an orderly disengagement of troops' with emissaries despatched to make contact with Nigeria's field commanders. He urged 'General Gowon, in the name of humanity, to order his troops to pause while an armistice is negotiated in order to avoid the mass suffering caused by the movement of population', adding that 'we have always believed that our differences with Nigeria should be settled by peaceful negotiations'.[20] General Effiong gave the names of Sir Louis Mbanefo, Prof. Eni Njoku, Mr. J. I. Emembolu, Chief A. E. Bassey and Mr. E. Agumah as members of the negotiating delegation, while the members of his advisory council, in addition to those already named, included Brigadier P. C. Amadi, Brigadier C.A. Nwawo, Captain W. A. Anuku, Wing Commander J. I. Ezeilo, Inspector General of Police P. I. Okeke, Dr I. Eke, Chief A. E. Udoffia, Mr. M. T. Mbu, Chief Frank Opigo and Chief J. M. Echeruo. Effiong repudiated the idea of a government in exile as he advised the civilian population to remain calm and thanked the foreign governments, friends, the Pope and the Joint Church Aid for their help.

That announcement was quite helpful in preventing the collapse of public order, and it made the then Colonel Olusegun Obasanjo the lucky recipient of the Biafran delegation as the Nigerian officer fortunate to be in command of the nearest section of troops at that time of increasing disillusionment among Nigerian soldiers. He made an announcement on 14 January 1970, praising himself for his accomplishment in crushing Biafra and asking those in hiding to come out and surrender themselves. He also announced a guarantee of safety for all law-abiding citizens and the cessation of the tactical movements of all troops. He thanked the men under his command, his commander-in-chief General Gowon and the citizens of Nigeria.

But that announcement did not restrain many of the rampaging Nigerian soldiers who were intent on fulfilling their lust for vengeance. Many women were raped and many others killed; much property was looted; and the soldiers, intoxicated by their unanticipated victory, soon became violent new gods in the former territory of Biafra, which was once again known as Eastern Nigeria but was now made up of three new states. In foreign countries there was genuine fear that the unbridled Nigerian soldiery would embark on an orgy of destruction. That fear was not unfounded, as later events proved.

Other foreigners had different anxieties, especially those who had supported Biafra in its darkest hour. 'When von Rosen heard of the defeat of Biafra', recalls Achebe, the Swedish count who had come out of retirement to fly Biafra's little war plane said 'it would take the world fifty years, at least, to understand what happened.'[21] That understanding was not the priority of the victorious Nigerian soldiers, or even of their commanders in Lagos. Neither could the civilian administration of Ukpabi Asika at Enugu restrain the victorious soldiers, and well into the 1970s there were numerous incidents of overbearing soldiers and their brutal acts. Still, General Yakubu Gowon in Lagos rose to the occasion as he inhaled the fumes of victory. His speech to declare the end of the civil war was perhaps the only achievement of his career.

Gowon announced formally that the attempt at secession had ended, marking the end of 'thirty months of a grim struggle'. He traced the history of the war, and, of course, blamed Ojukwu for it. He paid homage to the dead soldiers and innocent civilians and asked the living to heal the nation's wounds.

I solemnly repeat our guarantees of a general amnesty for those misled into rebellion. We guarantee the personal safety of every one who submits to Federal authority. We guarantee the security of life and property of all citizens in every part of Nigeria and equality in political rights. We also guarantee the right of every Nigerian to reside and work wherever he chooses in the Federation as equal citizens of one united country.... There is, therefore, no cause of humiliation on the part of any group of the people of this country. The task of reconciliation is truly begun.

He informed the people of the urgent task of rehabilitation and reconstruction, the importance of the new twelve-state structure and the need to provide relief in the war-affected areas. Gowon thanked all those who had helped Nigeria to prosecute the war, his armed forces and the civilian population. It was a flambuoyant speech that elevated Gowon into a significant Nigerian leader, but the interpretation of his speech by his soldiers was a different matter altogether. Many other people also interpreted it in their ways, and a public official went on record in the East Central state as saying that 'General amnesty should not mean general amnesia.'[22]

Chinua Achebe joined many of his former Biafran compatriots who were returning cautiously to their home towns and villages. He, particularly, had to be careful because his name was definitely on the list of those labelled as prominent rebels and his wife Christie was expecting their fourth child. In Ogidi the Nigerian soldiers had destroyed his family house. The state of disrepair in the area was astonishing; in some places the bush had reclaimed footpaths and all the abandoned property had been looted. Some houses that survived the bombs and bullets had been stripped of all their fittings. There was no family, either in Ogidi or in any other town in Biafra, that sadly returned home to find even their abandoned broomsticks intact. It was a terrible experience for a people who attached pride to the honest accumulation of property. Chinua Achebe in his philosophical way accepted his personal losses as part of the tragedy of the war; the international attention attracted by his books at least ensured an income that would enable him to recover.

He was asked to report to the military authorities at Enugu for clearance: these investigations became processes through which many important people were finally apprehended, old scores were settled and futile vengeance was fulfilled. Chinua Achebe went to Enugu for incessant and troubling interrogations, with questions designed to make him lose his temper.

> When the war ended ... I had to go through Police clearance. I had to submit myself to questioning by all kinds of people. 'What did you do as a rebel?' etcetera, etcetera. Or 'Write up a piece on what you did.' But never, not even for once, did I suggest that we made a mistake. And I'll never submit, that we made a mistake.

Achebe asked his own question some time later: 'Do you think we are mistaken? You have a responsibility to prove to us, now that you have won, that we were mistaken. I'm still waiting.'[23] Meanwhile there were other indications, as attempts were made to return life to normal, that the country regarded the inhabitants of the Eastern zone as a defeated group.

The new authorities were aware of Achebe's role during the civil war. S. G. Ikoku, who had been jailed with Obafemi Awolowo but was released as the war progressed and had become an official in Ukpabi Asika's East Central State government at Enugu, told Achebe: 'You gave us more trouble than the rest.'[24] The trouble Ikoku had in mind was the fact that Achebe had made public statements in support of Biafra. Achebe was aware that the soldiers could use flimsy reasons to detain him but he was not unduly worried, using the opportunity of the visit to Enugu to search for the manuscript of *How the Leopard Got His Claws,* which was being printed when Enugu fell. He recalls that when he went back to the site of the publishing house, 'it had been razed to the ground – it seemed to me that whoever did it didn't like publishing or at least this particular publishing house and perhaps this particular book.' One proof copy somehow survived, however, and

> a friend of ours, a relation of Christopher Okigbo's, had a copy of the galleys, fished it out and brought it to me. And so I made more changes, not major ones.[25]

It was also interesting that an intelligence officer with the Federal troops said to Achebe on one of those occasions when he was asked to report: 'You know, of all the things that came out of Biafra, that book was the most important.'[26] Others were continuing to be interested in Achebe's work, too, for in that year David Carroll published a book on his writings (*Chinua Achebe*) through the New York publishers, Twayne.

The retrieval of Achebe's manuscript was part of the slow return to normalcy in the former Eastern region. But the economic difficulties were enormous as the outside world learned through the news media. In London, for example, the television presentation of the enormous devastation and the attendant economic difficulties had a huge impact, as Ulli Beier remembers:

> The day after our arrival we learned that Biafra had collapsed. On the TV news, in a friend's house, we saw the first pictures of the devastated eastern region of Nigeria. Cyprian Ekwensi was shown, trying to make a livelihood by selling old bottles on the

market. This image brought home the tragedy more than a hundred newspaper reports. Here was a man whom we had known for years, who had made a reputation as a writer and a brilliant career in broadcasting and who was suddenly reduced to the level of barest existence. Reports also reached us that Chinua was in a state of deep depression – and how could it have been otherwise. Georgina and I decided on the spur of the moment to sell our collection of Nigerian paintings and send the money to our friends in Nigeria. What was the use of owning an art collection which was stored away in London, when some of our oldest friends were starving? We were watching that TV news in the house of Mrs Ella Winter, an art collector whose house was full of Paul Klees and Picassos. But she also had developed an interest in African art, because her husband Don Stewart (a former Hollywood scriptwriter) had once given a creative writing course for journalists in Ghana. She offered us £3,000 for our paintings. At a time when there was no market for such works at all, this seemed acceptable. We divided the money into several portions and sent it out to Lazarus Ukeje, Onuora Nzekwu and others, to help them acquire at least a few of the bare necessities of life. To Chinua I wrote a long letter saying that since he was surrounded by many of the country's most interesting writers, wouldn't it be a good idea to start a new literary magazine? I can't remember how much money we sent him, but it was certainly enough for the first issue and I had no doubt that others would go on supporting such a venture. This was the beginning of *Okike*.[27]

Both Beier's advice and his gift were welcomed by Achebe, whose mind was working in similar directions in spite of the tremendous difficulties of the time, made worse by harsh economic policies. Many years later Achebe wrote of this period with deep sadness:

> The civil war gave Nigeria a perfect and legitimate excuse to cast the Igbo in the role of treasonable felony, a wrecker of the nation. But thanks to Gowon's moderating influence overt vengeance was not visited on them when their secessionate State of Biafra was defeated in January 1970. But there were hardliners in Gowon's cabinet who wanted their pound of flesh, the most powerful among them being Chief Obafemi Awolowo, Federal Commissioner for Finance. Under his guidance a banking policy was evolved which nullified any bank account which had been operated during the civil war. This had the immediate result of pauperizing the Igbo middle class and earning a profit of £4 million for the Federal Government Treasury.... The Indigenization Decree which followed soon afterwards completed the routing of the Igbo from the commanding heights of the Nigerian economy, to everyone's apparent satisfaction.[28]

When those announcements were made as part of the insincere efforts to 'normalize' affairs in the Eastern states many   citizens felt the blow and their health deteriorated. In sorrow and anguish many prominent Biafran people who had survived the war died within two years of its cessation.

Chinua Achebe survived, although he had lost his books, some manuscripts, property and several relatives. Christie gave birth to their fourth child and second daughter on 7 March 1970 and they named her Nwando. It was a name given in anticipation that her arrival after the war in a period of relative peace would make her 'a child under which the parents would shelter'. That birth also coincided with the announcement that the academic and non-academic staff of the University of Nigeria, Nsukka should report at Enugu where Ukpabi Asika would address them. They reported but Asika could not address them; instead he delegated his secretary, who informed the staff and some of the students that a management and planning committee would be set up to resuscitate the university. This committee was eventually set up under the chairmanship of Chukwuemeka Ike, registrar of the university before the war. The task assigned to the committee was comprehensive since the university was in ruins. Buildings had been destroyed, office equipment thoroughly looted, furniture destroyed or carted away, books burnt and the premises deliberately neglected. Refuse had been dumped there and most of the houses and paths had been reclaimed by the encircling forest. It had been used as an army camp by the Nigerian soldiers and their abandoned vehicles and damaged tanks littered the landscape. With commendable zeal, however, Ike and his committee swung into action and their report was ready by May 1970.

Students reappeared without being summoned; the staff members were recalled officially. The deprivation of the war years enabled them to adjust to an environment which lacked water, accommodation and electricity. The university functioned without a vice-chancellor throughout the remaining months of 1970, although later a governing council was set up. It was a terrible time for members of the university community, many of whom slept on planks. The classrooms had no chairs and the students sat on cement blocks. Another problem arose from the fact that the university was ostensibly owned by the three Eastern states: East Central State, Rivers State and Cross River State. The university was reopened on the basis that the other states would join East Central State, in which it was situated, to administer it. Rivers State opted out but Cross River State agreed on condition that a campus of the university be established in their own state. Thus the University of Nigeria, Nsukka, commenced in 1970 without the financial power even to renovate its buildings or provide the necessary amenities.

Chinua Achebe was reabsorbed as a senior research fellow in the Institute for African Studies which had Dr S. N. Nwabara as its acting director. The institute had lost the services of several members of staff who had died: Professor J. C. Anene, Christopher Okigbo and Professor Kalu Ezera. In addition, all the collections of research material which the institute had made in ethnography, including books and rare documents, had been lost. The institute thus had to start afresh, but the doggedness of the staff enabled it to make a new beginning. The objectives of the institute were redrawn to respond to current realities. Chinua Achebe not only functioned as a senior research fellow in creative writing, but also taught courses in African literature for the Department of English and in the use of English for the Division of General Studies. It was a period of settling down for the writer after the desperate times of the war, but his creative instinct was still there and it surfaced in 'Lazarus', a poem in which he dramatizes a real-life incident in which a man said to have accidentally knocked down a pedestrian with his car is killed in revenge by the pedestrian's irate kinsmen on the erroneous assumption that the pedestrian has died. But the pedestrian, who has only been stunned, recovers. In shock, his kinsmen kill him because he has made them commit murder. Achebe extends the metaphor of the biblical Lazarus to capture the sense of disappointment aroused by Biafran survivors as they are reabsorbed into Nigeria:

> ...certainly that keen
> subordinate who has moved up
> to his table at the office, for
> him resurrection is an awful
> embarrassment...[29]

'Resurrected' Biafrans were indeed faced with situations in which former subordinates were unwilling to accommodate them in their former offices, even as they made efforts to survive the harsh, post-war economic conditions. At the University of Nigeria, Nsukka those efforts to survive also faced internal acts of humiliation such as the insistence that academic staff queue up for their salaries every month, while clerks subjected them to ridicule by shouting their salaries across the room to other clerks. Yet they and their students persevered.

It was a measure of the success of that dedicated group that in the entrance examination conducted that year more than 11,000 candidates qualified for admission, although the university could admit not many more than a thousand. While this academic reconstruction was going on, some people were only interested in cashing in on the situation. Achebe was disappointed at the behaviour of those officials and citizens of the state who were deliberately giving the impression that they had not been involved in the Biafran cause but had always been advocates of 'One Nigeria'. It was an attitude that was guaranteed to secure lucrative positions and financial gain. Achebe's response had much to do with the poem 'Non-commitment', written in September 1970. He cites Pontius Pilate and in particular the betrayal by Judas who

> alone in that motley crowd
> had sense enough to tell a doomed
> movement when he saw one
> and get out quick, a nice
> little present bulging his coat-pocket
> into the bargain – sensible fellow.'[30]

While the topical reference is clear, Achebe extends the poem, as usual, to serve as a parable on the human disposition to self-interest in other situations and locations. Another 1970 poem, 'An "If" of History', can also be read as a reaction to events in his country. He uses Hitler, asking a question about the possible development in the world if he had won his war, and thus finding a way to examine what would have happened to the current hypocrites if Biafra had won. Once again, however, his philosophical attitude transcends the immediate Nigerian situation: the poem is also a reminder that it is possible to emasculate truth in the euphoria of victory. Another parable with a clear application to post-war Nigeria is the poem 'He Loves Me; He Loves Me Not', provoked by the news that a street in Port Harcourt had been named after Harold Wilson. Here he questions whether a man who has armed one brother to kill the other can be regarded as a benefactor.[31]

While Chinua Achebe worked on these poems efforts were being made to make things normal and 1970 was coming to an end. Ulli Beier recalls a visit which he paid to Nigeria in 1970 in order to attend a conference organized by Michael Crowder, then director of African Studies at the University of Ife.

> I jumped at the chance: it was my first opportunity to visit Nigeria since we had left in December 1966. In Lagos I went straight to Onuora Nzekwu, who had been reabsorbed into the Department of Information. His wife cooked us one of those fantastic Igbo meals with vegetables that are not normally used in the West. In view of all this abundance of food we commented that it must have been a very hard task for a woman to feed her children during the war; but she said very firmly: 'Only a lazy woman found it hard to feed her children during the civil war.' She then explained that she would walk right through the fighting lines to trade on the Nigerian side and then return home with the food she had managed to buy.

Beier then borrowed a car and went to Nsukka in order to visit some friends as well as to see for himself the effects of the war there.

> Nsukka was then an exhilarating place. The buildings still showed the war damage. Most windows were broken and most furniture or other movable objects had been 'liberated' by the army. I was told that the Federal Government had no intention of re-opening the university so soon – after all it had been labelled the 'hotbed of rebellion' – but the students simply returned to the campus, cleaned up the mess and sent out for lecturers: 'We want to be taught.' The lecturers came and teaching was resumed somehow – with hardly any books and with the students sitting on the floor. But the morale was high – almost exuberant. The experience of war had been traumatic, but they said that it 'taught us what we are capable of!' Having met Mrs Nzekwu a week earlier, I had no difficulty in understanding what they meant.[32]

Beier reports that 'meeting Chinua after several years was exciting and it felt as if no time had passed, as if nothing had changed.'

In early 1971 the appointment of Professor H. Kodilinye as vice-chancellor was announced. Kodilinye had lived in England for almost 40 years, having gone to study there in the late 1920s, settled down, married, raised a family and in most respects become an Englishman. When he returned to Nigeria in 1971, Kodilinye revealed at his first press conference that 'I was born in the East, my parents lived in the North and I went to school in the West. I cannot speak any of their languages.'[33] Achebe remarked that the new vice-chancellor had said that 'he cannot recognize Nigerian food, let alone eat it. Given a chance he will appoint a European over a Nigerian to teach at his University.'[34] The general feeling as soon as Kodilinye assumed office was that his attitude was insensitive, arrogant and overbearing. In addition, his absence of forty years was a great handicap and he appeared strange to the people as he sought to establish a tradition based on what he had absorbed from the English culture. His idea of administration, moreover, did not meet the expectations of staff and students.

These alienating developments in the university worried Achebe and his colleagues; worse, they were part of a wider problem in the political affairs of Nigeria. Achebe had an invitation, for example, to visit Papua New Guinea and Australia, but when he applied for a passport the officials at Lagos refused to issue it to him.

> When I protested to the Commissioner for External Affairs he wrote me a nice letter with words to the effect – Dear Achebe, thank you for your letter in which you complained about difficulties which you thought you had with my officials ...[35]

It was apparent that a decision had been taken to make sure that those who had been involved in administrative activities in the former Biafra were covertly punished. Achebe's protest made it clear that further denials of his rights as a citizen would attract international attention. He did not get the passport, however, and he did not travel out of Nigeria in 1971. Fortunately his reputation was not hampered by such restrictions, even within the nation. In this year he was appointed a member of the East Central State library board, while Calpenny Productions in Lagos decided to make a film, *Bullfrog in the Sun*, which would be based on *Things Fall Apart* and *No Longer at Ease*. Calpenny had filmed Wole Soyinka's *Kongi's Harvest* in which the playwright had starred. For the production of *Bullfrog in the Sun* they recruited Princess Elizabeth Bagaya, member of a Ugandan royal family, and the Nigerian actor,

Orlando Martins. It was an ambitious project requiring formidable backing and production facilities, but Achebe was not directly involved.

Meanwhile at Nsukka Achebe's displeasure at the anomalies he had noticed both in his environment at Nsukka and in the wider society culminated in several projects. At Enugu there was the establishment of a Frantz Fanon Research Centre with Achebe as the first director. To Achebe, the centre reflected a search for continuity:

> We came out of the Biafran war full of zeal in all kinds of directions, and this was one of them. We think about structural changes of importance in our society, in our political system, in our economic system. There are Marxists among them, socialists and people of that general frame of mind, and the Frantz Fanon Research Centre was set up to organize the work of this group.

The centre produced a journal, *Dimension,* in which Achebe's poem 'Beware Soul Brother' was published. The centre did not last, however, because the founding group was soon dispersed by the

> capitalistic society of Nigeria in which there are all kinds of pressures, especially on the academic. We soon scattered in various places, we were no longer in one place but the idea survives.[36]

Another project expressive of continuity and survival was the new publishing house established at Enugu by Arthur Nwankwo and Samuel Ifejika with the support of Achebe, who was appointed one of its directors. This enterprising company, Nwamife Books or Nwankwo-Ifejika, published *The Insider: Stories of War and Peace from Nigeria* in March 1971. In that collection Achebe's story 'The Mad Man' demonstrates metaphorically and ironically the insanity of the past years. Nwibe, a man of distinction, is taking his bath in a stream when a madman takes his clothes. In blind rage he pursues the madman until they enter the market which leads Nwibe's people to assume that the occult forces of market squares have ensnared him. In a dramatic twist a charlatan who cures Nwibe suddenly has his reputation enhanced. Achebe ironically questions the normal concept of reality with telling accuracy. David Carroll rightly points out that in the story 'reality is dialectical; outraged respectability quickly turns into madness'.[37] It was a short story that enriched a collection in which several well-known writers like Flora Nwapa, Arthur Nwankwo and Samuel Ifejika had also been published.

Achebe was also interested in other aspects of publishing for he now decided to establish a journal that would enhance the discussion of African literature. In his role as a literary frontiersman he said that he established the journal *Okike*

> as an attempt to make sure our case is heard, to make plain that this is a culture with something to offer the world. There are other offerings, other attitudes, other ways of looking at the world; but this is the one we have and we have an obligation to present it for what its worth.

He added that

> the world is made up of different peoples and cultures, and all people, however modest their circumstances, have been working and creating. The world is poorer for not understanding this, for not looking for specific strengths of various cultures.

The obstacles facing the journal were glaring because

the territory into which it was born had been devastated physically and spiritually by war and defeat, its hopes of recovery cynically mocked by a Federal administration that combined slogans of reconciliation with punitive economic and banking policies. In addition to this peculiarly inauspicious environment the fledgling journal had also to contend with world-wide economic pressures which were making literary magazines notoriously short-lived everywhere.[38]

It was therefore a triumph when the first issue of *Okike*, edited by Chinua Achebe, appeared in April 1971.

The contents of that first issue of *Okike* included a poem each from Wole Soyinka, Gabriel Okara, T. C. Nwosu, E. N. Obiechina and Kevin Echeruo; two poems by Romanus Egudu and three poems each from Dennis Brutus, Chinua Achebe, Uche Okeke, Kalu Uka and Pol Ndu. There were three short stories: 'Vengeful Creditor' by Chinua Achebe, 'A Bull for the District Officer' by Nathan O. Nkala and 'Minus Everything' by Cyprian Ekwensi. Obiechina reviewed Ayi Kwei Armah's *The Beautyful Ones Are Not Yet Born*. The journal's cover was designed by Obiora Udechukwu from a traditional image of Ala, goddess of creativity, while Uche Okeke's vignettes and drawings illustrated the contents. The members of the editorial committee were E. N. Obiechina, M. J. C. Echeruo, Ulli Beier, Romanus Egudu, Wole Soyinka, Chukwuemeka Ike, Bernth Lindfors and Edward Brathwaite. A brief note from the editor acknowledged his gratitude to all those whose generosity had made the publication possible and in particular to Ulli Beier for his support. It was a gathering of distinguished African writers and Chinua Achebe's poems 'Question', 'Non-Commitment' and 'Vultures', in addition to his short story, illustrated his unique creative touch and helped to set the tone of the journal. 'The Vengeful Creditor', is the story of a poor girl named Veronica, who is minding a baby on the understanding that when he 'is big enough to go about on his own' her employer, Mr Emenike, will provide her with an education. But the promise is forgotten, although before going to live with the Emenikes Veronica had benefited briefly from a short-lived free primary education exercise in the country. The author juxtaposes the affluence of the Emenike family with the poverty of Martha, Veronica's mother. In the process he identifies the corruption, dishonesty, and insensitivity of the parliamentarians. When Veronica in desperation gives the baby red ink to drink and die so that she can go to school the Emenike family perceive it as an abomination. Veronica is dismissed and the 'Vengeful Creditor' cannot claim her right. In an ironic presentation Achebe shows that the ruthlessly pragmatic approach imbibed by Veronica in the home of the Emenikes is used against them in eliminating an impediment to her quest for education, which is the baby. The story satirizes the complacency, opportunism and selfishness that led to the violence of the civil war and is a good example of the thought-provoking material in that first issue of *Okike*.[39]

Okike indicated in that first issue that it would provide a voice for the African writer. Donatus Nwoga aptly describes it, looking back some years later, as

the fulfilment of a justified ambition in a renowned author to provide a medium for a new generation of writers to give expression to their talent. Chinua Achebe was playing the role of a wise Igbo elder, young though he was, to generate an environment which would allow those coming behind him to excel their elders.[40]

12

Constructing a Relevant Vision
Collections, Controversies & Conferences
1971–2

THE year 1971 was full of literary activities for Chinua Achebe. It appeared as if his creative urge, repressed by the demands of the war, had been released. He wrote short stories and poetry, edited several magazines simultaneously, and continued his role as editorial adviser to Heinemann Educational Books. Yet as he began to recover his rhythm of work the effects of the war lingered, and needed to be worked out of his system in several ways. Achebe was aware that it was impossible to go through such an experience without writing about it, even if one did not address the theme directly. Its influence on one's thinking about oneself and the rest of the world was bound to come through. But that awareness did not deter Achebe from pursuing new creative objectives. As Pius Okigbo remarks,

> fully conscious of his ability and of the need to move on if you are to be in front [Achebe] is constantly seeking new directions for expression: in novels, short stories, essays, poetry. It is this intellectual restlessness that has given Chinua, much to the chagrin of his inferiors, a seeming monopoly of fame.[1]

In 1971 that intellectual restlessness was manifested in Achebe's academic and social activities at the University of Nigeria, Nsukka.

In June 1971 Achebe's *Beware, Soul Brother,* a collection of 23 poems, was published. He dedicated the book to the memory of his mother who had died almost exactly four years before. Several of the poems he had published in journals were included and the enthusiastic publishers, Nwankwo-Ifejika, hailed a new beginning:

> A new book by Chinua Achebe is always a literary event. But in the last five years he has been almost silent – the years of the Nigerian crisis and the civil war. Now he speaks again in a voice he has not used before, the voice of poetry. These poems written during the war and immediately after reveal eloquently a sensitive writer's agony. Few of the poems speak directly about war but they all bear the mark of its distress and tragedy. We predict that Achebe's poems will become the kind of literary landmark he achieved with his first novel in 1958.[2]

The public welcomed the book for Achebe's reputation had grown tremendously, but the critics had varied opinions. Perhaps Donatus Nwoga's review took the measure of Achebe's achievement best, for he stressed both the strengths and the handicaps:

> Achebe's achievement in this little collection of 23 poems has given a stamp of authority, different in its own type from that of Okot p'Bitek, to poetry of simple language, that is, poetry, the logical sequence of whose lexical and imagistic elements can be followed without too much difficulty ... the simplicity of diction is then given validity by, and proves an adequate vehicle for, a subtlety of vision. The relaxed narrative movement, often prosaic, becomes the technique of a mythopoeic imagination ... the novelist in Achebe has not been completely submerged to the poet here....
> [T]here is a definite advantage to rhythmic movement of words and the poems in *Beware, Soul Brother* have unfortunately been deprived of this joy. The apparent irregularity of traditional verse is only a camouflage; the performance to dance or in solo recitation supplies the rectifying rhythmic and dramatic qualities to which the written poem has no access ... it is as if Achebe refused to be a poet and yet arrived at the peak of poetic purpose. *Beware, Soul Brother* is a significant contribution to African poetry. Its subjects and the humanism of its outlook enlarge our understanding of our recent past and give a warning on our future. Its varieties of tone – reflective seriousness, direct neutral statement, witty sarcasm, straightforward humour – enhance the entertainment of reading the poems. Above all, the subtlety of proverbial statement in simple language offers a valid alternative mode to creative talents not inclined by temperament or training to the older tradition of modern African poetry.[3]

Nwoga's judgement was to be echoed in different ways by other critics, depending on their literary, social or intellectual persuasions. The appeal of the poems in other climes was positive, for an Irish poet wrote to Achebe after reading the collection commenting that he was full of envy, wishing that he or any of his fellow poets in Ireland could write such grave and moving lines about the Irish problems. He called the collection Achebe's 'best work' and also 'the best war poetry that has come out from anywhere in a long time'.[4] It was a commendation that provided satisfaction of a certain kind for Achebe in terms of discovering that his creative efforts were appreciated beyond the borders of his country and in spite of the fact that they had been inspired by events in his own locality.

Such sources of satisfaction did not blunt the sensitivity of Chinua Achebe to disconcerting events at the University of Nigeria, Nsukka where Professor H. C. Kodilinye had assumed office as the vice-chancellor. Achebe's disgust at insensitive administration led him to establish another magazine known as *Nsukkascope*, with the motto 'Devastating, Fearless, Brutal and True'. It was a necessary act considering the timidity of most academic staff when it came to criticism of the overbearing administrator. Conceived as an internal 'watchdog', the magazine had Achebe as editor, Emmanuel Obiechina as associate editor, Ikenna Nzimiro as circulation manager assisted by Okechukwu Emodi, and Chimere Ikoku as treasurer. In the editorial of the first issue, Achebe observes that

> *Nsukkascope* makes its appearance at a time when an increasing number of thoughtful people are seriously questioning the place, the priorities and the performance of our universities: when the reputation of our intellectuals is at a very low ebb and deservedly so, if we must be honest.

The editorial condemns the fact that in the 'secluded citadel' of the university 'corruption, philistinism, favouritism, clannishness and other vices flourish under 'the aegis' of the academics, which is why

> *Nsukkascope* is committed to a total war on these evils in the fervent hope that the leadership of our universities may be shamed into rising to its proper role of standard bearer in the life of the nation.[5]

The contents of that first issue of *Nsukkascope* fulfilled the requirements of its motto for Achebe's editorial criticized the vice-chancellor for living in splendour in the midst of squalor, and also for neglecting (in particular) 15 assistant lecturers ejected from makeshift, burnt-out rooms and (in general) the hardship of staff and students. The issue of the unmerited standing accorded the vice-chancellor's son, recruited as a lecturer in the Faculty of Law, demonstrates most of the vices mentioned in the editorial. Ikenna Nzimiro, in his contribution, argues that Nigerian universities must be relevant to the Nigerian situation and urges that qualified Nigerian academics be attracted to take up positions. He concludes that recruitment of foreign academics should be

> on grounds of academic suitability and not on racial grounds based on neo-colonial mentality. When we adopt our international policy, let us make sure that it is not racism reversed. The National University Commission has warned and believes that indigenization is possible so that while cherishing the international values of universities, we shall not remain subservient to influences that are inimical to our security and national pride.[6]

Nzimiro's essay is also a response to some of Kodilinye's statements concerning his concept of a university.

A much more gloomy picture of the university is presented by Chimere Ikoku. Ikoku points out that the departments of chemistry, biochemistry, microbiology and pharmacy need both laboratory buildings and laboratory equipment, and that the inadequacy of the available accommodation is compounded by the large number of students. In addition the supplies of electric power (unavailable) and of water (inadequate) are said to exacerbate the problem. Ikoku suggests that the priorities of the university must be defined and the desired infrastructure provided through the setting up of a committee on reconstruction and development. He insists that the committee should recommend effective ways of erecting prefabricated laboratories and that basic research tools must be provided.[7]

An unsigned essay, 'The Plight of a Junior Lecturer', confirms the gloomy picture Ikoku presents for it describes the acute hardship experienced by some members of the academic staff as a result of lack of accommodation and the insensitivity of the administrators. In the editor's note at the end of the essay, Achebe writes that

> it is good to know that some accommodation has now been found for these members of staff. We think, however, that they should never have been subjected to this embittering experience. And we think also that UNAUT [University of Nigeria Academic Union of Teachers] ought to have come into this. It is the only way to break the barbaric tradition of leaving every man either to fight for his own rights or else seek succour through midnight conclaves of clan-heads.[8]

The other essays in *Nsukkascope* pursue the same line of attack. Emmanuel Obiechina's essay 'Just How Different are the Dons?' accuses the academics of exhibiting culpable subjectivity and harbouring superstitions incompatible with humanity, while Okechukwu Emodi, in 'Towards a Critical University', calls for a university community that is not swayed by sentiments and personal, selfish motives. The last item, 'A Focus on Faculties', is signed by a 'roving correspondent' who highlights the travesty of justice in the Faculty of Law in which Mr Kodilinye, the son of the vice-chancellor, is unfairly placed higher than Dr Otuka and Mr Ngoh.

The contents of that first issue of *Nsukkascope* emphasized Chinua Achebe's courage in fighting for justice, honesty and truthfulness. Again he had challenged a frontier, at a time when it was quite easy for critics to lose their jobs and when, with young children in his family, Achebe needed to be much more circumspect financially. But he was not deterred as he confronted a vice-chancellor who had constituted himself into a 'Lord of the Manor', with several stipulations as to how and when the academic staff could seek his attention.

It was clear that the administration at the University of Nigeria, Nsukka was becoming unpleasant to many members of staff. In September 1971 Chukwue-meka Ike, the registrar, resigned and accepted an appointment as the registrar of the West African Examinations Council, which had jurisdiction over Sierra Leone, Nigeria, Gambia and Ghana. Chinua Achebe persevered, however, hoping that his critical observations would influence the development of the university while he continued his editorial work for *Okike, Nsukkascope* and Heinemann Educational Books. At about this time he was visited by James Currey of Heinemann at the University of Nigeria, Nsukka.

> I remember visiting him in his house on the university campus which, like all the other houses on the campus, had blackened walls – there was no electric light, the whole university was a shell and had been through various military occupations. It was then that Chinua said, 'Look, during this period I've been unable to give you as much advice as I would have liked to have done. I think it should be handed over to another, and I would suggest that Ngugi be the adviser.'[9]

Achebe felt that he had made his contribution to the establishment of the African Writers Series and that, partly as a result of the reputation of the series, it was no longer an aberration to mention in other parts of the world that African literature existed. He had offered selfless service, for Alan Hill acknowledged that Achebe's 'ten years' editorship was entirely unpaid'. Heinemann Educational Books thus reluctantly accepted Achebe's decision that he relinquish the editorship the following year, 1972. Before James Currey departed they had also reached an understanding that Achebe would publish a collection of his short stories with Heinemann Educational Books.

In November 1971, *Bullfrog in the Sun,* the film version of *Things Fall Apart* and *No Longer at Ease*, was released by Calpenny Films. Like the first Calpenny production, based on Wole Soyinka's *Kongi's Harvest*, the film became contro-versial. Soyinka, who had played the lead role in the first film, had 'disowned' it; but the reaction to *Bullfrog in the Sun* was based on broader social factors. It was criticized by the Nigerian embassy in Bonn for portraying only the unpleasant side of Nigeria. Achebe was not satisfied with the adaptation, especially since the film incorporates aspects of the civil war which are not part of the novels. It was an ambitious project by Calpenny but it would have been a much stronger film if the socio-historical events had been woven into the story more skilfully. The juxtaposition of historical events and other narrative sequences, not to mention some of the technical problems, must have irritated not only Achebe but many other viewers familiar with the novels on which the film is based. Part of the problem with the screenplay by Fern Mosk, who also served as one of the executive producers with her husband Edward Mosk, was the desire to make the story contemporary. Achebe's lack of enthusiasm for the production did not make him a bitter antagonist, however, for he accepted the fact that the producers made use of their creative freedom.

Meanwhile he continued his literary activities at the University of Nigeria, Nsukka, where *Okike* No. 2 appeared in December 1971. It was another interesting issue with several poems, short stories and book reviews. Achebe's poem, 'Remembrance Day', explores the hypocritical contriteness exhibited at ceremonial 'remembrance days' for those who lost their lives in the service of the nation. He also published a short story, 'Civil Peace', which captures the uncertainties of life associated with the violence prevailing after the civil war. Achebe shows in this story the resilience of Jonathan Iwegbu, the major character, whose optimism at having survived the war with his wife and three of his four children alive is not affected by either the visit of thieves, who rob him, or the derelict state of his little house, abandoned during the war. Achebe depicts not only the spirit of survival that animated the people during the war but also the unintended dimensions of the violence that the war unleashed. In the end, though, it is Iwegbu's indomitable spirit that has the last word. He says after the robbery: 'I say let egg-rasher (*ex-gratia*) perish in the flames! Let it go where everything else has gone. Nothing puzzles God.'[10] That conclusion could also be said to reflect the kind of optimism exhibited by the staff and students at Nsukka who were making their own efforts to recover from the devastations of the war, despite the discouragement offered by the insensitivity of their vice-chancellor.

That discouragement was what Achebe and his *Nsukkascope* colleagues set out to eliminate. In January 1972 the second issue of the magazine appeared; with 70 pages, it was twice as big and considerably more varied than the 33-page first issue. In the editorial of this second issue Achebe writes:

> We would not say that we expected the birth of *Nsukkascope* to go unremarked – that would be dishonest but – neither did we anticipate the fall of comets. We are gratified by the enormous interest which we have stirred and are deeply touched by the many demonstrations of solidarity we have received.... Since the appearance of *Nsukka-scope* No. 1 a number of changes have occurred on the campus for the better. We do not wish to take credit for them (credit means nothing to us) neither shall we be lulled to contentment for a lot still remains to be done.[11]

Part of that refusal to be lulled, those many things needing to be done, were demands for more doctors at the university medical centre, for renovating the buildings of the centre, and for the provision of public toilets in the university.

Several letters either praising or criticizing *Nsukkascope* were published: A. U. Essien, an assistant registrar, praises the aims of the editorial committee but also admonishes them to be objective; Moses Ofodile, a porter, insists that *Nsukkascope* should be banned; a writer who signs himself 'Parrot George' from the Enugu campus of the university asks for diversification, while Otonti Nduka, who writes from the University of Ibadan, congratulates the editor and affirms that 'several of the *Scope*'s strictures are applicable to the academic communities in other parts of the Federation'.[12] It was a mark of Chinua Achebe's liberal attitude as an editor that he published dissenting views and it was also a practical demonstration of his personal philosophy that different shades of opinions must not be emasculated. All the same, the essays published were in the spirit of the magazine's objectives. E. N. Obiechina concluded his study of the dons and emphasized that they were clowns in fancy costume, amenable to genteel bribery, opportunistic and too self-centred to assert their rightful authority over the non-academic staff. That issue of the magazine was enlivened by the inclusion of poems by E. N. Obiechina, A. O. Morah and Dubem Okafor, in addition to two unsigned cartoons. Chimere Ikoku in his essay 'Appointments, Promotions and Staff Development: The Need for a New Look' offers both analyses and suggestions on how to improve the appointments and promotions procedure in the university, while E. N. Obiechina and Ikenna Nzimiro examine the collegiate system planned for the university. Their 24-page essay comprehensively examines the vice-chancellor's document and concludes that the important task that must be accomplished first is the provision of the basic but essential infrastructures. In a short essay, 'Four Types of University Intellectuals', Ikenna Nzimiro identifies the Progressives, the Conservatives, the Intellectual Ordinary Men and the Liberal academics, indicating their various characteristics. He regards the 'progressive intellectuals' as the tiny minority that 'possess the intellectual courage needed to uphold scientific objectivity and to defend truth'. This second issue of *Nsukkascope* certainly fulfilled the expectations of more readers and consolidated Chinua Achebe's reputation as a fearless editor.

Soon after the publication of *Nsukkascope* Chinua Achebe travelled to England in February 1972. It was a visit organized by Heinemann Educational Books and involved a celebration and the promotion of the hundredth book in the African Writers Series.[13] That book, appropriately, was *Girls at War*, Achebe's volume of short stories. As usual Achebe was sought out by several journalists wanting interviews. 'I don't charge into things frontally,' he told Paddy Kitchen. 'This is the first time I have travelled out since the war ended.' Nevertheless it was a hectic visit with Achebe granting three interviews and engaging in several other literary activities. Paddy Kitchen comments insightfully that 'writers do not usually experience either success or tragedy on so large a scale as Chinua Achebe' but he also adds that

> Achebe carries his mantle as the best-known African writer with an energy and responsibility that it is a pleasure to encounter. He appears to have not an ounce of conceit or temperament but gives himself up to the task in hand with total concentration.[14]

This remark was to be echoed by many others as the decade progressed. It was the creative work *Girls at War* that had brought him to London, however, and this was what attracted the attention of critics. The thirteen short stories in this collection range from short works Achebe wrote as an undergraduate to recent civil war stories. They had appeared in various journals, magazines and books, and many of them were written during the period when Achebe's major work was taking shape. It is thus possible to trace through them some of the themes and issues that had animated his first four novels. The more recent stories have a wartime setting and the title story explores the tragic effects of that horrendous conflict on morality, womanhood and ideals as a result of material deprivation and starvation. Achebe, as usual, writes with great economy of words while making the most impact with them.

The Heinemann celebration was a success and Achebe returned to Nigeria emboldened in his resolve to continue his creative enterprise. He now started work on a new novel with a basic plot involving four characters, but the story was not moving as he expected and since he usually wrote carefully and slowly he pushed the work aside and tackled other social and academic issues. At this time Nwankwo-Ifejika now renamed Nwamife Publishers, published *How the Leopard Got His Claws* which Achebe had written in collaboration with John Iroaganachi. There were now four people involved in the book: Achebe, Iroaganachi, Okigbo and the illustrator. It was through contact with some Norwegian acquaintances who had shown an interest in Biafra during the war – when the Scandinavian countries in general had been sympathetic to the embattled nation –

> that a Norwegian Firm decided to publish the story and they commissioned Per Christiansen, a leading illustrator of Norwegian children's books, to do the pictures. And then the Norwegians printed the book, though it was published in Nigeria.[15]

How the Leopard Got His Claws certainly had a chequered history and its publication in 1972 by Nwamife was the fulfilment of a five-year hope. It was also a reminder that Achebe was expecting Nigerian publishers to take the lead in producing relevant books, and of his continuing concern over the country's reading culture. In 'What Do African Intellectuals Read?', an essay published in the *Times Literary Supplement* of 12 May 1972, Achebe contemplates that disconcerting problem of reading habits.

Achebe admits in the essay that time is a limiting factor for the intellectual but he also insisted that the reading habit has not been cultivated. According to his private research a decade previously, 'Africans who went to the Library (at Enugu) did not go in search of literary pleasure'. He is forced to acknowledge that the literary background of 'today's African intellectuals', many of them 'eminent in their various academic disciplines and professions' is not encouraging. Although Achebe confirms that 'things have greatly improved' with books 'much more widely available in schools and public libraries', he also points out that 'the African intellectual's knowledge of the West (and he knows a lot more about the West than the Western intellectual knows about Africa) comes to him not from literature but from personal contact', since 'African intellectuals are among the most widely travelled in the world today'. Achebe believes that first-hand contacts between African intellectuals and the West 'are bound to decrease in significance as the overall population of African intellectuals increases and as African universities become more and more Africanized'. He speculates that in the future 'the African intellectual will come to rely for his knowledge of the West on myths and stock images from that kind of popular literature which most easily crosses cultural frontiers' and he hopes that 'this may be somewhat offset by a greater knowledge of himself, and of Africa, from his own literature'.[16] About thirteen years later Achebe was to discover through a newspaper controversy that his hope was still to be fulfilled. The essay is notable in that it marked a stage in his writing career when he turned his attention to general critical discussions in which he subjects prevalent notions and views to logical analysis.

An invitation from Dartmouth College in the United States afforded Achebe another opportunity to examine some of the controversial issues associated with modern African literature in terms of reading, language and the African intellectual. That invitation was extended to Achebe in order to confer on him an honorary Doctorate of Letters, awarded because

> whether your books are read for their literary merit or as serious treatises on social problems, they have been universally acclaimed as masterpieces.[17]

It was the first honorary degree Achebe received; there were to be 23 more over the next twenty years. Achebe's lecture was on 'Language and the Destiny of Man' and in it he considers the relationship between language and the society, examining what he regards as the ominous threat of language manipulation. He invokes the value given to language and literature in African mythology and draws on the works of other distinguished writers to stress his theme. He ends by focusing on

> the great myth about language and the destiny of man. Its lesson should be clear to all. It is as though the ancestors who made language and knew from what bestiality its use rescued them are saying to us: Beware of interfering with its purpose; for when language is seriously interfered with, when it is disjoined from truth, be it from mere incompetence or worse, from malice, horrors can descend again on mankind.[18]

It is in the West that language is most vulnerable, and Achebe's lecture on language and society never strays far from simultaneously considering the relationship between the West and the rest of the world.

In lectures like this one and in his critical essays Chinua Achebe was beginning to construct a relevant vision for his continent. That fact also made him a magnet to many people who either sought his opinion, invited him to visit them or visited him at Nsukka. Joseph Bruchac, an American, remembers how vividly the talk flowed during his own visit to Nsukka in 1972:

> I recall very clearly a conversation which I had in Chinua's home in Nigeria during the summer of 1972. The topic of the behaviour of the Church in the war was brought up by Emmanuel Obiechina, an Igbo poet and critic. He pointed out that many people were distressed with the way the priests acted. When the Onitsha market writers, famous for their rapidly written, entertaining and ungrammatical pamphlets, returned to their presses at the end of the war one of the first books published was named *No Heaven for Priests*.[19]

In Achebe's case topical subjects and controversies received a typically measured treatment which respected the complexity of reality and the traditional Igbo philosophy of the dual perspective, the consideration of all the relevant human angles. That approach also continued to be reflected in his editorial work as *Nsukkascope* and *Okike* both appeared for the third time. The September 1972 issue of *Okike* carried contributions from Gerald Moore, Francis Wyndham, Edward Brathwaite, Keorapetse Kgositsile, Quincy Troupe, Obiechina, Nathan Nkala, J. Kariara and John Haynes. The most significant aspect of this issue was the publication of three young Nigerian writers: Osmond Enekwe, Maxwell Nwagboso and Odia Ofeimun. It was to the credit of Chinua Achebe that he published Ofeimun when he was unknown, speeding his recognition as a poet of some merit.

Editorial work was not without its trying moments, though Achebe never permitted personal irritations to obscure his vision or the purpose of his journal. *Okike* was thriving: it had received support from distinguished individuals. The South African Ezekiel Mphahlele called it a 'beautifully produced journal' with 'a superb format' and 'literary material alive and vital' while another South African, Dennis Brutus, commented that 'we need much more material of this quality and it deserves to be very widely known'. Edward Blishen of the BBC enthused that the journal gave 'plenty of reason for excitement'; T. C. Nwosu labelled it a 'literary *tour de force*' and Molly Mahood found it 'full of good things'. The Nigerian *Daily Times* thought that it would serve as the 'pace-setter for African writers'.[20] Such praises encouraged Achebe for he also had to contend with perplexing reactions from some contributors:

> A young Nigerian poet living and teaching in New York sent me in Nigeria a poem for the literary magazine I edit. It was a good poem but in one of his lines he used a plural Italian word as if it were singular. And there was no reason I could see for invoking poetic licence. So I made the slightest alteration imaginable in the verb to correct this needless error. The bright young poet instead of thanking me wrote an angry and devastating letter in which he accused me of being a grammarian. I didn't mind that, really it was a new kind of accusation. But in his final crushing statement he contrasted the linguistic conservatism of those who live in the outposts of empire with the imaginative freedom of the dwellers of the metropolis. At first I thought of replying but in the end decided it was a waste of my time. If I had replied I would have agreed with him about our respective locations, but would have gone on to remind him that the outposts had always borne the historic role of defending the empire from the constant threat of the barbarian hordes; and so needed always to be awake and alert, unlike the easy-going, soft-living metropolis.[21]

Achebe, turning the incident into a joke, nevertheless thought it illustrated 'the predicament of the African writer in search of universality' who 'has been misled into thinking that the metropolis belongs to him'. Such encounters were often his lot as an editor and Achebe took them in his stride as he reflected on the varied aspects of creativity.

His own creative work demonstrated continuing experimentation in the ways he interrogated reality. In *Okike* No. 3 he published the poem 'Benin Road' and a short story 'Sugar Baby'. The story has a war-time setting and is a parable about unguarded desires. Cletus, the major character, has an overpowering yearning for sugar which leads him to lose his girl. As the narrator, Mike, weaves in the incidents to present the excesses of the characters and the humiliation of Cletus in his quest for sugar, the life of an immoral society coalesces as a single image. Achebe ends the story with the narrator's haunting comment:

> I realized how foolish it was and how easy, even now, to slip back into those sudden irrational acrimonies of our recent desperate days when an angry word dropping in unannounced would start a fierce war like the passage of Esun between two peace-loving friends.[22]

At one level this war story demonstrates Achebe's familiar concern with flaws in human nature that invariably lead to tragic events. There is evidence also of a philosophical attitude to reality clearly informed by a knowledge of Igbo oral tradition. An essay written at this time and based on his research at the Institute for African Studies gives a clear view of Achebe's philosophical interest in oral tradition. '*Chi* in Igbo Cosmology' ranges over the connotations and denotations of *Chi* as he argued that 'we may visualize a person's *Chi* as his other identity in spirit land' and 'without an understanding of the nature of *Chi* one could not begin to make sense of the Igbo world-view; and yet no study of it exists that could even be called preliminary.' In devoting his attention to the analysis of that pervasive and elusive Igbo concept, Achebe was playing the role of frontiersman once again.

He argues persuasively that *Chi* as the personal god is significant, through the names that the Igbo people bear or give their children and also through the ideas associated with *Chi* in Igbo beliefs generally. He extends the argument further, however, to interrogate the name *Chineke* as consisting of two parts and hinting at the possibility of a duality of godhead. Achebe's conclusions are tentative, but they exhibit an attractive logical sequence:

> And finally at the root of it all lies that very belief we have already seen: a belief in the fundamental worth and independence of everyman and of his right to speak on matters of concern to him and, flowing from it, a rejection of a form of absolutism which might endanger those values. It is not surprising that the Igbo held discussion and consensus as the highest ideals of the political process. This made them 'argumentative' and difficult to rule. But how could they suspend for the convenience of a ruler limitations which they impose even on their gods? For as we have seen a man may talk and bargain even with his *Chi* at the moment of his creation. And what was more, Chukwu himself in all his power and glory did not make the world by fiat. He held conversations with mankind; he talked with those archetypal men of Nri and Adama and even enlisted their good offices to make the earth firm and productive.[23]

The provocative observations of Achebe in this essay inspired other scholars to re-examine that concept of *Chi* in Igbo cosmology and even in other cosmologies: it eventually became one of his most quoted essays. But then, Achebe's reputation as an insightful and perceptive essayist had grown; now he could expect to be quoted and even misquoted, but never ignored.

Another interesting 1972 essay was 'Africa and Her Writers' which he presented at the Eliot House, Harvard University. It is an essay that commences with an emphatic statement on the relevance of art in spite of some of the prevalent views in the West concerning art for art's sake. Drawing his illustration from the traditional *Mbari* ceremony in Nigeria, Achebe asserts that 'there is no rigid barrier between makers of culture and its consumers. Art belongs to all, and is a "function" of society.' In identifying this role for art Achebe criticizes the 'human condition' syndrome as he argues:

> presumably European art and literature have every good reason for going into a phase of despair. But ours does not. The worst we can afford at present is disappointment. Perhaps, when we too have over-reached ourselves in technical achievement without spiritual growth we shall be entitled to despair. Or, who knows? We may even learn from the history of others and avoid that particular fate. But whether we shall learn or not, there seems to me no sense whatever in rushing out now, so prematurely, to an assignation with a cruel destiny that will not be stirring from her place for a long time yet.

Achebe singles out Ayi Kwei Armah as 'a brilliant Ghanaian novelist' who seemed to him 'in grave danger of squandering his enormous talents and energy in pursuit of the *human condition*':

> In an impressive first novel, *The Beautyful Ones Are Not Yet Born*, he gives us a striking parable of the corruption in Ghanaian society and of one man who refuses to be contaminated by this filth.

Achebe, who had been teaching the novel, feels that 'Armah's command of

170

language and imagery is of a very high order indeed' but he regards the novel as 'a sick book' which 'is sick not with the sickness of Ghana but with the sickness of the human condition'. Its hero is

> pale and passive and nameless – a creation in the best manner of existentialist writing [who] wanders through the story in an anguished half-sleep, neck-deep in despair and human excrement of which we see rather a lot in the book....

If 'ultimately the novel failed to convince' him, Achebe concludes, 'this was because Armah insists that his story is happening in Ghana and not in some modern, existentialist no-man's-land'.

The flaw in the novel, according to Achebe, is that 'just as the hero is nameless, so should everything else be'. Thus Armah 'imposes so much foreign metaphor on the sickness of Ghana that it ceases to be true' with the result that the novelist 'is clearly an alienated writer, a modern writer complete with all the symptoms' while

> unfortunately Ghana is not a modern existentialist country. It is just a West African State struggling to become a nation. So there is enormous distance between Armah and Ghana.

Achebe perceives Armah as an 'alienated native' and part of that flaw he attributes to the desire of an African writer to appear universal as a result of the anxiety generated by the name, Africa, which 'can still call up hideous fears of rejection'.[24] Achebe also illustrates his call for relevance with the example of Christopher Okigbo, a poet who 'sometimes had and expressed confusing ideas while producing immaculate poetry'. The true test is whether an African writer's inspiration is derived from Africa: it is relevance in this wider sense that Achebe wishes to endorse.

Achebe's comments aroused Ayi Kwei Armah's indignation and he wrote several rude and abusive letters to Chinua Achebe. Although Achebe must have expected a reaction he had not foreseen the anger and abuse. It pained him that Armah had misconstrued the purpose of his criticism and taken it as a personal affair. Achebe explained many years later that he 'was not trying to put Ayi Kwei Armah down' but that he was 'simply hoping (Armah) would not distort the talent which (Achebe) saw by his imitating the style and bias of some other people, imposing on his art' what Achebe called 'the foreign metaphor'.[25]

The episode unquestionably demonstrated that Chinua Achebe would not shy away from addressing issues he regarded as germane to African literature, even when his contributions were liable to be controversial. Nor did such controversies hinder the appreciation of his views by those who read either his critical or creative works – as was shown when a new edition of *Beware, Soul Brother* was published by Heinemann Educational Books in London. In the United States Doubleday published the collection under the title *Christmas in Biafra*. Nwamife Books had published it in Nigeria in 1971; in the 1972 edition Achebe 'retained all the twenty-three original poems in the present volume though some of them have been revised, a few rewritten completely, and one given a brand new name'. He also pointed out that 'in addition there are seven later poems bringing the total in the present volume to thirty – a more rounded, and to the mind, more restful figure than twenty-three'.[26] The success of the new edition was immediately recognized in the award of the first 1972 Commonwealth Poetry prize. The judges felt that the collection was worthy and it was selected from a list of works published in many countries. Alastair Niven confirms that 'the Commonwealth Poetry prize attracts entries from every part of the Commonwealth. It has recognized known and unknown poets and encouraged critical comparisons across continents'.[27] This prize was an addition to the honours that had been flowing Achebe's way for more than a decade. They meant wider notice for his creative works and brought him further invitations from various countries and academic institutions.

Such an invitation now came from the University of Massachusetts at Amherst, who wanted him as a Visiting Professor. That invitation came in September 1972; that it was associated with Harvey Swados, the American writer and academic who had visited Achebe in Biafra, persuaded him to accept it.[28] He was reluctant at first, believing his presence at the University of Nigeria, Nsukka, to be essential to the 'watchdog' role of *Nsukkascope* in censuring the excesses of the administrators. His acceptance of the offer, however, was to enable him to distance himself for a reasonable time from an intolerable academic situation while demonstrating to his adversaries that he was qualified to take up a high academic position in a prestigious American university. The departure of several other academics at about the same time could be attributed to the continuing insensitivity of Vice-Chancellor Kodilinye. But Achebe meant to be away for just one year.

His sojourn in America also meant the uprooting of several projects like *Okike.* Christie Achebe and their four children travelled to America with him. That move also coincided with Achebe's decision to stand down as Editorial Adviser for the African Writers Series after ten years and one hundred titles. Achebe had suggested that Ngugi wa Thiong'o replace him. But Ngugi, after consideration, turned the offer down as he feared it would divert him from his own writing. From then on Achebe was referred to in new titles in the series and in the numerous reprints of earlier titles as the Founding Editor.

In November 1972, Heinemann Educational Books celebrated the occasion at the Athenaeum Club in London. Alan Hill recalls that

> leading critics and authors such as J. B. Priestley, C. P. Snow and Angus Wilson gathered to pay tribute to Achebe, who gave a characteristically modest and humorous account of the years of his editorship.[29]

Although Achebe sought to underplay his achievement it was clear to those present that his contribution to the establishment and nurturing of the African Writers Series had been very significant. Appropriately, Achebe was made a director of Heinemann Educational Books, Nigeria in 1972.

In that busy November he also visited Franklin Pierce College, where he spoke and read from his collection of poems. Don Burness recollects:

> Achebe had dinner at our house. I remember his comment to me very encouraging – 'You are serious. I know you'll do well.' To be serious has been for Chinua the only way to live.[30]

His seriousness meant commitment to African values that were in danger of emasculation and degeneration in the bustling events of the 1970s. Achebe was also energized by the euphoria in America. When he was there in 1972

> it was pretty close to the 1960s, to the era of the Civil Rights Movement. There was the feeling that America was on the move. There was a lot of optimism and all kinds of new programs to bring the disadvantaged into the society.[31]

In Massachusetts, he found himself requiring a different approach to teaching from the one that had seemed most appropriate at the University of Nigeria, Nsukka. Moreover, as word got around invitations from prominent people and academic communities flowed in. His year at Amherst arose from a joint invitation extended by the English Department and the W. E. B. Dubois Department of Afro-American Studies. Although formally he was employed by the English Department he also had an office in the Black Studies Department. African Literature was generating a lot of interest although Africa was still a marginal notion to many people in America and Europe.

> I found that you couldn't isolate the novel from the poetry or the drama, or for that matter from the politics of Africa. So I found myself teaching a course on Africa seen through its literature. And I made sure that I always included works from Anglophone and Francophone areas as well as major works written in African languages.

It was a demanding responsibility, especially when the teaching was combined with the editorial work on *Okike* and creative writing. Fortunately the university derived its major satisfaction from the fact that Achebe's presence in the institution enhanced its reputation, and though the standard load for each professor was three courses Achebe had the privilege of teaching only one to a wide audience. He described that audience as consisting of

> American students, black and white, and members of staff. The American system is much more flexible than ours. They go all out to broaden the outlook of their students. You would not find only literature students in your class but all kinds of people; people from Mathematics, from Sciences and I found it quite challenging, I must confess.[32]

Achebe had hardly settled down at Amherst when one of his hosts, Harvey Swados, suffered a heart attack. His friend's illness affected Achebe keenly, and his sorrow deepened when Swados died in December 1972. Lyn Innes remembers her second encounter with Achebe at that time:

> I met Chinua Achebe again in December 1972. I had gone from Tuskegee in 1970 to work on a PhD at Cornell University, on a comparative study of Irish, African and Afro-American cultural nationalism, with a chapter on *Things Fall Apart*. I had applied for a teaching job at the University of Massachusetts, Amherst, and being aware that Chinua was there, sent this chapter with my letter of application. I was invited for an interview in early December and was asked if I would like to see Chinua. Of course, I did. He was very gracious concerning the chapter I had sent, and I think was helpful in encouraging the English Department to offer me an Assistant Professorship.... At the time [Chinua] was deeply grieved by the severe heart attack of Professor Harvey Swados, a close friend and supporter of the Biafran cause, who had also been instrumental in bringing him to Massachusetts. Harvey Swados died that week. I was particularly struck by Chinua Achebe's kindness in setting aside his own personal distress in order to see me and discuss my work.[33]

That ability to set aside his own pain in order to ameliorate the pain of others was exhibited several times during his sojourn in America, especially when news reached him of the deaths of various people in Nigeria. But now he was also accustomed to death as an inevitable part of life as he began to adapt to the rhythm of life in America with the dawn of 1973.

The rhythm was brisk, with invitations from several quarters and more responsibilities in his own home. Three of the children – Ikechukwu, Chinelo, and Chidi – were old enough to attend school, but the responsibilities that involved were minor compared with those incurred by the much younger Nwando. A new issue had arisen in the Achebe family which ensured that Chinua was exposed to the normal responsibilities associated with the nurturing of children. Chinua Achebe cites that development as one of the positive effects of the war in Biafra:

> The role of women in the society was very clearly demonstrated by the problems of the war. And thinking back on this, it is nothing new really, because women have always had an important role. It is just that in peaceful times people are not thinking about such things, but in a situation of stress, such as the war, the important things become highlighted.... One of the most interesting things I have noticed among the Ibo people since the war is the desire of the women to go back to school. Large numbers of housewives are going back to school with their daughters. At the end of the war my own wife, who is a teacher, went back to school for her Masters.[34]

That decision by Christie Achebe, which eventually led to her acquisition of a doctorate some years later, introduced Chinua Achebe to the responsibility of caring for Nwando. Nwando was

> just two and a half, and it was quite a problem, because I was teaching and my wife was anxious to do her doctorate in education, so we found her a little nursery school – and she hated it. I don't know why. I had the job of driving her there. She refused to speak English.... She refused to talk to her teachers and we realized that she was putting up a fight for language. So in the end, I promised to tell her a story every morning as we went to school and another story as we came back. She would look forward to this – and this was the way she overcame the trauma of the first alien experience.[35]

Another positive dimension of that experience was that it made Chinua Achebe aware of the implications of those folktales he told his daughter and he realized the need to refashion such stories, modernizing and embellishing them, and this led him five years later to publish more work for children.

Thus Achebe's teaching experience in America had two dimensions; the private one in his daughter's world and the public one in the university. He notes some of the virtues and weaknesses of the educational system he encountered:

> In America you are dealing with students who are coming out of a tradition where Africa is not really like anywhere else they know: Africa in literature, Africa in the newspapers, Africa in the sermons preached in the churches is really the other place. It is the Africa of *Heart Of Darkness*: there are no real people in the Dark Continent, only *forces* operating; and people don't speak any language you can understand, they just grunt, too busy jumping up and down in a frenzy. This is what is in the minds of these students as they come to African Literature. So I find that the first thing is to familiarize them with Africa, make them think that this is a place of *people*, it's not the Other Place, the opposite of Europe or America. This is quite a task. But once you've done it – going into the history of Africa, showing how this is something that could have happened to anybody – the reaction is quite often interesting. I remember a white American boy who came to me very tense, after reading *Things Fall Apart*, and saying 'This Okonkwo is my Father!' Now I'd never in my wildest dreams thought of Okonkwo as a white Anglo-Saxon Protestant! But this is what literature is about and why it's worth doing. Otherwise why go to America to teach African literature.[36]

That identification with a literary character created out of a different cultural context was very instructive. It was flattering, but it was also an affirmation of the fundamental unity in human affairs. That unity also emerged in an interesting inter-disciplinary context, as Christie Achebe discovered:

> A teacher used *Things Fall Apart* to teach mathematics in America. They were using concepts deduced from the novel to discuss mathematical equations. In numerous seminars they also used the novel and these were not black but white institutions. They were able to ferret out information from the books.

Much of Achebe's time in 1973 was divided between making the information in his novels clearer to readers through his teaching and responding to the high demand for his presence at conferences. There were so many of these that he often had to present the same ideas in two or three places. It was the importance he attached to those ideas that mattered to him, however, rather than how often or how widely they were presented. In the spring of 1973 an annual seminar organized by the African Studies Program of the University of Washington featured African writers and musicians in a course on 'Literature and Music in sub-Saharan Africa'. The organizers felt that

> one purpose of opening up [their] restricted seminar structure was to demonstrate to some doubting Faculty and administrators that students from many disciplines and backgrounds were interested in African Studies Courses.

The guests who featured included Chinua Achebe, Kofi Awoonor, Wole Soyinka, Dennis Brutus, Abraham Dumisani, Kwabena Nketia, Rodney Valask and Suito Suso. There was also the Oboade Drum and Dance Ensemble. Karen Morell recalls that Achebe's lecture was

> attended by well over 500 students, faculty and citizens from the community. The questions afterwards came from all three groups. The following day Achebe taped a television programme for KCTS/9 (the Campus NET Station) during which he faced questions primarily from literature students.... Because of Achebe's international reputation as a writer and political figure [these students who] already numbered 180 sat in and were frequently the ones who were most persistent in pursuing their point of attack; in particular, more African students attended this session than any other.[37]

In another session Achebe was introduced by Simon Ottenberg, a professor of anthropology in the same university who had done much work on Igbo culture. He told the audience that here was a writer who 'has moved from being largely a literary person to also being a political individual'. Achebe's subsequent address, 'Africa and her Writers' was the one he had presented at Harvard University, but the response at the University of Washington was no less enthusiastic. There was also a gathering in the home of John Pauker, rightly called 'an exchange of poetry', in which Achebe read some of his poems and listened to poems from each of the American poets present. That exchange produced a by-product of Achebe's visit to Washington, for one of his poems was selected for publication in *New Republic*, edited by Reed Whittemore and John Pauker.

Poetry also featured in a television discussion in which Achebe participated during the University of Washington seminar. He read three poems from the American edition of his collection of poems, *Christmas in Biafra*. The fact that the poems he read centred on the war obviously generated questions on that terrible experience. Achebe also revealed that he had written poems in Igbo and explained the implications of such creative enterprises. The questions Achebe answered were wide-ranging. He maintained his view that art should be in the service of a community, while acknowledging the role of emancipated Europeans like Ulli Beier in the Oshogbo art tradition. From a member of the audience on this occasion Achebe learned that his novels and the novels of Cyprian Ekwensi were popular at one of the Seattle public libraries. Responses during the University of Washington seminar indicated that the affinities between African cultural groups were quite strong. This idea was amplified the following month in a paper Achebe presented at a Conference on African Writing held at Dalhousie University and Mount St Vincent University in Halifax, Nova Scotia in May 1973. It was a gathering that attracted writers from Canada, South Africa, Tanzania, Ghana and Nigeria as well as scholars and critics from Canada, France, Britain, the United States and the Caribbean. The conference was spiced with an evening session open to the public at which Achebe, Nadine Gordimer and Peter Palangyo read from their novels and short stories. Achebe gave an address which he entitled 'Thoughts on the African Novel' in which he confessed that he had resolved 'not to make any further pronouncements on the African novel or African literature or any of these large topics unless he dreamt up something really novel and spectacular to say'. Nevertheless, he agreed that 'perhaps the day-to-day thoughts and worries are just as important, being always with us'.

It is on those 'day-to-day thoughts and worries' that he bases his observations as he identifies the complexity of a creative mind as a novel is being written; he also mentions the salient issues confronting the African novel and the controversies associated with the language in which that novel is written. Achebe criticizes the notion that works of African literature are expected to imbibe what are erroneously regarded as universal issues. His illustration from the works of critics and his personal experience add an element of authenticity to his conclusion in which he emphasizes that

> all these prescriptions and proscriptions, all these dogmas about the universal and the eternal verities; all this proselytizing for European literary fashions, even dead ones, all this hankering after definitions may in the end prove worse than futile by creating needless anxieties.

He assures his audience that he has

> no doubt at all about the existence of the African novel. This form of fiction has seized the imagination of many writers and they will use it according to their differing abilities, sensibilities and visions without seeking anyone's permission. I believe it will grow and prosper. I believe it has a great future.[38]

This is a statement of hope from a practitioner who relies on his literary experience to interrogate current critical notions. Not for the first time, Achebe's contribution to debate on controversial issues and contentious literary attitudes emphasizes his dedication to the construction of a relevant vision for Africa, its literatures and its societies.

13

An American Expedition
New Light on the Heart of Darkness
1973–5

IN the years that Chinua Achebe resided in America in the 1970s, his appearances at conferences, seminars and other public academic occasions were marked by a conscious effort to present to his audience the idea that, in spite of technological progress in the world, there were still numerous vices that militate against the search for knowledge. It was probably this idea that made George Adams comment that Achebe's presence was bound to

> have many beneficial effects. He will leave behind a deeper and more sympathetic understanding among Americans of Africa's literature and, perhaps more important, of Africa's role in the world.[1]

Many miles away in France, Achebe was having an impact too, for Thomas Melone had written a critical study of Achebe's works, *Chinua Achebe et la tragédie de l'histoire,* which was published in Paris in 1973 by Présence Africaine.

Achebe certainly believed that literature and society needed to be understood together, which was why whenever he addressed an audience he encouraged his listeners to search for beneficial knowledge from works of African literature. He also pointed out that this search could be constrained by internalized preconceptions that were contradictory to reality, and that in the case of Africa such preconceptions often generated erroneous views and attitudes. It was not a defence of Africa but an attempt to present a reality that was not often accorded the respect it deserved. Thus even when Achebe spoke of his personal experiences the narration remained critical in spirit, forcing his audience to attend to the broader social perspective. One of those personal narratives was the autobiographical essay, 'Named for Victoria, Queen of England', in which Achebe describes the advent of the missionaries to Ogidi and the childhood experience which leads to the dropping of his English name, Albert. The insight gained through his education and acquaintance with books in the home helped to widen the implications of an Ogidi boyhood. The essay yielded critics an opportunity to glance beyond the structure of his novels and relate their interpretation to his personal experiences. That essay was one of the highlights of two weeks of intensive study and discussions of African and Caribbean literatures at the University of Missouri, Kansas City, 9–23 June 1973. Part of the activities there focused on a dialogue between Chinua Achebe and the Guyanese writer Wilson Harris. Reinhard Sander reports that

> it is true that creative and critical differences between those two outstanding modern novelists often seemed to hamper the intended dialogue between Africa and the Caribbean, but because of this encounter the participants were challenged to forget their preconceived, simplistic notions of Third World writers.

Sander adds that

> both writers participated throughout ... answering questions, reading from their works and attending more informal gatherings such as picnics, play and poetry readings, and the occasional party.[2]

It was a revealing conference for the participants and it further illustrated a growing dimension of Chinua Achebe's presence in America: as an expedition from Africa, its objective to inform and educate.

In a half-dozen interviews featuring Chinua Achebe, Michel Fabre was able to distil that aim to inform and educate, but with particular reference to the fictive vision of *Arrow of God*. To Fabre, Achebe revealed that *Arrow of God* was 'inspired in part by [his] desire to re-evaluate [his] culture' and that the title 'relates to how Ezeulu stands for the instrument, the weapon of the god he serves'. Citing appropriate examples from his tradition Chinua Achebe demonstrates that

> in Igbo traditional society there were built-in means of discouraging people from becoming too powerful or too rich, or rather of encouraging them to trade that power and wealth against honors and titles.

In recalling that tradition Achebe was at the same time revealing how a viable culture had been disorganized by foreign interventions which ultimately forced the people to adopt a world view and values that threaten their survival. Achebe also provides an insight into the ending of *Arrow of God,* especially with reference to the statement that 'thereafter any yam that was harvested in the man's fields was harvested in the name of the son'. Achebe reminds his audience that

> in general terms, the end of a story is only an end in one sense. It is a beginning in another sense because it is an open-ended kind of end. At the end of a page, another page is projected, like an echo or the pebbles you throw in a pond, and it goes on and on.

He explains, however, that

> This specific ending has all sorts of meanings for me. There is a suggestion of Christian ethics in 'the name of the son', nearly in a caricatural sense. There is a bit of parody there, but it is not really parody because Christianity is not a joke, and suddenly what will happen to the Ibo culture is not going to be a joke. But there is an even deeper possibility in which the harvest in the name of the son becomes a reversal of the natural order. In the society we have been looking at in this story, you do not do things in the name of the son but in the name of the father. The legitimacy is with the elders, the ancestors, with tradition and age. We now have a new dispensation in which youth and inexperience earn a new legitimacy. This is something new and different. Wisdom belongs to the elders but the new wisdom is going to belong to the young people. They are going to go to school, to go to church, and will tell their fathers what it is. This almost amounts to turning the world upside down. I think that Ezeulu

himself sensed it coming, he had some kind of psychic vision. This is why he sent his son to the British. Something told him that it might be necessary. He found some other explanations for doing it, but in fact he sensed what he was doing. This was confirmed the first time he was interviewed by the English administrator Clark, and Ezeulu looked up and the image in his mind was that of a puppy, something unfinished, half-baked, too young; and yet there was authority. Now, this reversal itself is tied up with the colonial situation. There is no other situation in the world where power resides with inexperience and young people. A young man would not approach the seat of power in England, but in a colonial situation he is given power and can order a chief around. In a very deep sense this reversal is the quintessence of colonialism. It is a loss of independence. These are some of the ideas that are implied at the end of the novel.[3]

It is very apparent from Chinua Achebe's response that he is capable of insightful interpretation of his own works. Although diffidence did not permit him to embark on such studies, his comments often reveal a number of hidden dimensions. Particularly interesting is his attitude to language through which we glimpse some of his creative motivations. He regards himself as a conscious artist because he 'often makes conscious attempts at recreating the turns and phrases of the vernacular while using English'. But he also insists that

> I do not feel much kinship, basically, with the English tradition although I use the English language. I have no thorough respect or worship for it. It is a very fine instrument, but not an object of ritual. I respect ritual but it tends to make objects irrelevant to present-day situations when it extends to areas outside religion.[4]

Several readers and critics have suggested that Achebe's characters experience a sense of failure. To the question, 'Why do your heroes always fail, as Ezeulu does?' Achebe answers,

> Now, I sometimes use the word 'fail' myself, and cannot blame anybody for using it. But I use it in a special way, because there is a very deep sense in which one can talk about Okonkwo or Ezeulu failing. It is a sense in which you see those two people standing for something. They stand for a way of life, a people, a vision of the world. Now, if a man knows what he stands for, it is difficult to say that he fails. However, both men succeed in much the same way Christ can have been said to succeed.... At the same time I am not sure that Okonkwo's or Ezeulu's set of values really die. The simple fact that we are telling their stories and that some people may think, 'Here is a man after my heart', means something, some kind of return or regeneration in the lives of their descendants. It is certainly hasty to apply words like 'failure', you know.[5]

The essential truth of that remark is demonstrated in the persistent interest in the stories of those characters, and once again we find Achebe the writer in debt to Achebe the critic. This would not surprise Lyn Innes:

> When I joined the English Department at the University of Massachusetts in September 1973, I also began attending the course in African literature taught by Achebe. The writers covered included Senghor, Okigbo, Awoonor, Ngugi, Soyinka, Armah and others. Because the students insisted, he also included one or two of his own works, although he usually asked someone else to conduct the class in which they were taught (I remember Professor Joseph Skerrett taking a class on *A Man of the People* and I took one on *Things Fall Apart*). This did not please the students, however, who wanted to hear about the novels from the horse's mouth.... [In the following year] Chinua Achebe took the class on *Arrow of God*. This was most illuminating, and despite his feeling that his novels ought to speak for themselves, or

with the help of other critics or readers once he has written them, I have to say that in this case Chinua Achebe seemed to me far and away his own best critic.[6]

Lyn Innes attended Achebe's class out of interest, while at the same time she was one of his colleagues: she was thus in a good position to appraise his influence on the students.

Chinua was a most conscientious teacher. The classes were always carefully prepared, and he provided useful information and stimulated plenty of interest from the students. I particularly remember the classes on Okigbo, Awoonor and Soyinka's poetry as being packed with information and insights and have continued to find the notes from them useful in my own teaching.

Those class discussions certainly involved the students and their teacher in a dialogue that was necessary for an appropriate assimilation of significant aspects of African literature.

What impressed me also was his extraordinary patience with the students, whose questions about works by himself and other African writers often revealed dreadful racist assumptions, and all too often they insisted on reading these works as anthropological texts rather than as poetic or fictional creations. Rather than dismiss such questions or respond with annoyance, which would have been most understandable, he always attempted to use the occasion to educate and help the students understand more clearly what their assumptions were and where they were leading, never humiliating the students in the process.[7]

Obviously Achebe was conscious that a major part of the problem was ignorance and the uncritical assimilation of prejudiced notions and views from the newspapers and television. His expedition in America, and particularly in the teaching situation, was geared towards performing the delicate task of a frontiersman in a cultural environment where people have internalized unpleasant ideas and must be confronted with appropriate knowledge in order to initiate a dialogue that will contribute to changing their views gradually.

That role of frontiersman with its sometimes daunting responsibilities depended on the kind of people Achebe encountered. He was in Australia in the summer of 1973, and interacted with writers and students there. Of his meeting with A. D. Hope, one of Australia's leading poets, Achebe recollects that

He said wistfully that the only happy writers today were those writing in small languages like Danish. Why? Because they and their readers understand one another and knew precisely what a word meant when it was used.

Achebe had not thought of it that way, believing that 'the English-speaking Union was a desirable fraternity', but he now realized that

there was an important sense in which [A.D. Hope] was right – that every literature must seek the things that belong unto its peace, must in other words, speak of a particular place, evolve out of the necessities of its history, past and current, and the aspirations and destiny of its people.

It was this awareness that made Achebe mentally prepared for the reaction of another Australian.

On another occasion, a student at the National University who had taken a course in African Literature asked me if the time had not come for African writers to write about 'people in general' instead of just Africans. I asked her if by *people in general* she meant *like Australians*, and gave her the bad news that as far as I was concerned such a time would never come. She was only a brash sophomore [and] expressed herself with passionate and disarming effrontery.

Nevertheless Achebe was convinced that

this girl was only making the same point which many 'serious' critics have been making more tactfully and therefore more insidiously. They dress it up in fine robes which they call universality.

Reviewing his Australian journey, Achebe adds:

I hope I do not sound too ungracious. Certainly I met very many fine and sensitive people in Australia, and the words which the distinguished historian, Professor Manning Clark, wrote to me after my visit are among the finest tributes I have ever received.

Clark had written

I hope you come back and speak here, because we need to lose the blinkers of our past. So come and help the young to grow up without the prejudices of their forefathers.[8]

It was testimony from a sensitive mind who had perceived reality, in Achebe's words, from a neglected perspective. Such encounters enabled Achebe to understand many prevalent misleading impressions concerning African literature and also provided opportunities for him to point the minds of other people in unexplored directions.

Lyn Innes recalls that Achebe's office in the African Studies Building was 'the headquarters for *Okike* magazine and where he most frequently worked'. After Achebe asked her to help with *Okike*, she 'worked in the office one or two days a week with Kathy, his secretary'.[9] Thus was *Okike* successfully transplanted in Massachusetts, where the fourth issue of the journal came out in December 1973. That issue carried an apology which explained that

Okike has not appeared regularly in the last one year. The problems that caused this are now happily over and with this issue the magazine will be published thrice a year.[10]

In *Okike* No. 4 there were book reviews by Omolara Leslie and Kalu Uka; short stories by Anele Ebizie, Ossie Enekwe, John Munonye and Rasheed Gbadamosi; essays by Chinweizu and Ezekiel Mphahlele; and poems by Curtis Lyle, Quincy Troupe, Enekwe, Chinweizu, Ifeanyi Menkiti, Jayne Cortex, John Pauker, Ihechukwu Madubuike, Jenudo Oke, Micere Githae-Mugo and Chinua Achebe. The Achebe poem was entitled 'Flying' and Innes recollects seeing early drafts:

Once when I was working in the *Okike* office alone and looked into the waste paper basket to see if an address I needed was on an envelope I had just thrown away, I discovered draft after draft of a poem Chinua had been working on – 'Flying', I believe, – and realized how carefully and meticulously he wrote and polished his work before it was published.

Perhaps that was why work on his fifth novel was not proceeding as fast as he desired, although his busy schedule and interactions with numerous people may also have affected his writing. Certainly those who worked with him at this time remember it as a positive experience

Chinua treated all those who worked with him with a deference and courtesy unusual in the States ... or anywhere else for that matter, and I think Kathy [the secretary] felt that was an important and efficient part of the *Okike* enterprise. The office was a centre of work, discussion, occasional social gathering for others in the Africana Studies Centre – Michael Thelwell, the novelist and critic, John Bracey the historian, Esther Terry who taught drama and produced a dramatic version of *Things Fall Apart* at the University Theatre, Nelson Stevens, an artist whose work was sometimes printed in *Okike*, Irma McClaurin, a young poet and teacher who was to become the United States representative for *Okike* when Chinua returned to Nigeria. Letters and contributions came from many well-known authors – John Updike, Ezekiel Mphahlele, Doris Lessing, Nadine Gordimer.[11]

Achebe's presence was sufficiently magnetic for the university to consider retaining him as a permanent member of staff as 1973 drew to a close. Achebe was not so overwhelmed by such attention, however, as to neglect his main intellectual preoccupation: this was consciously and consistently to refine a vision of reality based on his Nigerian and African experience. He thus accepted an invitation to attend a conference at the University of Ife, Nigeria, in December 1973. It was an International Conference on Publishing and Book Development which attracted several participants from African countries, Europe and the United States of America. In Achebe's paper, 'Publishing in Africa: A Writer's View', he asserts that there

> is a tendency when we speak of books to forget or to give inadequate thought to the simple fact that our central purpose is a dialogue, or the desire for a dialogue, between writers and their readers, that everybody else in the business is a facilitator.

Nevertheless, Achebe agrees that

> our primary concern this week [16–20 December 1973] must centre on publishers because that is what we have been invited to talk about but also, I think, because a publisher is really more crucial than the other intermediaries ... [because] the crucial decision of whether this particular book is to be or not to be belongs to the publisher [and] the publisher is the primary go-between from writer to reader in what I see as a dynamic social artistic relationship.

He then locates his view of the publisher's role within his evolving vision of the writer and his community:

> If I am not entirely deluded in my vision of the writer and his community moved together by a common destiny; of the artist and his people in a dynamic, evolving relationship, if I am not totally misguided, then the go-between, the publisher, must operate in the same historic and social continuum.... What we need is an organic interaction of all three elements – writer, publisher and reader – in a continuing state of creative energy and in which all three respond to the possibilities and dynamics of change.

Achebe calls on the local publisher in Nigeria to 'learn from others' and at the same time 'make his own way in the world', especially in seizing 'upon the peculiar characteristics of a place and [making] them a strength for his task' while his 'book-keeping should be so scrupulous that writers will not hesitate to place their manuscripts in his care or booksellers to do business with him'. Achebe also asks established writers 'to support indigenous publishers who display the necessary qualities of intellect, creativity and organization', before ending by pointing to the need for state support even in a 'free-enterprise African setting' and while recognizing the positive and negative aspects of state publishing.[12]

Participation at that conference enabled Achebe to meet several individuals like the man he regarded as a 'bright academic from Tanzania' who was saying, 'Well, socialism in Tanzania, it's got its negative aspects.' Achebe recalls that when the Tanzanian began to recite those negative aspects he said to him:

> Look here, this matter comes down very simply to this: would you prefer to have Tubman of Liberia running your country? This was before the old man's death; he happened to be on my mind at the time, for although presiding over a country with perhaps the lowest *per capita* income in the whole world, Tubman had just purchased for himself the most expensive yacht afloat. So it comes down to this: would you like Nyerere or Tubman?[13]

That exchange emphasized Achebe's appreciation of genuine attempts at leadership: he looked in vain for these in Nigeria at the end of 1973 as he travelled to other parts of the country visiting relatives and friends. Evaluating the military government in Nigeria, he could not help perceiving some of the excesses of those associated with the Gowon regime. It was disheartening to notice a new spirit of opportunism in the country, especially with the boom generated by the oil wealth which was leading the military leaders to dream up many grandiose projects and feeding corruption in the transactions related to those projects. Achebe was saddened that the enormous opportunity for development offered by oil wealth was likely to be frittered away. He sent an open letter to the newspapers which was published in the mass-circulation *New Nigerian* in 1974. He deliberately chose this publication strategy in order to reach the military establishment, which was said to regard the *New Nigerian* with respect.

It is a critical letter in which Achebe admonishes not only the leaders but also the people for he argues that the only protection the people have against the worst ravages of corrupt government 'is a vigilant populace' and that the country is a long way from 'having a citizenry that can compel probity in the management of national affairs'.[14] Achebe also criticizes the hypocrisy, self-deception and timidity of the citizenry. His letter greatly encouraged the few opposition voices that had been raised occasionally in the country. It was clearly the aptness and courage of those remarks that made a Kano businessman tell A. P. J. van Rensburg that 'Achebe stings, but he's beautiful. He has alerted a lot of us to what is going on around us and changed our thinking about priorities.'[15] The sting noted by the businessman was not an idle metaphor, for Achebe criticized any aspect of social behaviour he considered anomalous, especially corruption. His criticism of corruption and abuse of power was informed by a personal experience. As he revealed some time later:

> A girl from Lagos got my address from a newspaper and wrote to me at the University of Massachusetts to help her gain admission to a University in the United States. She had little mathematics and less science. But she had a Federal Government scholarship to study engineering! I think that a country which can do this kind of thing to itself has probably gone beyond mere inefficiency and corruption into absolute cynicism.[16]

While Achebe was contemplating disconcerting realities at home, he also found himself compelled to address issues of continental scope, especially in the area of literatures from Africa. One continental forum was the Association for Commonwealth Literature and Language Studies conference in Kampala, Uganda in January 1974 which Achebe was invited to attend. It was the fourth conference of that association since its foundation in England in 1964, when Achebe had also been a keynote speaker. In Kampala he presented a paper on 'Colonialist Criticism' which, as usual, created much interest with the participants reacting in varied ways. Achebe's views are presented in a manner likely to affect even the most insensitive critic, which must account for the constant stream of references that resulted. He fears that his use of the word 'colonialism' in his title may be inappropriate because it is 'associated in many minds with that brand of cheap, demagogic and outmoded rhetoric' which rests on 'a tendency to blame other people' and also because 'it may be said that whatever colonialism may have done in the past', it has 'become a symbol of a new relationship of equality between peoples who were once masters and servants'. The latter-day colonialist critic 'sees the African writer as a somewhat unfinished European who with patient guidance will grow up one day and write like every other European.' While

> most African writers write out of an African experience and out of commitment to an African destiny. For them that destiny does not include a future European identity for which the present is but an apprenticeship.

Thus he criticizes the idea of creating 'universal' African literature as well as the cultivation of self-contempt in some African novels as part of that colonialist perspective. At the same time Achebe protests that 'meanwhile the seduction of our writers by the blandishments of colonialist criticism is matched by its misdirection of our own critics'. One of the major flaws he identifies is the fact 'that the colonialist critic, unwilling to accept the validity of sensibilities other than his own, has made particular point of missing the African novel' with 'lengthy articles to prove its non-existence largely on the grounds that it is a peculiarly Western genre, a fact which would interest us if our ambition was to write "Western" novels'. Instead of prolonging Western parochialism, he suggests,

> let every people bring their gifts to the great festival of the world's cultural harvest and mankind will be all the richer for the variety and distinctiveness of the offerings.[17]

Achebe's conclusion does not deny the achievements of the responsible and insightful foreign critic but it intimates that there is a need to rid criticism of prejudices and also racist notions. The paper aroused very strong reactions and two differing responses best illustrate the areas of contention. H. H. Anniah Gowda regards Achebe's criticism as 'very sober advice and a mighty challenge for critics from all the ex-colonial countries',[18] while Kirsten Holst Petersen with obvious irritation pronounces that

> in the political field the African has every right to lay down the law about foreign behaviour in his country (like everybody else), but in the field of literary criticism he must – like everybody else – admit that he has not sole copyright to the thoughts expressed by his literature and that he therefore cannot prescribe what others are going to think and write about it.[19]

Ironically it was the prescriptive element in 'colonialist criticism' that Achebe had chosen to attack. Despite the controversy, Achebe had illuminated the issues he raised and also helped to advertise the fact that African writers possess varied views. He returns to the theme of that variety when describing an aspect of the conference later:

> We were talking about Ayi Kwei Armah (incidentally, I object to being classed with

Armah and Ouoloquem on the matter of commitment, because we are committed to different things, completely). The argument was on Armah's *The Beautyful Ones Are Not Yet Born* and the whole generation of young people at this conference said, 'Oh, he is committed, he is a committed writer.' This was going on for some time, so I asked, 'What is he committed to?' And then there was silence, for about two seconds – it completely threw them, as you would say. Then somebody with presence of mind thought very quickly while the others were still confused and said, 'He is committed to social change.' And I said, 'Ah yes, he is committed to social change.' Well, that is a nebulous thing to be committed to. Social change from what to what? I mean, to be [merely] committed to social change doesn't help. You must find out what is going on in the society. Even in anger you must feel kinship to your society, not alienation from it.[20]

The expression of such strong views inevitably created antagonists. But Achebe felt convinced that, if his views were justified, such antagonism would not detract from that justification.

If evidence were wanted that his views as well as his creative works were relevant to the African continent, it could be found in the fact that more and more Africans were attaching importance to them. An experience at Kampala airport after the conference brought this home forcefully to Achebe. It was about midnight when he walked through the lobby carrying his travel bags in order to board a plane on his way to the United States. He handed his ticket to the woman at the check-in with the words: 'I am going to Boston, USA.' The woman accepted it routinely and then something struck her for she suddenly shouted the name she read in disbelief. 'Chinua Achebe!' It was the African writer in blood and flesh. That shriek attracted even those at the control tower and everything virtually came to a standstill. Some minutes later Chinua Achebe found himself surrounded by porters, clerks, other travellers and even customs officers who were alerted by the clamour of the check-in woman. Achebe was pressed to enjoy a drink while the crowd regaled him with their impressions of the novels, short stories and poems that he had written. It was an encounter that made clear to him the nature of his literary responsibility to the tens of thousands of readers of his books in Africa who were among the hundreds of thousands worldwide. Such encounters made Achebe committed to the positive use of his literary works in the interest of Africa, which accounted for the strong views that sometimes aroused controversy. Another of these strong views was expressed at a ceremony in Stockholm.

Achebe and the other guests had come to honour Heinrich Böll, the Nobel prize winner. One of the members of the Nobel committee said something which Achebe found unpleasant. He was annoyed and he told the man off. A friend of Achebe's was amazed and reminded the writer that the man he had just told off was very powerful because he was a member of the Nobel Academy and 'he is one of those who control the Nobel prize'. Achebe's reply was succinct: 'And so what?'[21] Such reactions did not always endear him to influential people but then his acquiescence in a derogatory remark made in his presence would have amounted to a clear abdication of his moral responsibility as an African who was present in the audience. It was the same characteristic candour that he exhibited when he visited London in early 1974 for a question and answer session under the auspices of the Africa Centre. He said on that occasion that in spite of the fashionable insistence that henceforth African writers must only produce works in African languages, 'the first step towards that goal should be to teach these languages in schools and colleges'. He also informed his audience, however, that he had written some poetry in the Igbo language. It was in that forum, too, that Achebe predicted that 'literature from Nigeria will bear marks of the civil war' which he felt formed 'part of the twentieth-century phenomenon'. In reaction to a question on whether he would write a novel about the United States, Achebe answered that he did not think he would 'feel able' to do it in spite of his observation that 'the novel in the United States is doing what it should not do and people are losing patience with it and turning to journalism'.[22] The answers from Achebe were candid and his remarks relevant which made that visit to London important, although his primary objective in coming to England was to honour an invitation from the University of Southampton.

Explaining his university's decision to honour Achebe, the academic registrar of the University of Southampton speculates that

> it is unusual for Southampton to confer an honorary degree on someone who had no Southampton connections whatsoever. The citation does not indicate that there was some special link with Dr Achebe. However, the then Vice-Chancellor, Professor L. C. B. Gower, had worked in Nigeria. From 1962–65 he was Adviser on Legal Education in Africa to the British Institute of International and Comparative Law; Adviser to the Nigerian Council of Legal Education; and Dean of the Faculty and Professor of Law in the University of Lagos. It may be therefore that the connection in this case was Professor Gower's link with Nigeria.[23]

There were others at the University of Southampton, however, who had a good knowledge of Africa and Chinua Achebe, as the citation which preceded the award showed. The Professor of Modern History, J. C. Bromley, gave an inspiring oration prefaced by an amalgam of interesting quotes from Achebe's fiction.

> The least that can be said of him, as our Vice-Chancellor knows, is that he has rendered signal services to education in Nigeria.... Achebe's novels explore with difficult and often terrifying candour, the fractures in ancient cultures, the contemporary confusion of values and alienation of intellectuals in a pluralistic society whose people have responded to change at an uneven pace and in conflicting styles.... Achebe holds strongly that art has everything to do with real life; he is deeply committed to the cause of salvation. And yet his art brings each generation and all kinds of men, himself included, to judgement.[24]

Deservedly honoured, Achebe went back to the United States where his intellectual objectives, resolutely African, continued to declare themselves even in quite ordinary incidents.

> A young Nigerian woman doing a higher degree in America said to me, I hear you teach Tutuola? It was not a simple statement; her accent was heavy with accusation. We discussed the matter for a while and it became quite clear that she considered *The Palm Wine Drinkard* to be childish and crude and certainly not the kind of thing a patriotic Nigerian should be exporting to America.[25]

Such incidents provided Achebe with the 'raw material' of ideas that he elaborated in his essays, as another incident illustrates:

> In the Fall of 1974 I was walking one day from the English Department at the University of Massachusetts to a parking lot. It was a fine autumn morning such as encouraged friendliness to passing strangers. Brisk youngsters were hurrying in all

directions, many of them obviously freshmen in their first flush of enthusiasm. An older man going the same way as I turned and remarked to me how very young they came these days. I agreed. Then he asked me, if I was a student too. I said no, I was a teacher. What did I teach? African literature. Now that was funny, he said, because he knew a fellow who taught the same thing, or perhaps it was *African history* in a certain community college not far from here. It always surprised him, he went on to say, because he never had thought of Africa as having that kind of stuff, you know. By this time I was walking much faster. 'Oh well', I heard him say finally, behind me: 'I guess I have to take your course to find out.' A few weeks later I received two very touching letters from high-school children in Yonkers, New York, who – bless their teacher – had just read *Things Fall Apart*. One of them was particularly happy to learn about the customs and superstitions of an African tribe.[26]

Reflecting on the encounter and the letters, Achebe points out that

the young fellow from Yonkers, perhaps partly on account of his age but I believe also for much deeper and more serious reasons, is obviously unaware that the life of his own tribesmen in Yonkers, New York, is full of odd customs and superstitions and like everybody else in his culture, imagines that he needs a trip to Africa to encounter those things.

He adds that 'the other person being fully [his] own age could not be excused on the grounds of his years and that 'ignorance might be a more likely reason; but here again … something more wilful than a mere lack of information was at work'. That wilfulness Achebe identifies as the desire or the need

in Western psychology to get Africa up as a foil to Europe, as a place of negations at once remote and vaguely familiar, in comparison with which Europe's own state of spiritual grace will be manifest.[27]

It was that tendency that Achebe often questioned as he visited other cities and talked to numerous audiences.

He also found time to engage in creative writing, for a revised edition of *Arrow of God* was issued in 1974. In the preface Achebe reveals that it was the novel he was likely to be caught reading again and in the process he had become aware of 'certain structural weaknesses' which he has taken the 'opportunity of a new edition to remove'.[28] The changes include the provision of additional information for some characters and settings; a modification of syntax to reflect emphasis and word order; the reconstruction of some phrases and the removal of some wordy explanations. Some of those changes reflected a desire by the novelist to make the statements more accurate or to improve the English words. There was an artistic pruning of words which eliminated the few obvious indications of attempts to explain the Igbo words to a foreign audience. The changes enhanced the development of the themes and the dramatic delineation of character. Bruce King asserts that

while the themes, characterization and narrative form have not changed, the second edition is better written, technically more satisfactory and focuses more on the drama of individual emotions than on reporting community life.

He argues that

the author of the revised edition is a more mature craftsman, less concerned with explaining local culture to Europeans; he has a more secure control of English and relatively, is more interested in the drama and role of his main character within a period of cultural transition.[29]

The revision illustrated that Achebe was not averse to criticism and that he often subjected himself to self-criticism. That attitude was what had enabled him to perform the function of editor for the African Writers Series and *Okike*. It was an attitude impossible without tolerance and patience and reminds one that Lyn Innes said of him at Amherst that 'he was patient and tolerant in social gatherings'. Innes explains:

> I remember a dinner party at which the host announced that he would advocate that each member of his department be allotted a salary rise and 'thirty-five native girls'. Embarrassed and annoyed by the sexism and racism inherent in this light-hearted remark, I glanced across to Chinua, to see him catch his wife, Christie's eye, and raise his eyebrows ironically. However, neither of them made any remark at the time, the 'joke' passed without comment from any one else, and Chinua and Christie have, I believe, remained on friendly terms with the host and his wife, who are in many ways generous and good people.

Achebe was likely to have made a private rather than a public admonition and his anger would emanate publicly only when that effort failed, unless it was a matter of delivering an 'urgent antidote to a festering wound'. Innes adds that she remembers another dinner where

> Chinua was addressed rather persistently by an American Professor of English who kept asking him whether he should not disapprove morally of the tactics of the [kidnappers of] Patty Hearst, the Californian heiress. Chinua calmly but very pointedly replied that he was not an American and could not speak for or be held to account for the activities of Americans, black or white. He also commented that in cases of survival, the usual notions of morality could not always be relevant.

Innes doubts whether

> the Professor took either point, and he did not seem to see that his assumption that all 'Black' people could be lumped together and assumed to think in the same way was a problem.

She also reveals that the man

> was one of the many English Professors upset by Chinua's public lecture attacking Conrad's *Heart of Darkness*, a novel which, as Chinua pointed out, was probably taught more frequently than almost any other in the United States university courses.[30]

That public lecture would be delivered in 1975, some months in the future. Meanwhile, Achebe produced a sixth issue of *Okike* in December 1974 and included in it his poem, 'The Old Man and the Census'. The poem is a satirical discussion of the amazement created by the census figures: after a civil war the population is still notably higher, not lower. Achebe has the old man reflect that

> decimation
> by miscount however grievous
> is a happy retreat from bolder uses
> of the past

– obviously referring to the misuse of census figures in the 1960s and the attempt to reduce the population of some ethnic groups through massacres. Achebe predicts in the poem that even in the future 'depending on which Caesar orders the count',

new conurbations
may sprout in today's wastelands
and thriving cities dissolve
in sudden mirages.[31]

That prediction of mirage cities and people was to be fulfilled years later when another census exercise was conducted, and the poem as a whole indicates the writer's keen awareness of political events in his country in spite of his residence in America.

The same issue of *Okike* carried a controversial article by Chinweizu, Onwuchekwa Jemie and Ihechukwu Madubuike, 'Towards the Decolonization of African Literature', also published in *Transition* edited by Wole Soyinka. The opening sentence of the article launched its major thesis:

There is a failure of craft in Nigerian poetry in English. Despite the high praises heaped upon it from all sides, most of the practitioners display glaring faults e.g. old-fashioned, craggy, unmusical language; obscure and inaccessible diction, a plethora of imported imagery; a divorce from African oral poetic tradition, tempered only by lifeless attempts at revivalism.

They criticized some of the poems by J. P. Clark, Christopher Okigbo, Wole Soyinka and M. J. C. Echeruo. Their conclusion was that J. P. Clark 'has a few glaring faults' but 'he attains no great heights either', 'whereas Soyinka begins with the brilliance of "Telephone Conversation" and descends to the contorted opacity of "Idanre", for Okigbo the journey is from the first foundering steps of "Heaven's Gate" to the assured stride and sweep of *Path of Thunder*'.[32] The crux of the essay is a suggestion that an infusion from the African oral traditions would enhance the creation of modern African poetry. The impact of that essay endured; it was quoted increasingly in other journals and in university communities in Africa. Clearly *Okike* had created a rupture and African literary criticism was destined not to be the same again after the appearance of Chinweizu, Jemie and Madubuike.

But 1975 also brought new honours for Chinua Achebe, as the Scottish Arts Council awarded him their second annual Neil Gunn International Fellowship in succession to Nobel Prize Winner Heinrich Böll, adding to the honour in 1974 (some months before) by the Modern Language Association of America which elected him an honorary member, placing him in a select group of only forty persons who represent the highest level of achievement in world literature. It was destined to be a year in which Chinua Achebe would be remembered for the range and power of his literary contributions. On 18 February he delivered the second Chancellor's Lecture at the University of Massachusetts, Amherst. The Chancellor's Lecture series recognizes distinguished members of the faculty of the University of Massachusetts

and by providing an opportunity to reach a varied audience from the University community and beyond ... also serves a wider purpose in celebrating learning, scholarship and creativity, the intellectual values at the heart of the academic enterprise.

At the end, each participant is awarded the Chancellor's medal,

the highest honor bestowed on individuals who have rendered exemplary and extraordinary service to the University of Massachusetts at Amherst.[33]

On the reverse side of each medal is engraved the recipient's name and the date. Achebe's lecture, 'An Image of Africa', centred on racism in Joseph Conrad's

Heart of Darkness. Achebe suggests the novel reinforces a racist view of Africa, emphasizing the image of the continent as a place of negation that makes Europe's 'spiritual grace' manifest. Although many members of the audience had read the novel, very few had assessed fully the negative implications that the lecture highlighted. Achebe illustrates that

> *Heart of Darkness* projects the image of Africa as 'the other world', the antithesis of Europe and therefore of civilization, a place where man's vaunted intelligence and refinement are finally mocked by triumphant bestiality.

He draws attention to the use of derogatory adjectives by Conrad and comments that

> when a writer while pretending to record scenes, incidents and their impact is in reality engaged in inducing hypnotic stupor in his readers through a bombardment of emotive words and other forms of trickery, much more has to be at stake than stylistic felicity.

Achebe develops his argument through appropriate examples from the novel's setting, language and characters. In as much as 'the primary narrator is Marlow' whose 'account is given to us through the filter of a second, shadowy person' Achebe is convinced that if

> Conrad's intention is a *cordon sanitaire* between himself and the moral and psycho-logical *malaise* of his narrator his care seems to me totally wasted because he neglected to hint clearly and adequately at an alternative frame of reference by which we may judge the actions and opinions of his characters.

Achebe now confirms the uncompromising central thrust of his lecture:

> the point of my observations should be quite clear by now, namely that Joseph Conrad was a thoroughgoing racist. That this simple truth is glossed over in criticisms of his work is due to the fact that white racism against Africa is such a normal way of thinking that its manifestations go completely unremarked.

Even the argument that Africa is only a setting is perceived by Achebe as implicitly racist, for this is Africa as setting and backdrop which eliminates the African as a human factor, Africa as a metaphysical battlefield devoid of all recognizable humanity, into which the wandering European enters at his peril.

The real question is thus the 'dehumanization of Africa and Africans which this age-long attitude has fostered and continues to foster in the world'. Achebe ends by observing that 'in all this business a lot of violence is inevitably done not only to the image of despised people but even to words, the very tools of possible redress', and also that, though the 'work of redressing which needs to be done may appear too daunting', he does not believe 'it is one day too soon to begin' because 'Conrad saw and condemned the evil of imperial exploitation but was strangely unaware of the racism on which it sharpened its iron tooth'.[34]

It was certainly a disconcerting lecture and many of the English Department professors were upset. At the reception that followed the lecture, Achebe recalls, an elderly English professor walked up to him and said: 'How dare you!' and stalked away. Somebody else said to him: 'He is not talking about Africa. This is literature. You have no sense of humour.' However, he also remembered that a few days later another English professor said to him: 'After hearing you the other night I now realize that I had never really read *Heart of*

Darkness although I have taught it for years.'[35] The lecture and the reactions it elicited epitomized Achebe's American expedition, which was something like a missionary journey in reverse. This time it was a journey to break down the deaf walls of racist assumption in Europe, America and other parts of the world that he visited. It was also one of the prominent issues he discussed in his collection of essays, *Morning Yet on Creation Day*, which Heinemann Educational Books published in 1975. The fifteen essays were originally published or read between 1962 and 1974 and they illustrated that the basic convictions of Achebe as a writer had not altered drastically over that period. It was also clear that they had played an important part in literary and social developments in Africa. The journal *Research in African Literatures* carried a review of the book which notes that

> one of Achebe's favourite proverbs concerns the need to understand 'where the rain began to beat us'. This collection of essays will contribute much not only to our understanding of 'where the rain began to beat' but also to the building of a sturdier and roomier shelter.[36]

The publication of the essays enhanced Achebe's reputation further, as did another award that came his way at this time, the 1975 Lotus Prize for Afro-Asian Writers.

Despite his busy year – in March, for example, he was honoured with a 'Certificate of Appreciation for Outstanding Literary Contributions to Nigeria, Africa and the World Community' by the Nigerian Students Union of Pittsburgh – Achebe still found time to write an 'Introduction' to the South African exile poet, Keorapetse Kgositsile's *Places and Bloodstains* (*Notes for Ipelang*). In doing so he confirmed an abiding interest in the peculiar problems of apartheid South Africa. It was that same interest in apartheid, and commitment to eradicating it, which made Achebe accept an invitation to the first conference of the African Literature Association in Austin, Texas, in March 1975, where he spoke on Black South African literature. His paper stressed the political imperative in African literature by illustrating that even a writer who claimed to be apolitical was making a political statement, because a refusal to question the establishment was indirect support for it. He explained that the feeling of commitment operated through the same process for he argued that

> to play the game of the colonialist is not to be neutral; it is to be on the side of the colonialist. And I think we African writers are largely aware of this. It is only those who don't have our problem who are not aware of it. I mean if I were European, I think my position would be different, but from where I stand, I don't have an alternative.[37]

However, that conference was to offer an opportunity for a Nigerian graduate, Charles Nnolim, who was then launching a professional academic career, to meet Achebe. Nnolim described his motive at that meeting:

> When I met Achebe ... I felt encouraged to approach him. Did he know one Simon Nnolim, a former policeman in Enugu, I ventured to ask, and did he read his book entitled *The History of Umuchu* from which much of *Arrow of God* seems to have been drawn? Yes, he said, he knew him. He went further: he admitted that while working for the Eastern Nigeria Broadcasting Service he interviewed Nnolim in 1957[?]. He was visibly shocked to hear of his death. He reminisced that Nnolim and one Mr Iweka who wrote *The History of Obosi* (to which Nnolim himself alluded as the source of his inspiration to write a similar book) were rare people who collected invaluable

information that was of historical and anthropological interest. Nnolim had never mentioned the writer of *The History of Obosi* by name. Achebe filled in that gap for me. Achebe also added that he and the officers of the ENBS interviewed Nnolim in our home town Umuchu; that the object of the interview was Night Masks who performed for them; that they stayed about three nights in Umuchu; but he did not remember reading Nnolim's book.[38]

Nnolim, a brilliant but sensation-seeking critic, was to make a mountain out of that encounter. There was further communication on the issue in which Achebe who never had the reputation of a prolific letter writer wrote down details of his discussions with Simon Nnolim in 1958, especially with reference to the real-life Umuchu priest who was imprisoned by the white district commissioner and the subsequent inability of the priest to perform his duties. But Achebe underestimated the ambitions of Charles Nnolim, which became all too clear in an article the latter published in 1977. Meanwhile the conference which provided an opportunity for Nnolim and Achebe to meet came and went: it marked the origin of a radical association that was destined to grow positively.

There seemed to be no end to the honours bestowed on Chinua Achebe in 1975, for soon he was receiving an honorary doctorate from the University of Stirling. Alastair Niven comments on that award:

> As a consequence of the close interest in African literature and history at Stirling I was one of a number of people who proposed that Achebe should be given an honorary doctorate. Achebe came to Stirling where he renewed acquaintance with the then Head of the English Studies Department, Professor Tommy Dunn, whom he had known in Nigeria. I entertained Achebe in the house and began what I hope has been an occasional but genuine friendship.[39]

This was not the only doctorate to come the way of the Achebe family in that year. Christie Achebe graduated with a PhD in Education after completing her studies at the University of Massachusetts. Lyn Innes says that 'Chinua took great pride in his wife Christie's achievements, and held a party in her honour' and that 'Chinua himself did much of the cooking for the party, which had a large attendance.' This was not unusual, for according to Innes

> He enjoys the company of others, quickly puts others at ease, and is the first to enjoy a good joke, even one against himself (or especially one against himself).... He also took much delight in his family and friends, and I heard from him many stories about Nwando, his youngest, who was just beginning school when I knew him in Amherst.[40]

Nwando was a lively and questioning child who, Chinua Achebe recollects 'asked me why she didn't have *chi* in her name. She thought it was some kind of discrimination, so she took the name Chioma, which means Good Chi'.[41] It was an interesting sign of the rapport between Chinua Achebe and the members of his family. A similar rapport between him and his colleagues at Amherst made him 'a welcome guest at many parties, dinners and social gatherings in the academic community'.[42]

Thus his decision to accept an offer of appointment at the University of Connecticut in Storrs in 1975 was received without enthusiasm at Amherst, Massachusetts. The sadness was shortlived, however, when it turned out that Achebe was still within 'calling distance'. Clearly, many members of staff and students had felt enriched by Achebe's sojourn with them. Michael Thelwell,

Chairman of the Afro-American Studies Department, paid tribute to him. He pointed out that in Achebe's novels African people could read about their own culture from an indigenous perspective, and of the 'profound understanding' Achebe had opened up. Thelwell personally felt so close to Achebe intellectually that he named his son Chinua and that friendship has continued. Nevertheless, Achebe went to the University of Connecticut, Storrs, as University Professor of English in succession to the classicist Rex Warner.

14

Going Back to the Roots
Return to Nsukka
1975–9

ACHEBE commenced work at Storrs, Connecticut with the same energy he had shown at Amherst, Massachusetts. But it was clear that he was increasingly drawn by the political situation in Nigeria. A military coup had occurred on 29 July 1975 in which General Gowon, who was attending an Organization of African Unity (OAU) summit in Kampala, Uganda, was removed as head of state. It was a bloodless coup but the most striking aspect of it was the manner in which Murtala Ramat Mohammed, the new head of state, exhibited his leadership qualities. It was a radical departure from the flamboyance and pageantry of the Gowon regime. Mohammed had earned a reputation as a tempestuous officer but he operated as a distinguished head of state, announcing himself with the declaration: 'Fellow countrymen, the task ahead of us calls for sacrifice and self-discipline at all levels of our society. This government will not tolerate indiscipline. This government will not condone abuse of office.'[1] It was a declaration that Mohammed implemented with great determination. In Connecticut that change in leadership style was seen by Chinua Achebe as a more positive sign, although he still felt that military regimes were an aberration. There were also indications from the new military regime that it would accelerate the democratic processes towards handing over to a civilian government. In anticipation of that aim the *New Nigerian* newspaper in Kaduna serialized Chinua Achebe's *A Man of the People,* illustrating the novel through a series of specially commissioned drawings to remind people of their past. Achebe himself was in Nigeria to deliver the October 1975 lectures organized by the Nigerian Broadcasting Corporation in Lagos.

It became apparent as 1975 drew to an end that, even if he had shown other tendencies in the past, Murtala Mohammed really was a transformed soldier dedicated to the development of his country. Achebe wrote of that period several years later:

> On the morning after Murtala Mohammed seized power in July 1975 public servants in Lagos were found 'on seat' at seven-thirty in the morning. Even the 'go-slow' traffic that had defeated every solution and defied every regime vanished overnight from the streets! Why? The new ruler's reputation for ruthlessness was sufficient to transform in the course of only one night the style and habit of Nigeria's unruly capital. That the

194

character of one man could establish that quantum change in a people's social behaviour was nothing less than miraculous. But it shows that social miracles can happen.[2]

Achebe also knew, however, that to

effect lasting change it must be followed up with a radical programme of social and economic reorganization or at least a well-conceived and consistent agenda of reform which Nigeria stood, and stands, in dire need of.

Nevertheless, a few steps had been taken in the right direction and that realization increased his desire to return to Nigeria in 1976. Although he felt that the transformation of the society 'had begun to fade'[3] by February 1976, the death of General Mohammed in that month's abortive coup by B. S. Dimka was unwelcome news; it was also a terrible shock to many Nigerians. When the situation came under control, Olusegun Obasanjo became head of state. Obasanjo lacked the dynamism of Mohammed, however, and his announcement that he was taking over against his 'will and personal conviction'[4] symbolized the cautious, even timid nature of his regime in all parts of the country except the Eastern states, where he was blatantly overbearing.

Achebe was aware that a chance to transform the country had been lost even as he made conscious efforts to settle down at the University of Connecticut. Charles Owen, a professor in the same department, recalls that

Chinua Achebe and his family lived here and became a part of the community. I remember entertaining him and being entertained at dinner parties at our house and at his. He had a house on Storrs Road between the university's property and Four Corners, well back from the road.[5]

Another professor at Connecticut, Joseph Cary, valued Achebe as a colleague and an eye-opening critic.

My wife and I knew Chinua and his wife enough to have dinner together several times. She, a professional social worker as I recall, felt isolated in the little town of Storrs, and I don't think was very happy here. He, with his regular duties in our department, seemed less frustrated. But I think they both preferred to live in the livelier town of Amherst.... Chinua had given his marvellous lecture on Conrad's *Heart of Darkness* the year previous in Amherst and he gave me – a great admirer of Conrad and a frequent teacher of that story – a copy of it. I found it judicious and disturbing in what seemed to be its moral perspective, and I never again taught that tale without referring to Achebe's masterly reading of it. It opened my eyes and I've always felt grateful to him for doing so.[6]

In spite of making a positive impact, however, Achebe felt the need to return to Nigeria and informed the University of Connecticut authorities that he would not continue as university professor beyond the end of that academic year. The change in the administrative leadership at the University of Nigeria, Nsukka, where Professor Kodilinye had been replaced by Professor J. O. C. Ezeilo, was also an incentive, although Achebe had been promoted to the rank of professor many months previously under the old university regime. His American expedition had enabled him to overcome some painful memories, moreover, although he still reflected that he found it difficult 'to be coherent about the civil war' because 'there are some parts that are simply not possible to talk about. We just don't have those forms of words.' He also revealed that 'it is something that has affected one, and that one is trying to recover from, to come to terms with. I think the experience has left something in my conscience which is coming out all the time.'⁷ In 1975, in response to the question whether his stay in America was getting to him, he had told William Lawson:

> After a while anywhere you go you begin to respond to signals. But I haven't too much as yet, I don't think. That would be a warning to move again, because, I think, one can only handle so much. I mean, I don't really feel called upon to handle the American world. You only have one lifetime, you see. That's the way I operate, anyway.⁸

When that warning to move again was obeyed by Achebe the administrators at the University of Connecticut did not welcome the news; Rex Warner, the former university professor, had been there for ten years and Achebe had been expected to stay for another ten. Before he left for Nigeria the University of Prince Edward Island, Canada, made him an honorary Doctor of Law, citing his dedication as a creative artist to

> a land losing its heritage, losing its connection to the soil and its dedication to hard work, losing its young to the lure of the cities and the promise of easy money. He writes of an educated class who forget that they were once poor and refuse to aid their countrymen.⁹

This latest honorary degree was awarded by a university with the motto, Faith, Knowledge and Service, and service emanating from knowledge was what Achebe hoped to render to Nigeria on his return. In a short interview given on 27 June 1976, he told Ossie Enekwe that from the personal angle he expected to accomplish three things on his return:

> I'd like to complete the novel I'm working on. I had hoped to have at least the first draft ready here before going back. Secondly, I want to see the work of the magazine *Okike* developed in its natural soil, with people who share the same kind of vision as I have. Thirdly, I'd like to pursue my own understanding and study of Igbo culture, which excites me more and more every day.

In the same interview Achebe confesses that several factors have stimulated his desire to write a fifth novel, in spite of the impediments:

> I want to do what I believe is important. And so I've been thinking, I've been working out things in my mind, and part of it is the Nigerian crisis. I have to ask myself 'What happened to Nigeria? What happened to my relationship to Nigeria? What happened to the Igbo people in relation to Nigeria? And how are we going to deal with this future? Should this kind of thing ever happen again, how would we deal with it? How does Nigeria move on into this stage of evolution?' And these are very important questions. And I don't think you can answer them if you're busy churning out one novel after another.¹⁰

Thus Achebe was returning to confront the reality of his country: the devastations of the past, the anomalies of the present and the uncertainties of the future. It was a homecoming in which he sensed enormous advantages and disadvantages. John Agetua, who interviewed him soon after his return to the University of Nigeria, Nsukka on 16 August 1976, observes that the interview took place

> on the 2nd floor of an imposing, but rather old-fashioned building appropriately called *The Institute of African Studies*. In the background lay charred and damaged armoured vehicles, sad reminders of the bloody civil war. Chinua Achebe's office which was no more cheerful served to remind one of the hard times on which the University of Nigeria has fallen; all I saw in the name of furniture were a disconsolate fan, two rickety trays and equally rickety chairs. No more.¹¹

It was a far cry from the offices Achebe had used in America but this did not deter him. John Agetua's observation also illustrates that the much vaunted reconstruction, six years after the civil war, was fraudulent.

In the Agetua interview Achebe identifies some of the policy issues that could effect positive changes in the nation. Although he is responding to specific questions, his answers indicate clearly the underlying ideas that were agitating the mind of the writer. He feels, for instance, that 'given an enlightened government concerned about communal culture and aesthetic values, its role will be that of a patron of the arts', which makes him insist:

> Give artists the recognition due to them. Secondly, the government can set up in every state capital a museum and an art gallery. The museum will preserve our traditional arts and artifacts and the gallery will do the same for the outstanding work of modern artists so that we don't lose it all to European and American visitors and tourists. The government can create or encourage facilities for publishing books cheaply and competently in Nigeria so that our writers will not have to seek overseas publishers.

Among other fundamental issues Achebe discusses a view of history, seen as 'a growth, as a cumulative process in which we make use of the things in our past, even our mistakes, without waging war'. He criticizes the Nigerian intellectual for not being

> committed to the intellect but two things: status and stomach. And if there's any danger that he might suffer official displeasure or lose his job, he would prefer to turn a blind eye to what is happening around him.

At the same time Achebe was also critical of artists, for he was convinced that 'artists who say they do not care about communication delude themselves'. He expresses his hopes for the country:

> I would like a free and democratic Nigeria, I would like a Nigeria with a greater, much greater sense of social justice in which the disparity between the peasant and the well-to-do is much, much narrower.

Achebe insists that bad leadership cannot be excused because 'the man who is put there has undertaken this role of leader' and 'his role is to lead, to be a priest, to do all the things that his office demands. And as I said, I think that he can do more than we think by giving the example and the leadership.'[12]

The return of Achebe to Nigeria imposed diverse academic responsibilities. He was soon invited by S. O. Biobaku to contribute to a book on *The Living Culture of Nigeria*. Achebe wrote the essay 'Contemporary Literature', a survey of Nigerian literature which appeared when Biobaku's book was published in 1976. In the essay he highlights the problem of language and the vibrancy of the literature in assessing the achievements of Nigerian poets, novelists and playwrights. A much more challenging responsibility was his teaching role at the University of Nigeria, Nsukka, where he offered a course in modern African fiction. He discovered that the tradition of reading nurtured in his secondary school days was not practised in many of the secondary schools that produced the students admitted into the Department of English.

> To many students coming to the University, reading a novel is a huge chore. To plough through a novel is intimidating to many of them. Some will even run away to go to study linguistics because they imagine there is very little reading required there. So you have to coax them into literature. Many of them had never read before except for what they had to read for their school certificate.

That realization made Achebe adopt a new method of teaching:

> What I did was to introduce short stories, African short stories, that anybody could manage: the scope is small, the time required is small and there are some stories that can really trigger off discussion and interest. People could really come alive in discussing what happens in this story in a way that they would never have imagined before: they had thought of these stories as something dead, that you had to struggle to master. Once this was done with the shorter things then they were readier to tackle a longer novel.[13]

Achebe was not prescriptive, but operated on the principle that it was better to excite the imaginations of the students. The books he recommended reflected the wide expanse of modern African fiction from the East, West, North and South.

While Achebe was settling into this teaching towards the end of 1976 he was visited by a delegation from the organizers of the Second World Black and African Festival of Arts and Culture (FESTAC), scheduled for January 1977 in Lagos. The delegation informed Achebe that he should write the words for an anthem that would be used for FESTAC. Achebe, who was not in the habit of writing without proper reflection, was unwilling to engage in that exercise at such short notice, but he was pressured by the delegation and reminded that it was an act of national service. Part of Achebe's discomfiture was related to the fact that the organization of FESTAC had become very controversial with the altercation that attended the resignations of Hubert Ogunde and the popular musician Fela Anikulapo-Kuti. It later transpired that Fela Sowande, the musicologist, had been approached to provide the music for a FESTAC anthem and had insisted that he would do it only on condition that Chinua Achebe wrote the words, which was why the delegation had come to Nsukka. After much labour Achebe finally produced the words for an anthem and the delegation departed with a promise to send adequate remuneration. The words he had produced were not used, however, for in the tradition of waste that has characterized both civilian and military regimes in Nigeria the delegation discarded it on their return to Lagos. That did not stop Achebe from selflessly making both solicited and unsolicited contributions to the development of the nation as he became more fully involved in his academic duties at the University of Nigeria, Nsukka.

Many of the students found it exciting to be in his class and took pride in announcing to their colleagues that the famous novelist was their lecturer in the Department of English. The new university administration was equally interested in the presence of the novelist, appointing him to a disciplinary panel that investigated an examination leakage involving the Faculty of Law at the Enugu campus in 1977, a task that was accomplished to their satisfaction. Achebe was also appointed to the Anambra State Arts Council and nominated as external examiner for the University of Lagos, which took him to that city as often as his presence was required. On the campus, student organizations extended invitations to him to deliver public lectures, which he accepted depending on a schedule which now included acting as chairman of the Ceremonials Committee and as the university's public orator. That appointment meant that Achebe had to organize the Convocation ceremonies as well as writing and reading the citations on various individuals scheduled to receive honorary degrees. It was not an easy task: the public orator is expected to possess the clear delivery and commanding presence that make up the one clear impression formed by many of those who attend convocation ceremonies. These quite onerous responsibilities – the functions of the Ceremonials Committee and the public orator were later separated – did not deter Achebe from proceeding with his creative work and writing essays, according to his mood and inclination.

At about this time in early 1977 Charles Nnolim – who had discussed his uncle, Simon Alagbogu Nnolim, with Achebe during the African Literature Association conference in 1975 – found a way of drawing attention to himself as a critic. In an essay entitled 'A Source for *Arrow of God'*, published in *Research in African Literatures* of Spring 1977, Nnolim contends that

> although Achebe has never admitted it publicly the single most important source – in fact, the only source – for *Arrow of God* is a tiny, socio-historical pamphlet published without copyright by a retired corporal of the Nigeria Police Force. His name was (he died in 1972) Simon Alagbogu Nnolim and the title of his pamphlet was *The History of Umuchu.*

Nnolim adds that Achebe 'lifted *everything* in *The History of Umuchu* and simply transferred it to *Arrow of God* without embellishment', although he admits that Achebe 'fictionalized his source, created characters other than that of Ezeulu, and provided thematic and dramatic centres'. Nnolim then proceeds, leaving the realm of criticism well behind, to speculate – in spite of his interview with Achebe in 1975, in which the novelist informed him that he had met Simon Nnolim who told him the story of a real life incident – that 'it is very probable that Nnolim, being a generous man, had made a present of his book to Achebe'. Nnolim compares only five passages – consisting of a few sentences related to the amalgamation of Umuchu, the story of Umunama, the festival of the pumpkin leaves, the sacrifice of coverture (pregnancy curve) and the arrest of the chief priest – to establish his view. He nevertheless feels able to assert that 'it would only be fair to conclude that Achebe's *Arrow of God* is little more than a fictional expansion of *The History of Umuchu* by Simon A. Nnolim'. And he is emboldened to add that Achebe seems to have owed further debts to C. K. Meek's *Law and Authority in Nigeria* in writing *Arrow of God* and *Things Fall Apart*. This observation appears to be an afterthought, given his earlier conclusion that his uncle's work is the '*only* source for *Arrow of God'*.

Charles Nnolim is not totally insensitive to the nature of his assertions, for at the end he makes an attempt to qualify his remarks. Yet even then he cannot avoid what sounds like gratuitous insult:

> In conclusion, the reader must be warned that the foregoing is in no way intended to denigrate the great artistic achievements of Achebe as a creative writer and novelist. But my study does establish a few facts about Achebe and his sources. First, we must admit that Achebe is a careful researcher of his facts, which shows great intelligence, for no one has been able to complain that his depiction of Igbo society is distorted or falsified. Secondly, one must admit that it takes painstaking and diligent research to organize and bring alive such complex material. Thirdly, though Achebe is a great observer of Igbo cultural life, the evidence tends to show that his sources are not solely oral; Achebe did not write from personal observation alone, nor merely from a combination of personal observation and the great stories told him by his father and grandfather. He definitely made use of printed sources in writing *Arrow of God*.[14]

Achebe did not bother to reply to Nnolim for he felt that it was unreasonable to insist that the novel, *Arrow of God*, of 230 pages, is merely an expansion of a historical pamphlet (*The History of Umuchu*) of 17 pages. But in the wake of Nnolim's trenchant assertions other critics proceeded to examine the available material. Lyn Innes, in her article 'A Source for *Arrow of God:* A Response', published several months later in *Research in African Literatures* of Spring 1978, notes that the claims of Nnolim 'concerning overwhelming evidence' led her to

> read on with great interest and, indeed, some concern for the reputation of Achebe, against whom these accusations of artlessness, lack of creativity and failure to 'admit sources publicly' were being levelled. The evidence, however, was far from 'overwhelming'. Despite repeated statements by Nnolim that passages from *The History of Umuchu* were rendered 'verbatim' or 'set down almost verbatim' in *Arrow of God ...* on the contrary, they varied significantly in detail, structure, length and phraseology. In one instance only could it be argued that Achebe uses words very similar to those in *The History of Umuchu,* and these are the sacrifice of Coverture, words given by Simon Nnolim in Igbo. This comparison between Charles Nnolim's translation and Achebe's might seem more telling if one were not aware that such a ritual prayer would be widely known and also that Charles Nnolim has considerably altered his original's translation in order to make his point.

Innes argues that on 'the evidence of Nnolim's article alone, then, the charges of faithfulness to sources' and of 'lifting everything without embellishment were clearly disproved by the very examples compared'. Innes reports that she has

> read *The History of Umuchu* in both the original (1953) and revised (1976) versions. It is a fascinating history, full of details which one feels would have been of great interest to Achebe and which he might well have included in his novel had he known about them – the story of the six sons of Echu and the founding and history of the original six villages prior to amalgamation.

She concludes, however, that

> *only* those passages quoted by Charles Nnolim – a total of five pages – have any relevance to the rituals and events described in 230 pages of *Arrow of God*. That simple fact alone makes nonsense of the claim that Achebe 'lifted everything in *The History of Umuchu* and simply transferred it to *Arrow of God* without embellishment'.

Innes's dismissal of Charles Nnolim's article is admirably succinct:

> One of those sources [in the writing of *Arrow of God*] might have been *The History of Umuchu* but Charles Nnolim's claims that it is the only source and that Achebe must have had it before him as he wrote are unconvincing and irresponsible. Like Achebe's Ofoedu at the meeting to discuss the road labor, he appears to have 'opened his mouth and let out his words alive without giving them as much as a bite with his teeth'.[15]

Many critics felt that Innes had made an appropriate and telling response. Bu-Buakei Jabbi was another critic to respond, in an article that appeared in *African Literature Today,* the journal edited by the respected Eldred Jones. Jabbi finds that in Nnolim's essay

> an unfortunate ineptness in source attribution couples with a basic interpretative myopia to seriously mar what is otherwise an impregnable array of evidence for the historical authenticity of Achebe's background materials. Even his own account of the geography of Achebe's home town in relation to Umuchu, a plausible source of the elements of myth and ritual in the novel, is enough to discredit Nnolim's absolute certainty that Achebe must have had before him the pamphlet entitled *The History of Umuchu* as he wrote his novel. He has obviously grossly overstated his case.[16]

This controversy affected neither Achebe's teaching in Nigeria nor his reputation, for those who were interested examined the evidence and their conclusions did not differ materially from those of Innes and Bu-Buakei Jabbi.

The University of Massachusetts at Amherst, meanwhile, invited Achebe to return in order to accept an honorary degree. On 21 May 1977 he thus became a Doctor of Humane Letters: in the words of the citation, 'Few have made more powerful music with letters in any language, and few with such power have been more gently and truly humane.'[17] It was a fitting reminder and recognition of the contributions he had made during the years of his American expedition.

Back home in his native Nigeria, Achebe had mounted another kind of literary expedition, aimed in this case at arousing self-awareness in his fellow citizens. Through his course in modern African fiction he had discovered 'a certain condescension among [his] students towards Amos Tutuola's *The Palm-Wine Drinkard'*.[18] Achebe made efforts to counter such condescending attitudes, especially when students wrote in their essays that Tutuola was incapable of writing correct English. On one occasion he drew the attention of the other students to a grammatical error, in the very next sentence, by a student who had insisted in his essay that Tutuola was illiterate. At the same time Achebe moved beyond that elementary stage of nurturing the appropriate attitude to critical discussion by pointing out the importance of the artistic elements incorporated in the novel. It was thus not surprising that when Achebe was invited by the University of Ibadan to deliver the first Equiano Memorial Lecture on 15 July 1977 he should choose to speak on 'Work and Play in Tutuola's *The Palm-Wine Drinkard'*. Achebe points out that 'Tutuola's art conceals – or rather clothes – his purpose, as all good art must do' for it centres on what 'happens when a man immerses himself in pleasure to the exclusion of all work; when he raises pleasure to the status of work and occupation'. He suggests that '*The Palm-Wine Drinkard* is a rich and spectacular exploration of of this gross perversion, its expiation through appropriate punishment and the offender's final restoration'. Achebe explores that novel through the principle that 'Tutuola's moral universe is one in which work and play in their numerous variations complement each other', and that 'even a moderately careful reading of *The Palm-Wine Drinkard* reveals a number of instances where Tutuola, by consistently placing work and play in close sequence, appears quite clearly to be making a point'. The fulcrum of his study is that the Drinkard's fault 'is that he attempted to subvert the order of things and put play in the place of work. He does this because he has an appetite which knows no limit or boundary. His punishment is exact and appropriate.' Achebe also shows how the 'law of boundaries' operates in the novel in addition to the 'principle of unfulfilled promise' in various episodes. At the end he argues that 'relevance' is a

> word bandied around very much in contemporary expression, but it still has validity none the less. In *The Palm-Wine Drinkard* Tutuola is weaving more than a tall, devilish story. He is speaking strongly and directly to our times. For what could be more relevant than a celebration of work today for the benefit of a generation and a people whose heroes are no longer makers of things and ideas but spectacular and insatiable consumers?[19]

In the course of another public lecture, an incident occurred which illustrates another aspect of Achebe's new mission to raise the level of awareness – of the relation between art and life, this time. His novel *A Man of the People*, which predicts a military coup, had coincided with the 1966 January coup in Nigeria. The feeling that he had foreknowledge of the coup had thus been expressed in certain quarters, especially during the war. Achebe recalls:

> Long after the civil war I was questioned rather closely on this matter after I had given a lecture in one of our universities. Rather annoyed, I asked my questioner if he had read the book and he said vaguely yes. Did he remember, I asked him then, that before the coup in my story there was first a blatant rigging of an election, civil commotion in the land, murder and arson, which happened to be paralleled also by similar events in Nigeria before the January coup. Was he suggesting that I too planned those upheavals in Ibadan and elsewhere? Did he remember that my story specifically mentions a counter coup, a prophecy which, alas, was also fulfilled in Nigeria in July 1966. Was he suggesting that I sat in on the planning of that as well? In general, did he think that a group of dissident army officers planning to overthrow their government would invite a novelist to sit in on their plot, go back to their barracks and wait for two years while the novelist wrote up the book, had it edited and produced by his publishers, and only then spring into action and effect their coup to coincide with the book's publication? Such a theory might have been excusable in 1966 for the armed soldiers who had gone in search of me first to my office and then, fortunately, to a house I had already vacated. How could they know that the offending book had taken two years to write and publish? But a university teacher in 1977![20]

Achebe had never felt a need to distance himself from controversy: his reaction in this instance was motivated by the need to correct a blatant display of literary myopia by an academic in a citadel of learning. Such encounters made him realize the enormity of the task that he had to tackle in Nigeria, especially in terms of creating the appropriate attitudes in responding to intellectual challenges. He also realized that an academic capable of harbouring such misconceived thoughts was incapable of nurturing the young minds of the students properly. Above all he felt acutely the necessity of writing more books for such young minds, and especially for children, in order to inculcate in them essential moral, social and cultural values.

In 1977 he published two books for children, *The Flute* and *The Drum,* through Fourth Dimension, the publishing house in Enugu, Nigeria. The books were based on two folktales widely known in Igboland, but Achebe applied his artistry in their recreation.

> I have used oral tradition in two kinds of stories; one is called *The Flute.* Now this is the story of a child who forgets his flute on the farm. It is a fairly common story in Africa. When the child and his family reach home at dusk he remembers his flute and wants to go back for it. But that is not permissible. You see, the world is divided. Spirits have their own time. So if you go there at night, you are breaking the law of jurisdictions and you can expect all kinds of problems. So when this boy wants to go to the distant farm at night his parents beg him not to go. But still he does. And so in a sense this is a story about disobedience. And true enough, the boy meets the spirits. All of this is in the tradition. What is not there is the king of the spirits saying to the boy: 'Why did you disobey your parents?' Being a spirit, you see, he has seen far away right into the boy's home, before he came. So he says, 'What about your mother? Didn't she offer to buy you another flute on the next market? Why did you disobey your mother?' The boy looks down, he knows he is beaten, you see, he knows about disobedience. He rallies and says, 'That flute, I made it myself, it is the only thing that I could call my own.' Now I put that in, quite shamelessly, you see, because I think you require that kind of justification for disobedience. Children may not ask you, but it will be bothering them you know, if you tell them, 'You should obey your parents.'

Why is it that this boy didn't and yet he is rewarded in the end? Now I insist the question should be asked. So the boy gives a good answer and the spirit says indulgently: 'Well that is not good enough. But I like your spirit, I like your guts.' So the point is made that obedience is still the rule, but courage is also important. And we make the point that the song which the boy makes about his flute lying out there all alone, in the cold, is another saving grace. And so, making things – a flute or a song – adds to build up the story, I think. And that way, the idea of making things which I feel very strongly about is injected into the story without destroying it.[21]

That explanation illustrates that Achebe not only considered his use of narrative devices carefully, but also the moral purpose of the tales he adapted. The same creative vision was reflected in Achebe's second adaptation:

The other story I did for children is called *The Drum*. That again is from tradition, a traditional story about the doings of the tortoise during a time of great famine in the land of the animals. He goes in search of food; he's just wandering, miserably, and then he stumbles, by sheer accident, into the world of spirits, and he is rewarded with a drum that produces food. So the tortoise takes this home and beats it and feeds the animals. Now I decided to make a political story out of this, by making the tortoise want to use the power that he has over the other animals to attempt to become their king. And he is succeeding! One can see the kind of king tortoise would become from what is already happening, and the way he is carrying on. He sets up a committee for the Coronation, and makes the biggest animal his drum major! The elephant beats the drum too heavily and breaks it. It is a very desperate situation. The tortoise tries to patch it up but it won't work. So he says to the animals: 'Well, don't worry; after the coronation, I'll go back and get a new one.' But the animals reply: 'No drum, no coronation.' So the tortoise is compelled to go on a second journey which is faked and this is the whole point of the traditional story. Adventure, fine. Faked adventure, no. Because in faking it, all the things that happened by chance before are now contrived and false.... The tortoise goes away from spirit-land lumbering a heavy drum which he discovers on his way does not dispense food but assorted punishments – masquerades that whip, bees and wasps that sting. The tortoise decides when he returns home that it is only fair that the animals should share his unhappy experience just as they had shared his feasts. I don't think I have altered the meaning and flavour of the story. In my own estimation what I have done is to make it applicable to our situation today. And I believe that this is what the makers of these traditions intended to do – to tell stories that would be applicable to that day, and I believe these stories are evolving slowly through the millennia until our own time.[22]

That elaborate description of his creative enterprise highlights the fact that Achebe has never taken any aspect of his creativity for granted – a characteristic that critics have noted, among them Kate Turkington, whose *Chinua Achebe* (the fifth book on Achebe's works) was published by Edward Arnold in 1977.

In the same year he revised his collection of short stories, *Girls at War*, with the same creative carefulness, eliminating the undergraduate works 'Polar Undergraduate' and 'In a Village Church'. They were replaced by the war story 'Sugar Baby' which had appeared in *Okike*. He also edited further issues of *Okike* which had returned to its home environment at Nsukka. All these activities did not affect his teaching: a second set of students was now studying modern African fiction under him in the 1977/8 academic session. The first set of students, meanwhile, had discovered after the sessional examinations that Achebe was a very strict but careful and fastidious examiner who read their papers thoroughly before he awarded marks. Achebe also earned their respect through his modesty, for there was nothing about him of the flamboyance of film stars or other successful Nigerian personalities. The only thing that gave his success away was the impressive American car he was using at that time. Perhaps that was why he abandoned it within a few years and depended instead on the less conspicuous *Okike* Peugeot. He dressed simply but with good taste in harmonious colours and well-tailored clothes. It was a harmony that the students also noticed in his lectures. One of Achebe's students told *Newswatch* magazine that Achebe

> never made anyone look stupid and he has the patience, an uncommon trait, to listen to any viewpoint. In particular, he makes sure his students look at the world differently, through African eyes.[23]

The same ex-student confessed, however, that Achebe was so sensitive that he always wondered how he managed to retain his sanity in the face of the realities of contemporary Nigeria. It is also significant that Achebe downplayed the harsh and often controversial criticism that one notices in his essays while introducing the works of other African writers to his students with extensive illustration of their artistic accomplishments; and he did not teach any of his own books. Emmanuel Obiechina, a professor in the same Department of English at that time, usually taught Achebe's novels; the second set of students in the 1977/8 session studied *Arrow of God*. Although Achebe's discussion of African writers highlighted their virtues, he did not sing their praises unnecessarily. But he sustained the interest of the students, and was especially good at arousing their desire to read and write. Many of them came to appreciate that the name Chinua Achebe belonged to another human being, and that they could aspire to write, too. Among Achebe's second set of students, four wrote and produced their own plays before the end of the session. It was in the same academic session that Kalu Uka, then a lecturer in drama in the Department of English, adapted *Arrow of God* under the title *A Harvest for Ants*. It was an epic production with a cast of 60, produced first at Nsukka and later at the National Theatre in Lagos. Sunbo Marinho was a co-producer in Lagos and that combination of Marinho and Kalu Uka turned it into one of the most memorable adaptations of Achebe's novels. Thus the literary awareness which Achebe created as that session progressed was reflected in drama, in literature and even in his lifestyle. One lecturer told his students that Achebe had demonstrated that 'it is possible to combine a happy married life with a successful writing career'.[24] On some evenings the students going to their classes or their hostels would encounter Chinua and Christie strolling along the campus streets.

Christie certainly gave him ample support. Only rarely, though, was she seen calling on him at his Department of English office. No doubt she was conscious of the freedom that he needed and she was equally busy making a success of her own career. The students that Christie taught in the Faculty of Education often regaled their room-mates with stories concerning marital incidents that she used to illustrate her lectures. The freedom that she secured for Chinua Achebe allowed him to devote his energies to his string of creative and academic activities as he wrote, taught the students, edited books and functioned as external examiner of the University of Lagos.

It was on one of those trips to Lagos that Achebe said he saw

> a startling sight right under a multi-million *naira* flyover in Lagos. A beggar was crouching in the middle of the road scooping something into a bowl while furious cars

dodged him on all sides. As we got close I realized that the brownish-white stuff he was collecting was not pure sand but a mixture of sand and salt. A salt bag must have fallen out of a van and broken there and he had come on the scene rather late. The friend driving me said, 'This is one Nigerian whom the oil boom missed.' I could not get over the gigantic, almost crude irony of that scene: the multi-million modern bridge overhead, a beggar defying instant death to scoop sand into a bowl for his soup.[25]

Such observations that would not have affected many of his privileged fellow citizens sensitized Achebe to the enormity of social injustice in his society. It was an experience that only Lagos could have spawned.

It was also on one of these visits to Lagos in 1978 that Achebe met Ebun Clark, the wife of John Pepper Clark who had been Achebe's close friend before the circumstances of the civil war in Nigeria turned them into antagonists. Ebun Clark invited Chinua Achebe to lunch and insisted until he was forced to accept, for she said: 'I do not know what has come between you and your friend [J. P. Clark] but you must come to lunch.' When Achebe arrived at the home of the Clarks, the reconciliation was not spontaneous, but it clearly took off from there. Whenever Achebe went to the University of Lagos as external examiner and he had the time, he would call on the Clarks, until gradually the friendship was restored. It was on one of those visits that he met the Ghanaian novelist Ayi Kwei Armah, who had taken exception to Achebe's criticism of his first novel *The Beautyful Ones Are Not Yet Born*. Chinua Achebe had not bothered to reply to the abusive letters that Armah had been writing to him concerning that criticism, so when Armah met him in Lagos he felt that it was an opportunity to confront Achebe. An argument ensued and Armah, who was very worked up, told Achebe: 'If you had anything against my novel you could have told me privately.'[26] He was deeply hurt but Achebe had not the time nor the inclination to pursue that kind of disagreement.

There was no doubt that he was too busy in 1978 to engage in futile disagreements or personality conflicts, for the editing and publishing of *Okike* was a full-time activity. *Okike* No. 12 (April 1978) carried an editorial which noted that

> because of the many practical problems we have encountered in uprooting *Okike* from Amherst, Massachusetts and replanting it in Nsukka, Nigeria, we find ourselves running almost one year behind publication schedule. We do apologize to everyone. In spite of this temporary setback it is good to be home and we are excited by the prospects of sound continuous growth in our native soil.[27]

In the same issue of *Okike* Achebe published a poem, 'The American Youngster in Rags', informed by his recent encounter with America where some youngsters find their comfortable lives boring and therefore seek new experiences among the poor. Achebe cautions in the poem that the reality of the poor is not a subject for clownish and hypocritical simulations of the state of poverty. The same criticism of fake attitudes even in the creative enterprise appeared in his essay, 'The Truth of Fiction', which was presented as a convocation lecture at the University of Ife in 1978. The University of Ife had awarded Achebe an honorary degree on that occasion, after an impressive citation read by Professor Wole Soyinka in which he praised Achebe for 'making the life of his fellow men better through literature'.[28] It was the sixth honorary degree to be awarded to him and the first from a Nigerian university. Achebe appreciated the honour and the convocation lecture he delivered was in keeping with the reasons given for honouring him. Achebe's theme is 'man's constant effort to create for himself a different order of reality from that which is given to him, an aspiration to provide himself with a second handle on existence through his imagination'. He insists that 'just as man is a toolmaking animal and has recreated his natural world with his tools so he is a fiction-making animal and refashions his imaginative landscape with his fictions', but he also points out the 'richness, the sheer prodigality of man's inventiveness in creating etiological fictions' and that 'not all his fictions are equally useful or desirable'. Thus he insists that 'there are fictions that help and fictions that hinder. For simplicity, let us call them beneficient and malignant fictions.' Achebe finds the great virtue of literary fiction in its helping to 'locate again the line between the heroic and the cowardly when it seems most shadowy and elusive, and it does this by forcing us to encounter the heroic and the cowardly in our own psyche' which convinces him that 'the life of the imagination is a vital element of our total nature' because 'if we starve it or pollute it the quality of our life is depressed or soiled'.

Achebe also sets out, on the other hand, the terrible dangers to which fiction is exposed: the belief in superior or inferior races, for example, or the belief

> that some people who live across our frontiers or speak a different language from ourselves are the cause of all the trouble in the world, or that our own particular group or class or caste has a right to certain things which are denied to others, the belief that men are superior to women and so on.

Achebe stresses that holders of such fictions 'are really like lunatics, for while a sane person might act a play now and again, a madman lives it permanently'. He identifies privilege as 'one of the great adversaries of the imagination; it spreads a thick layer of adipose tissue over our sensitivity'. He ends by restating his positive vision of fiction, now understood in a fuller perspective:

> The fiction which imaginative literature offers us [does] not enslave; it liberates the mind of man. Its truth is not like the canons of unorthodoxy or the irrationality of prejudice and superstition. It begins as an adventure in self-discovery and ends in wisdom and humane conscience.[29]

In the final analysis Achebe is insisting on the use of literature in the interest of humanity, particularly in Africa. He is thus returning to the theme of 'Commitment and the African Writer', an essay published in 1976 in *Readings in African Humanities: African Cultural Development*, edited by Ogbu U. Kalu. Part of Achebe's personal commitment lay not only in producing literary works on themes relevant to his society, but also in publicizing the work of those other writers who had created relevant literary works. He cooperated with Dubem Okafor in editing *Don't Let Him Die*, an anthology of memorial poems for Christopher Okigbo published in 1978. A preface by Achebe that illustrates the effervescence of Okigbo's character leads off a worthy collection, while 'the variety of tributes assembled here bears witness to the power of his personality, his poetry, his life and death'.[30] At about this time Achebe himself was the subject of a collection of essays edited by Bernth Lindfors and Lyn Innes, *Critical Perspectives on Chinua Achebe,* which Three Continents Press published in 1978.

This was also the year in which Achebe was involved in producing a new Nigerian national anthem. On 1 October 1976, in his Independence Anniversary message to the nation, Head of State Olusegun Obasanjo had announced a decision by the federal government that the existing national anthem was inappropriate to Nigeria's national circumstances, mood and aspirations. A competition was launched through the federal Ministry of Information, inviting entries from Nigerians for the first part of the competition, which was the composition of the words of the anthem. On 4 March 1977 it was announced that a total of 1,500 entries had been received by the close of the competition on 28 February 1977. A further announcement was made on 1 October 1977 that five entries had been shortlisted and the secretary of the selection committee asked for views and comments to enable the committee to take a decision. In the end the committee decided that the five shortlisted entries should be used as sources from which to produce a final version of the anthem. Several distinguished Nigerians were invited to Lagos in 1978 to help in that exercise, among them Chinua Achebe and Emmanuel Obiechina. The invited academics were split into two groups and they worked independently with the same material. Achebe was in one group, Obiechina in the other, and the two groups submitted what they had produced to the selection committee. The two works were subsequently passed on to General Obasanjo: he selected the work produced by Obiechina's group, and Nigerians were informed in May 1978 that they had a new national anthem. The five Nigerians whose works served as the raw material were given ₦100 each.

In September 1978 Achebe was at Canterbury, Kent for the Conference on African and Caribbean Literature, attended by high school and university teachers, librarians, writers and publishers. The conference discussed the reasons for teaching African and Caribbean literature in British universities and schools, the books and authors that were accessible and how educators and publishers could cooperate to make those literatures produce positive effects. Achebe's paper was on 'The Uses of African Literature' and in it he asserts that African literature 'shares common approaches with other literatures' although it 'assumes a social purpose' which he attributes to the affinity between modern African literature and the oral tradition. He illustrates his statement with two Nigerian fables to stress the social purpose of the literature. Achebe adds that 'the modern African writer, unlike the makers of fables', has had 'to mediate between his indigenous culture' and

> the foreign conquerors of his people. Naturally the contents of his new fable can no longer be concerned merely with the dynamics of autonomous societies, but [must deal] also with the relationship between his old culture and the invading culture of his masters.

To Achebe the essential role of performing for the benefit of the writer's people has not changed, as he illustrates with the fiction of Equiano and the poetry of Senghor, David Diop, Agostinho Neto, John Ekwerre and Lenrie Peters. Achebe concludes that

> a writer who feels a strong and abiding concern for his fellows cannot evade the role of a social critic which is the contemporary expression of commitment to the community. And this concern is at the very heart of African literature, past and present.[31]

His paper was an interesting introduction to a new world of literature for many of the participants who were coming to African literature, as readers and teachers, for the first time.

Achebe's own focus, meanwhile, reverted to literary developments in Nigeria and the kind of teaching that he had to do at Nsukka. 'Teaching, which is one aspect of my life, I have been doing with pleasure', he declares in an interview in 1978, since 'literature is something I have believed in all my life'. Achebe feels that 'it is a pleasure to make this literature available to younger people' and also that 'one is in a position to try out ideas that one has been building up over the years. I'm in a position to experiment with the teaching of African fiction.' He hopes that 'the students are gaining something from my presence here'.[32]

As 1978 drew to a close, Achebe was also concerned about the attitude to literature, arts and culture in his society, in spite of the flamboyance of FESTAC. In an interview he observes that he does not 'think that Nigeria staged FESTAC because it has come to believe in the arts' because 'if you look at the national style now, there is more vulgarity'. He complains that

> our major problem is the style of the country today. One has to cope with that, the vulgar materialism [and] coping with those problems slows you down because you spend a great deal of energy wrestling with basic things that should have been taken care of by somebody else.

Achebe reflects that it is very easy 'to despair of teaching, preaching, writing or talking' to his own generation 'or people slightly older'. Nevertheless he believes that 'literature has the capacity to engage the imagination of children, so that they will see it is better to be fair-minded than to be unjust, that it is better to be kind than cruel, better to be humble than arrogant and so on'.[33] But he is also interested in the planned elections for a return to civilian rule in 1979, in spite of the unpleasant effects of General Olusegun Obasanjo's official visit to the University of Nigeria, Nsukka, where he embarrassed the assembled university community that 'rose respectfully to its feet on his entry' (into the Niger Room of the Continuing Education Centre) by asking them to recite the National Pledge. Achebe describes the response to that unexpected demand:

> A few ambiguous mumbles followed, and then stony silence. 'You see,' said the general, bristling with hostility, 'you do not even know the National Pledge.' No doubt he saw in this failure an indictable absence of patriotism among a group he had always held with great suspicion.[34]

But the impending elections appeal to Achebe in a special sense, for he perceives Nigeria as being

> in a transitional state, technologically, spiritually, politically. We are about to get back to civilian government again. One wants to be around as these things are happening.[35]

National preparations for those civilian elections had commenced with the lifting of the ban on politics, so 1979 began with a heightened tempo of political activities. But that did not distract Achebe's attention from the educational system in Nigeria, especially its relevance and values. In an essay on 'Continuity and Change in Nigerian Education', presented at the University of Lagos under the auspices of the Government College, Umuahia Old Boys Association and later published in *The Umuahian*, their Golden Jubilee publication, Achebe argues that it

> is possible to transform ourselves by vigorous effort into a modern, prosperous and just society. The most important single tool for this transformation is education. Or perhaps I should say an educated citizenry.

He regards the introduction of the Universal Primary Education scheme as 'a matter of great joy' and the 'king-pin of modernization'. But he reminds his audience that

in revolutionary times it is so easy to underrate the past or be impatient with tradition. And let's face it, the past can sometimes be a burden; and tradition can become a reactionary subterfuge. That is why we must speak of tradition not as an absolute and immovable necessity but as one half of an evolving dialectic – the other part being the imperative of change.

He criticizes the former Ukpabi Asika administration of East Central State for its 'anti-history tendencies' for he insists that

the right step for a government to take in the face of disparities among its educational institutions is not to reduce basic facilities all round, but to begin to introduce them where they do not exist.

He also criticizes some of the arguments concerning university admissions, although he agrees that 'the closing of the educational gap between different parts of this country is a national imperative that calls for bold departures and innovation'. Achebe also says that changes should not contravene the old and tested educational principles of selection, instruction and evaluation. He does

not question the value of making special concessions under certain well-controlled situations to secure temporary relief. But such a measure is called a palliative not a cure. Anybody who for whatever reason prescribes easy educational pain-killers as a cure for the imbalance in the country is either a very careless doctor or an unscrupulous one.

He asserts that the introduction of an ethnic sieve will produce both institutions and students that are third-rate. He is convinced that Nigeria can produce a large corps of trained men and women but that

first it must instil in its youth the rigorous habit of stretching themselves to the fullest in open competition rather than seeking, like some exotic plant, the special soil and climate of a green-house.

Finally he delivers a warning and a challenge:

God forbid that we should be the generation that had the resources in men and material and got so close to creating Africa's first truly modern state but frittered away the chance in parochialism, inefficiency, corruption and cynicism.[36]

It was an incisive and frank examination of Nigerian education and it confirmed Chinua Achebe's reputation as a fearless and bold commentator on the life of his society.

The seriousness of his interest in education at this time is demonstrated in *Okike* No. 13 (January 1979), which is devoted to the issue and includes an educational supplement edited by Emmanuel Obiechina. The editorial points out that the

idea is to expand the magazine's interests and responsibilities to accommodate a deliberate attempt to speak to a younger, school-going and educationally attuned audience for whom literature has increasingly become a nightmarish subject that terrorizes the hard-pressed classroom teacher and his awe-struck, frightened student.

The supplement was therefore created, according to the editorial, 'to augment the efforts of formal teaching of literature in our post-primary institutions'.[37]

In *Okike* No. 13 Achebe also published two poems, 'Knowing Robs Us' and 'Pine Tree in Spring', dedicated to Anna and Leon Damas respectively. In 'Pine Tree in Spring' the poet conceives Damas as a 'flag-bearer of green memory', a loyal tree 'standing guard/alone in emerald glory' but which is 'now lost in the shade/of traitors in flamboyant revelry'; he pleads at the end of the poem, 'can't you vouchsafe me/your stubborn constancy?'[38] Achebe never shied away from paying deserved tributes in his creative works, or from criticizing ideas and writers in his critical works – as in the 1979 essay on 'The Bane of Union: An Appraisal of the Consequences of Union Igbo for Igbo Language and Literature', published in the first volume of *ANU* magazine.[39] Achebe regards Union Igbo, an attempt to create a central Igbo dialect by an English classical scholar, as a 'hideous Esperanto' and 'a real disaster'. He perceives it to be a great disservice to the Igbo language and his essay, highlighting its detrimental consequences, insists that Igbo writers should forget it and write in their own dialects. The essay draws attention to another dimension of Achebe's cultural vision which relates to the creation of works in his native Nigerian language.

That concern with language was also reflected in 'Impediments to Dialogue between North and South', an essay he read at the Berlin International Literature Festival which formed part of Horizons 79, the first Festival of World Culture held from 21 June–15 July 1979. Achebe was among twelve African writers invited to Berlin. His paper points out that in the relationship between Europe and Africa the latter 'is seen as a beast of burden' and that this view 'has ruled out the possibility of a dialogue'. The other contributory factor to the impossibility of dialogue he identifies as 'too much transmission and too little reception' in Europe. A major fault in that attitude is 'Europe's reliance on its own experts' with the result that they 'exclude African testimony'. Another method adopted by Europe to evade dialogue with Africa is the 'phenomenon of the *authentic* African. This creature was invented to circumvent the credibility problem of the white man talking to himself.' It means the use of Africans 'unspoilt by Western knowledge'. Achebe ends by discussing the work of V. S. Naipaul in this context of 'authentic Africans', deciding that Naipaul is a 'modern Conrad'. He states the terms for dialogue thus:

> The new evasion will have its day and pass on leaving unsolved the problem of dialogue which has plagued Afro-European relations for centuries, until Europe is ready. Ready to concede total African humanity. 'We are the whiteman's rubbish,' says an Athol Fugard character, '… his rubbish is people.' When that changes, dialogue may have a chance to begin. If the heap of rubbish doesn't catch fire meanwhile and set the world ablaze.[40]

That warning was appropriate in a city where in the years 1884–5 the European powers held a conference to determine the partitioning of Africa among them, their arbitrary and hasty decisions sowing the seeds of so many future disasters. Achebe was aware of the shadow of history as he talked to his audience, participated in the conference literary activities and returned to Nigeria.

He arrived in time for the presidential elections of 1979, contested by Nnamdi Azikiwe of the Nigerian People's Party (NPP), Obafemi Awolowo of the United Party of Nigeria (UPN), Abubakar Waziri of the Great Nigerian People's Party (GNPP), Shehu Shagari of the National Party of Nigeria (NPN) and Aminu Kano of the People's Redemption Party (PRP). Shehu Shagari was declared the winner and a legal wrangle between him and Obafemi Awolowo ensued. The court upheld Shagari, however, on the basis that he won in 12⅔ of the states. It was a legal solution that did not convince popular opinion. Nevertheless, the election paved the way for the exit of Obasanjo and his fellow soldiers. President Shehu Shagari was sworn in on 1 October 1979, at about the same time that Chinua Achebe was honoured as an Officer of the Federal Republic (OFR) and awarded the first Nigerian National Merit Award (NNMA) for excellence. These awards were not undeserved but some Nigerians feared that they would make Achebe less critical of government actions. It was a groundless fear:

> Now one of the weaknesses of Nigeria is failure to accept merit and quality, in various areas, in the sciences, in the arts, in everything. Politics is all that matters here … when in a fit of absent-mindedness or whatever, the Nigerian nation says we recognize your achievements as a writer and we give you a medal, I don't see that I should reject it. Not that I need that medal. Of course I didn't need it and this was all the more reason why I thought I could take it because I really didn't need it. But for me, it meant that for the first time literature was being accorded a certain recognition. And while I was going to receive it I was also writing a speech, this was before anybody else knew that this was to happen, a speech in which I was going to say precisely this: that nobody is going to buy me with honours and I think that this will not be the end because we should have a situation in which national honours are given to writers, given to painters, given to sculptors, given to journalists.[41]

In his NNMA acceptance speech, 'The Metaphor of the Rain and the Clock', he assures the writers, critics and citizens of Nigeria that

> Most writers are inveterate critics of their fellow men and of society – a role imposed on them by their multiple vision, their natural scepticism and individualism. They are not good material for government Information officers and public relations operatives. Show a writer the glittering sky-line of your expanding metropolis and he will be looking down instead into your swollen, foul-smelling open drains. Point out to him the graceful sweep of your ultra-modern concrete and aluminium fly-overs and he will spy out the beggar living prehistorically under the rock shelter. That is the writer's nature and strength. To wish him to be otherwise is to wish impotence upon him and deny society the full vigour of his creativity. A writer who finds himself in perfect drill formation would almost be obliged by a natural cussedness, if you like, to shuffle and drag his feet. When he gets up to dance with his fellows he is apt to hear in his mind's ear the rhythms of a different drummer. In the words – frightening words – of Joyce Cary, 'he is doomed to be free'.[42]

Achebe uses the timing of the award to great effect in his closing remarks:

> I think I am on safe ground if I say that Nigerian writers are not planning to send a delegation to President Shehu Shagari to pledge their unflinching support. Flinching support is more in their line of business. But I do hope that the military government's last-hour precedent of honouring writers at the highest level will be maintained by Shagari and succeeding regimes so that Nigeria may become an example of enlightenment to Africa and other parts of the world.

It was a necessary hope.

15

Setting Up More Structures
Education, Culture, Politics
1979–83

AN administrative problem faced the Department of English at the University of Nigeria, Nsukka at the beginning of the 1979/80 academic session. A head of department for the current academic session had to be found from among the senior members of staff: Professors E. Obiechina, D. I. Nwoga and Chinua Achebe. But Achebe had clearly stated when he accepted the professorship at Nsukka that he would not want to be involved in administration and the university had agreed, since such activities would hamper his creative work.

D. I. Nwoga was due for his sabbatical leave that academic year, however, and had made preparations to proceed to the United States of America. At the same time E. N. Obiechina had an opening as a Smithsonian Scholar which would lapse if he failed to utilize it. After much argument the university administration decided that if they could convince another senior member of staff to be the head of department, both of them would be given permission to be away. Thus they solicited the help of Chinua Achebe, whose own international engagements were not in doubt but who could also afford to dictate some of the terms if he so desired. Achebe magnanimously agreed to assume duties as head of department to accommodate his two colleagues, although he emphasized that he would work in that capacity for only one year. This additional responsibility meant that Achebe was very busy as 1979 ended and the new year of 1980 began. It was in this new year that the civilians in government began to demonstrate their deficiencies in terms of corruption, indiscipline and numerous social vices. It also became clear that the former military administration of General Obasanjo had created certain unwise economic structures in which corruption flourished. Achebe followed these events with increasing disappointment as 1980 progressed; it was becoming clear to him that purposeful leadership would have made all the difference.

Despite the demands of the English department, Achebe accepted an invitation to visit Australia in March 1980 which enabled him to be a guest at the Writers' Week in Adelaide. At that forum Achebe delivered an address on the theme of myth, symbol and fable in African literature. He did not make the same conceptual divisions between those terms that are current in the Western world, but rather acknowledged the primacy of myth as the raw material and the substance of stories. Achebe found the writers he met excessively concerned with their individual positions, each preoccupied with not being like any other Australian writer, 'somebody very different from everybody else'. He met several visitors from other countries like Ian Creighton-Smith, with whom he discussed the problems arising from regional languages in Britain. Achebe also visited an aboriginal college where he read some poems. As he explains in an interview with Suzanne Hayes:

> When I thought about what to do (what I could possibly read? What I could say?) I saw that even in my collection of poems which I wrote for a different occasion, a very different time and place (the end of the civil war in Nigeria), there were things which could be said to have relevance. And one of the poems occurred to me. It's called 'Benin Road' and it is simply the meeting of force with lightness, the force represented by a car and the lightness by a butterfly, and they meet tragically – for the butterfly, of course – in this paved tunnel. You know, it's a human situation: a strong, materialistically strong culture meeting one which is gentle and very old and that sort of thing – it's very tragic.[1]

Achebe used that poem to evoke for his audience the similarities between the African and Australian colonial experiences. He elaborates on his view of colonialism in the interviews he granted Jim Davidson:

> Colonialism creates the kind of man who sees government as 'they'. Government isn't in fact the white man. Government is always the people involved, the way they are administered, the way they are taxed, the way they are represented…. Once you are pushed to the state where you say 'they', you are lost. And this is the tragedy I think of colonial status. It's worse in Africa than it could possibly have been in the dominions when they were colonies because in a way 'they' were the same kind of people as yourselves, your cousins. In Africa 'they' is a very different kind of person. So it's all too easy to adopt the attitude that I will not cooperate.[2]

What Achebe highlights is that the attitude of those in government to public funds and property is negatively influenced by the colonial experience. It is not strange that such issues should have occupied him at a time when the civilian administration in Nigeria was failing to sustain the hopes of the people.

Achebe discusses other constraints that have affected his creativity in an interview with Rosemary Colmer:

> This year, this last year has been particularly difficult in terms of time. I've never really complained about time until now, because I've always had enough time for anything I wanted to do; but this year I am doing something that I never thought I would do, which is administrate a department. I thought all that was behind me. I did my administration in radio nearly 20 years ago and I thought I'd done my bit. But this year something exceptional happened, so I've not had as much time as I wanted. Maybe at the end of this year I should be able to give more time and get the novel out of the way. I think it's time, too, I think it's probably time that I wrote another novel.[3]

Achebe returned to Nigeria in the middle of March 1980 but did not find the time to continue work on that novel. In the following month he flew to the United States for a conference of the African Literature Association in Gainesville, Florida, between 9 and 11 April. It was at that conference that he met James Baldwin for the first time, although Achebe had read *Go Tell it on the Mountain* about twenty years before. At that meeting which Achebe describes as 'a memorable encounter in the *Jungles* of Florida', he dramatically greeted

Baldwin thus: 'Mr Baldwin, I presume.' Baldwin enjoyed the meeting too, and explained that he had asked for the dialogue between himself and Achebe because 'It's very important that we should meet each other, finally, if I must say so, after something like 400 years.'

Mildred Hill-Lubin also reports that words such as 'confrontation', 'connection' and 'symbolic' were used to describe the event. She also reports that Achebe in reaction to a question answered that the African and the black American writers are engaged in the process of creating themselves again 'after having been shaped and controlled by others', while Baldwin regarded the exercise as 'nothing less than an excavation of a buried and denied history, a history never written down'. Hill-Lubin says that 'while they stressed the significance of the coming together as a metaphor for all black writers, they rejected the notion of racial exclusion'. The two writers also agreed on the social purpose of art and that African art had a foundation of morality. The dialogue between the two writers took in such issues as Negritude and women in African societies. The encounter between Achebe and Baldwin did not end without drama of a less pleasant kind, for as their dialogue was in progress an unknown voice came over the public address system and threatened Baldwin: 'I am coming up there Mr Baldwin. We can't go along with this kind of stuff. We can't stand all this kind of going on.' It was a shocking intrusion but, according to Hill-Lubin, Baldwin answered 'Mr Baldwin is nevertheless going to finish his opening statement and I will tell you wherever you are; and if you assassinate me in the next two minutes, it no longer matters what you think. The doctrine of white supremacy on which the white world is based has had its hour, has had its day.'[4] Achebe describes that memorable meeting:

> As we stepped into a tremendous ovation in the packed auditorium of the Holiday Inn, Baldwin was in particularly high spirits. I thought the old preacher in him was reacting to the multitude. He went to the podium and began to make his opening statements. Within minutes a mystery voice came over the public address system and began to hurl racial insults at him and me. I will see that moment to the end of my life. The happiness brutally wiped off Baldwin's face; the genial manner gone; the eyes flashing in defiant combativeness; the voice incredibly calm and measured. And the words of remorseless prophecy began once again to flow.[5]

In spite of that negative incident the meeting between Achebe and Baldwin reaffirmed the affinities between Africans and people of African origin all over the world. Their acceptance of the invitations extended by the African Literature Association was also a boost to the image of that organization which was at that time still struggling to assert itself.

At this conference Chinua Achebe granted an interview to Kalu Ogbaa on 11 April 1980, in which he responds to several issues associated with African literatures. Ogbaa wanted to know Achebe's view of Igbo literary critics, especially in the interpretation of his works. Achebe answers that 'there have been outstanding examples' of critics who 'have done very serious work on [his] novels or generally on Igbo culture as seen through our literature' but he also mentions 'others who have been somewhat casual or even negative in their attitude' like 'a certain fellow who was claiming that *Arrow of God* was written by his uncle, which led to the rather curious situation in which the fellow was dismissed as irresponsible by a white critic'. He adds that he considers critical responsibility not only important but also essential for cultural survival because 'a culture can be damaged, can be turned from its course not only by foreigners' although the Igbo culture was 'disturbed very seriously' by Europe. Defining a standpoint, he says that

> If we are ready to take challenges, to make concessions that are necessary without accepting anything that undermines our fundamental belief in the dignity of man, I think we would be doing what is expected of us.

Achebe has found that sense of purpose emerging in the criticism of the day, for he notes that

> the high standard of criticism from people like David Carroll and many others has raised the tone of our criticism immensely in the last several years and that we no longer see the kind of critical dilettantism we saw initially from people who were not really qualified either by temperament or training to get into it. They were doing it maybe because nobody else was. And now we have some very acute, some very sharp people.

These remarks acknowledge the prominent strides that African literature has made in other parts of the world as well as in Africa itself. Achebe adds that teaching and criticism are performing similar roles, and that 'the teaching of literature should go on and even increase because [it is] very important'. This leads him to the observation that 'literature is not a luxury for us. It is a life and death affair because we are fashioning a new man. The Nigerian is a new man.' If writers, critics and teachers are to win the battle for the mind of that New Nigerian,

> it is something solid and permanent that we must put into his consciousness. That is what he reads, what he believes, and what he loves. We must dramatize his predicament so that he can see the choices and choose right.[6]

That decision to utilize creative works in the service of the nation was not unexpected: it had become clear that the self-image of Nigerians was adrift in the negative economic realities spawned by a plethora of selfish political decisions. Achebe was concerned especially for the minds of impressionable children. In an interview with Jonathan Cott in the summer of 1980 in London he says:

> Our responsibility as Nigerians of this generation is to strive to realize the potential good and avoid the ill. Clearly, children are central in all this, for it is their legacy and patrimony that we are talking about. If Nigeria is to become a united and humane society in the future, her children must now be brought up on a common vocabulary for the heroic and the cowardly, the just and the unjust. Which means preserving and refurbishing the landscape of the imagination and the domain of stories, and not – as our leaders seem to think – a verbal bombardment of patriotic exhortation and daily recitations of the National Pledge and Anthem.[7]

Part of Achebe's efforts to refurbish the landscape of the imagination revolved around delivering lectures and the discussion of literary issues with his students in a way that was expected to sustain their interest. He was aware, of course, that 'a writer [in Nigeria] is known by the younger age and hardly known by those of his age and older age who are the policy makers'.[8] Achebe's remark may have been true of other Nigerian writers but in his own case his reputation had been assured locally and internationally by works read by young and old. Further confirmation came with the publication of Robert Wren's *Achebe's World: The Historical and Cultural Context of the Novels of*

Chinua Achebe by Three Continents Press in 1980, and also from the statistical fact that *Things Fall Apart* had sold two million copies. There was no doubt that his audience was growing in size while the number of Africans he had influenced positively was also increasing. An incident at the 1980 Noma Award ceremony at the University of Ife, which Achebe attended as a special guest, said more than all the statistics. It was there that he met Mariama Bâ, the Senegalese writer and winner of that first Noma award. Achebe and Mariama Bâ exchanged greetings but Achebe could not speak good French while Bâ could not speak English, and thus after the exchange of a few words they parted and Achebe went to talk to some other people. In the midst of that conversation, however, Achebe noticed Mariama Bâ coming back with a man who turned out to be a bilingual Cameroonian. The man translated the conversation of the two writers and in the course of discussion Mariama Bâ told Chinua Achebe that she started writing after reading *Things Fall Apart*. Even in translation, then, that landmark novel had made a deep impression.

Achebe was making a deep impression on his students, too, and his classes were increasing in size. He had to devise new methods of involving as many of the students as possible in class discussions in the Department of English. His close class contact with the students revealed certain deficiencies in the students and he confessed in 1980 that

> there's a real decline in education in my country. One notices that students – even third year or final year students in English – require more direction than one used to think necessary. So in that kind of situation, you find yourself doing more of the teaching, direct teaching. I would have preferred the seminar, the kind of discussion with groups that you get with more mature students. But you have to do both.[9]

As head of department, moreover, Achebe couldn't help noticing the various academic difficulties emanating from the classroom activities of other lecturers, and it became clear to him that there, too, the standard of education was falling. One incident which shocked him was an invitation card sent to him as head of department to attend a local graduation ceremony in the village of one of the best graduate students of that year. The student had added a handwritten note in which Achebe found grammatical errors that he would not have expected from a student adjudged to be one of the best graduates produced by the department. He read that letter at a departmental staff meeting as an example of the kind of product coming out of the department. He then set up a departmental enquiry and asked every member of staff to compile a list of the most serious and frequently encountered errors in the use of language. The idea was to publish a handbook of common errors which could be used to tackle the problem. At about this time a student in a degree script wrote that 'Macbeth was a Russian General who went to fight in Norway.' Professor D. S. Izevbaye was the external examiner for that year and the department was embarrassed. Achebe felt that 'the problem with language was passing the stage of confusion to that of incoherence'. It was also noted by the department that the decline coincided with the decision of the senate of the University of Nigeria to remove proficiency in the English language as a compulsory qualification for securing admission. Achebe explained that his plans for a rectification of the problem of language 'was something that needed time to be fully implemented'. He added, however, that despite falling standards he still met 'very bright students' in his classes.[10] Indeed, some of the students produced by the department went on to become significant creative writers and literary critics. One of the consequences of his concern with falling standards was that even lecturers who had been noted for their laxity in grading scripts became reasonably strict. A number of students were unhappy at that development but it was a necessary medicine.

The worry that if standards were not maintained education would degenerate troubled Chinua Achebe throughout 1980. He encouraged his fellow members of staff to make periodic evaluations of student scripts, while the students were made to understand the difficulties that could arise from an inability to express oneself appropriately. Several students benefited from that exercise while some others expressed their resentment by writing graffiti on the walls like the one which read: 'You wicked man. You gave me a 'C' grade'[11] – a signal, nevertheless, that awareness of the problem was growing. Achebe taught his students, graded their scripts like other members of staff, administered the department and still occasionally found time to accept invitations to visit other countries.

His two weeks in Upper Volta, now renamed Burkina Faso, were enlightening:

> I spent two weeks in Upper Volta which is often listed as the poorest or second poorest country in the world, and which perches precariously on the edge of the Sahara Desert. To my utter astonishment there was no power failure throughout my stay in Ougadougou; the taps in my hotel room not only ran all the time but ran with the kind of pressure one sees in Europe and America. My hotel room was modest but impeccably clean; you could use the towel in the bathroom without wondering, as you must do even in four-star Lagos hotels, whether it was washed after the last lodger left. The food was excellent and the waiters were courteous and well-trained. I was not charged the earth or compelled to make a crippling initial deposit.[12]

Clearly Achebe perceived the treatment he received in that country as an apt illustration of a people managing their limited resources to the best of their ability. It was that attitude he expected in his country, too, but the political culture of President Shehu Shagari left much to be desired. It was also that attitude of making the best use of limited resources that he expected from his students, though he was nevertheless contemplating further ways of improving university education in Nigeria as he came to the end of his stint as head of department.

If Achebe ended 1980 without the responsibility of administering a department, that did not prevent the university from calling on him to fulfil his responsibility as chairman of the Ceremonials Committee. There was ceremony of another kind at Enugu for Chinua Achebe, however, when Fourth Dimension organized a book launch to coincide with his fiftieth birthday. Several books published by Fourth Dimension were presented to the public and one of them was Alexander Madiebo's *The Nigerian Revolution and the Biafran War*. In the address he delivered that day Achebe comments that

> many accounts on the Nigerian civil war though interesting and useful in their way have been inadequate for two main reasons. First, some have suffered from the author's limited knowledge of the major issues involved. Second, and much worse, some accounts have been quite frankly self-serving, inspired primarily by the desire of their authors to rig the verdict of history in their own favour or in favour of their group and faction.

He predicts, however, that Madiebo's account

> will maintain its superiority for generations and generations to come [because] he

confronts our recent history boldly and squarely. He is dispassionate in his analysis and quite merciless in exposing our hypocrisy, our ineptitude, our cruelty. In this process some cherished illusions are knocked on the head; some popular idols are sent tumbling down from their pedestals of deceit and chicanery; some reputations that were unfairly damaged by jealousy, spitefulness, ignorance, misunderstanding and mass hysteria are rehabilitated.

Achebe recommends the brilliance of the author's style as that of 'an army General who writes like an angel' and also as 'a fine example of effective prose, such as is becoming extremely rare these days'. Turning to Fourth Dimension's decision to honour him, he appreciates 'the thought of launching these publications to coincide with [his] fiftieth birthday', but this is an honour which he

> does not deserve and only accepted with some embarrassment. I think that the only people who are entitled to inflict their anniversaries on other people are accredited saviours of mankind – like Christ and Mohammed and others of like stature. I have saved nobody yet, not even myself.

He goes on to nurse his audience to 'wage a battle of the mind with the weapon of books. We must remember our history so as not to be condemned like clowns, to keep bumping into the same disasters over and over again.'[13] The address confirms that Achebe never missed an opportunity to appeal to the minds and souls of his compatriots in order to galvanize them into positive action. It was also on that occasion that a Nigerian soldier, Mamman Jiya Vatsa, found a novel way to sing Achebe's praises:

> We celebrate the coming of age,
> of the writer of the people.
> When *Things Fall Apart*, we are *No Longer at Ease*,
> And we look for *Arrow of God*,
> to aim at *A Man of the People*.
> *The Girls at War* sing, *Beware, Soul Brother*,
> To the steps of *The Drum* and *The Flute*,
> On *Morning Yet on Creation Day*,
> As *Chike and the River*
> Tell the story of *The Trouble with Nigeria*,
> And *How The Leopard Got His Claws*.
> There are shouts of *Don't Let Him Die*.
> Our man of genius give us more, We celebrate.[14]

Among the academics who visited the university at this time was Professor Emmanuel Ayandele, invited to deliver a General Studies lecture following a similar visit by the economist, Dr Pius Okigbo. After his lecture in early 1981 Ayandele, in a conversation with C. C. Ifemesia and Chinua Achebe which veered towards the war, confessed to them that he rated the *Ahiara Declaration* 'the best document that came out of the war'.[15] Ayandele did not know that he was talking to the authors of the document and in particular to the chairman of the National Guidance Committee of former Biafra, Chinua Achebe, who edited and refined it: everybody had assumed that it was written by General Ojukwu. Achebe also played host to Alan Hill and his wife Enid at Nsukka in February 1981 as the visitors toured Nigeria. Another visitor to Nigeria that year was Jimmy Carter, former president of the United States, who said that he and his family were avid readers of Achebe's books.

In March 1981 Achebe was invited to India by H. H. Anniah Gowda, editor and publisher of *The Literary Half-Yearly*. He spent a week at Mysore where he gave two lectures on 'The Truth of Fiction' (previously presented at the University of Ife in 1978) and 'The Nature of the Individual and his Fulfilment'. He was excited by his encounters with such brilliant, if abrasive, writers as Ananta Murti and others. In the second essay Achebe, after reviewing the various concepts of fulfilment and how the individual is affected, argues that

> the idea we have to seek is, in my view, the one which combines freedom for the individual and the safety of society. A society which represses the individual spirit will rapidly degenerate into stagnant mediocrity. But without society there can be no meaningful individuality to exercise and no civilization.

This general truth has a specific application to particular societies:

> Every culture that truly desires excellence will have to redress the balance between the two realities of individual freedom and social responsibility in accordance with the excesses of its own past practices.... Those that have sat too heavily on the individual will have to restore liberty to him and those that have denounced ties of responsibility must learn that without ties there can be no fulfilment in the complex conditions of modern life.[16]

On his return to Nsukka, the Department of English asked him to address the staff and students. He spiced that address with jokes and anecdotes about the Nigerians he had met in India, his detailed narrative showing that he never failed to observe his fellow human being closely and keenly.

Achebe next accepted an invitation to present an address at the launch of *Expo 77*, a novel written by his friend Chukwuemeka Ike, now a prominent Nigerian novelist. His account of Ike's work emphasizes its range and relevance.

> Chukwuemeka Ike has explored a wider spectrum of Nigerian life than any other novelist. Each of his six novels [then] takes a different perspective of our story, drawing its material from a different facet of his own rich and diverse experience.... *Expo 77* is new not only in its subject matter; it is in a totally new mode: an essay into detective fiction.... [Ike] sees examination malpractices as a symptom of a deep and dangerous national disorder for what the adult society – not the children – are ultimately responsible.

Characteristically, he ends by stressing the regenerative role of fiction: 'Ike has us all in his debt for telling us the truth; whether we are big enough to learn from our past mistakes is another matter.'[17] Achebe's support for the book launch was evidence of his continuing encouragement of his fellow writers, a role he had developed as editor of the Heinemann African Writers Series and *Okike*.

In June 1981 a special issue of *Okike*, No. 18, was dedicated to the late Angolan poet and president, Agostinho Neto. Achebe, who had never met Neto, was so touched by his death that he wrote a poem, 'Agostinho Neto', for the memorial issue. His appreciation is summarized in the last stanza:

> Neto, I sing your passing, I
> Timid requisitioner of your vast
> Armoury's most congenial stories.
> What shall I sing? A dirge
> Of gloom? No, I will sing tearful songs
> Of joy; I will celebrate
> The man who rode, a trinity

Of awesome fates to the cause
Of our trampled race!
Thou healer, soldier and poet![18]

In June of 1981 he visited Britain as a member of the executive committee of the Commonwealth Arts Organization and conducted a series of readings and lectures in various places. It was on that visit that he granted interviews to Lindsay Barrett and the trio of Anthony Appiah, John Ryle and D. A. N. Jones at the University of Cambridge. In the interview with Lindsay Barrett, Achebe is asked to comment on the main thrust and impact of *Okike*. He answers that a magazine

> should not dictate, but should provide a forum for discussion and we have been quite active in that area. It has provided a forum for new writers. There are some people, I am glad to say, who were first published, first saw the light of day, so to speak, in the magazine.

He also believes that the journal has provided a context 'in which to discuss the ideas behind literature'.[19] In the second interview which Achebe granted to Appiah, Ryle and Jones, his answers were as varied as the questions. Achebe provided biographical details concerning his childhood and education and discussed his attitude to the Igbo language, especially the 'esperanto' known as 'Union Igbo' and the purpose of fiction. On the last topic he offered the view that 'the attempt of the politician to deceive with words is countered by the efforts of the writer to go behind the words to show the meaning'. Achebe also expressed the view that colonialism created 'the Warrant Chief' syndrome in which a ruler is

> chosen not by his people but because a foreigner approved of him – it is that heritage that we are really suffering from. In fact what happened here was that the accountability which was part of the traditional system then disappeared. The check which tradition had on the leader was removed. He only had to be acceptable to the British resident.[20]

By the 1980s Chinua Achebe had established a reputation as a writer who reacted wisely and reasonably to issues and events. His emerging role as a father figure was emphasized by the invitation he extended to Nigerian writers to gather for a convention at Nsukka. This Convention of Nigerian Authors could be seen as a new extension of the structures Achebe was constantly setting up in Nigeria, Africa, America and Europe in the interests of literature. He wanted his fellow Nigerian writers to come together and consider the setting up of a formal organization. He conceived of it as partly a trade union for writers through which they could discuss their common interests and responsibilities, including specific issues like royalties, and partly as a forum where 'one can feel the pulse of the writers'. The event took place between 26 and 28 June at Nsukka. The formal opening on 27 June, at which the Kenyan novelist Ngugi wa Thiong'o was an honoured guest, was addressed by the vice-chancellor of the University of Nigeria, Professor Frank Ndili, who welcomed the writers as he recalled 'that this university has played certain crucial roles in the development of modern African literature': he mentioned the poetic vocation of Christopher Okigbo and the novels of Chukwuemeka Ike. Ndili considered the occasion as an historic one and he expressed the pride of the university in being associated with the birth of the Convention of Nigerian Authors. He was particularly pleased that the convention was bringing together writers in English and in various Nigerian languages. I am sure that the interaction of these different traditions holds out great potentialities for a vigorous and rich national literature.[21]

The Minister for Social Development, Youth, Sports and Culture, Chief Paulinus C. Amadike, declared in his own address that 'the writer in Nigeria has to make up his mind who his public is and cut his expectations according to the inherent character of the public.' He pointed out that 'the artist wears a mantle of leadership whose sustenance depends on his public performance, the image he and his peers present and the influence they exert on the public'.[22] In his convener's address Chinua Achebe expressed gratitude at the response of the minister, the university community and his fellow Nigerian writers to his invitation, although he prefaced his address with the announcement of the death of a pioneer writer in the Hausa language, Abubakar Imam.

The convener gave the reasons for setting up the convention as including the need to tackle the business side of writing, the importance of offering assistance to new and aspiring writers or help to writers in distress, and the necessity to maintain 'the freedom and safety of writers in society'. He illustrated the need for such safety in an organization with two incidents which demonstrated the unchecked arrogance of power in Nigeria:

> The other day a state Governor said to an airport press conference: 'Damn it, I am the government!' and he received an ovation and delighted laughter instead of shocked silence. About the same time another chief executive told an audience at this University, 'Politics is power, and nobody gives up power peacefully.' He was applauded. By academics! In a seat of enlightenment.

Chinua Achebe explained to his audience that his concern was

> not what politicians say or do but the absence of a countervailing tradition of enlightened criticism and dissent [which meant that] a writer who must be free [has] no choice really but to run great risks. And we had better know it and prepare for it.[23]

At the end of the business meeting a formal organization of Nigerian authors was set up and the gathered writers unanimously elected Chinua Achebe as its President.

Soon after that convention Achebe informed the university of his intention to retire. It was apparent to him that after ten years of active teaching in Nigeria and the United States he needed to turn his attention to other activities. His announcement was not expected to take immediate effect, although the Department of English organized a send-off ceremony in his honour in July 1981. The Paul Robeson Drama building was the setting for several literary activities: Emmanuel Obiechina discussed Achebe as a novelist; Donatus Nwoga evoked him as a poet; Juliet Okonkwo examined him as a critic; while Kalu Uka celebrated 'Achebe, the Man'. Uko Akpaide, a lecturer in fine and applied arts, and Ezenwa-Ohaeto performed poems, while the talented Esiaba Irobi produced one of his interesting plays. Kalu Uka regaled the audience with a memorable story of the modesty of Achebe whom he once saw standing in a queue at the university medical centre waiting for his turn, long before the military rulers of his country thought of the queueing culture as part of the 'war against indiscipline'.

Achebe continued his services to the university after that ceremony, since his retirement had not taken effect. Thus he was still an active member of the university staff when there was a major altercation between Professor Frank Ndili, the vice-chancellor, and Professor Anya. The quarrel degenerated to the extent that both parties were not even on speaking terms and it threatened to disrupt administrative activities in the university. Inevitably it was referred to the governing council for discussion and solution, and the council scouted for an individual of known probity who would be the chairman of a panel to investigate the case. Chinua Achebe was their choice and he yielded to their appeal in the interests of the university. It was almost the last assignment performed by Chinua Achebe and among the members of his panel were Professor Donatus Nwoga and Professor Nduka Okafor. The chairman of the governing council at that time was Alhaji Ali Monguno, and he appealed to the investigating panel to submit its report quickly in order to recover administrative stability in the university.

The panel conducted interviews, discussed many issues, examined numerous documents and interviewed the parties involved in the quarrel. The members worked late into the night at the university guest house, in candlelight when there was no electricity. They were under great pressure and towards the end of their investigations, when they were discussing and putting together their report, some members of the panel wavered instead of taking firm decisions, which consumed more time. At one point the secretary to the panel blew up and scolded some members who could not make up their minds. Achebe rebuked him for his rudeness, reminding him that he was not really a member of the panel but a secretary. At the end, when the panel submitted its report to the council, the members were horrified at the magnitude of the offence.[24] Professor Anya was reprimanded and it was the least that the council could do. It was an act of courage on Achebe's part to accept a responsibility which was likely to earn him the displeasure of the blamed party, but we have seen that it was not in his character to shirk from what he perceived as his duty to his society. He also performed these duties in spite of his international commitments. In October 1981 he was in Tokyo, Japan, for a colloquium with the theme 'Diversified Evolution of World Civilization'.

Achebe recalls that at 'that forum the participants were attempting among other things, to define the cultural ingredient or as one of the Japanese scholars put it the *software* of modernization'. A family anecdote related at the colloquium by Professor Kinichiro Toba of Waseda University, Japan, made an intellectual impact on Achebe.

> My grandfather graduated from the University of Tokyo at the beginning of the 1880s. His notebooks were full of English. My father graduated from the same university in 1920 and half of his notes were filled with English. When I graduated a generation later my notes were all in Japanese. So ... it took three generations for us to consume Western civilization totally via the means of our language.

Achebe found the remark significant for

> we can conclude that as Japan began the count-down to its spectacular technological lift-off it was also systematically recovering lost ground in its traditional model of cultural expression. In one sense then it was travelling away from its old self towards a cosmopolitan, modern, identity while in another sense it was journeying back to regain a threatened past and selfhood.[25]

As usual, Achebe applied this insight to the reality of his country as he urged his compatriots to comprehend the positive dimensions of that experience in Japan. There was no doubt that the lesson was needed by Nigeria. Its economic, political and social realities were a source of anxiety for all sensitive minds. Perhaps the need to devote more time to that aspect of the Nigerian reality was part of his reason for retiring.

That retirement took effect at the end of 1981. It was a decision that enabled him to devote more time to the *Okike* project which had grown beyond the stage of publishing only the journal. There was now a separate *Okike Educational Supplement*, some occasional publications and the organization of an Okochi festival in which traditional poets and writers in the Nigerian languages performed. Achebe maintained a link with the University of Nigeria, Nsukka, for he still lived on the campus where his wife Christie was a lecturer in the Faculty of Education. In appreciation of the services he had rendered to the university, Achebe was nominated for the award of an honorary Doctor of Letters. He accepted and at the December Convocation of 1981 duly received a seventh honorary degree.

Stepping aside from the bustle of academic work enabled Achebe to devote more attention to political activities in Nigeria. It was clear to him, as 1982 began, that the politicians had not changed from the type he had satirized in *A Man of the People*. There were indications of shocking corrupt practices, misuse of power and an excessive adherence to the pomp and pageantry of public office. Achebe, whose acquaintances included people from the five registered political parties, was not simply saddened and concerned. He was beginning to lose patience with his country. At other times he had found his fiction to be an adequate means of expressing his disappointment and displeasure, and so he picked up the novel that he had been working on for the past ten years. He had left it on one side for quite some time and needed to read the chapters that he had written carefully in order to become reacquainted with the story. The four characters he had chosen were in place but it seemed to him that he had not found an adequate story to carry the themes he had in mind. Achebe spent some time on that novel in the course of 1982 but later abandoned it again, thinking that it was the end of his pursuit of that particular creative enterprise.

Other creative enterprises engaged him and one of them was the celebration of ten years of *Okike* publications. It was a ceremony that Achebe had planned the previous year to coincide with the inauguration of the Convention of Nigerian Authors but he was wisely advised to separate the two activities. The anniversary celebration now took place on 29 April 1982 at the Continuing Education Centre of the University of Nigeria, Nsukka. Present at the ceremony was Dr Alex Ekwueme, a patron of *Okike* and vice-president of the Federal Republic of Nigeria.

The celebrations included the presentation of several books published for *Okike*. Selections of stories and poems from previous issues of the journal made up *Rhythms of Creation: A Decade of Okike Poetry*, edited by D. I. Nwoga, and *African Creations: A Decade of Okike Short Stories*, edited by E. N. Obiechina. In the preface to the collection he edited Obiechina describes how 'manuscripts poured unremittingly into the offices of the editor of the fledgling magazine' so that 'ten years afterwards, there has accumulated a literary harvest which, for variety, freshness and depth of insight, constitutes the most significant phenomenon of the African literary scene'.[26] Another publication was *Aka Weta*, an anthology of contemporary Igbo poetry, and it was launched by Dr Alex Ekwueme. It was significant that the contributors to that anthology were encouraged to use their various dialects, a reminder of Achebe's strong opposition to 'Union Igbo'. Achebe explains, in an address he called 'The *Okike* Story' that

> the doggedness with which *Okike* triumphed over its early environmental dangers was born out of a conviction that a man chastened by the humiliation of defeat often had deeper insights to report than his conqueror, and that out of the trauma of the Biafran experience something good and valuable might be recovered for Nigerian and African literary development and civilization.

He acknowledges the financial support which *Okike* received from Ulli Beier, Alex Ekwueme and Arthur Nwankwo, pointing out that 'Ulli Beier came to our aid totally unasked; Ekwueme and Nwankwo responded to appeals that had gone out to several Nigerians in different parts of the country.' He expresses deep gratitude to the Ford Foundation in New York for its substantial grant to *Okike* and also acknowledges the help received from the National Council for Arts and Culture. Achebe stresses that in addition to the journal *Okike* there was also the *Okike Educational Supplement* aimed at tackling 'the abysmally low quality of literary instruction'. Furthermore he highlights the organization of Okochi Festivals in which

> traditional poets and singers of excellence have been invited to Nsukka to perform not as decorative or peripheral fillers but serious and honoured guests, as repositories of our endangered civilization.[27]

The celebration itself was enlivened by the performance of an Igbo minstrel, Afam Ogbuotobo, and later that evening a three-hour Okochi festival was held at the Princess Alexandria Auditorium on the university campus.

Thus the celebration served the twin purpose of assessing the achievements of *Okike* and sensitizing the Nigerian public to its merits. Several Nigerians responded positively and it became apparent that there was widespread academic support for the journal; Achebe consolidated both the intellectual and social goodwill. Soon after, he was invited by the University of Kent to receive his eighth honorary degree, and in July 1982 travelled to Canterbury for the ceremony, in which the Archbishop of Canterbury, Dr Robert Runcie, and Mr U. B. Alexander also received honorary degrees. Professor Robert Gibson, the University of Kent orator, told the audience that Achebe 'is now revered as Master by the younger generation of African writers and it is to him they regularly turn for counsel and inspiration', which Gibson regarded as 'a heavy responsibility'.[28]

After the award Chinua Achebe found time to call on his former English tutor at Government College, Umuahia, Adrian Slater, who was living in Canterbury during his retirement. Achebe gave Slater an autographed copy of *Arrow of God* in which he had written: 'To the man who taught me respect for language.' It was a touching mark of recognition for Slater, who had taught at a Nigerian college about forty years before, and, as he recalled, had work from his Government College classes that surpassed what he got later from the English pupils he taught in England.[29]

This was also the year in which Achebe was made an honorary member of the distinguished American Academy of Arts and Letters. But these visits he made to other lands only magnified his by now acute dissatisfaction with the state of political affairs in Nigeria. Especially influential was the visit he made to Ireland as a guest of the Irish government for the centenary of James Joyce. Achebe describes how he

> sat with other guests and thousands of Dubliners in a huge municipal hall waiting for the President of the Irish Republic to arrive and inaugurate the event. I noticed that [there were] two minutes to go and I had still not seen any signs of [the President's] arrival. On the exact dot of five a tall fellow walked on to the stage followed by *one* man in uniform. The Chairman of the event (who incidentally was a writer and not the Irish Minister for Social Affairs, Sports, Children, Women, Trade Unions and Culture) motioned the audience to stand. So that was the president! His ADC gave him his speech which he read and came down to sit in the audience to listen to [other] tributes to Joyce.[30]

Such incidents served to convince Achebe that Nigerian political culture needed to be restructured through a change in the attitude of the leaders. Thus he took a decision to become active in politics and, after examining the five parties, accepted the invitation of Mallam Aminu Kano, one of the most selfless politicians that his country had ever produced, and joined the People's Redemption Party (PRP) in late 1982. Achebe preferred an interventionist role to that of a mere critic for he obviously believed that a political rupture was necessary. He attended meetings and engaged in several discussions about new structures since the general elections would be held the following year, 1983. His entry into politics did not lessen his contribution as president of the Association of Nigerian Authors – the official nomenclature adopted at their annual conference at the University of Ife in November 1982 – or as editor of *Okike* with its associated activities.

In 1982 the *Okike* committee decided to establish a journal to be known as *Uwa Ndi Igbo* with Professor Chieka Ifemesia, a historian, as its first editor. According to Ifemesia, the idea 'developed from a discussion of cultural and literary affairs by the Okike Committee. The journal is to be used to meet the challenges of our times especially in documenting relevant materials.' It was a journal made for the ordinary man which could be used to discuss issues and subjects like traditional science, technology, literature, history, psychology and all aspects of life. Ifemesia recalls that 'what bothered the Journal was the passing generation of people who had so much knowledge in their head which had not been documented'.[31] Thus *Uwa Ndi Igbo* considered the documentation of the minstrels in whose works were embedded so much history, drama and literature: they were tape recorded, transcribed and put in writing as ways of conveying the meaning and nuances of the original works.

These literary and political activities kept Chinua Achebe busy as the year 1983 began. It would be a year of political elections, since the first term of the elected president, governors, senators and legislators was coming to an end in Nigeria. Achebe's membership of the PRP involved him in several political activities with various individuals and groups, including his friend and publisher Arthur Nwankwo who was campaigning to be elected as governor in Anambra State. In response to the need to appeal to the intellect of the electorate, Achebe started working on a social study of Nigeria. Although it was a book aimed at catching the attention of the public before the elections, Achebe in his careful way also had in mind its relevance beyond the elections.

While the PRP was working towards the elections and Chinua Achebe was writing his book, however, the party became embroiled in an internal altercation. The crisis led to Michael Imoudu declaring that a faction of the party was loyal to him while Aminu Kano, the veteran politician, presided over the rest of the party. The party's Kano State governor, Abubakar Rimi, and Balarabe Musa, a former governor of Kaduna State, also became political rebels. These developments did not trouble the party unduly because the influence of Aminu Kano was strong in those two states. Thus Aminu Kano continued his campaign and many Nigerian citizens anticipated the election as an opportunity for effecting political change, especially after a spate of incidents of arson in which public buildings were burnt. The most notorious of those incidents was the burning of the gigantic 37-storey Nigerian External Telecommunications (NET) building in January 1983. In addition incidents of corrupt practice were numerous, especially among the officers of the ruling National Party of Nigeria, and President Shehu Shagari appeared unable to either call his lieutenants to order or generate a climate of accountability. Furthermore the various national and local political leaders, from all the political parties, were exhibiting unpleasant signs of intolerance for opposition. These were among the enormous difficulties that Chinua Achebe perceived as he worked on his pre-election book.

While the local political scene did not offer him cause to be joyful, Achebe received the consolation of more international awards that proved to him the importance of the writing career on which he had embarked. He was made a member of the Royal Society of Literature and a Governor of Newsconcern International Foundation. He also became the patron of the Writers and Scholars Educational Trust, London, Amnesty International's publishers. In Nigeria, he was made a member of the National Festival Committee and the offer of the Commonwealth Foundation Senior Visiting Practitioner award for 1983 made it another good year for Chinua Achebe's reputation as a distinguished African writer.

16

The Trouble with Nigeria
An Ambassador for Literature & Justice
1983–7

H IS engagement in political activities in 1983 made Achebe more sensitive to the need to refashion the political culture in Nigeria. It became a preoccupation that was pursued with vigour as he reflected upon the various aspects of the society in the book he was writing. He had discovered, even within the political party of which he was a member, that it was easy for individuals without definite principles to break their promises and act in ways that generated disillusionment for the ordinary Nigerian. At the same time he was aware that the leader and presidential candidate of his political party, Aminu Kano, was exemplary in the way that he conducted his affairs without pursuing enormous wealth at the expense of ordinary people. The programme that Aminu Kano advocated late in March 1983 confirmed that view: he urged Nigerians to cultivate a sense of pride in their agricultural development in order to meet the country's food requirements, suggesting the introduction of agricultural science in all post-primary and higher learning institutions in Nigeria.

As the elections approached it was clear that the incompetent Shagari administration and his political party, the NPN, were becoming desperate. The PRP was engaged in a well-articulated political programme for the elections – scheduled for 3, 13, 20 and 27 August and 3 September 1983 – in spite of an internal crisis, the common fate of all Nigerian political parties at the time. The inability of the Federal Electoral Commission to produce a reliable voters' register remained a worry.

Achebe attended several meetings of PRP officials in various parts of the country. At a press conference after such a meeting in the second week of April 1983 Aminu Kano presented his vice-presidential candidate, Mrs Bola Ogunbor. He explained that the party believed in the transformation of the society and that women should be given the freedom to contribute in the struggle to improve conditions. 'If we don't make women part of our struggle, we shall not succeed.'[1] After that meeting in Kano on Saturday, 16 April, Chinua Achebe returned to Nsukka in the company of Chief Sylvester Nwodo, the deputy leader of the PRP in Anambra State. On Sunday, 17 April news reached him that Mallam Aminu Kano had died. It was unbelievable; he had conversed with the man the previous day. Chief Nwodo came to his house that Sunday convinced that the news was not true. He told Achebe that it was propaganda meant to discredit the PRP. But it was true. A tribute published in *West Africa* of 25 April declared that Kano

> will be missed by his party, but also by millions of other Nigerians for whom he had symbolized the national conscience, a shining example of selfless service, in a country where all too frequently to serve is also to grow rich.[2]

It was indeed the loss of a man who had battled incessantly to remove a system of power which he perceived as oppressive to the mass of the people.

With Kano's death so close to the August presidential elections his party lost its momentum, since it had to refashion its organizational structure. In addition the loss of the national secretary of the party, S. G. Ikoku, who resigned and became a member of the NPN in the same month, meant that a fundamental solution had to be found to the crisis in the PRP. In early May 1983 the party held a two-day meeting in Kaduna at the end of which the new party officers and political candidates were announced. Alhaji Hassan Yusuf was the party's new presidential candidate, with Mrs Bola Ogunbor as the vice-presidential candidate, while the widow of Mallam Aminu Kano, Hajia Aishatu, became the grand patron of the party. At that meeting, Chinua Achebe had been offered the position of party leader, which he declined, accepting instead the position of deputy national vice-president. Comrade Uche Chukwumerije became the national secretary while Sidi Sirajor became national publicity secretary and Una Akpan his assistant.

Shortly after that meeting the book that Achebe had written to coincide with the presidential elections was published by Fourth Dimension Publishers at Enugu as *The Trouble with Nigeria*. It was a work of no more than 68 pages, but it was Achebe at his satirical, critical and interrogative best. The publishers called it 'a savage indictment of the current system and a message of hope for the future', as well as 'a book that must be read by all Nigerians who care about their country, who feel they can no longer stand idly by and "wring their hands in anguish" while Nigeria is destroyed by bad leadership, corruption and inequality'.[3] The thesis of *The Trouble with Nigeria* is presented by Achebe on the first page, where he asserts that 'the trouble with Nigeria is simply and squarely a failure of leadership' and 'the Nigerian problem is the unwillingness or inability of its leaders to rise to the responsibility and to the challenge of personal example which are the hallmarks of true leadership'.[4]

The book is clearly an indictment of the élite class and also a criticism of the anomalies in the society. But it ultimately generates the hope that the future could be transformed. It is a work that is compulsory reading for all concerned Nigerians who are willing to act positively in the interest of their society. But more especially it is a challenge to the people to abhor bad leadership, corruption and inequality. He condemns tribal politics and the false image which the citizens have of themselves. The political activities of Chief Obafemi Awolowo and Dr Nnamdi Azikiwe, in particular, come in for criticism and their acolytes are censured for imbibing some of the same political deficiencies. Achebe feels that social injustice emanates from the practice of tribalism and that it ultimately leads to the cult of mediocrity. He argues that 'indiscipline pervades our life so completely today that one may be justified in calling it the condition *par excellence* of contemporary Nigerian society',[5] and also that 'corruption in Nigeria has passed the alarming and entered the fatal stage; and Nigeria will die if we keep pretending that she is only slightly indisposed'.[6] His discussion of the Igbo problem leads to the conclusion that 'when Nigeria learns to deal fairly with all its citizens [its] prospects for progress and stability will be infinitely brighter'.[7] He condemns President Shagari for his insensitivity to the problems of corruption and in the final chapter he offers the example of Aminu Kano by juxtaposing him with Awolowo and Azikiwe. Achebe concludes that

> Aminu Kano had the imagination and intelligence to foresee the danger which our unjust social order poses for society and renounced the privilege of his class and identified himself completely through struggle with the fate of the down-trodden.... Nigeria cannot be the same again because Aminu Kano lived here.[8]

The Trouble with Nigeria was a bombshell, for it had criticized sacred cows like Awolowo and Azikiwe, and it had not spared the other political leaders, either. But it was generally regarded as a truthful book and Achebe's assessment of Aminu Kano was widely accepted. President Shehu Shagari seemed to recognize the extent of public respect for Kano when he announced in May 1983 that the Kano airport was henceforth to be known as the Aminu Kano International Airport. Meanwhile, the crisis within the PRP was being resolved gradually with the reuniting of the two factions, one led by Michael Imoudu and the other led formerly by Aminu Kano but now by Hassan Yusuf with Chinua Achebe as deputy leader. Alhaji Balarabe Musa, formerly of the Imoudu faction, became the new national vice-presidential candidate of the reunited party in the elections of 1983, which were marred by massive electoral malpractices. At the end the NPN of President Shagari was declared the winner of the presidential election while Awolowo's UPN, Waziri's GNPP, Azikiwe's NPP and the reunited PRP were said to have lost much of what they had won in 1979. The newly registered National Advance Party (NAP) did not win a significant portion of votes although it received a few thousand in Imo State.

The violence that erupted after the elections was unprecedented and in Anambra, Oyo and Ondo states, where the incumbent governors lost due to the manipulation of election results by their opponents, the political battles were bitter. The incumbents went to court but it was clear that the NPN, in control of the judiciary, was unwilling to relinquish power. In Ondo State the electoral victory of the NPN was overturned by the Supreme Court but in Anambra and Oyo states those fraudulent electoral victories were confirmed. The consequence was a strong feeling of disenchantment, especially as the court cases dragged to an end in the latter part of 1983. Achebe, whose book *The Trouble with Nigeria* had warned against political, social and economic injustice and the inevitable consequences of abused democracy, was greatly disappointed. Achebe made his views known in an interview he granted Mike Awoyinfa of the *Sunday Concord,* published in October 1983.

Awoyinfa called it 'a long-running interview covering all you had ever wanted to know about Nigeria's most famous novelist'. Achebe is asked if the Nigerian politician had changed from the way he portrayed him in *A Man of the People.* He replies:

> I think, if anything, the Nigerian politician has deteriorated. The corruption of Chief Nanga of *A Man of the People* was on a minor scale compared with today. Today, we

are talking about millions. People are stealing millions. In the day of Chief Nanga, if they stole ten thousand it was very bad news. Today, Ministers are in business and there are all kinds of scandals. I think the situation is really much worse and this is one of the reasons why one has to come out and really say something that may sound harsh but, in my estimation, necessary.

Asked to comment on the conduct of the 1983 presidential elections, Achebe answers:

What has happened is a wholesale disregard of the rules – the rules of election, the rules of fairness. If you don't have the attitude of fair play then you cannot have a democratic system. There is no doubt that from the very beginning even before the actual elections, the people in power – I don't mean just the Federal government, I mean those in power all around – did not want anything that would upset them where they are in power. They wanted something that would upset somebody else. There is absolutely no doubt in my mind that there was widescale rigging of results. This is quite clear to me. It is left to those who can analyse it in the law court and all the other people to produce the evidence. But [by] the evidence of my eyes and my ears [it] appears that there was widespread rigging of the elections. And what this suggests is that we do not really care for democracy.[9]

One interesting question put to Achebe by Awoyinfa is whether there is 'any overt or subtle clash between him and Wole Soyinka?' 'No there is not,' Achebe answers categorically. 'Why should there be?' He is asked further if there is 'any literary competition between them' and he replies: 'There may well be but again that's not great news. There's competition between people in the same profession everywhere. The purpose of all that is not to say that you discredit the other man or anything like that but that you try to excel.' He adds that

Fortunately, in the case of artists, every artist is a unique person just as every individual is unique to a considerable extent. So you are not really competing about the same thing. It's not like you are scrambling for scarce resources. Each person has his own little area where he can excel without trampling or stepping on someone else's toe.... If you know me, I'm not highly competitive. So it is not great news. Somebody else may have a different notion of our relationship appropriate to people like us but to me it is normal.[10]

It was an illuminating comment that clarified several issues.

At about this time Achebe was in London to honour an invitation from Alastair Niven, director-general of the Africa Centre.

I remember [Achebe] giving a public talk to a packed house but it was not an evening without its drama. There were a number of Young Turks in the audience who felt strongly that Achebe was of the old guard. I remember that the evening was chaired by Dr Lyn Innes. A member of the audience, a radical Marxist from Senegal, said in a speech from the floor that Achebe had 'betrayed the African revolution', a remark which visibly shook Achebe.

Niven adds that Achebe 'was expected to stay for a dinner that night but did not do so. He gave, as always, a marvellous address and it was a distinguished evening, but I do not think that he enjoyed it as much as I had wanted him to do.'[11] The irony was that this criticism had come at a time when Achebe was involved in momentous political events and was becoming increasingly worried that ordinary people in Nigeria were being cheated by their leaders. The accusation was new to him and seemed to be motivated by the fact that he had not proclaimed dramatically and hypocritically that he was either a socialist or a Marxist. All the same, the accusation made him more sensitive to the nuances of human reactions and assumptions concerning his writing, his person and the events in his own country.

Those events were generating feelings of great disappointment, confirmed by the events that unfolded within the PRP itself when Achebe returned to Nigeria. The party had succeeded in capturing only the governorship of Kano State, through the obvious influence of the late Aminu Kano, but the man who became governor, Bakin Zuwo, was a different person altogether. A tall, boisterous man who was impervious to the plethora of political gaffes he made with both words and failures of logic, Zuwo's sole aim was to control the PRP. Unfortunately he had neither the vision nor the mental attitude to assume such a leadership position but he commenced using the state wealth within his control to achieve his aim. The national president was in his pay and that fact led Zuwo to take excessive liberties in party affairs. But there were members of the party in Kano State, like the academic Dr Junaid Mohammed, who took exception to the behaviour of Governor Zuwo. Mohammed criticized the party for several of its deficiencies which angered Bakin Zuwo, who retaliated with a campaign to hound Mohammed out of the party. It was not a campaign that Zuwo could orchestrate alone, however, and when the matter came to the attention of some national officers of the PRP like Uche Chukwumerije, the secretary, he refused to join the campaign and insisted that Junaid Mohammed must be given an opportunity to explain himself. That decision angered Zuwo, who turned on Chukwumerije with the intention of expelling *him* from the party. It was this second battle to expel Chukwumerije, the party secretary, which brought the crisis to a head at a national meeting. At that meeting Chinua Achebe challenged Bakin Zuwo, since the national president Hassan Yusuf was too afraid of Zuwo to call him to order. But Zuwo was not ready to yield to reason and a serious quarrel erupted between him and Achebe. It was so serious that the two men nearly came to blows and Zuwo exacerbated matters by making unguarded ethnic allusions to the effect that 'the Igbos are coming again'.[12] At that point it became quite clear that the national president Hassan Yusuf was powerless and Achebe walked out of both the meeting and the People's Redemption Party.

The party was again on the verge of collapse as the meeting ended in disarray. The chairman of its eastern branch, Arthur Nwankwo, wrote a strong letter in November 1983, after the quarrel between Achebe and Zuwo, informing the national executive that until Bakin Zuwo apologized the branch would suspend its membership of the party. Achebe confessed later that his experience in the PRP after the death of Aminu Kano 'was very bad' because

> there were people who wanted to use your name. They have no intention of doing the things you say should be done, or the things you believe or the things even the party stands for. There will be the raw politician who wants power – that is all he wants – and he will go for it. I saw many people who did not even understand the national nature of the party. They thought it was just their own and that those of us who were coming from the South were just there to decorate their show. I saw the intellectual at his worst.

Achebe further observed that they would 'sit and have debates' but when the moment comes to stand up [for the decisions] you find them sneaking away and then coming up with excuses later. The fundamental weakness of the party was that there was no follow-up after Aminu Kano. Aminu was there with a lot of experience, a lot of ideas but he had no one to succeed him.[13]

It was undoubtedly a serious disappointment, which Achebe had to overcome in order to deliver a speech on 'The Purpose of Education' at the Federal Government College, Lagos in November 1983. It was, as usual, a speech in which Achebe urged his listeners to put the values of education to positive use in the Nigerian society. Such cultural activities, and even social activities such as the send-off party for Alan Hill at Ibadan when he retired as the Chairman of Heinemann Educational Books, were quite helpful in lifting Achebe's political gloom. Alan Hill described the occasion as one 'graced by many affectionate speeches from all authors and rival publishers, and not least from Aig (Higo) and Chinua'.[14] In addition the annual conference of the Association of Nigerian Authors held at Benin enabled Achebe to achieve a distance from politics in order to reflect fully on the nature of his society. In the presidential address on that occasion he considers the role of the association: 'If I may put it crudely the reason for this association is to give the work we do and the ideas we stand for as writers a stronger presence in the life and affairs of this nation.' He insists that 'fashions may change surface appearances but the inner values remain' and 'they do manifest themselves in this stubborn refusal to bow to external dictation and are ultimately indispensable to the creative experience'. On the theme of commitment Achebe argues that 'Nigeria is a highly political country. And so when we speak of commitment, it is inevitably political commitment with all its Nigerian implications.' Thus he warns: 'As individuals and citizens what we do in politics is our business. But as an association of writers, our role is clear: keep out!'[15] His major contention is that the political hypocrisy and tribal distinctions surreptitiously emerging in the assessment of Nigerian literature must be eliminated.

As far as his personal political affairs went, the fact that the national executive had not bothered to reply to the protest letter of the Eastern chairman of the party made it fairly obvious that Bakin Zuwo was tightening his grip on the PRP. That was the situation in December 1983 when Achebe granted a television interview. In the course of the interview he was asked what he thought of President Shagari's Green Revolution Programme and he replied that 'it was a disaster which gave plenty of food for thought and nothing at all in our stomach'. That statement gave great offence. Press comment included the observation that Achebe should not have been asked to comment on agriculture because he was not an expert in that field. But Achebe felt that little academic expertise was needed to tell 'us when our stomach is empty'.[16]

In December 1983 the Nigerian soldiers returned to the political scene through a coup on the last day of the year. It was like turning a full circle, except that a majority of the people welcomed the removal by force of the corrupt, wasteful and extremely incompetent Shagari regime. The first announcement by Brigadier Sanni Abacha on 31 December referred to the 'harsh intolerable conditions under which we are now living'.[17] In his broadcast to the nation on 1 January 1984 Head of State General Muhammadu Buhari highlighted the same reasons and ended with the statement that 'this generation of Nigerians, and indeed future generations have no other country than Nigeria. We shall remain here and salvage it together.'[18] With this patriotic and moving statement Buhari took up the reins of government, with Tunde Idiagbon as his chief of staff and Ibrahim Babangida as chief of army staff. It became clear that the Buhari regime was committed to the adoption of a tough posture when many of the politicians were arrested and soon after several probe panels were set up to determine the degree of corruption associated with the toppled Shagari regime. Military rule was not a new occurrence in Nigeria, however, and Chinua Achebe, like most of his discerning compatriots, was aware of the various factors that could deflect even the most patriotic objectives.

That awareness was reflected in a lecture that Achebe delivered at the University of Port Harcourt on 8 February 1984. In 'Reflections on Nigeria's Political Culture', Achebe notes a fundamental characteristic of the Nigerian political class as 'a drive towards absolute power'. He condemns the manner in which the politicians 'turned their attention to modern institutions whose independent existence and powers of initiative had thus far been taken for granted – the universities, the mass media, business and industrial establishments, etc.' and he notes that this development had taken place steadily 'over the years since independence' until the institutions concerned had been brought 'into line by a domineering political command post'. Achebe mentions that the politicians in the Second Republic 'had virtually completed the destruction of independent and honest businessmen and captains of industry and replaced them with roving bands of corrupt and incompetent party contractors'. His major criticism, however, is devoted to the ways in which the mass media and the universities 'have become attractive to the politician and vulnerable to his power-garnering appetite'. Achebe illustrates his lecture with the example that throughout 1983 'Nigerian newspapers, radio and television demonstrated amazing vituperative vigour', while in Anambra State

> we were given the spectacle of the general manager of the Nigerian Television Authority on the screen dancing up and down the arena of an NPN rally; and we saw another senior executive of the station line up his production staff on the last day of campaigns to make brief speeches of support for the NPN – openly on the screen! [I] had taken the opportunity of a visit to NTA Lagos earlier in the year to complain to the director-general about the truly sickening excesses of his Enugu staff. He wouldn't let me finish. Anambra, he said, was a war zone; the staff had his permission to go all out; when the elections were over we could all go back to normal broadcasting. That was the politician and his obsession with the short term.

Achebe emphasizes that 'reputations are always built under conditions of strain when the temptation is strong to opt out now and fight another day'. His choice of NTA 'does not mean, incidentally, that they were the only, or even the worst offenders, in the media disaster of 1983', but that it had 'a special responsibility' in his view to 'uphold decent professional standards; and it failed abysmally'.

In the same manner Achebe examines the universities, criticizing the manner in which the names of politicians have come to be associated with such institutions. He takes the example of the University of Nigeria, Nsukka and the names given to its halls of residence, refectory, library and stadium.

> Here is the grasping political mentality at its most brazen, respecting neither excellence nor good taste nor history at the very citadel of learning. And incidentally inaugurating a tradition of self-adulation by politicians which, a little later, was to give us Ahmadu

Bello University and later still, and slightly less brazenly because [it was] accomplished through surrogates, Obafemi Awolowo University.

He wonders 'why Nigerian politicians and their surrogates are not prepared to wait for history to honour them. They seem somehow to be afraid of history.' The result, he points out, 'is that their actions have imposed on the nation a shabby and unhealthy legacy which we must repudiate if we are ever to attain anything like a decent and viable political culture'. He reminds his audience that 'human civilization has to strike a fine balance between the variable and the constant, between what can come and go and what must abide like the proverbial anthill to tell the savannah of last year's bush fire'. Achebe points out that the interest of the politicians in the university does not end with 'the naming of halls and streets after himself. He wants ultimately to control what is going on there' and it

> is therefore imperative that the university order its affairs in such a manner that it can command respect in the land, as this is the surest way to safeguard its integrity from political encroachment. And the university must also be ready to show courage in the face of threats. This is hardly possible unless the management of its own affairs is unimpeachable.

The mission of a university, Achebe declares, is 'to nurture itself into a centre of free enquiry and intellectual excellence whose aim is to produce, conserve and transmit knowledge and culture'; he concludes that 'this is a terrible responsibility which we assume when we enrol to teach or learn in a university. Not everyone can fulfil it. But those who do will influence for good the life and political culture of Nigeria.'[19]

The essence of this lecture was particularly relevant in early 1984, when many of the academics in the universities had succumbed to the temptations of politicians; quite often they re-enacted the political conflicts on campus in their efforts to show support for the political leaders. The displeasure of Chinua Achebe at such activities was clearly motivated by a sense of the appropriate moral consciousness that should obtain in a university, a sense he derived from his association with several distinguished universities in other countries. Mount Allison University in New Brunswick, Canada became the latest of these when it invited him to accept an honorary degree. Achebe went to Canada for that award on 14 May 1984, which coincided with the 130th anniversary of the founding of the Ladies College as part of the Mount Allison Wesleyan Academy. The citation highlighted Achebe's accomplishments as 'the first African novelist in English to blend fictional art with moral purpose' and also mentioned his commitment to 'a world view beyond the dividing-lines of race and colonial history'.[20]

Achebe's tenth honorary degree would soon follow from another Canadian institution, the University of Guelph in Ontario. This honour coincided with the Commonwealth Foundation Senior Visiting Practitioner Award which enabled Achebe to spend two months between May and July 1984 at Guelph. G. D. Killam recalls that 'at the suggestion of Mr Ric Throssell, Director of the Commonwealth Foundation, I nominated Chinua for the award of a Senior Commonwealth Practitioner which after a period of deliberation he accepted'. He adds that this was

> the beginning of a two-month visit which was memorable in many ways – for his

meeting again with Margaret Laurence, a friend of long standing; for a memorable meeting with Northrop Frye and a memorable visit to give a talk at the McLuhan Institute at the University of Toronto; for active participation in teaching workshops with colleagues and friends from Cameroon; and in presenting a 'letter from Canada' to Nigeria on the overseas service of the Canadian Broadcasting Corporation.[21]

It was a hectic schedule but wherever Achebe went he offered evidence of the special insight into different social contexts which had come to be associated with him. In the 'letter from Canada' he was as honest as ever as he examined his country in relation to Africa and the rest of the world. His contribution to the workshop on the educational and literary uses of folk orature, sponsored by the Guelph–Yaoundé Project on Education for Self-Reliance, was equally relevant. In that address Achebe insists:

> Let me say once more, let's not inhibit the collection [of folktales]. I think that those who collect or bring in the material should go out and do it. Thereafter comes the editorial stage where the final decision on the literary quality; on the content, on the ideological – yes even the ideological content of the story is discussed. Incidentally we must be ready to plough through masses of collected material to discover a few nuggets of real quality.

He cautions against an insensitive acceptance of oral literature because 'not all oral literature is of acceptable quality', but he was convinced that 'if you have a group sensitive enough to good writing, to good stories, to the needs of Cameroonian education they will know what to do'.[22]

Achebe also addressed the graduands of the Arts and Social Science colleges on the day that he received his Doctorate of Letters. According to G. D. Killam, his convocation address was judged by the president of the university, the vice-chancellor and the dean of the college 'to be among the most compelling presented to Guelph Convocations'. Achebe tells the graduands that 'they are inheriting a world which differs fundamentally from the world [their] fathers inherited – differs indeed from the world ever inherited by any previous generation of mankind'. He believes they 'have a responsibility to try to save the world' for themselves, even if they assume that they do not possess the power. He reminds them of

> another kind of power. The power of creation. The power that the creation myths of all peoples bear witness to – the power of the mind and the word. I suggest that the force that enables one thing to create another can be available to you. Your education in a University that takes its international vocation seriously is one aspect of it. Your personal commitment to redress the parochialism and prejudices of the past is another. The new world is not some starry-eyed utopian metaphor. It is a practical question of life and death. Either a *new* world or a *dead* world. I wish you success.[23]

His address received an ovation and the citation that preceded the award of his honorary degree was greeted with another. It described Achebe as 'Nigeria's foremost man of letters' and noted that 'the University of Guelph has become well and favourably known for its leadership in the study of Commonwealth Literature – a commonwealth of ideas and ideals, to which our candidate has made uncommonly important contributions'.[24]

Before 1984 was out, his novel *A Man of the People* was listed by Anthony Burgess in *Ninety-nine Novels: The Best in English Since 1939;* in New York Benedict Njoku published *The Four Novels of Chinua Achebe*[25] in which he makes efforts to probe the fictional world of Chinua Achebe from both the realistic and naturalistic perspectives. On 26 October Achebe was a speaker at a special plenary session of the African Studies Association meeting in Los Angeles. Don Burness recalls that he was on the panel with Achebe, Bob Wren and I. N. C. Aniebo, and that 'Chinua was very stern when an African, probably a Nigerian, in the audience referred to the Igbo "dialect". Chinua told him not to forget that Igbo is a *language* not a dialect.'[26] Achebe was in America because he had been appointed a Regent's Professor of English at the University of California at Los Angeles. He gave the Regent's Lecture in November 1984 on 'The Writer and His Community' in which he argues that one of the consequences of the transition from oral traditions to written forms of literature 'is the emergence of individual authorship', but also points out that part of his

> artistic and intellectual inheritance is derived from a cultural tradition in which it was possible for artists to create objects of art which were solid enough and yet make no attempt to claim, and sometimes even go to great length to deny, personal ownership of what they have created.

That art form he describes as the *Mbari* tradition. The principle of individualism which has dominated Western thought, by contrast, does not identify creativity with the spiritual wealth of the community, although the dazzling achievement of Western technology often gives the impression of its association with the right values. Achebe goes on to argue, drawing on the discussion of technology and values in Cheikh Hamidou Kane's *Ambiguous Adventure,* that neglected non-Western values may possess insights capable of enriching the process of modernization around the world.

Part of that error of omission, he insists, is reflected in the idea that the novel 'was designed to explore individual rather than social predicaments' and he asks: 'If the novel came about in particular ways and circumstances must it remain forever in the mould of its origin?' Achebe argues that many of the ideas attributed to the West, including individualism, are as old as human society itself, but he adds that in the Igbo society the 'artist and his people are in very close communion' even when they disagree. In addressing the issue of the make-up of his personal community, Achebe tells a story which highlights the fact that 'the singer should sing well even if it is merely to himself, rather than dance badly for the whole world'. His conclusion reiterates his view:

> I can see no situation in which I will be presented with a Draconian choice between reading books and watching movies; or between English and Igbo. For me, no either or; I insist on both. Which, you might say, makes my life rather difficult and even a little untidy. But I prefer it that way. Despite the daunting problems of identity that beset our contemporary society we can see on the horizon the beginnings of a new relationship between artist and community which will not flourish like the mango trick in the twinkling of an eye but will rather, in the hard and bitter manner of David Diop's young tree, grow patiently and obstinately to the ultimate victory of liberty and fruition.[27]

The Regent's Lecture thus provided Achebe with the opportunity to clarify a number of issues clouding a true understanding of literatures from Africa. His ambassador's role was dedicated not only to a heightened appreciation of literature but also to the identification and illustration of its basic values and relevance. It was an act that was needed in a world where African countries and cultures were subject to negative perspectives in foreign news media.

International literary ambassadorial activities did not draw Achebe's attention away from Nigerian developments for long. He gave his support to the Association of Nigerian Authors; he wrote a foreword to the book *Igbo Arts: Community and Cosmos* (edited by Herbert Cole and Chike Aniakor and published by the University of California Press) and he responded to the criticism of Nolue Emenanjo's review of an anthology of Igbo poems, *Aka Weta*, in an essay ('Editorial and Linguistic Problems in *Aka Weta:* A Comment') published in the first issue of *Uwa Ndi Igbo,* the journal he had established.

Emenanjo had criticized the fact that contributors to the volume of poems had been encouraged to write in their own dialects as well as the 'central Igbo' encouraged in schools. Achebe's response is that 'the great tragedy of Igbo is to have been saddled one generation after another with egoistic schoolmen who have been concerned not to study the language but to steer it into narrow tracks of their particular pet illusions'. He also insists that 'language is *never* created by grammarians' but 'made by the people and enriched by their poets'.[28] In the same critical way Achebe's foreword to *Igbo Arts: Community and Cosmos*, written while at the University of Guelph in June 1984, thoughtfully describes the 'Igbo World as an area for the interplay of forces' and also notes that the 'artistic deployment of motion, of agility which informs the Igbo concept of existence' makes the masquerade 'so satisfying to the Igbo disposition'.[29]

There was no doubt that Achebe defended whatever literary positions he adopted vigorously and persuasively. It was in the same spirit that he granted an interview to Okey Ndibe of the *Concord Weekly* (Michael Awoyinfa of the *Sunday Concord* used some of the extracts as a cover story). In the major part of the interview, published in the *Concord Weekly* of 28 January 1985, Achebe says that there 'is the need to serve every community as fairly as possible' but 'merit is not what you can [get] on the basis of quota'. He insists once more that 'Nigeria as a nation has not been founded up to now' and that the man who will do some of the things he enumerated in *The Trouble with Nigeria*

> is the man who will be called by posterity the founder of the Nigerian nation. But it is difficult, he's going to rise beyond all that we know today, to be possessed by this vision of Nigeria as a modern state in the 21st Century. He can't be mucking around with tribalism, with petty religious arguments.

He explains that Nigeria 'has never had it so bad' and also that the 'rest of the world, especially the more developed countries, are marching ahead and every day puts them so many miles ahead of us'. Achebe agrees that 'the army tends to do things in the area of discipline. But they do not often understand that a country is not a parade ground.' He states emphatically that he 'cannot accept the permanence of military rule' and that 'the democratic resources of Nigeria will assert themselves again'. He warns that 'whenever it is, whenever the time comes' to hand over to civilians, 'if they do not hand over they will soon hear about it'. Achebe argues that elections 'should not be left to the man who is struggling to save his neck' and that 'public servants are public servants and they should be open to criticism, open to examination, open to exposure'. Thus he comments that Shagari must be held accountable for his tenure as president because 'when somebody becomes president, he swears an oath to uphold the constitution and if the constitution is not upheld, then he's guilty already. He does not have to be guilty of petty thieving, it's enough that the president is guilty of mismanagement.'[30] Achebe's remarks were always literary events, which was why he was sought after by journalists. In response to one of the questions concerning the standard of education in Nigeria Achebe says that it has fallen so low that even professors can no longer communicate well. This remark was published in the *Sunday Concord* of 20 January 1985. Achebe is quoted as expressing dissatisfaction with what he describes as 'the absolute, almost illiterate level at which even Professors had their discourse'. He adds:

> This must come from the fact that they do not read, they have no mastery of the language of the discourse, or of the linguistic equipment which is very important even in science. They don't have the equipment for internalizing the knowledge so they pour it out as it is in the text book.

Achebe notes by way of illustration that

> the chances are that inside a plane in other parts of the world, you'd find a large number of people engaged in reading but in Nigeria once the lounge is over and you get into the plane, people are either still attempting to hold loud conversation or if they cannot, they have nothing to do.

His conclusion is that 'there is a great, almost cataclysmic fall in quality and level of education in Nigeria'.[31] The following week Michael Awoyinfa interviewed some professors at the University of Lagos asking for their comments. In the *Sunday Concord* of 3 February 1985 he published an article under the headline 'Dogs Eat Dog: Professors Attack Professor Achebe':

> Some Professors at the University of Lagos have exploded over the claim made by novelist Chinua Achebe that educational standards in Nigeria have fallen to the point where even Professors cannot communicate well. 'I don't know what University he is referring to,' remarked one angry professor who declined to be quoted on grounds that the issue was too 'trivial' for him to discuss. 'I can't comment', he said, 'because I don't consider Achebe as a professor in the academic sense. He only has a first degree, I agree he was made a professor but I see him as a performer, a practitioner. It's just like making Sunny Ade a Professor of music.' 'I do not want to join war with Achebe', said another professor, Abiodun Adetugbo, who is a professor of English Language at the University, 'I respect Achebe. He is a fine writer, but I want to believe the spoken English standard of an ordinary undergraduate today is better than his. The problem with language is that everybody is an expert. It is my field. I get annoyed when people get up to talk like this and that.' Professor Adetugbo explained that the standards of spoken English these days have risen [higher] than in the past 'when we had bookish English as the standard.' He added that more kids of today speak fluent English than in the past. Professor O. Oloko of the Sociology Department said that the students produced from the department 'have gone to other universities abroad and have obtained higher degrees in record time which shows the quality we produce is high.' According to him, that is one way of measuring the rise in educational standards. The other measure, he said, is that 'the quality of books and the quality of development in the field has been on the increase'. Professor Oloko said that Achebe's method of comparing the educational standards of the past to the present and concluding that standards have fallen is 'unscientific'. He accused the novelist of comparing the 'best of the past to the worst of today'. He said there is need for him to do a 'close comparison' before arriving at a conclusion. A Professor of Economics, F. O. Fajana, said that he has no time for reading novels but 'I don't think I lose anything.' He explained that he spends most of his time 'reading all the relevant journals, magazines and periodicals in my field which sufficiently equip me to express myself'. Dr Joseph Omoregbe who heads the Department of Philosophy also admits not reading novels regularly. 'But when you talk of language, my field has its own style of presentation', he said.[32]

Two weeks after the publication of that report the response of Chinua Achebe was published in the *Sunday Concord* of 17 February 1985 as a letter to the editor headed 'I'm an original Professor … professing Literature':

Your issue of February 3 carried a front page report by Michael Awoyinfa on the reaction of some Lagos University professors to my contention that educational standards have fallen badly in Nigeria. In a way I am grateful to the five gentlemen. Nothing I could have said would have made my point as well as the sub-standard quality of their argument. The first professor chooses quite sensibly, it seems, to fight behind a shield of anonymity. He begins by dismissing the issue as too trivial to engage his attention and then goes on to wonder what university I was referring to. I thought I had made it clear; I was talking about Nigerian universities including Lagos. But his real *coup de grace* was thus: 'I don't consider Achebe as a professor in the academic sense. He only has a first degree etc.' Professor Anonymous obviously believes that having a degree is the same thing as having an education, and that the more degrees you have the more educated you become. This is, of course, a species of superstition commonly encountered among the half-educated. The danger is that this class of people is now storming the very citadel of Nigeria's academia. Ignorance is bad enough; but combative ignorance trumpeting its own values is a threat not only to education but to civilization itself. I have no desire whatsoever to be considered 'a professor in the academic sense', by my Lagos colleague. I am quite content to be a professor in the original sense professing my subject which is literature, both here in Nigeria and anywhere else I choose. Professor Adetugbo flatters me as a 'fine writer' but is also convinced that 'the spoken English standards of an ordinary undergraduate today' are better than mine. He should know because he is better than a mere 'fine writer'; he is nothing less than a language specialist! And he concludes like the specialist he is by comparing the 'bookish English' of the past unfavourably with the (bookless?) English of today. I was an external examiner in Lagos University before Adetugbo achieved his professorship. I do not recall meeting any of his spell-binding undergraduates but I certainly read some awful scripts. Professor Oloko of Sociology makes several claims: that his students go abroad and get higher degrees in record time; that 'the quality of books and the quality of development in the field have been on the increase'. Since he has accused me of being unscientific, I take it he considers the above allegations of his as constituting scientific proof of rising educational standards. From Dr Omoregbe, head of the Department of Philosophy, comes the following: 'When you talk of language my field has its own style of presentation.' I think we all know that every discipline has its own jargon. But we also know that the brightest people in the discipline are usually the ones who can dispense with its jargon. Bertrand Russell, mathematician and philosopher and one of the most educated men of the 20th century, knew the jargon of the two disciplines and yet was able to win the Nobel Prize in literature for the elegance of his writing. But perhaps the most amazing statement of all comes from the Professor of Economics – a self-confession (no less) to illiteracy! Professor Fajana does not waste his time on novels and such like, but devotes himself entirely to reading journals and magazines in his field. 'I don't think I lose anything', he says. I have bad news for him. He not only does lose a lot in general awareness and culture but he will not even be a good economist! He might be satisfied with his performance but any road-side mechanic can tell him he is 'missing fire'. Although I knew that our universities were in deep trouble I never suspected that a reporter could dredge up all those calamities at such [short] notice and in one institution alone! Neither did I think that university people could flaunt their ignorance so boldly in the world's face as some beggars do their grotesque deformities. God help us![33]

It was a comprehensive response questioning several fundamental issues from a man who had sincerely professed literature, an objective that had taken

Achebe all over the world for readings and lectures. Not long before the controversy started Achebe had delivered the Senate Lecture at the University of Jos. It was also clear, however, that controversies did not deter Chinua Achebe from either telling the people what he thought was appropriate or cautioning the soldiers who held positions of civil authority in his country. His criticism of the military regime in Nigeria was particularly important because General Buhari was ruling with such severity. He had promulgated several decrees, the most obnoxious being Decree No. 4 which stipulated very stiff penalties for publications that contained even slight errors. It was this decree that was used to penalize two journalists working for the *Guardian* newspaper. In an interview which Achebe granted to the *New Nigerian* newspaper in April 1985 he warns the Buhari regime against the

> attempt to clamp down on expression, free expression. I think that is definitely something that is neither desirable nor even useful. I've said this before, that I do not see what advantage this regime can derive from having a kind of running battle with journalists. My people say that if you have too many enemies you take palm wine to some of them. You make friends with some of them. Because unless you do that you are finished.... I don't really see why you want to be fighting on all the fronts. You need support, you need some people who are in favour of everything in detail. Don't alienate them. The press is one of these groups.

Achebe nevertheless points out that one of the achievements of Buhari was the 'business of holding people accountable for what they did. I think this is something new in Nigerian political culture' because 'it is very crucial that from now on anybody who aspires to be a leader, when he wakes up in the morning, sees the vision of Kirikiri [maximum security prison] ahead of him'.

Achebe, lamenting that Nigeria has not been founded, argues that one 'of the greatest betrayals of modern times' was the 'chance to turn Nigeria into one of the great nations of Africa, perhaps the leading Black nation' which was frittered away. But he is convinced that the issue of leadership in Nigeria must be taken seriously 'because nobody is forced to be a leader of Nigeria. You offer yourself so you know that there are difficulties and it is really your responsibility to deal with them.' He points to some of the problems a leader must deal with, like the 'many young able-bodied Nigerians, unemployed'. Achebe regards them as 'a waste of the most important resource we have. There are millions of these people and some programme has to be evolved that will engage [them]' so that they will not be 'available to be recruited into all kinds of anti-social behaviour'. Achebe perceives some of those instances of anti-social behaviour in politics and feels that any political system can work in Nigeria 'if you want to apply it honestly. We are not from Mars, we are human beings like other people who are governed under these systems'. He emphasizes that 'our task is to find the answer to the question: the president presides over Nigeria, who presides over the president? Part of the answer, Achebe feels, is people in leadership positions performing their duties efficiently. He believes that 'all good literature [does] a little bit of crusading' because 'every good story always brings something out. It is not just words for the sake of words, at the end there must be some position which you take so that somebody who encounters this book is not quite the same person when he has read it.' On the other hand, Achebe warns, a 'writer can never get into rigid positions. I think rigidity by its very nature is anti-art. This is why I can create a villain who is quite attractive.'

He adds that 'this is not ideological because if it were ideological a villain should have a very bad image, but that doesn't create literature. Literature is often created by the paradox.'[34] It was an insightful interview; but the warning Achebe gave to Buhari was unheeded and that military leader was to pay for it later in 1985, although his difficulties would come from unexpected quarters.

Achebe's literary engagements in 1985 were varied and significant. Heinemann Educational Books published *African Short Stories* which Achebe selected and edited in collaboration with Lyn Innes. That collection of twenty short stories included work from Western, Eastern, Northern and Southern Africa. In his introduction Achebe hopes the collection will serve as 'a manageable and enjoyable introduction into the art and the world of African fiction'.[35] In addition to this kind of literary activity Achebe was at the Franklin Pierce College in the United States in May 1985, where he gave the commencement address and collected another honorary degree. The citation referred to Achebe's achievement as writer, poet and teacher:

> With seriousness and acumen you have provided a renewed sense of African heritage, history and tradition. Like oral historians and storytellers of the village, you have continued through the written word to be a teacher of your people. You, who write with clarity, precision and irony, are acclaimed by elders and by students, and equally importantly, by other African writers. Because of your work, other Africans have gained the confidence to take their wares to the market places of the world where words, imagination and social reform matter. Outside of Africa you have been helping others to appreciate your society. Within Africa you have been seer and prophet. Disgusted by the selfishness of political leaders who have forgotten the wisdom of the ancestors, you have inspired the young to do better.[36]

The acclaim noted again in that warm citation was matched by cold statistics: *Things Fall Apart* alone had sold over two and a half million copies by 1985, in which year the University of Nigeria, Nsukka appointed him Professor Emeritus. At the ceremony, the university's public orator, Professor Emmanuel C. Okafor, described Chinua Achebe as 'a man whose humility, transparent honesty, inner peace, and yet a keen sense of humour have fascinated his colleagues and friends'. He added that 'his pen has edified and inspired peoples the world over' by producing 'clear and eloquent ideas [which] have endeared him to millions of readers'. His own university's verdict was that Achebe 'has always performed the noble role of a teacher, a seeker after truth, whose exemplary leadership the community has fully recognized and appreciated'.[37] The honour meant that Achebe was entitled to an office and would be there for occasional consultations, in addition to the lectures he could give when the spirit moved him.

At about the same time a second book on Achebe written in French, and the ninth book on his works – Denise Coussy's *L'Oeuvre de Chinua Achebe* – was published by Présence Africaine in Dakar and Paris. While Achebe welcomed the foreign recognition and critical studies of his works all over the world, a significant incident now occurred. He received a letter of invitation from Stockholm for a Second Conference of African Writers scheduled for the following year, but replied:

> I regret I cannot accept your generous invitation for the simple reason that I do not consider it appropriate for African writers to assemble in European capitals in 1986 to discuss the future of their literature. In my humble opinion it smacks too much of those

constitutional conferences arranged in London and Paris for our pre-independence
political leaders. Believe me, this is not an attempt to belittle the efforts and concern
of your organization or indeed of the Swedish people who have repeatedly demonstrated their solidarity with African aspirations in many different ways. But I strongly
believe that the time is overdue for Africans, especially African writers, to begin to
take the initiative in deciding the things that belong to their peace.[38]

Achebe felt that African literature had developed to the extent that it could be
discussed in Africa, where important seminars on Africa should now be held.
Thus he rejected the invitation, even though Stockholm was the seat of the
Nobel Prize committee and his response might well eliminate him from nomi-
nation for the award of that prize. He had been a strong contender for several
years and it was emphasized in 1985 that it was about time the Nobel Prize
came to Africa. Achebe's letter to Stockholm affected his chances since from a
'prize-giver's point of view a writer who would reject such an invitation might
be likely to reject a prize based on similar reasons and such decisions would
definitely be scandalous', as one critic pointed out.[39] Achebe's letter was also a
clear indication that Africa would always be the centre of his literary activities.
Ayi Kwei Armah was another who rejected the invitation to attend that Stockholm conference: in this instance, he and Achebe were in agreement.

Meanwhile the creative drought which Achebe the novelist had experienced
for almost two decades was over. He began work again on that fifth novel which
had refused to develop, *Anthills of the Savannah,* and this time, to Achebe's
amazement, it started to come. In a later interview he tries to explain why the
writing of the novel became possible in 1985:

I picked the thing up again and reread it in order to get acquainted once more with the
characters, and the story seemed to be there this time. I don't fully understand,
perhaps the fact that I had rested and thought about our condition and written a rather
angry essay about this, *The Trouble with Nigeria,* perhaps all that helped to ease the
passage of the new story.[40]

Thus Achebe started creating what he regarded as a summation of both his
vision and the different strands in his previous novels.

In the midst of this creative exercise the warning Achebe had publicly
offered the military government of General Buhari in the *New Nigerian* proved
well founded. On 27 August 1985 Buhari's former colleague Ibrahim Badamosi
Babangida, army chief of staff, carried out a coup. He arrested and detained
Buhari loyalists who were in the country. The chief of staff, Tunde Idiagbon,
was on a pilgrimage to Mecca but he bravely returned several days later and
Babangida put him in detention. Achebe felt that it was the stubborn streak in
Buhari which had paved the way for this overthrow of his regime; but he was
also convinced that Ibrahim Babangida, who assumed the title of president and
commander-in-chief of the Nigerian armed forces, was incapable of providing
the kind of leadership that Nigeria required.

That conviction soon proved to be justified as Babangida commenced a
theatrical style of leadership with tactical moves that embroiled Nigerians in
time-wasting debates. Achebe was saddened not only by these developments
but also by the way in which they prevented Nigerians from grasping the reality
of their existence in the wider world. In an interview with J. O. J. Nwachukwu-
Agbada in October 1985 he criticizes the irresponsibility exhibited by Nigerian
leaders and particularly the corruption that has materialized in the society.

Achebe answers other questions in that interview: when asked whether being awarded the Nobel Prize for literature would remove some of his misgivings about the politics of the West, he replies that 'his views are not negotiable'. He insists that

> what we have to do is clear: we have to stick to our vision, no matter what [because] our vision of what is important, is not what is important to, say, an American. Americans think what is important to you is not important. Therefore, the thing for us to do is to stick to our priorities.

He regrets that unfortunately there are so many writers and spokesmen acting against such a vision but he feels that he cannot 'get into that kind of act'.[41]

One of the acts that Achebe did find relevant, however, was encouragement of the Association of Nigerian Authors to develop and progress. Thus he was at Abuja in early December 1985 for the annual conference of the association which had Major-General Mamman Jiya Vatsa, poet and Minister for the Federal Capital Territory, as its host. It was an interesting conference which attracted as many established writers as the inaugural meeting at Nsukka in 1981, but after the elections Achebe announced that he would not continue as president of the association when his term expired the following year, 1986. He had set up the association; now it would be able to develop further under the guidance and direction of other people. In his presidential address Achebe sounds a cautious, practical note:

> I hope we shall be able in our business session to take a hard businessman's look at our organizational problems. I must urge you to bear this in mind and find some time individually and in groups to reflect on the structural and other weaknesses of our association. If we are to succeed in our plan to make next year's convention an occasion for celebrating two hundred years of Nigerian literature (if you like, from Equiano to Ekwensi) then we must set things in motion now lest our grand theme should become what a British Prime Minister once described as a grandiloquent label on an empty luggage.[42]

Some days after the end of the conference at Abuja, the writers who had attended and many other Nigerians were shocked to hear an announcement that a group of soldiers plotting a coup had been arrested. Among the names mentioned was Major-General Mamman Vatsa. It was unbelievable because at the conference he had given his time and resources liberally for the success of the event, and given no indication of his involvement in a dangerous plot.

It was thus with confusion and anxiety that Nigerians waited for further announcements concerning the coup plot. In the midst of this anxious wait, in December 1985, Achebe granted an interview to Okey Ndibe and C. Don Adinuba for the *African Guardian*. He presents the view that

> military regimes are part of the problem of Africa, part of the problem of under-development; of foreign control, of irresponsible leadership, of interference by the major powers. Africa is caught in all these problems and therefore Africa is unstable. Military regimes occur as an indication of the in-built instability of African nations at this time in their history.

His assessment of the Buhari and Babangida regimes is that 'it is a question of plus here and minus there'. His general view of the society contains the insight that 'in the struggle for the improvement of society, for the elimination of oppression, you must see reality wholly and steadily'. He argues that 'clarity does not lie in being blind or half blind' and that it 'should confer on you the ability to see the picture as untidy' because 'the reality of our existence is untidy'.[43] He adds that fanaticism in politics, ideologies, or even religion is part of the unwillingness to perceive that reality from the proper perspective.

Achebe's anxieties about narrow and uncompromising political outlooks were closely related to the reality of Nigeria in early 1986. On the second day of that year he gathered as many members of the Association of Nigerian Authors as he could round up, in spite of the fact that he was recovering from a bad dose of malaria. They produced the draft of a plea to the federal military government for a fair and public trial of Mamman Vatsa and other military officers arraigned with him for treason. Achebe recalls that 'Cyprian Ekwensi was to take the statement and motor all the way to Lagos that same afternoon and hand it to the Secretary General of the Association', Odia Ofeimun.[44] In confirmation of Achebe's fears, however, the trial of the arrested soldiers accused of plotting the coup was pursued with the same military fanaticism that had ruptured the society on several previous occasions. The trial, which started secretly in late January 1986 at the Brigade of Guards headquarters, Victoria Island, Lagos, ended on 25 February. The tribunal agreed that Mamman Vatsa 'had long nursed grievances against the President', and neither Vatsa's statement that he had served the country for 24 years without nursing political ambitions or grievances, nor his warning that 'the day [members of the Nigerian Army] start insulting [themselves] others will join', nor his confidence that 'this sentence shall not be my final hour, for I have God's promise on that, God's judgement is the last' swayed the tribunal.[45] In the end Vatsa and nine other officers were sentenced to death, though Vatsa's only link to the coup plot was the statement that one of the plotters, Bitiyong, claimed to have procured money for its organization from him on the excuse that he, Bitiyong, would use it for a farm. (Bitiyong also claimed to have obtained money from Babangida himself which he used to finance the meetings of the plotters.) Various procedures by the military bodies (so it was claimed) confirmed the sentence and the condemned men awaited the decision of Babangida's Armed Forces Ruling Council scheduled for 5 March 1986.

In early March, Chinua Achebe was in Lagos for some other commitment and in the process he met John Pepper Clark. Clark thought it would be a good idea if he, Achebe and Wole Soyinka made efforts to meet Babangida and request clemency for the condemned men. Clark contacted Soyinka, who supported the idea, and on 4 March 1986 they sought audience with and were received by President Ibrahim Babangida. It was Chinua Achebe's first visit to Dodan Barracks. After the closed-door meeting the three writers emerged and made available to the press copies of their statement which read:

> Our appeal is straightforwardly based on the need for clemency as an essential element in the attainment of that healing process which the present national leader swore to embark upon, on taking oath of office. Without being superstitious, we cannot but observe how a 10-year cycle of blood-letting appears to have become an incubus on the very life of the nation's armed forces – 1966, 1976 and 1986. You possess the will to break this jinx. You have the moral duty to exercise that will.... The truth is unavoidable; the very persistence of this cycle shows only too clearly that death has never proved a deterrent for men determined on seizing power for reasons of patriotism or personal ambition, but against the nation itself. In attempting to

redress the situation, therefore, we the offended parties, the would-be victims, have a responsibility to ourselves to ensure that we do not also inflict further injuries on our very being.[46]

It was a moving statement and before they departed Babangida made a promise to consider their request. Their visit was given prominence on the national television network news that day.

It was thus with shock that Nigerians received an announcement, made by General Domkat Bali the next day, 5 March, at 8 pm, that the condemned soldiers had been executed three hours previously. Part of the irony was that the military in their announcement appropriated part of the statement for clemency made by Achebe, Soyinka and Clark. The military decision received the support of the politician Obafemi Awolowo, who said that 'It is a just punishment if you shed blood in the execution of legal process' and that 'crime will flourish if those found guilty are not punished' – this was another irony, for 22 years previously, when Awolowo had been found guilty of coup-plotting (his accomplices later confessed that they were all guilty), he was not executed but jailed. Chief Awolowo's statement came on the same day, according to *West Africa* magazine, that President Babangida had sent a 'glowing testimonial to the Chief on the occasion of his 77th birthday'.[47] Another prominent politician, Alex Fom from Plateau State, supported the Awolowo view, but many other Nigerians agreed with the students of the Kwara State College of Technology, Ilorin, who rightly warned that 'the killing of the 10 coup plotters is a sign of the insensitive nature of the government to the true feelings and aspirations of the people and it is a threat to democratic rights'.[48] Chinua Achebe, who had no doubt that Mamman Vatsa had been murdered, felt devastated. It was a terrible disappointment, and it was only a prelude.

17

What Literature Has To Do With It
Leaders, Prizes & *Anthills of the Savannah*
1987–9

I F 1986 was a year of literary and social achievement for Achebe, it was also shadowed by a feeling of devastation associated with the execution of Mamman Vatsa. Making the strenuous emotional effort required to come to terms with that feeling enabled him to continue writing his fifth novel. His international reputation continued to soar: *Things Fall Apart* had now sold more than three million copies and had been translated into 45 languages, while *No Longer at Ease* had also reached the million mark. Bernth Lindfors, considering Achebe's impact in Asia by the late 1980s, confirms that

> because Achebe's works have been able to cast their spell on readers all over the world for more than thirty years, he has gained recognition, in India and elsewhere, as Africa's leading literary guru, an enchanter and sage whose words carry extra weight. And because his popular following continues to grow year by year, he will surely remain a guru – perhaps India's only African guru – for many years to come.[1]

Achebe's reputation was just as high in London, where in July 1986 he attended a two-day celebration of the African and Caribbean Writers Series by Heinemann Educational Books. There were discussions and readings at the Institute of Contemporary Arts in London, and public re-issues of some modern African classics, including *Things Fall Apart*.

The central theme was the question of the appropriate language for African writers. Debates centred on whether a writer should use a language imposed on him, and whether that language could adequately represent the writer's culture. Ngugi wa Thiong'o asserted that language 'is part of the neo-colonial structures that repress progressive ideas'. Achebe, however, in a public conversation with the Somali novelist Nuruddin Farah which was chaired by Lyn Innes, insisted that he can write in both Igbo and English, in addition to the fact that the reality of Nigeria made English necessary for communication. Although Achebe agreed that 'every writer must deal with this very complex problem according to his situation', he also felt that if a writer has at his disposal the tools of more than one language, he should use them freely: 'Why not? These are advantages you have. Why turn advantage into a liability?' Patricia Morris reports that the impression Achebe gives in the flesh is of a man completely at ease. Achebe's ability to contain diversity and to parry effortlessly with young radicals, places him in the position of the great man, the wise father, who arouses the ire of his sons. Unthreatened he absorbs the force of their blows, almost welcomes them. Not for nothing has he been called the Father of African Literature.

The Achebean tendency to contain adversity was illustrated on that occasion, Morris observes, when he was 'challenged by a young man who suggested that as a product of colonial times, Achebe is out of touch with the new world view'. The 'father figure' replied:

If the world has changed so that the young people with their new education can see it differently, then let them write the books that reveal this new perception. There's no point in quarrelling with me. You go ahead and write about that view that replaces my own view of the world. And the book will speak for itself. There's no quarrel. The diversity I was talking about is something to be happy about. There are now 60 or 100 writers in Nigeria instead of three or four. That's wonderful.[2]

Accommodation of other antagonistic views was not motivated by a reluctance to protest in times of personal danger for, as he told Robert Moss in a brief interview, he had been admonishing Nigeria's leaders rather boldly. 'I am not exaggerating my bravery. One's reputation has a little to do with it. When I do want to say something, I really go ahead and say it.'[3] And indeed, he returned to Nigeria, to say what be felt the urge to say at that time.

The National Merit Award Lecture, delivered at Sokoto in Nigeria in August 1986, seven years after the award, gave him an opportunity to speak out in the interest of the nation and its people. In a long citation that preceded the lecture, the eminent economist, Pius Okigbo gave some biographical details of Achebe as well as listing his honours and accomplishments. For Okigbo, Achebe brought 'together the metaphors and emotions of an unlearned people with those of the learned, the primitive and popular with the modern and fastidious', while 'behind his small soft exterior lies an iron soul and an iron will'. Okigbo's is a deep-going assessment, free of the rhetoric and platitudes that often mark these occasions. In Achebe he finds 'a man of very strong convictions tenaciously held because they are arrived at only after careful thought. Chinua epitomizes for those around him that final quality in humility which borders on pride.'[4]

After that introduction Chinua Achebe delivered a lecture entitled 'What has literature got to do with it?' He reminds his audience that 'we might say that a nation becomes what it honours; and how it does it is a paradigm of its national style'. In his review of recent Nigerian history Achebe compares his country with Japan and considers that 'the history of Nigeria from, say, 1970 to 1983 can be characterized by contrast as a snatching of defeat from the jaws of victory', which he attributes to the 'one-tracked mind, the simplistic mind, the mind that cannot comprehend that where one thing stands, another will stand beside it'. This narrowness 'appears to dominate our current thinking on Nigeria's need for technology'. Thus he criticizes the desire to emphasize science at the expense of liberal arts education, which contradicts the fact that education is a complex creative process. In that process literature, including animal fables, can combine 'in a most admirable manner the aesthetic qualities of successful imagination with those homiletic virtues demanded of active definers and custodians of society's values'. He does not perceive the role of literature as providing just 'latent support', however, for he identifies its offer of the 'kinetic energy necessary for social transition and change'. The relevance of literature to the aim of a new Nigeria is that it provides the creative energy of stories to initiate and sustain the work of creation. Achebe shares a vision in which

> literature, whether handed down by word of mouth or in print, gives us a second handle on reality; enabling us to encounter in the safe, manageable dimensions of make-believe the very same threats to integrity that may assail the psyche in real life; and at the same time providing through the self-discovery which it imparts, a veritable weapon for coping with these threats whether they are found within our problematic and incoherent selves or in the world around us.

And he ends with an insightful question:

> What better preparation can a people desire as they begin their journey into the strange, revolutionary world of modernization?[5]

The audience reacted appreciatively to that lecture from a man now rightly assumed to be one of the wise men of his generation, a prophet at home as well as abroad. In America at this time the composer Steve Burnstein was setting one of Achebe's poems, 'After a War', to music. At home, Sina Odugbemi of the *Vanguard* newspaper interviewed Achebe at Sokoto. Odugbemi wants to explore the notion that recognition, 'when it comes to a writer of Achebe's stature, does bring its enormous burdens' because members of the public expect him to be a moral leader, and one who leads by personal example. Achebe admits that 'there is a bit of that', because

> where I am a little known intimately the feeling is even stronger. I'm sure that if people heard that I embezzled funds belonging to the University or Town Union they would be quite shocked. You are held up there.

But when Achebe is asked if his reputation would be hurt if some people heard that 'Chinua Achebe had loads of girl friends', he replies:

> That would depend entirely on whether or not it harms my image. It depends on the society. In some societies it would enhance your image. In Nigeria people would not be extremely perturbed, because of our attitude to women. I doubt if I would be hurt by that.... In many parts of the world artists are almost given permission to be awkward. What I don't find myself saying is: artists are supposed to have a string of girl friends and so I must do likewise. There is no personality you can call the artist's personality. A lot of young people mess themselves up because of trying to be fashionable. Anything as artificial as that is false. An artist must have integrity – be true to his nature.... I was never intending to monopolise the depiction of the Nigerian or the African, or the black man. There are obviously different traditions. It is the business of the writer to depict the tradition he is familiar with.... I don't believe an artist needs to be rowdy. Most artists may well be bohemian but they cannot impose that on others. The ultimate judge of an artist is his art.[6]

The publicity which his Merit Award lecture received was not unexpected, for Achebe had come to be associated in Nigeria with a truthful and honest attitude to the discussion of his country's affairs. Another opportunity for speaking out came a month later in September 1986. The context was the national debate on the political future of Nigeria instituted by the Babangida government. Achebe was invited to participate in one of the debates organized for the university community at Nsukka. On 23 September 1986 he presented a paper on 'The University and the Leadership Factor in Nigerian Politics' which gave him an opportunity to reply to the critics of *The Trouble with Nigeria*. He identifies and rejects as unconvincing the two main criticisms of his contention that the trouble with Nigeria is a failure of leadership: that his view of the Nigerian predicament is élitist; and that his diagnosis identifies individuals rather than an economic and political system as the source of the Nigerian problem. Achebe proceeds to examine the three components of national development: the system, the leadership and the followers. He argues that the basic problem with bestowing pre-eminence to systems 'is the inability to explain how an abstract concept can bring itself into being autonomously', while on the notion that followership should be pre-eminent 'it is enough to say that no human enterprise has flourished on the basis of followers leading their leaders'.

As for his third component, Achebe emphasizes that

> leadership is a sacred trust like the priesthood in civilized humane religions. No one gets into it lightly or unadvisably because it demands qualities of mind and discipline of body and will [extend] far beyond the needs of the ordinary citizen.

He argues boldly that the élite factor is an indispensable element, but agrees that there are uses and abuses of such a system, illustrated by the example of a national army. An élite can be turned into a counterfeit élite, and for Achebe the real problem with leadership is recruitment. He nevertheless believes that the society can demand basic competence in all those who desire leadership positions: even in traditional monarchical systems, he argues, there were the élite, the king makers who were ineligible for selection as kings but were qualified to insist on competence and other attributes of good leadership. In effect, Achebe perceives the university and other élite centres as capable of playing the role of king makers, though he points out that the universities have not lived up to expectations because they have allowed the erosion of their own prestige. He ends with a call to the universities to 'produce that salt of excellence which the nation relies on' to drop 'into the boiling soup of Nigerian leadership'.[7]

Achebe's argument was aimed at the heart of the problem with his society. Perhaps that was why the Anambra State government felt that he possessed the right ideas and appointed him as pro-chancellor of the Anambra State University of Technology in Enugu. It was an appointment that provided him with an insight into the administration of a Nigerian university from another level. It coincided with the television adaptation of *Things Fall Apart*, produced by the Nigerian Television Authority in both the English and the Igbo languages. The adaptation acknowledged the accomplishments of a now classic novel which had done much to enhance the reputation of modern literature from Africa.

One of the practitioners of that literature – Wole Soyinka, playwright, essayist, novelist and poet – was awarded the Nobel Prize for Literature in October 1986. It was the first time the award had been made to an African and was a major event in literary circles. In Nigeria the news was received with excitement by the media and while one group of journalists waited for Soyinka at Lagos, another group proceeded to the University of Nigeria, Nsukka, to interview Chinua Achebe. The Nobel Prize enthusiasm was dampened to an extent by the murder of a Lagos journalist, Dele Giwa, but it surged out as the shock of Giwa's death subsided. Achebe granted an interview to the journalists who besieged him and in his statement congratulated Wole Soyinka, praising his 'stupendous display of energy and vitality' which made him 'most eminently deserving of any prize'.[8] The two events, Giwa's death and Soyinka's Nobel Prize, combined to keep Nigerians talking as 1986 wound to a close. Soyinka went to Stockholm for the Nobel ceremony and at home was made a commander of the Federal Republic, which brought him into closer contact with Ibrahim Babangida, a relationship that was to generate much controversy for him.

The December 1986 conference of the Association of Nigerian Authors was attended by the three writers J. P. Clark, Wole Soyinka and Chinua Achebe. Achebe's five-year term had witnessed the consolidation of the Association. In his final presidential address he reviewed its achievements and again congratulated Soyinka on his award.

> This is the year of Wole Soyinka's Nobel Prize. We rejoice with him on his magnificent achievement. A lot has already been said or written about it and no doubt more will be said. For me what matters is that after the *Oriki* and the celebrations we should say to ourselves: one of us has proved that we can beat the white man at his own game. That is wonderful for us and for the white man. But now we must turn away and play our own game.

The award and its significance clearly generated reactions, and Achebe's call for sober reflection was intended to lift the performance of those who would be playing 'our own game' in literature.

> I want us to hold the orphan image firmly in our minds. We may be feted by kings and princes on occasion. But if we remain true to our vocations then we are, as Joyce Cary once said, doomed to be free. And that means free to return to the punishment and poverty of orphans.[9]

As Achebe relinquished one responsibility as president of the Association of Nigerian Authors, the citizens of his home town urged him to accept another. Thus before the end of 1986 he was elected president-general of the powerful Ogidi Town Union for a first term of three years. It was a post he accepted reluctantly, but he saw it as part of his contribution to the culture and environment that had nurtured him. At that time the town had problems with managing money and the citizens wanted an individual they could trust, and who could provide the right leadership. Interestingly, Achebe refused to accept a chieftaincy for the simple reason that he '[did] not want to be a chief'. Although the villagers joked that a 'man without a title cannot make laws for titled men', they accepted his principled position.[10] While Achebe felt compelled to accept this new post, he also felt that he had done enough for the *Okike* journal to exist without his direct involvement. He thus relinquished the position of editor of *Okike* at the end of 1986 and Ossie Onuora Enekwe, who had been assistant editor for some years, became the editor from the twenty-fifth issue.

Local responsibilities at Ogidi did not prevent Chinua Achebe from honouring some international and national engagements and receiving further awards. He became an honorary life vice-president of the Onitsha Chamber of Commerce for his 'distinguished career' in January 1987. Soon after, he travelled to India for a conference that brought together a number of important novelists, playwrights, poets and significant female writers. The many fine minds assembled made it an occasion for the free flow of ideas, although it had been indicated that no papers would be presented. Achebe discovered, however, that the discussion in which he took part stimulated the need to present a brief paper. Christie Achebe, who was there too, was struck by the depth of his responses considering the short time it had taken Chinua to write his spontaneous contribution. It was in the course of this conference that Achebe met Vikram Seth, who autographed one of his books for him.

Soon after their return to Nigeria it was announced on 19 May 1987 that the veteran politician, Chief Obafemi Awolowo, had died. As usual Nigerians, accustomed to glossing over the deficiencies of their fellow citizens at death, or making the most of an opportunity for self-promotion, erupted into eulogies recounting both the man's real achievements and some imaginary ones. That Awolowo possessed a large number of followers among his ethnic group added intensity to these eulogies and exaggerated their scope. At one point Chuk-wuemeka Odumegwu Ojukwu, the former leader of Biafra, claimed that 'Awolowo was the best President Nigeria never had.'[11] That remark was a further tonic to the excitement of the crowd of sympathizers and politicians who never missed an opportunity to advance themselves. The climax was the initiation of a debate by some of the politicians asking the Babangida government to accord a state funeral to the late Obafemi Awolowo. In the midst of the hullabaloo Chinua Achebe felt compelled to point out to the nation some of the things that Awolowo had done which made him undeserving of such an honour.

In a statement on 26 May under the title 'Awolowo's Apotheosis', Achebe pointed out that

> Chief Obafemi Awolowo was a great leader, in so far as he was both a Nigerian and a leader. But his contributions to Nigerian public affairs in the last years did not qualify him as a great national leader, rather he was a champion of a section of the geographical expression called Nigeria.

Awolowo, he pointed out, 'was rejected by the Nigerian electorate every time he offered himself to lead them'. He regarded the call for a state funeral as amounting to a national swindle and rejected the notion that there was a 'North–South divide' on the issue. Achebe insisted that the issue was being hyped by

> a minority of Nigerians ready to use their control of the apparatus of government and the mass media to foist their narrow, reactionary obsession recklessly on the majority.... Despite the clowning circus of ex-politicians and would-be politicians in Ikenne in recent weeks, there is no doubt that serious-minded Nigerians are highly critical or even contemptuous of the expensive hocus-pocus which is now being staged in their name.

Achebe felt that the true status of Awolowo was a decision to be made not only by those whose cause he championed and that 'no nation thrives on expediency and prejudice or by subverting principle' and rules.[12] The kind of support which Awolowo had among his ethnic group made a strong reaction to Achebe's statement inevitable. Awolowo's supporters made angry comments and published equally angry letters to the editors of some of the Lagos-based newspapers. They hurled insults at Achebe and the sometimes cantankerous Ebenezer Babatope, former director of publicity for Awolowo's defunct political party, was 'sorry that Chinua Achebe had continued in this game of frivolity, attacking Awolowo even when the man is no longer present'. He added that he 'used to admire Achebe for his seeming leaning with progressive ideas and opinions' but that his views on Awolowo portray him 'on the contrary'. Lateef Jakande, who was a governor of Lagos state as a member of Awolowo's political party, said that Achebe was entitled to his opinion but he ought to be very objective when commenting on a man such as Chief Awolowo; he was also 'convinced Achebe was wrong'.[13] One indication of support for the Achebe view came from a popular Lagos musician, known for his radical music and lifestyle, who was quoted as saying that the death of Awolowo was good riddance, for he had introduced tribal politics to Nigeria. A sober, conciliatory comment came from a young man, Nick Dazang, who wrote in the *Sunday Concord* that

> we may not like the primeval politics of our founding fathers – which is salutary and healthy to our task of national reconstruction. But we must not be bitter, which is why I ask Achebe the gentleman and indeed fellow Nigerians to forgive Awolowo. Forgiveness is an elixir, a healing balm to the soul.[14]

Awolowo was buried at Ikenne with many people attending the funeral.

Achebe meanwhile had travelled to Kenya on an assignment in the interest of Africa as a whole and not of Nigeria (or a section of it) only. He had made his observation and it was left to interested Nigerians to take whatever decisions they considered appropriate in honouring Awolowo. The project in Kenya involved the formulation of a realistic time frame for Africa's future development and for the broadening of policy and research agendas beyond the current limits of the continent. The project meeting – sponsored by the African Academy of Sciences of Nairobi, the Council for the Development of Economic and Social Research in Africa (CODESRIA) of Dakar and the Alan Shawn Feinsten World Hunger Program of Brown University, USA – was held in the Tea Hotel, Kericho, over five days at the beginning of June. The participants were divided into groups and the group consisting of Chinua Achebe, Göran Hyden, Calestous Juma, Kwesi Prah and Mahendra Shah produced a presentation they entitled 'The Big Lift: A Journalist's Account'. It made use of a fictitious character, Kwame, to examine various impediments to development in Africa, including a lack of self-reliance, self-scrutiny, and political democracy. Kwame also identifies Africa's priorities: the need to develop an African industrial base; the development of indigenous scientific and technological capacity; the organization of society on a private, yet cooperative and egalitarian basis; the utilization of women's organizations; and the effective resistance to threats from other regions of the world. The ideas identified by Kwame were similar to many of the ideas that Achebe had identified in his own literary and other works.[15]

Unsurprisingly, similar ideas were part of the vision of Chinua Achebe's fifth novel, *Anthills of the Savannah*.[16] This story is woven with thematic strands that include love, hate, passion and friendship. Such a potent mixture often results in violence, especially with political and natural disasters as part of the background of the novel. In Achebe's fable the perennial city and village conflicts, as well as military and civilian confrontations, dramatize the tension of modern Africa. Though there is anger in the writing, Achebe gives an artistic portrayal of contemporary Africa. This is also a novel of hope, for the author shows that even the most devastating political and emotional turmoil gives way to renewal.

Anthills of the Savannah was short-listed for the 1987 Booker McConnell Prize, Britain's most prestigious literary award. The *New Statesman* called it Achebe's 'most complex, enigmatic and impressive work yet' while *The Guardian* said, 'it is a masterly tour de force, written with elegance, irony, hope' and the *Financial Times* added that 'in a powerful fusion of myth, legend and modern styles, Achebe has written a book which is wise, exciting and essential, a powerful antidote to the cynical commentators from "overseas" who see nothing ever new out of Africa'.[17] Achebe's quintessential Africa includes the view of struggle as useful, especially when it issues as a statement through which resistance becomes known; the magnification of the female characters; the utilization of memory; the anatomy of power and the hope in the young and the future. *Anthills of the Savannah* was launched in London on 17 September 1989 amidst wide publicity, for as Emmanuel Ngara remarked, 'the name of Chinua Achebe is synonymous with the rise and development of modern African literature because Achebe is a pace-setter.'[18]

Perhaps the fullest and most significant response came from Africa, in a review in *West Africa* by the novelist Nuruddin Farah:

> I've always held Chinua Achebe's writing in the highest esteem, believing it to be the most singular contribution the continent of Africa has made to world literature. Some people may not like me for saying it, but the truth is [that] he has no equal among us and that many of us whether we admit it or not, owe a great deal to him; many have even learnt the craft from him. Rhetoric, polemic and the theatrics of pamphleteering aside, Achebe is, in my opinion, Africa's best novelist and craftsman, and one of the world's greatest, living or dead.... *Anthills of the Savannah* is as different a novel as each of Achebe's has been from the one preceding it, or others that have come after it. But this latest is tidier, with a narrative structure that is earthy, and a language which, on the whole, is spare, and a telling that is direct. Now and again, there is a stylistic stutter. Often the points in the novel are made in a roundabout way or else in a cryptic manner and sometimes the reader becomes the proverbial man who's lost a camel for which he looks in a milk container. Nevertheless this is a charming novel, a book of metonyms, a rich treasure of transferred meanings.... *Anthills of the Savannah* is a most engaging and a hugely successful novel. There is a great deal of poetry in it, and the quality of the writing is charged with informedness, an awareness of high things and high thoughts. This is an outstanding novel by Africa's most accomplished writer. *Anthills* calls for a celebration.[19]

That celebration did not include the Booker Prize. Writing in *West Africa*, Kaye Whiteman thought that 'if it was a pity [the book] did not win, it was good exposure for a writer who has long deserved the recognition that has already been accorded him by his sales figures'. Perhaps Achebe's own views on the matter of prizes and the criteria of judges were concealed diplomatically in his comment, during a television interview before the event, that 'if you want to see a masquerade, you don't stand in one place'.[20] Several interpretations are possible, one of which is that literature and prizes should not be perceived from a single point of view.

The value in that caution on the viewing of the masquerades was reflected in an interview Achebe granted to Yusuf Hassan of *African Events*. Achebe tells him that the real value of a work of art, and indeed of a good teacher, is that they start something in the mind of everybody, not just the élite, not just the writer. Not just the one person. But you engage the whole people in evaluating their condition and you do give leads, because ultimately the fundamental values are clear enough. Humaneness, decency, justice, fair play and so on.

Clearly it is the non-recognition of those fundamental values by non-Africans that makes Achebe insist that Africans

> should not be unwilling to deal with the complexities [of life]; we should not be bent on the one-solution approach. Africa is not a one-solution continent. We are not a one-issue continent.[21]

Achebe's appeal for a many-sided vision was echoed from an unexpected direction when Queen Elizabeth II sent an assistant to him requesting permission to quote from the title poem of *Beware, Soul Brother* in an address she intended to present at the Commonwealth Institute. She delivered that speech on 6 November 1987 and part of it read:

> The comparison is often made between the Commonwealth and a family, so often that it has become a somewhat hackneyed one. It is, nonetheless, a good one. The family still stands – a solid support to all its individual members. The same goes for the Commonwealth. The principles for which it stands are quite simply those which would, if universally applied, make the world a better place. We often fall short of the targets which we set for ourselves, but no man is the worse for keeping those goals in his sights, and for striving to reach them. Nor does it hurt to set those goals before our children. In the presence of the author, I quote some lines which struck home to me when I read them: 'Remember also your children for they in their time will want a place for their feet when they come of age and the dance of the future is born for them.'[22]

Quotation by the Queen was another signal that Achebe's efforts in clearing the frontiers for literature from Africa had not been in vain: even in the cosy comfort of a royal world, it seemed, it was possible to absorb something of what he had conveyed in his creative works. The universal reach of his readership emerged even more clearly when Achebe's publishers took him on a tour across Europe in order to promote the new novel and meet his readers. He visited Sweden, Denmark and Germany, and fulfilled a series of engagements in various parts of London.

More readers also meant more books of criticism, such as Emmanuel Meziemadu Okoye's *The Traditional Religion and its Encounter with Christianity in Achebe's Novels*, published by Peter Lang in 1987. An invitation from the University of Massachusetts also enabled Achebe to travel widely in America once more. He had been invited by the university's Institute of Advanced Study in the Humanities and the W. E. B. Dubois Department of Afro-American Studies. Patricia Wright in *Campus Chronicle* quoted Jules Chametzky, the director of the institute, on Achebe as the 'centrepiece of one of the greatest collections of black writers in the world'. The presence of Achebe was intended to coincide with the probable presence of James Baldwin on the same faculty. The university had also recruited John Wideman, while regular staff like Michael Thelwell and Julius Lester were expected to complement the 'collection' of distinguished black writers. Chametzky also noted that 'many people here have sterling memories of Achebe's earlier visit, and we consider it quite a coup to have gotten him to return'.[23] Part of the academic responsibilities

Achebe was expected to fulfil in his busy programme as Visiting Professor of Afro-American Studies included the teaching of a class in African literature, conducting a year-long inter-disciplinary seminar for faculty and peers, and at least one public presentation of either a lecture or a reading. Christie was also invited to lead a separate institute seminar as an expert on educational policy.

The return of Achebe to Amherst, where he had delivered his lecture on 'An Image of Africa: Racism in Conrad's *Heart of Darkness*', was not without its own positive consequences. When he arrived at Amherst another professor told him that he had not agreed with him after that lecture on Conrad thirteen years previously, but had come to agree with him since.[24] Sadly, on the other hand, the envisaged literary reunion between Achebe and James Baldwin did not take place because Baldwin died on 30 November. At the memorial service for Baldwin held on 16 December 1987 Achebe presented an address in which he recalled his encounter with the works of James Baldwin and later with the man himself 'in the jungles of Florida in 1980'. Achebe says that during those four days he saw 'how easy it was to make Jimmy smile: and how the world he was doomed to inhabit would remorselessly deny him that simple benediction'. In the same address Achebe laments the murder of the articulate visionary Captain Thomas Sankara, the head of state of Burkina Faso, a man whom President Mitterand of France had characterized with the remark: 'Sankara is a disturbing person. With him it is impossible to sleep in peace. He does not leave your conscience alone.'

Achebe concludes that 'principalities and powers do not tolerate those who interrupt the sleep of their consciences' for the death of Sankara was the termination of 'one of the few hopeful examples of leadership in Africa'. He links the death of Sankara to the miracle of the fact that Baldwin 'got away' with that same attitude of prodding the conscience of his society 'for forty years' in his writing career. And does so still:

> As long as a tiny cartel of rich, creditor nations can hold the rest in iron chains of usury; so long as one third or less of mankind eats well and often to excess while two-thirds and more live perpetually with hunger; as long as white people who constitute a mere fraction of the human race consider it natural and even righteous to dominate the rainbow majority whenever and wherever they are thrown together; and – the oldest of them all – the discrimination by men against women, as long as it persists; the words of James Baldwin will be there to bear witness and to inspire and elevate the struggle for human freedom.[25]

The Baldwin family gave his briefcase to Achebe with the words: 'We think he would have wanted you to have it.'[26] His memorial service speech was effective as well as affecting; it drew lucid attention to the cogent issues in the works of James Baldwin. Some of those issues were also present in the address that Achebe read at the third convocation ceremony of the Anambra State University of Technology (ASUTECH) in Nigeria, as its pro-chancellor. On the same occasion the first chancellor of the university, Alhaji Suleman Adamu, the Emir of Bauchi, was installed. Achebe's address was entitled 'Turning the Mind to Things that Matter', at a time when the Nigerian society was in dire need of that advice. Achebe first addresses the graduands, informing them that he hoped they had passed *through* the university and not *under* it because

> passing through is the very essence of education. It implies a process – a beginning, a

middle and an end; but an end which turns out always to be a new beginning. My wish for every product of the ASUTECH process is that your education should never cease and also that nobody seeing you hereafter will have cause to wonder whether you indeed passed through or merely achieved a certificate by some short-cut or mango trick.

In the same way he asks the new chancellor not to consider geographical impediments in his relationship with the university because 'making light of geographical distance in that way is an attitude of mind – a predisposition to go out; to reach out and touch other people'. Achebe emphasizes the dream embedded in the establishment of the University of Technology as a necessary part of the objective of developing the society, but he regrets the manifestation of negative activities in both the institution and the society. Thus he laments the scores of imminent catastrophes

> facing our nation in population, health, industry, education, agriculture, etc., to which we pay scant attention, wrapped up as we are in our obsession with who should exercise power – a pitiful parody of power – over whom; busy fighting for the captaincy of a ship that is sinking.

Achebe warns those he considers the 'warring factions' in the institution to desist and concludes with a call to those 'excited by this challenge of ASUTECH'[27] to join him in building a reputable university.

The address was clearly part of the counsel – periodic warnings, advice, caution, and suggestions – that Achebe freely offered his country in the decade of the 1980s with the hope that his society would embark on the path of progress. But an incident occurred at this time which made that hope appear unattainable. It began with an invitation to him from Lagos State University to accept the award of an honorary degree. In January 1988 he was thus one of the invited guests; the university paid his fare and put him up in its guest house, where he waited for the commencement of the ceremony. Several months earlier, when he was sent the invitation, Achebe had 'accepted without hesitation. I thought it was a wonderful idea and began to get ready'.

Having arrived on the Sunday, however, Achebe found himself in an embarrassing situation:

> The following day, Monday, Dr Olumide, the Vice-Chancellor, turned up at the Lagos State University guest house in the afternoon. He said it looked as if there was a problem. People were trying to disrupt the convocation but he was battling against it. He came back again at 6 p.m. looking so dejected. I was sorry for the Vice-Chancellor. He seemed to have this vision which I thought was very useful for the country. He seemed shattered by the failure of his efforts.[28]

The cancellation of the convocation 24 hours before it was due to start was unbelievable. But it reflected the background to Achebe's comment: 'This country has big problems. The greatest of which is hypocrisy. I'll keep bashing away at this. The day I lose hope in Nigeria, I will stop talking about it.'[29] Astonishingly, the event was not discussed in the Nigerian press, though an autonomous function of a university had been grossly violated. The reputed 'social critics' in Nigeria did not raise their voices. It was said, however, that the convocation of Lagos State University had been stopped because there was opposition to the inclusion of Achebe's name among those to be honoured. The decision to cancel was thus linked to the reaction in some of the Western states

256

to the criticism Achebe had made concerning the funeral of the late Obafemi Awolowo. It was no coincidence that Achebe's books had been banned in some of those states. In an interview which Achebe granted later in the year he argued:

> If we are still running universities the way we pretend they are run, I don't see how the opinion anybody holds of me can impinge on what this university wants to do in this regard. I'm not short of honorary degrees as you know. I have more than any other Nigerian who has ever lived, except Dr Dike. I will have two more from abroad. So, I'm not short of honorary degrees. The Lagos State University degree will not add a particular glamour to me. But what I'm talking about is that this is something seriously wrong.

Told that his books had been banned, Achebe answered that it was 'so much worse for Lagos State University. So much worse for the Lagos education system' and that 'if any school in Nigeria wants to ban my books, they are welcome to do that. What they are doing is imposing limitations on their own children'. He regarded it as part of the 'nervousness and lack of civilization in our society that people should behave this way'. And he expressed his concern at the 'incredible erosion [and] debasement of Nigerian literature by people who ought to know'.[30]

At home amidst familiar problems or engaged in other activities elsewhere, Achebe never hesitated to interrogate any issue he considered important or detrimental to the human society. Thus in February 1988, the month the American edition of *Anthills of the Savannah* came out, he was at the University of Texas, Austin, where his literary engagements included a lecture on 'The Writer and the Society'. Lydia Foerster reported in the *Daily Texan* of 19 February 1989, that Achebe had said, among other things, that history for him 'does not have a past and present unless somebody can tell me the date when the past ended and the present begins. It seems to [him] rather naive to think in those terms.' She also reported that Achebe argued that the 'purpose of literature really is to revitalize people who are alive'.[31] A complementary report was published in the *Austin American-Statesman* of 21 February 1988 in which Enedelia J. Obregon highlights Achebe's comment that 'change is imperative, especially in the African situation' but that the need is not felt strongly in the West

> because things are generally all right from your view. That's because the West runs the world. But from the view of Africa and Third World countries, the world is upside down and needs to be totally reordered. When people say my books are too political, this is the reason.

Achebe is convinced that 'people in the United States and in other Western countries need to be more open to different ideas and different cultures' and should not 'choose to be isolated. It's not as if the world were closed. You are self-contained. It's dangerous if in addition to being the policeman of the world you're trying to control, you make the wrong decisions based on insufficient knowledge.'[32]

Achebe's remarks highlighted the human dimension of African literature, to which he believed the West needed to open itself. It was that intrinsic human dimension in literature, as well as in the interactions of human beings, that featured in a conference address he presented at the University of Massachusetts between 22 and 23 April 1988. The conference was organized as a tribute to James Baldwin, whose participation had been anticipated before his death.

Achebe was introduced by Michael Thelwell ('The world has listened to him, as you will do now') and Ketu Ketrak, who confessed that 'it has been a great treat to have Chinua Achebe here with us at the University this academic session as Fulbright Professor' because she had learnt

> a great deal from him by simply listening to him and have marvelled at his great skill in telling stories, at his wisdom, which is often cloaked in the most deceptively simple and lucid expressions, at his manner, which is always gentle, even humble, and also at his lively wit and sense of humour.[33]

Achebe did not disappoint them. In his address, 'Spelling Our Proper Name', he reiterates the achievement of the late James Baldwin as a writer who 'wants to lift from the back of Black people the heavy burden of their blackness, to end the oppression which is visited on them because they are Black and for no other reason (to use his own phrase)'. He perceives that role as important because

> to answer oppression with appropriate resistance requires knowledge of two kinds. Self-knowledge by the victim means in the first place an awareness that oppression exists, that the victim has fallen from a great height of glory or promise into the present depths. Secondly, the victim must know who the enemy is. He must know his oppressor's real name, not an alias, not a pseudonym, not a *nom de plume*.

This identification of one's oppressor is explained by Achebe as related to the issue of a proper definition and awareness of one's identity. Moreover, he regards literature as essential in that task of identification because

> the cure which literature can bring to human anguish is to prove its truth and history and so make it familiar and possible to live with. Unfortunately, the truth, the history about Black people has been so deeply buried in mischief and prejudice that a whole army of archeologists would now be needed to dig it out.

Thus Achebe perceives the way Africa has always been reflected in the mind of the colonizer as deliberately and erroneously conceived to justify the self-interest of the colonizer as synonymous with moral necessity. He refers to some historical records to counter some of the myths associated with Africans and the slave trade, especially the false notion that Africans willingly sold their kinsmen into slavery. Achebe recommends the reading of appropriate historical works by Cheikh Anta Diop, Chancellor Williams and Chinweizu; he praises Diop for giving 'black people a foundation on which to begin a reconstruction of their history'. He ends on the positive note that 'good writers have a good nose' for information that will empower their readers: he cites John Wideman, Alice Walker, Toni Morrison 'and a host of other novelists and poets'.[34] In addition to the address, Achebe gave a reading from *Anthills of the Savannah*, and he also read a poem he dedicated to Christopher Okigbo. In the last part of the conference, a panel discussion, Achebe concluded his comment by insisting that the significance of Baldwin is that he

> stood quite clearly and quite firmly on the side of the artist using his talents to call things by their name, including saying that the emperor has no clothes. And if you say this, you're not going to be very popular with the emperor, but you will be doing your work.[35]

That task of telling the emperor or the world the truth had found expression almost fourteen years previously in Achebe's insightful essay on Joseph

Conrad's *Heart of Darkness*. That essay was selected, in spite of its carefully argued but devastating comment on the novel, by Robert Kimbrough for his Norton critical edition of *Heart of Darkness*, published in 1988. Kimbrough rightly points out in his introduction that 'the three most important events in *Heart of Darkness* criticism since the second edition of his book are the public remarks of Chinua Achebe on Conrad's racism, the film *Apocalypse Now* and the publication of Ian Watt's *Conrad in the Nineteenth Century*.[36] But in the bid to achieve a balance of views Kimbrough published three more essays: two by Wilson Harris and Ponnuthrai Sarvan defending Conrad, the other by Francis B. Singh supporting the Chinua Achebe view. Clearly the discussion of Conrad would never be the same again and the Fulbright professorship at the University of Massachusetts enabled him to re-examine the effects of that 'Conrad racism' on contemporary America and world affairs. When Achebe was told that many critics interpreted his essay as saying, 'Don't read Conrad', however, he explained: 'It's not in my nature to talk about banning books. I am saying, read it – with the kind of understanding and with the knowledge I talk about. And read it beside African works.'[37]

His appointment at Massachusetts did not prevent Achebe from travelling, and the invitations were numerous in 1988. Early in the year he attended a writers' symposium in Dublin, Ireland. It was organized by the Irish Arts Council to commemorate a thousand years of the founding of the city of Dublin and the theme of the symposium was 'Literature as Celebration'. Achebe said that though some of his colleagues found the theme disconcerting, in his view it reflected a basic truth associated with his own traditional literary inheritance. The symposium was a major event and the *Irish Times*, in a story it published on the day Achebe gave his brief paper, called him 'the man who invented African literature'. Before he presented his paper Achebe dissociated himself 'from that well-meant but blasphemous characterization'. He insisted that it was not as a result of modesty but that his

> refusal was due rather to an artistic taboo among [his] people, a prohibition – on pain of being finished off rather quickly by the gods – from laying a proprietory hand on even the smallest item in that communal enterprise in creativity which [his] people, the Igbo of Nigeria, undertook from time to time and to which they gave the name *Mbari*.[38]

The reason Achebe proffered was genuine. It was that adherence to the truthfulness of his experience as an artist in the service of his people that made his creative works intrinsically invaluable, locating them within the *Mbari* tradition. It was also at that forum that Joseph Brodsky told Achebe after listening to his comments on Conrad: 'I do not see any racism there; perhaps prejudices, but then all of us are prejudiced.' Achebe answered: 'Yes, I know you do not see it. That is why I am talking about it; if you saw it there would be no point talking about it, I raise it because intelligent and sensitive people like you who ought to see it, do not see it.'[39]

Further recognition of the 'communal' aspect of his creativity came in May when he gave a reading at the Schomburg Center for Research in Black Culture, a branch of the New York Public Library in Harlem, where an old black man walked up to him and said that when he read *Things Fall Apart* he knew both the food described and the people. It was testimony from a man who had never been to Africa and Achebe remarked that such responses pleased him because they meant that there 'is enough memory of who we were for us to begin to build bridges again'. The need for such bridges was reflected in other ways, like the contents of the bulky envelope which turned out to be from a class in the women's college of a university in South Korea: 'they had read *Things Fall Apart* in their class' which made 'all 34 of them decide to write a letter' to Achebe. What touched him most was the connection which those women saw between their own history and Nigerian history, 'the way they saw British colonization as similar to Japanese colonization of Korea'.[40]

Such encounters were insightful as well as satisfying to the writer as he continued his task of consolidating the literary frontiers he had cleared, shuttling between Nigeria and the other parts of his still expanding world. On one of those trips back to Nigeria in May 1988, Achebe met a man in the aircraft taking him to Enugu and described that encounter thus:

> This chap I happened to be sitting [with] looked at me and said, 'You're Professor Achebe?' And I said, 'Yes'. He said, 'We are on the same board.' I said, 'What board?' He said, 'Of the Radio Corporation of Nigeria.' And I said, 'Is that so?' Mark you before then my son had telephoned and said, 'this is in the news.' And I said: 'Is that so? Maybe I'll get a letter soon.' But I didn't get any letter for months. And I came back for something else and ran into this man on the plane and he says, 'We are on the same board.' I asked, 'How many meetings have you had?' He said: 'Fifteen. Somebody is standing in for you. Now I'm going to tell the Director-General that I saw you.' And I said, 'Tell him you saw somebody like me.' So, when I got to Enugu, two days later the Secretary to the Corporation and the Lawyer came with a letter from the Minister. Well to cut a long story short, I was not able to accept.[41]

The appointment which Achebe rejected was that of Chairman of the Federal Radio Corporation of Nigeria. His decision must have been influenced by the excesses of the Babangida military administration at that time in Nigeria. It was a courageous and principled refusal, for such appointments meant access to several privileges that would have increased his material standing. He was serving Nigeria at both the state and town levels at that time, though his state-level appointment as the pro-chancellor of ASUTECH ended that year. Achebe must have felt that service at the state and local levels had more to do with ordinary Nigerians than an appointment by visionless soldiers who lacked principles. That high-minded concern with principles was shown in an interview he granted Patricia Wright at the University of Massachusetts.

Wright describes Achebe as possessing a skin that is 'a deep brown, and there is the most wonderful long *seam* around his mouth.' She adds that 'his eyes are very sharp and very dark behind thick spectacles. And when he hears something that amuses him, those eyes go *dancing*.' She also reports Achebe as saying that he 'was created by a moment in history. *Things Fall Apart* was created by the same forces. There was no way one could have evaded writing that book.' Patricia Wright clearly agrees:

> Achebe moved something that justice demanded be moved.... Fortune is dealt to individuals but individuals also direct fortune. Achebe is a fortunate man, but also a man who took fortune by the throat.[42]

Her comment emphasizes the transformation that the fiction of Achebe achieved. A story that came to him when he went to lecture at the University of

California in Berkeley illustrates that transformation. He narrates the story of Judge Wolfgang Zeidler thus:

A librarian there showed me a letter she had received from a friend of hers in Germany to whom she had once introduced my book *Things Fall Apart*. This friend, according to the letter, had then loaned the book to a neighbour who was a distinguished Judge. The reason for the loan was that the Judge was planning with much enthusiasm to emigrate to Namibia after his retirement and accept the offer made to him to become a constitutional consultant to the Namibian regime. He planned to buy a farm out there and spend his retirement in the open and pleasant air of the African veldt. His neighbour, no doubt considering the Judge's enthusiasm and optimism rather excessive if not downright unhealthy, asked him to read *Things Fall Apart* on his flight to and from Namibia, which he apparently did. The result was dramatic. In the words of the letter shown to me the judge said that 'he had never seen Africa in that way and after having read that book he was no more innocent'. And he closed the Namibia chapter. Elsewhere in the letter the Judge was described as a leading constitutional Judge in Germany, as a man 'with the sharpest intelligence'. For about 12 years he had been President of the Bundesverfassungsgericht, the highest constitutional court in Germany. In short he was the kind of person the South Africans (the white regime then) would do much to have in their corner; a man whose presence in Namibia would give considerable comfort to the regime there. His decision not to go was obviously a triumph of commonsense and humanity over stupidity and racial bigotry. But how was it that this prominent German jurist carried such a blind spot about Africa all his life? Did he never read the papers? Why did he need an African novel to open his eyes? My own theory is that he needed to hear Africa speak for itself after a lifetime of hearing Africa spoken about by others.[43]

Achebe rightly felt that the story of the judge, Wolfgang Zeidler, 'is a companion piece to the fashionable claim made even by writers that literature can do nothing to alter our social and political condition; of course it can'.[44] It was that knowledge that made Achebe utilize the opportunities that came his way to convey the appropriate view of Africa to the world. One of those opportunities came in a television interview which Achebe recorded on 27 July 1988 at Chancellor Joseph Duffey's house on the University of Massachusetts campus entitled 'Listening to Africa'.

That filmed interview by Bill Moyers was premiered on 12 September and ran for 10 weeks. At the beginning of the interview Achebe is shown strolling on the Amherst campus with two university students, Kathleen Melley and Habib Enayetullah, early in the morning. Enayetullah told Stacey Chace of the *Campus Chronicle* that Achebe 'didn't have any airs' and that he felt the writer had 'an incredible knowledge of Indian literature'.[45] The film was part of a public affairs television series, 'Bill Moyers' World of Ideas', consisting of conversations with thoughtful men and women about issues and ideas shaping America. Achebe answers numerous questions concerning literature and art but the comment and advice that he gives to Western viewers is the heart of the interview. He says that the West should

see Africa as a continent of people – just people, not some beings that demand a special kind of treatment. If you accept Africans as people, then you listen to them. They have their preferences. If you took Africa seriously as a continent of people, you would listen.[46]

He emphasizes that issue because he is convinced that Western attitudes should be changed since 'the traditional attitude of Europe or the West is that

Africa is a continent of children'. That attitude, Achebe points out, underlies the disposition of world affairs, and he emphasizes that 'the world is not well arranged, and therefore there's no way we can be happy with it, even as writers'. In addition, that lopsided arrangement is supported by the fact that 'the withdrawal of the colonial powers was in many ways merely a tactical move to get out of the limelight but to retain the control in all practical ways'. The colonial experience was more devastating than the world imagines because there is 'no way you can inculcate democracy through dictatorship. The colonial system in itself was the very antithesis of democracy' although 'there was democracy in many parts of Africa before colonial rule came'. Achebe insists, however, that a rectification of that abnormality cannot be made without an understanding of the people involved, which is why he concludes that the Western world must realize that Africa

> is made up of human beings; we are people. We are not funny beings. If you took up any newspaper here, you probably won't see Africa mentioned at all for months. Then perhaps one day, you'll see some strange story. It has to be the kind of story we've come to associate with Africa. I would simply say: look at Africa as a continent of people. They are not devils, they are not angels, they're just people. And listen to them. We have done a lot of listening ourselves.... It is important that we develop the ability to listen to the weak. Not only in Africa, but even in your own society, the strong must listen to the weak.

Those issues – concerning the re-examination of Africa and the need for the strong to listen to the weak – were not occurring to Achebe for the first time. His collection of essays, *Hopes and Impediments: Selected Essays (1965–1987)*,[47] published by Heinemann Educational Books in 1988 illustrated the same basic concerns. The fifteen essays in this book reveal both Achebe's awareness of his African background and his sensitivity to the reality of the rest of the world. Thus the essays capture the ambivalences, the uncertainties and the frayed linkages between human societies and peoples in the world. But in his perceptive examination of those human issues Achebe remains sincere, reasonable and logical. Chris Dunton reviewed the essays in *West Africa*:

> No one reading Achebe's fiction or listening to him in an interview can fail to be attracted to his temperate, fine-tuned humanism; the essays in his new book remind us also how tough-minded, how properly insistent, he can be in exposing false and demeaning ideas about Africa and its culture.[48]

The analytical spirit of those essays augmented the objectives of the novel *Anthills of the Savannah*, which sold briskly in Nigeria when the paperback edition finally came out through the local publishers: a year behind schedule and six months later than the Kenyan edition, negotiated six months after the conclusion of the arrangement between the publishers in Nigeria and Heinemann Educational Books in London.

The delayed emergence of the book in Nigeria did not affect the tour that Achebe's London publishers organized to enable him to participate in two major book-launching events for *Anthills of the Savannah* in Copenhagen and Oslo, to coincide with the publication of the Danish and Norwegian translations. In Oslo Achebe participated in a symposium with André Brink of South Africa as part of a bookfair. In Sweden he met academics, writers and journalists in the cities of Umeå and Stockholm, though the Swedish translation appeared some time later. His public lectures generated interest in the fate of his country and the role of the writer. Responding to questions, he offered, not for the first time, his hope that 'literature should make it possible for us, by observing the tragedies of fictional characters and fictional societies, to circumvent them; we should not have to go through the same thing once again.[49]

From Scandinavia Achebe returned to Nigeria. As usual, journalists trailed him to Nsukka, where he granted several interviews. He told Okey Ndibe of the *African Guardian* that 'what somebody says when he comes to power doesn't really signify very much' because 'it's like a salesman giving you the virtues of his product'; instead, he insisted, 'it's the press who ought to be telling us our condition'. With obvious reference to the Ibrahim Babangida regime he added: 'It's the press who ought to say that what we saw, we are not seeing anymore. Banning obviously is part of repression, not part of human rights. So if you have bans, restrictions, detentions, these are contrary to human rights.' Yet he thought that these political challenges had much to do with the exciting nature of literature from the Third World:

> Life in the Third World is much more problematic; much more demanding and challenging [and] problems help to create literature; the tension of having to struggle is one ingredient. But this is not to say that we should therefore stay in problems so that we can create good literature. We must not stay in sins so that grace may abound, as the Bible says. God forbid! But problems are a necessary ingredient in the creation of important literature. The West and the more comfortable parts of the world may not, in fact, have anything very important to worry about now. And so they create literature that is easy-going, personal, even frivolous.[50]

In another interview Achebe talked to the persistent Onuora Udenwa of *Quality Weekly*. He assessed the impact of the military regime:

> Nigeria is becoming a closed society; very, very slowly. And closed societies are dangerous, they are totalitarian, fascist and that's not where we are supposed to be heading. We are supposed to be heading in the direction of human rights, of discussion etc. That's what we are told.

When the interviewer sought Achebe's opinion on what had affected him most in his life, the state of Nigeria was still his theme:

> I come to tears almost every day on Nigeria. On the missed opportunity of Nigeria; the fact that nobody has had the imagination to say, 'Look I'm going to transcend all this pettiness and become the leader and founder of modern Nigeria' because this is important for Africa, this is important for the black man. The black man is looking to Nigeria. So, let's stop all this nonsense about religion, about tribe and so on. Let's organize Nigeria and make it a working entity so that it can fulfil its mission in the world.[51]

The interviewer insisted on obtaining Achebe's view concerning remarks in several Lagos-Ibadan newspapers that he was neither a relevant nor an effective writer since he was not awarded the Nobel Prize in 1986. Achebe had to contextualize the issue in a way that would educate and inform.

> My position is that the Nobel Prize is important. But it is a European prize. It's not an African prize. It's not a Nigerian prize. Those who give it, Europeans who give it are not responsible to us. You can't go and ask them. 'Why are you not giving it to so and so?' It's not your prize!... They have their reasons for setting it up. They have their rules for determining who should get it. And so, what we should be saying is 'Okay,

we are happy they have given one of us their prize'. But to go from there to say, 'Ah now this is the *Ashiwaju* of African literature', is so absurd. Now, that is something I would like to take on sometime and explain, that a European prize does not make anybody the *Ashiwaju* of Nigerian literature. And we must put things in their proper perspective.... Let us not forget that we are Nigerians, we are Africans. And this is not one of our things. Literature is not a heavyweight championship. Nigerians may think, you know, this man has been knocked out. It's nothing to do with that.[52]

This part of the interview was extracted and used as a cover story with wide publicity, providing ample ammunition for those seeking confirmation of the idea that Achebe must be jealous. It led to another spate of reactions in the press with some writers either supporting or disagreeing with him. As Achebe had said in the major part of the interview, published a week later on 10 November, 'I guess my greatest fault is that I don't accept standards that may be okay for other people for the sake of peace.'[53]

In December 1988 Henry Chakava of Achebe's Kenyan publishers invited him on a tour of Kenya during which he gave talks to numerous school children. They came out in their hundreds and thousands in every centre that Achebe visited. He explained that

there are about twelve schools in every district and they all came together in one place with all their teachers; and it was like they were saying, 'we found ourselves in literature'. I had the biggest book signing in my life.[54]

Back in Nigeria there was a literary celebration of *Anthills of the Savannah* at Enugu on 26 January 1989. Heinemann Educational Books (Nigeria) gathered book lovers, friends, critics, students, professors, administrators and ordinary men and women to celebrate the publication of Chinua Achebe's *Anthills of the Savannah* and his daughter Chinelo Achebe's *The Last Laugh and Other Stories* at the Hotel Presidential. It was not an occasion for the formal handover of the mantle of creativity to a member of the younger generation but the juxtaposition of a distinguished craftsman and a promising fledgling debutante. The chairman of the occasion was Dr Pius Okigbo and the celebration was as modest as any one would have expected considering Chinua Achebe's legendary restraint in such social affairs. Although the guests were distinguished and varied there was an unmistakable infusion of the bonhomie of writers' gatherings. It was thus a literary celebration in which jokes were abundant. Aig Higo, the publisher, aroused laughter through his comments on the various colours of traditional caps worn by some of the eminent guests which, he observed, did not signify traditional titles or wealth. Professor of English Ernest Emenyonu continued the fun by confessing that his own cap was worn to hide a receding hairline. Emenyonu also reviewed the two books with commendable insight and then the master of ceremonies invited Chinua Achebe to make brief remarks as the 'big masquerade'. Achebe thanked the guests for coming to the celebration, especially those who came from distant places. He revealed that the members of his family are not noted for making speeches through an anecdote concerning the wedding of one of his cousins where he was asked to make a speech and declined, and the man who had made the request retorted: 'Silent family!' – for his brothers had declined, too. He was able to share his happiness at the fact that the responses of ordinary people in the country had encouraged him and made him feel that the task of a writer 'is invaluable'. He revealed, to applause, that the greatest contributor to that literary celebration was his wife,

Christie, who had made it possible for father and daughter to show the world the harvest of their literary efforts. And finally he noted that the writer in Nigeria was saddled with numerous problems that included the personal, the social, the economic and the political – but the only solution was to continue writing, in spite of those impediments.[55]

This central belief in the importance of the act of writing, against and through all impediments is illustrated in *Anthills of the Savannah*. He elaborates on it in an interview with Chris Searle:

If you look at the things that are happening in the society; the struggle itself, the inspirer to struggle, the story of the struggle; when you put all these things together and ask what is the most important, then the choice falls upon the *story*. It is the story that conveys all our gains, all our failures, all we hold dear and all we condemn. To convey this to the next generation is the only way we can keep going and keep alive as people. Therefore, the story is like the genes that are transferred to create the new being. It is far more important than anything else.[56]

18

The Legacy of an Eagle on Iroko
Masquerades, Celebrations & Survival
1989–93

Many scholars from all parts of the world interested in African literature assembled at Nsukka. They came from all the continents. The distinguished Michael Thelwell came from America with Bernth Lindfors and John Povey; G. D. Killam from Canada, Denise Coussy from France, Alastair Niven and C. L. Innes from Britain, Gareth Griffiths from Australia, Raoul Granqvist from Sweden, Wolfgang Zach from Austria and A. L. Imfeld and Ulla Schild from Germany. It was a magnificent gathering. The voices of countless writers and critics, the books they had authored and the ebullience of their greetings as they paced backwards and forwards sent smiles into every heart. For the first time in living Nigerian memory, over one hundred and fifty papers were delivered on a single writer in a conference in Nigeria when the literary world went to Nsukka.[1]

THAT account, with its respectful allusion to *Things Fall Apart*, captures an honour that Chinua Achebe received in 1990. It was not unexpected, for the impact of his novels was universal and the sales figures available from Heinemann Educational Books show that by 1986 Achebe's novels were selling as much as 33 per cent of the combined turnover of the 270 titles in the African and Caribbean Writers Series. Alan Hill maintained that it was those sales that sustained the series, making it possible for scores of titles that could not otherwise 'have lasted for more than a week to be kept in print'.[2] The translation of his novels into more than 45 languages, meanwhile, ensured access to them for people of other world cultures.

His work as a writer, it would seem, had led Chinua Achebe to an ever-deeper contemplation of the nature of African societies and their relationship with the rest of the world. In March 1989 he was invited to the 25th anniversary meeting of the Organization of Economic Cooperation and Development (OECD) in Paris. Many of the participants came from the rich societies of Europe, America and Australia. Achebe was the only writer in the midst of these bankers and economists reading their papers and discussing the structural adjustment programmes imposed by the West on so many countries of the Third World. It seemed to Achebe that what they were saying was something like:

You are not managing your affairs well – you are in debt. So if you need more loans, this is what you will do: you have to remove subsidies on agriculture and this and that; and if you obey our rules, more loans will come your way. These are a few things that you will have to adjust; it may impose some hardship on you, but we know it's going to work.

Achebe heard the chairman of the Central Bank in Kenya say: 'A country like Zambia has been practising this for two years – but they are no better off after all this.' And he heard the authors of the structural adjustment idea answer thus: 'No, you have to give us a little more time. This thing has to work in the end.' It was then that Achebe got very angry.

> I am beginning to understand why I am here. I have been wondering what a fiction writer is doing among world bankers and economists. But now I realize that what you are doing here is fiction! You talk about 'structural adjustment' as if Africa was some kind of laboratory! Some intellectual abstraction. You prepare your medicine, you mix this into that; if it doesn't work, you try out another concoction. But Africa is people, you know? In the last two years we have seen the minimum wage in Nigeria fall from the equivalent of fifteen pounds a month to five pounds a month! That's not an abstraction; somebody is earning that money and he has a wife and children you see. You are punishing these countries because they are in debt but America is the biggest debtor of all; and nobody is asking America to adopt policies that would bankrupt their citizens. But Africa – the Third World – they are places where you can try out things because you believe that Africans are not really people, they are expendable.[3]

As he delivered his speech Achebe could sense the shock in some of his audience, as if they had 'realized for the first time that Africa was not just a conglomeration of different formulas'. In his speech he was confronting the kind of mentality that had always created problems for his society, whether in art or literature or economy or politics. Making the speech was part of his task of defending the interests of Africa, and his reputation added weight to his succinct observations.

The honours and appointments which continued to flow his way were often offered in recognition of his role as a fighter for Africa's literature and its economy. He was appointed a Distinguished Professor of English at the City College of the City University of New York in 1989, and also given the 1989 Callaloo Award 'in recognition of invaluable contributions to World Literature'.[4] Recognition flowed not only from learned institutions but equally from ordinary students like Mohammed B. Taleb-Khyar from Mauritania, who told Charles Rowell after Achebe had given a reading and lecture at the University of Virginia in April 1989: 'In this [Western] culture, you meet knowledge, you meet erudition, you meet expertise, but not wisdom. Mr Achebe speaks and writes wisdom.'[5] It was in recognition of that wisdom that David N. Dinkins, then president of the borough of Manhattan before becoming mayor of New York in 1990, honoured Achebe's literary career, his role as a thinker and 'the expression and transmission of knowledge and truth through his writing and teaching'.[6] As part of the presentation Dinkins proclaimed Thursday, 25 May 1989 as Chinua Achebe Day in the borough of Manhattan. It was an unexpected and touching gesture for Chinua Achebe, who was fulfilling the requirements of his position at the City University of New York.

On 19 May 1989 Achebe was made Doctor of Humane Letters by Westfield State College, Massachusetts, which was celebrating its 150th anniversary by honouring 'the recent 30th anniversary of the publication of Chinua Achebe's first novel, *Things Fall Apart*'. This was Achebe's twelfth honorary degree, awarded 'not only for his moving prose and clear vision, but also for serving as such a bridge between cultures'.[7]

When the Open University of Great Britain awarded Achebe an honorary degree soon after, the citation appeared to have been written by someone who had taken the trouble to grasp the dynamic of his career as a writer:

> Chinua Achebe embracing the inexorable logic of his people's history is a writer with a cause. He seeks to be the voice of his own people.... His work challenges the misrepresentation of the history of the African people and their culture. He explores the prospects of a future with living roots in a rich cultural heritage to be built by the African people themselves.... The power of his art has made accessible to those of us who are not African a world of rich tradition and cultural achievement, a perception of the complexity of contemporary Nigerian society. Our encounter with it teaches us something about ourselves. Through his writing he has enriched all humanity.[8]

In confirmation of his universal appeal and stature, in 1989 Achebe was appointed to a seven-person international jury by the Indian government to award the annual Indira Gandhi Prize for Peace, Disarmament and Development. He was to serve for three years.

This great harvest of honours and international recognition did not insulate Achebe from the residual bigotry and insensitivity in Western attitudes to Africa.

> I had a very curious experience in Holland, where I was put up as President of International PEN. An older, much older man, a Frenchman, was put up also – or he put himself up after he saw my name. And he won. But the interesting thing is that he had no conception – and didn't want to have any conception – of the literature of Africa. He kept quite clearly and studiously avoiding any mention of African literature, and at some point he said something like this: 'How can we expect the Third World, with all its problems, to produce great art?' Now this is the kind of mind or mentality I'm talking about. It remains alien to me though I encounter it frequently. It is alien to me because my whole life has been ordered in such a way that I have to know people. This is one of the penalties of being an underdog, you see. The overdog doesn't need to know about the underdog; therefore, he suffers severe limitations, and the underdog ends up being wiser because he knows about himself and knows about the overdog.[9]

It was that knowledge which the position of the writer from Africa enabled him to acquire – seeing things from below – that made Chinua Achebe's contributions distinct and relevant.

Hostility and insensitivity did not inhibit Achebe's interrogation of prevalent Western ideas that he considered blinkered and negative. As he says in an interview with Charles Rowell in May 1989, 'One small corner of the world cannot wake up one morning and call its artifact the 'Great Tradition'. Great Tradition makes sense only if you're not aware of other people's tradition.' He also questions the idea that history from the African continent

> should be measured in terms of paper. So whenever you don't have a piece of paper, somebody says there is no history. And we seem to be quite ready to accept it. So you would find historians going to archives in Portugal, for instance, to see what some sailor from Portugal had said when he came to Benin in the fifteenth century. We don't ask the condition of this sailor when he was making his entry, whether he was drunk or sober. He is on a piece of paper and therefore reliable – more reliable than what you might gather in the field by asking people.

The way in which Achebe persuades his listeners to re-examine their own original concepts was an attribute that enhanced his reputation as a wise man as the 1980s drew to a close. His vision of the responsibilities and role of the literary critic in the new Nigerian society is an example of his emphasis on constant and flexible revaluation.

> Today when the [work] is down in print on paper, I think the role of the critic has become a lot more complex and this is a lot more important. It is important because there is need for mediation. Since I'm not going to go around and meet the people and answer their questions as a story teller would do in the past, actually meet them face to face and experience their support or disagreement, somebody else is called into existence to perhaps explain difficult parts, or perform all kinds of functions of a mediating nature. Also, there is so much which is produced, there is so much that is written, all of it is not of the same quality and a certain amount of discrimination is necessary just to survive the barrage of production in the modern world, the sheer number of books. I think therefore the role of the critic is important. Also, I think the critic is there to draw attention to this community that I was talking about, to the tradition. How does this new work relate to what has happened before, and how does it relate to writers who were here before, how does it even relate to those who did not write their stories but told them? So I think there is a new and necessary and important role for the critic.[10]

Achebe's preoccupation with finding a way forward for Africa which breaks the intellectual fetters of a colonial past and uses traditional resources in creative new ways emerges from a conversation he had with Ulli Beier at Iwalewa Haus in Germany on 1 July 1989. Achebe had visited Germany as a lecturer for the Sonderforschungsbereich (special research area programme). There are people who doubt that Africa will ever recover from its tribulations, he reflects, but 'the assessment is not quite fair – because if our leaders failed they were not leaders which we have chosen [but] the leadership they [the West] installed'. Achebe declares that in Africa 'if we win the battle for the minds, the first thing which will go is that rigidity of mind that has come to us with the so-called "higher religions", this fanaticism that can make a man go to war over a matter of belief'. And he looks forward instead to a rediscovery of the meaning of the old saying that 'the world is a Dancing Masquerade'.[11]

Achebe was calling for a greater awareness of the variety in the world, and for a variety of viewpoints to match this 'dancing masquerade'. 'Rigidity of mind' had its say again when, in 1989, an angry British critic used the opportunity of Achebe's involvement in a documentary for the BBC to denounce the 1975 lecture on racism in Conrad's *Heart of Darkness*.[12] The dance of the masquerade, meanwhile, was leading Achebe to the Harare Book Fair in Zimbabwe, where in August 1989 he was an honoured guest in the company of President Robert Mugabe and other distinguished participants.

The masquerade led him further afield. In October of 1989, in America, Achebe published the maiden issue of *African Commentary: A Journal for People of African Descent,* for which he wrote the foreword, 'Our Mission'.

> Africa is more than a geographic reality; it is a spiritual phenomenon, born, truly enough of a painful history – the history of slavery – but it is a history which binds every *Black* person to Africa. It is for this reason that *African Commentary* is a journal for people of African descent – whether they are African-Americans, or Africans in Europe, the Caribbean, or in the homeland.

Looking back at lost opportunities, Achebe emphasizes the urgency of the mission:

> It is not long to the twenty-first century: we are indeed running out of time. The goal of *African Commentary* is, in part, to ensure that Africa and the rest of the black world step into the next century with dignity and a restored sense of initiative. In the three decades since many African nations became independent, the question of forging African unity has often been raised and sabotaged by African leaders themselves. With just about ten years to the twenty-first century, it is clear to us that Africa cannot make it on the individual steam of diverse countries.

Beyond lost opportunities lay a past with a part to play in the future:

> *African Commentary* is committed to reclaiming the rich heritage of Africa, and re-drawing the contours of African history. Beyond reclaiming the African past, the pages of *African Commentary* will be open to some of the best minds in Africa and the Black world to ponder the question of Africa's and its descendants' place in the world today.[13]

It was thus in order that the first issue of the journal should be on 'The Identity Question' and the consulting editor, Okey Ndibe, suggested the scope of *African Commentary* when he wrote that it 'is a unifying symbol which will gather the scattered shards of the Black World. To do this, the magazine will visit all black people wherever they may live to examine their political, economic and social affairs.'[14] The list of contributors, reflecting some of the best minds available, emphasized the importance of the mission undertaken by the publisher: Chinua Achebe, Sam Ajiri, Kofi Awoonor, A. M. Babu, Dennis Brutus, Chinweizu, Larry Diamond, Augustine Esogbue, Nuruddin Farah, Ibrahim Gambari, Nadine Gordimer, Okechukwu Ikejiani, Leonard Jeffries, Fela Anikulapo-Kuti, Ali Mazrui, Ifeanyi Menkiti, Toni Morrison, Gloria Naylor, Olusegun Obasanjo, Ben Obumselu, Chuba Okadigbo, Pius Okigbo, Mokwugo Okoye, Ben Okri, William Strickland, Michael Thelwell and Obiora Udechukwu.

African Commentary was meant to give a voice to Africans everywhere in the world, as Achebe made clear: 'I agree with the late reggae star, Peter Tosh, when he sings that wherever you come from, once you are a black man, you are an African.' Essays published in the first and subsequent issues tackled that task of presenting the African/black perspective on issues of world importance so that 'Africa and the rest of the world step into the next century with dignity and rekindled optimism'.[15] In several interviews granted by Chinua Achebe in November 1989 he reiterated these views. The occasion of his fifty-ninth birthday gave one opportunity to the journalists who sought him out. In an interview granted to the *Nigerian Statesman* and published on 14 November 1989, Achebe told the team of interviewers:

> I have been travelling, I have time to take my message beyond Nsukka wherever the spirit moves me. I was saying to a group in New York a few months ago that I was a missionary in reverse. Your people brought the message to us once upon a time, now it is my turn to bring my message to you. So I see myself in that way too.

Achebe was a missionary in a new medium, with a different message.

> The whole purpose of African literature in my view is to change the perception of the world as far as Africans are concerned, and for me that's being a missionary. So I have been very busy spreading that good news that Africans are people, that we are not savages and cannibals.

He did not pursue his missionary calling to the neglect of his own society, insisting that Nigerians have the responsibility and the ability to effect changes in the nation's intellectual culture and economy.

We must do that and even if it is going to take a generation to do it, we must do it. A right step, you know this cliché, is a step in the right direction. It is a cliché but it is a very, very meaningful cliché. A step in the right direction is very important. Ten steps in the wrong direction are useless. If your intention is to go there and you face the other way and start taking steps, you are not ever going to get there.[16]

In an interview granted to the *Daily Champion* and published on 18 November Achebe provides one reason for the inability of his country to move in the right direction.

Nigeria can have good leaders. Other countries have had good leaders. Good leaders don't come every day either. But some societies prepare themselves for good leaders. Others prepare themselves to oppose the emergence of good leadership. So this is why it is important to be talking about it so that people will know it is possible. It happens once in a while. But if we set up a system which celebrates mediocrity, then this system will make sure that good people do not have a chance.

Vigilance against mediocrity and the defence of merit were necessary conditions of the emergence of a new Nigeria.

If something keeps happening and happening, or if somebody keeps failing and failing in Igboland he will go and consult an oracle. They call it *Iju Ase*. But frankly, I would say that the moment we decide to put merit aside and bring up whatever other considerations, that society is bound to be in trouble and I think that's one of the things that has happened to us. And the modern world has not been created on considerations outside of merit.

Always ready to state plainly what he saw as fundamental Nigerian values, he could also employ the ironic perspective of the novelist.

The Greeks or Romans or some Europeans of antiquity said that something new is always coming from Africa and we seem to be living up to that reputation. In Nigeria, we have a situation where before an election the government forms parties. This is a totally new thing, Nigeria's contribution to political thought. One is still watching to see how it develops.

He had watched to see how his role as chairman of the council at ASUTEC would develop, and decided not to serve a full term: 'Half-way through my tenure they thought twice about it. I'm not going to sit in any place and be somebody else's mouthpiece.' In his view the university teachers had added to the problems of Nigerian higher education institutions.

We academics have presided over the liquidation of the university system. One of the ways we have done it is our obsession for office. Twenty-five years ago, university professors were held in very high esteem. Today, I don't think anybody thinks very much of them and, quite frankly, I think it is of our own making.

He gives the example of

what happens when a university Vice Chancellor is about to leave office. You ought to see the trips made up and down to government houses and to Lagos, begging for position. Why? Because people are looking for positions and the independence of the university has been eroded.

Achebe spoke authoritatively: he had been associated with Nigerian universities for 23 years.

In the *Daily Champion* interview he also looks back at his literary output over those years, revealing that in his creative work he has been

> covering the same story from different angles, and I happen to believe that there is no such thing as one story. This is why you keep circulating in terms of style, in terms of time, in terms of perspective in order to approach what you might call the truth.

One of the questions Achebe was asked was whether five novels were enough.

> It's not in my place to say whether five novels are enough or not but that's what I've been able to present. If anyone feels strongly about gaps he can fill them. I did not sign a contract with anybody that I will be giving them one novel every two years. There is a certain philistinism in Nigeria which is based on all kinds of things, jealousy, spite etcetera.... There are some writers who write a lot, and there are some who don't write a lot. One of the greatest American writers, Ralph Ellison, wrote one great world shaker called *Invisible Man* and you can't talk about black American writing without mentioning Ralph Ellison, and right on top too.[17]

The same issue of true quality versus the philistinism of the literary marketplace was highlighted in another interview which Achebe granted the *Daily Times* and which was also published on 18 November 1989. In his assessment of literature in Nigeria he remarks that

> creativity will show where it exists; it will not be evident where it does not exist. No amount of self-promotion or publicity or anger is going to make a bad text work. Our writers must be ready to work as apprentices and not see themselves as instant stars.

Asked to define greatness in literature he spoke of a

> literature which alters the situation in the world. A good and important book does that and nothing can be done without reference to it. It has made a statement which changes the relationships and perceptions of the world. But one shouldn't worry about whether one can write a great book. I think one should write the best book one can write,

At the end of the interview he was asked what he thought his generation of writers had done.

> I think what we did was literally to create modern African literature. I think that's what history expected us to do. We were at the crossroads: we just happened to be there. That is something which cannot be denied. There may be different opinions about the quality of particular texts but nobody anywhere who lays any claims to being knowledgeable can ignore African literature now.[18]

The *Daily Times* editorial in the same issue of the newspaper acknowledges the relevance of what Achebe has done for Africa and humanity.'as a gifted storyteller and fabulist' who

> has counselled the entire world with the truth of his fiction.... He has not only wrestled at the luminous crossroads of culture and racial encounter; he has won great victories as well, like the eagle on Iroko. Achebe is now perched on the summit of fame which others may attempt but hardly surpass.... We have no doubt that for Achebe at 59, it is morning yet on creation day.[19]

The day before, Achebe had received one more feather of glory with the award of a fourteenth honorary degree from the University of Ibadan where his talents had been nurtured.

Others were looking back, like the academic and critic Louis James who thought that *Things Fall Apart* could now be seen as a catalyst which had altered the orientation of commonwealth literature.

> In 1989 it requires an act of imagination to realize its pioneering achievement. It was not only the language which had to bridge a cultural gap – the formal elements of narration and qualities of sensibility and emotional structure all had to be redefined.... After *Things Fall Apart*, literature already written in the Commonwealth took on a new emphasis: this, too, could be assessed against the metropolitan culture with a new clarity.[20]

Honours and responsibilities were flowing so thick and fast that Achebe could not always be present to receive them in person. Thus in 1989 he was elected the first president of PEN's Nigerian chapter in his absence from the ninth Association of Nigerian Authors annual conference in Calabar, and re-elected in his absence for a second term of office as president-general of the Ogidi Town Union. Elections, appointments and invitations ranged from Africa to America to Europe. He addressed the annual conference of assistant head-masters of English in the New York City school system, who all came to listen to him because at some point they had to teach or introduce *Things Fall Apart* in their schools. At a conference in Budapest he challenged some French partici-pants who were lamenting the ruin of civilization because 'the written word is dying'. Achebe told them he did not believe that 'the story is dead' and reminded them that 'it may well be in their own interest to say that no more stories should be told'. He felt convinced that 'the story is very much alive'.[21]

And should be written. His awareness of the necessity for the narration of the story led him to declare, at the height of the Salman Rushdie *Satanic Verses* controversy, that 'writers across the world were generally outraged by the passing of a death sentence on a writer for his writing'. He added that a writer 'has to be conscious of the possibilities of offence and resentment' but that 'the consequences should not include passing of a death sentence. The conse-quences can include people refusing to read the book or writing against the book; reviewing the book adversely.' A book's right to publication seems to Achebe to be closely related to the right to existence of a human life. In his own case, certainly, the books were the fruit of the life.

> I think all you need to tell the stories that I have told is to live the life that I have and keep your eyes and senses open and working. It seems to me very simple. I've never had any strain trying to present my condition beyond the strain of having to present the story, to write it, to find the most appropriate words to carry the message. Sometimes you succeed well, sometimes not so well and it is a part of the frustration of creating a story out of an experience that is not verbal.

Recognizing the connection between the right to life and the right to write en-forces, he believes, a spirit of tolerance. Despite, for example, his own impatience with a trend towards 'heroicism' in the new literature of memoirs and biog-raphies in his country,

> any writing is better than no writing. And if anybody wants to write his own heroics by all means let him. The answer to a bad book is a good book; it is a better book. If somebody puts himself in print, you should welcome it, read it and if you somehow

don't agree, then you have a good opportunity of saying so. The more we come out with what we've done and what has been done in our lives the better for us. I don't think we can complain. Let everybody write. It will be a good starting point in digging out the truth.[22]

For Achebe that truth was not divorced from the public life of Nigeria, where events were again taking a disturbing turn. He advised the military government of Ibrahim Babangida against witch-hunting innocent citizens after violent demonstrations caused by the structural adjustment policies of the International Monetary Fund (IMF) because 'people are not told by radicals that they are hungry'. The legitimation of these oppressive policies seemed to him to depend on a situation in which the leaders operate 'as if they are mentally living abroad'. His advice is that 'there are certain points you cannot cross when you are dealing with people; they are not a formula. When they are driven beyond that point, they take to the streets.'[23]

As Nigeria's leaders remained at home (while 'mentally abroad') to tighten the screws of austerity policies imposed by the priorities of international interests, Chinua Achebe was venturing abroad again to contest the role of his country (and his continent) within a rapidly changing international order. At the beginning of 1990 he accepted an appointment that was to last from January to March at Dartmouth College as a Montgomery Fellow and Visiting Professor of English. It was further honour from an institution that had awarded him the first of his fourteen honorary degrees. Perhaps Achebe accepted the appointment in order to register his appreciation, for 1990 gave him early signs of a busy schedule. Significantly, in view of the changing balance of world power, the Academy of Sciences of the USSR gave him a citation in 1990 too. It was the beginning of the last decade of the century and he had warned his continent to take the competing priorities of a changing world into consideration in devising development plans.

Achebe's sensitivity to the many-sidedness of words had been described in Lawrence Baugh's account of an interview with him fifteen years before. Words have 'strange personalities' and

> many faces depending upon the user and often to whom they apply. People don't take the time to analyse all the meanings of words so their horizons unfortunately become very limited in scope and consequently the realities of certain situations are distorted.[24]

Achebe seems to have had the 'strange personalities' of words at the back of his mind as he delivered the South Bank lecture as part of the London Weekend Television South Bank Show in January of 1990. His topic was 'African Literature as Restoration of Celebration' and he used the opportunity to elaborate on the talk he had given in Dublin in 1988. He describes the unique *Mbari* ceremony in Igboland as 'a celebration through art of the world and of the life lived in it', explaining that 'it was performed by the community on command by its presiding deity, usually the Earth goddess, Ana [who] combined two formidable roles in the Igbo pantheon as fountain of creativity in the world and custodian of the moral order in human society'. The development of his theme turns on a fuller examination of one of the key words in his title.

> The problems some of my colleagues had in Dublin with the word celebration may have arisen, I suspect, from too narrow a perspective on it. *Mbari* extends the view,

274

opens it out to meanings beyond the mere remembering of blessings or happy events; it deliberately sets out to include other experience – indeed, all significant encounters which man makes in his journey through life, especially new, unaccustomed and thus potentially threatening encounters.

Mbari illustrates art 'in its social dimension', as a 'celebration of reality', of the 'creative potential in everyone' and of 'the need to exercise' it for 'communal cooperative enterprises'. Achebe illustrates the insistence on human presence in the traditional *Mbari* art and contrasts this with its absence in the works of Joseph Conrad and John Buchan. He links the deliberate denial of human presence, human feelings and human values in these writers with the justifications offered by the wider society for the devastation of Africa by the slave trade and its colonial legacy. Drawing examples from his personal education, Achebe emphasizes the respect for human values in Africa. He also points out that African writers have used both the inherited colonial language and their own indigenous languages in asserting those values. He perceives 'the emergence of modern African literature as an assertion of human values and also a return of celebration' but he assures his audience that 'celebration does not mean praise or approval', although 'praise can be part of it, but only a part'. His conclusion looks both inwards and outwards, and suggests that other continents might do the same. 'The new literature in Africa is aware of the possibilities available to it for celebrating humanity in our continent. It is aware also that our world interlocks more and more with the worlds of others.' If we accept that 'then we had better learn to appreciate one another's presence and to accord to every people their due human respect'.[25]

Achebe had highlighted celebration in the cause of truth, in which the essential human values are preserved and rendered significant through creative works. But a celebration of a different kind was associated with him in February 1990 when a conference entitled 'Eagle on Iroko: Chinua Achebe at 60' was organized at the University of Nigeria, Nsukka. It was the idea of Edith Ihekweazu, a professor in the Department of Modern Languages and dean of the Faculty of Arts. Professor Ihekweazu became chairperson of the symposium committee, Obi Maduakor was its secretary, B. N. Igwilo was in charge of finance and Virginia Anohu was responsible for fund-raising. According to Obi Maduakor, 'the Faculty was enthusiastic, the vice-chancellor, Chimere Ikoku, gave financial support and the responses were tremendous from both national and international bodies. Contacts were made in Europe and America and many people received the idea with enthusiasm.'[26] The birthday symposium was held during 11–15 February 1990 although Achebe's birthday was not until November. The idea was to avoid clashes in dates, since it was presumed that other universities, institutions, groups and associations would organize literary activities commemorating Achebe's sixtieth year. Achebe himself, however, regarded 60 as an arbitrary age to celebrate because 'we are growing all the time and we are learning: There is continuity as we grow, as we learn. This is why we must go on growing, doing the kind of things you think are important.' While 'perhaps there are things that you see clearly' with age, for him

> the important things have always had to do with pioneering, with finding out the meaning of my existence. To the very last moment, I think we should be pioneering, finding out more about ourselves, trying to tell our story better so that the next generation can have all the background that we can give.[27]

It was the credo of a writer who was still projecting his vision, his energies and his talents in the interest of his society and the true tradition of his culture.

When the symposium activities commenced at Nsukka on 11 February 1990, it was clear, as Chidi Amuta wrote in the *Daily Times* of 12 February, that 'this, indeed, is Achebe's hour'. Amuta thought that for 'those intent on understanding today's Nigeria and changing it for the better, there is something in every Achebe work for us all'. He congratulated the conveners, who

> could not have chosen a better [venue or] theme. Nsukka, fountain head of Azikiwe's legendary wisdom. Nsukka, death place of Christopher Okigbo and Chukwuma Nzeogwu! And the title: Eagle on Iroko. There is no translation that can do justice to that ancient Igbo idiom. Put simply, it says Achebe is man at the summit. Such men never die.[28]

Vice-Chancellor Chimere Ikoku, in his address, drew attention to the social role. Achebe had 'been in the forefront of constructive criticism and has in no small measure impacted our national life, ethos and aspirations.' The spirit of variety recommended and exemplified by Achebe's works was reflected when Edith Ihekweazu, in her speech of welcome, emphasized that 'while focusing on the serious scholarly discussion, the symposium will be embedded in a variety of other modes of artistic expression – music, drama, painting and sculpture, because no art is an island unto itself'. She added that her 'faculty has in fact concurred in emerging as a multi-coloured masquerade, harmonizing all her specialized abilities into a single purpose and concept'.[29] It was an apt cultural interpretation of an academic and literary phenomenon which the symposium title reflected in its metaphor: the eagle is king of birds in the mythology of the people, and the iroko is a giant among trees. Thus the eagle's perch is beyond the reach of the bullets of hunters – whose dane guns, in the past, were incapable of sending bullets to the top of an iroko. That metaphor, applied to human beings, 'refers to a person whose achievements have gone beyond the stage of being destroyed by rivalry or malicious comments'.[30]

Variety had been promised, and the symposium delivered it. Participants were thrilled by masquerade performances from several parts of Igboland. It was a magnificent spectacle as varied masks in their dignified and enthralling costumes swayed and danced to the intricate music of traditional instruments. An exhibition was mounted by the university's Department of Fine and Applied Arts, consisting of the recent works of thirteen lecturers exhibiting the *Uli* motif. The well-known *Oba Koso,* a play by the late Duro Ladipo, was performed on the second night by a group who gave a fascinating interpretation of Yoruba cultural traditions. The other play was Emeka Nwabueze's adaptation of Chinua Achebe's *Arrow of God,* to which he gave the title *When the Arrow Rebounds.* The director of the play, Eni-Jones Umuko, discusses the play in a prefatory note:

> *When the Arrow Rebounds* creates its own victims, whether or not such victims violate cosmic precepts or are just pawns in the hands of the gods. Ezeulu is only an arrow in the hands of his god. In fighting for Ulu and seeking revenge against his people, little did he know that that arrow could rebound and turn predator into prey, the pursuer into the pursued…. In this fall of the god's surrogate, we [i.e. the Director and his audience] believe, in spite of the universal echo, the playwright's views, or the novelist's omniscient conclusion that victory is shared. The 'victory' for the missionaries is far from total.[31]

It is in this concept that Emeka Nwabueze's adaptation differs from that of Kalu Uka.

Other aspects of the symposium provided equally interesting and significant avenues for literary interactions. The keynote speakers, Michael Thelwell and Emmanuel Obiechina, gave a good account of themselves. Thelwell emphasized the unanimity of struggle in world literature as he cast Achebe and James Baldwin as the pivots of his essay, while Obiechina stressed the interstices between the teacher and the writer in Achebe through the complexity of his literary contributions. Several distinguished scholars presented their works in special sessions under such subjects as the depiction of womanhood, literature for children, Christianity and Igbo cosmology, the novelist as teacher, Achebe as critic and so on. It was significant that despite the plethora of critical works on Achebe the scholars and critics managed to generate fresh insight into his works, subjecting both his theory and his subject matter to renewed scrutiny. Many papers highlighted Achebe's narrative skill, his selection of subject matter and his critical vision. Some expressed dissatisfaction with the Achebean tragic vision that plunges characters like Okonkwo, Ezeulu, Max, Ikem Osodi and Chris Oriko to their deaths, though others defended this creative vision as preferable to fairy-tale happy endings.

Achebe's status as a great writer was not in doubt, but the response to the symposium from his Nigerian compatriots and international literary acquaintances alike exceeded even the most optimistic expectations. The indefatigable efforts of Edith Ihekweazu and her committee were so successful that all the hotels in Nsukka were fully booked and some participants had to sleep at Enugu, many kilometres away. The attendance and support ranged from the Commonwealth Secretariat, the ambassadors of West Germany and Austria, and the diplomatic representatives of the United States, Britain, France, the USSR and Sweden to the university's Vice-Chancellor Ikoku and Pro-Chancellor Mrs Tejumade-Alakija. Achebe's fellow writer Wole Soyinka sent him a white ram. The Nsukka town authorities renamed a major street 'Chinua Achebe Avenue', while the Association of Nigerian Authors gave the celebrant its first Triple Eminence Award. Even the question and answer session with the Somali writer Nuruddin Farah was conducted in a spirit of celebration. On the last day there was a festival of life organized by the Association of Nigerian Authors during which readings, recitals, performances and music were presented. As G. G. Darah wrote in the *Daily Times:*

> Those who still insist that prophets are not recognized in their countries should have been at Nsukka. Here were gathered people from all the continents of the earth to pay homage to one of the most eloquent interpreters of their experiences: Chinua Achebe.[32]

Joseph Bruchac observed that Achebe's 'gifts to all of us have been so great that we can never hope to repay', only strive to emulate his 'example, to do what good we can with our own lives and gifts'.[33]

The end of the symposium did not provide Chinua Achebe with an opportunity for rest; there were many other invitations and requests that he had to honour. Any refusal would have created the impression that he was arrogant and disrespectful to those who issued the invitations. Fortunately, Achebe found in these occasions ideal opportunities for the enunciation of his views and providing an African perspective on the affairs of the world. These ever more numerous engagements did not alter Chinua Achebe's family commitments. Christie Achebe commented, on the occasion of the 'Eagle on Iroko' symposium, that his constant travels did not affect the family adversely because

> you miss people when they haven't done their job. You get angry when people haven't done their job and they leave you. But if people have done their job, laid a good foundation and made sure you are not lacking in anything then you appreciate their external commitments.

She added that the family 'would like to have him for longer periods' but that the children had been brought up to value the fact that their father had a commitment. Besides, 'He phones us and writes us and makes sure we know where he is at any time, any moment we know how he is getting on, his difficulties, joys. You feel that spiritually he is around with you.'[34] Achebe's awareness of the extent of his commitments and their role in his life as an African artist came out in an interview with Angela Jackson:

> There's so much to do. I mean you look to the right and there's work waiting to do, left, front, behind and really it's very, very difficult, but it's also very exciting because this is what makes our lives different from the life of poets and artists in cultures where poetry and story-telling are no longer taken seriously.... Art is still very important and this is why people can be thrown into prison or worse for writing a poem, for writing a novel and this is our situation; it is a very, very important and real situation because we are dealing with real issues, with things that touch society deeply.... I'm involved in so many things. There are so many things I want to start.[35]

One aspect of those numerous activities was a constant shuttle between Nigeria and other parts of the world. On 22 March 1990, while Achebe was on his way to Lagos in order to fly to the United States to fulfil an engagement at Stanford University, he had an automobile accident. It occurred at Awka, on the double carriageway that links Enugu and Onitsha, when the axle of the car inexplicably gave way and the car somersaulted. His son Ikechukwu and the driver were not seriously hurt but the car literally fell on Achebe, seriously injuring his spine. The news stunned people in Awka, but was confirmed by the local doctor who administered first aid when the injured writer was conveyed to his clinic. Achebe was later taken to Enugu and after some days flown to the Paddocks Hospital in Buckinghamshire, England, where he was admitted to the spinal section. A vigil commenced in Nigeria as the story circulated all around the country.

The *Weekend Concord* published a selection from a big batch of 'Get Well Messages for Achebe' on 21 April 1990. The selection reflected the spectrum of emotions the accident had aroused and the variety of people Achebe had touched through his writings. Some of the messages read:

> Achebe's *Things Fall Apart* has provided an artistic thought which I intend to translate on canvas and for this I will need him alive, healthy and hearty to witness *Things Fall Apart* a product of his imagination retold in a plastic medium. (Victor Ecoma)

> The whole world clamour for your works; so we are all praying for you to be on your feet soonest. (Fidel Eseka)

> To me Professor Achebe is too precious to this country to be involved in such a calamity and I wish God in his infinite mercy and tender love will give him a quick recovery. (Uchenna Chukwu)

We nearly lost a book bound in flesh and blood, we nearly missed him – we nearly missed Professor Chinua Achebe. Truly Chinualumogu is your name. (Edem U. K. B. Ikpong)

I thank God for saving the life of our dear writer, Achebe, and I wish him a quick recovery. (Robinson Nwonye)

I wish to join all those who are praying for the speedy and full recovery of Professor Chinua Achebe. In fact the whole nation should pray for him. (Abimbola Ogunsula)

You have landed with the glory of accomplished flight; not yet the perching of a spent force, so wake up and celebrate again the Ozo title of a rich barn of letters. Wake up and live, Achebe, wake up and live! (Nezer Mabayoje)

I nearly ran mad when I heard of the accident. I pray the media houses to always keep us informed and I urge the doctors handling him to apply the best medicines available so as to facilitate the recovery of the born again writer and calm the anxieties of those of us who are his readers. (Silas Nwanya)

The drums still beat, the dancer still dances, the audience still watch, the curtain is yet to fall, the Devil is a liar, he will walk again. (Ben Ezumah)

May almighty God grant Achebe speedy recovery so that he can bring to completion his volume of works awaiting completion, until when it is God's wish to call him peacefully and not through any mishap. (Tony Emeka Ohanete)

Things shall not fall apart. His fingers shall continue to hold the pen. He will be at ease. (Ricky A. Ajayi).

Be strong! Nothing falls apart for it is the snare and sophistry of the devil and he does it in the shame of cowardice. The Lord will heal you of your wounds. (Anonymous)

You are too big to be neglected because a writer like you is hard to come by. Get well soon and bring peace to the anthill of the people. (Adewale Adedeji)

I pray for God's protection and your quick recovery. (Prince John I. Aitalegbe)[36]

The same feelings were reflected in all the other messages published in various newspapers and magazines, and in the large number of personal letters sent to Achebe's hospital bed in England. In addition several individuals made efforts to see him there.

After several weeks in hospital, Achebe's condition became stable, but by July 1990 it was clear that he would be confined to a wheelchair. He was still in the hospital when he was awarded an honorary doctorate of Humane Letters (his fifteenth degree) at the commencement ceremony of the Georgetown University Law Centre in May 1990. The citation emphasized his contribution to our understanding of

> societies that are forcibly moved from the outside; of the personal demands upon common men and women during times of dramatic political and social change; and of the difficult consequences that flow when hope of freedom, dignity and democracy are thwarted by the use of force.[37]

The news that Achebe, so 'forcibly moved from the outside' himself a short time before, had passed successfully though the danger zone was welcomed on all sides.

While Achebe was battling for his health, an attempted military coup led by Gideon Orkar on 22 April 1990 almost toppled the regime of Ibrahim Babangida. In the broadcast made by Orkar 'on behalf of the patriotic and well-meaning peoples of the Middle Belt and the southern parts of this country', he informed the country of 'the successful ousting of the dictatorial, corrupt, drug baronish, evil minded, sadistic, deceitful, homosexually-centred, prodigalistic, unpatriotic administration of General Ibrahim Badamasi Babangida'.[38] Luck saved Babangida, the coup failed, and the business of governance proceeded after the execution of those arrested and convicted through the mysterious processes of 'military laws'. Such periodic violent upheavals confirmed Achebe's view that the problem with Nigeria was a question of leadership.

Achebe was discharged from the hospital in August 1990 and in September accepted an invitation to be Charles P. Stevenson Professor of Literature at Bard College, New York State. Professor Leon Botstein, the president of Bard College, had approached Achebe during his stay in hospital with the offer of that specially endowed chair. Botstein explains that 'I went after Chinua Achebe because he is one of the great intellectual and ethical figures of our times.' In his view, 'a great deal of the discussion of multiculturalism today is canned. It reduces and essentializes African and black experience. I thought it important for students to hear Achebe, who combines multiculturalism and wisdom.'[39] The impact of that wisdom, arduously gained and tested, was soon felt by students as Achebe started teaching. For his part, Achebe was grateful that Bard College had given him 'the peace that he needed to mend and begin writing again'.[40]

The news that Achebe was at Bard College in order to 'mend' did not abate the appreciation of his literary importance in Nigeria where, on 16 November 1990, his sixtieth birthday, the *Sunday Times* devoted a magazine essay to him in which, after an elaborate discussion, the authors concluded that

> Eagle on Iroko was an apt metaphor for depicting that the man has attained the summit of his career. But great artists are ageless because great works of art are timeless. Achebe, therefore, is not just Eagle on Iroko, he is Eagle above seasons. And while he lives, it is, in his own words, morning yet on creation day.[41]

The article also quoted the view of James Currey, who had worked with Achebe at Heinemann Educational Books, that 'Chinua Achebe more than anyone else reshaped the literary map of Africa'.[42] G. D. Killam develops that view:

> [Achebe] has a central place in contemporary literature, because he, more than any of his peers, reflectively and unobtrusively has modified the traditions of fiction. He derived forms which are distinctively his own for the purpose of envisaging and conveying experience which is deeply convincing. Deceptive profundity, discriminating insight, mental and moral fastidiousness, elegance and lucidity, these are the hallmarks of Achebe's art.[43]

Several critics broadened that view in 1990 with the publication of a flood of books discussing Achebe's writings. They include Kofi Yankson's *Chinua Achebe's Novels: A Sociolinguistic Perspective,* Ada Ugah's *In the Beginning: Chinua Achebe at Work,* C. L. Innes's *Chinua Achebe* and the work edited by Kirsten Holst Petersen and Anna Rutherford entitled *Chinua Achebe: A Celebration.*

Through all the tumult of acclaim and near-tragedy, constancy is a theme that links Achebe, the views of his critics, and those who have known him personally like Ulli Beier:

> There is one thing I had learned about Chinua: his friendship does not have to be nourished by continuous encounters and interchanges. You may not have seen him for months or even years – you may rest assured that when you meet again, he will be the same person you remembered. He may have become older and wiser, but his relation-

ship to you has not changed. Chinua is one of the most reliable people I know. You can rely on his political integrity as much as on his emotions and his personal loyalty.[44]

It was this quality above all, perhaps, that brought together American scholars, writers, poets, journalists, teachers, anthropologists and civil rights fighters to pay tribute to him in late 1990. They met under the auspices of the New York Society for Ethical Culture in conjunction with the Frederick Douglass Creative Arts Centre and Poets House, and Amma Ogan reported that the 'tenor of the contributions revealed a new world that had been lost or was searching for a sense of itself by people for whom Achebe was clearly more than a Nigerian writer'. John Wideman described the metaphysical excitement of 'seeing another man of colour' affirming his own reality while Toni Morrison spoke of doors 'Chinua had figuratively opened' for her. Jerome Brooks described him as 'a necessary angel who has restored for us something that slavery took from us'. Testaments to Achebe's influence came through the literary contributions of Grace Paley and Amiri Baraka, also known as Le Roi Jones. Jayne Cortex read a poem, 'Everywhere Drums', dedicated to Achebe, while Quincy Troupe, Allen Ginsberg, Toni Morrison and Larry Mcmurty read passages from Achebe's works. Amma Ogan's report mentioned that 'Wilfred Cartey added a sense of drama to the occasion' with his presence, for 'sightless he spoke with his eyes closed, his head leaning slightly backwards, in a musical voice whose rhythmic ebb and flow traversed a wide terrain of continents and experiences'. Cartey recalled that when he had first met Achebe in 1963 there was no such thing as African literature and reminded his audience that 'to articulate is to celebrate'. Ogan confirmed that the 'proceeds from the tribute were to be given to Achebe towards payment for his treatment'.[45] The convalescent Achebe was not present, although the family was represented by his daughter Nwando.

In February 1991 at the University of Port Harcourt in Nigeria a sixteenth honorary degree was bestowed on Chinua Achebe in his absence. The citation was delivered by Professor Ola Rotimi, who stated the facts of Achebe's life but mid-way in the citation changed style and proceeded in the manner of a traditional performer. 'Chinua, son of Achebe, let me from this point on, address you in the style of traditional African oratory.... Speaker in proverbs, we salute you. Exponent of the values of Africa's cultural heritage I say it is you we greet.' Rotimi praised Achebe who ventured 'into the forest of world literature and came back a hero'. The university orator resorted to an invocation for emphasis:

> If Danger aims its arrows at you again,
> The arrows will never fly.
> If they do fly,
> They will not hit you.
> If they do hit you,
> They will not wound you.
> If they do wound you,
> You will not weaken.
> If you do weaken,
> You will not fall down.
> If you do fall down,
> You will not faint.
> If you do faint,
> You will not ... die!

'Indeed,' Ola Rotimi insisted, 'you will last long in our midst; kolanut lasts long in the mouths of those who value it!'[46] The award was received on behalf of Achebe by his daughter Chinelo. In that year, too, there were three new books of criticism: *Reading Chinua Achebe: Language and Ideology in Fiction* by Simon Gikandi, *Approaches to Teaching Achebe's* Things Fall Apart, edited by Bernth Lindfors, and *Chinua Achebe: New Perspectives* by Umelo Ojinmah.

Meanwhile, Bard College had extended several privileges to Achebe, including the construction of a special house and the availability of a special vehicle. Thus Achebe was able to 'pick up his life' and commence a process of gradual adjustment and recovery. In 1991 the spate of honorary doctorate degrees turned into a flood. Skidmore College of Saratoga Springs, New York awarded him the seventeenth on 26 March 1991, hailing him as 'the greatest of a new generation of African writers'.[47] Achebe gave a reading for the annual Frances Steloff Lecture on the same occasion. The new School for Social Research of New York awarded him an eighteenth degree on 21 May 1991 with a moving citation that concluded

> Not content with art alone, you feel compelled to teach and to act, asserting as a political man, the value of the individual. With eloquence, generosity and courage, you inspire us to grapple with the moral issues in political life and the goals of justice.[48]

That reference to teaching was in order, for Achebe, although in a wheelchair, had started effective teaching at Bard College. Another indication of his renewed interest in literary activities was the republication by Heinemann Educational Books of *Contemporary African Short Stories* which he edited with C. L. Innes. It was an improvement on the 1985 edition and the new volume, with 20 stories, reflected the full range of African literary styles. Achebe's teaching at Bard College drew on the same wealth of diversity. Karen Winkler playfully reports that Achebe

> says he prefers not to teach his own work, but [that] when he does so students often object to his portrait of an African culture in which men like Okonkwo beat their wives. But this year was different. He taught *Things Fall Apart* at Bard and no one raised the question.

Winkler quotes Achebe:

> Finally I said, there is a question about Okonkwo that I am usually asked. My students said, Oh, people do that in lots of cultures. They had the sense that this is another human story. I had very little more to tell them.[49]

That universal human element was one of the qualities cited when Hobart and William Smith Colleges awarded the nineteenth degree: 'The first truly African novelist, you wield the language of one culture to pierce the truth of its interface with another'.[50] The twentieth degree also came in June, from Marymount Manhattan College, citing the world-embracing journeys of the Ogidi boy and his works:

> You have travelled from Ogidi, your village in Eastern Nigeria, to points around the globe, but the distance measured in miles is almost inconsequential when compared to the distance your words have travelled, spreading understanding and knowledge, and dispelling myths.[51]

When Heinemann Educational Books celebrated 30 years of literary excellence in 1992, the company also declared that Chinua Achebe's *Things Fall Apart*

> set the standard for the next three decades and has gone on to become the masterpiece of African literature. More than eight million copies have been sold world-wide and students study this classic text from countries as diverse as Singapore, Australia, Sweden and Canada. It is a truly internationally acclaimed book.[52]

Karen Winkler confirms that Achebe 'has become very much a figure in Western literary circles, one of the main authors to be added to the literary curriculum in the name of multiculturalism'. Bernth Lindfors estimates that '*Things Fall Apart* is probably the African novel most taught world-wide. It is one of the best answers to the story of Africa told by Europeans.' Kwame Anthony Appiah, a professor of Afro-American Studies at Harvard, has found that 'Chinua Achebe is one of the people every one in African Studies wants to have an opinion about. He has played a key role in shaping African literature.' Similarly Gerald Graff, a professor of English at the University of Chicago, considers that in multicultural studies Achebe 'is one of three or four writers who are the obvious choices, and a lot of people outside African literature are turning to his work'. Graff adds that in his classroom discussions on the relationship between art and politics 'Achebe makes the point as well as any one I have read. He is succinct – upfront but not crude.'[53]

In New York in 1992, meanwhile, Anchor/Doubleday had reissued all his novels, and in celebration of that event asked other literary minds to offer judgements on Chinua Achebe. Margaret Atwood considers him 'a magical writer – one of the greatest of the twentieth century'. John Updike declares that '*Things Fall Apart* is a great book, and everything Achebe writes bespeaks a great, brave, kind, human spirit'. Barry Lopez has found that 'although we recognize the situations Chinua Achebe brings to life in his novels, we do not know them until he speaks. He offers us a remarkable, revisionist Africa, an indispensable illumination of the forces of our time'. For John Edgar Wideman, 'it's as if the great antiquity, wisdom, poise and dignity of traditional African culture begins to speak to me through the eloquent voices of a tribal elder'. Yusef Komunyakaa, winner of a Pulitzer Prize for poetry, tells Achebe in 'Keeper of the Vigil' that

> you helped me steal
> back myself. Although
> sometimes the right hand
> wrestles the left, you
> showed me there's a time
> for reed flutes
> and another for machetes....

Maya Angelou's experience is that 'with *Things Fall Apart,* all readers meet their brothers, sisters, parents and friends and themselves along Nigerian roads. I, too, find myself among its pages as accurately as I see my mirror reflection.' The respected Nadine Gordimer delivers the succinct consensus that Achebe 'is gloriously gifted with the magic of a generous ebullient talent'.[54]

Along with the praises of fellow writers came a steady flow of visitors. Several people who visited Achebe at Bard College in 1992 confirmed that he had started writing gradually. Chukwuemeka Ike was impressed by the extent of his recovery and Don Burness said that on his visit Achebe had told him: 'Christie saved me.'[55] It was a tribute to the support of an understanding wife in a world where marriages had become temporary liaisons.

Achebe told Bradford Morrow 'it was almost as if everything I had ever done in life was a preparation for my accident'. He added that some people at the hospital said to him: 'Why should such a thing happen to you?' and he answered. 'Why not? Those to whom this sort of thing happens, did they commit any sort of crime? Not necessarily.' However, Achebe confessed that 'when you begin to wrestle with the physical problems of not being able to get up and move, and all kinds of other things, and having to learn your body again, that's a terrible difference to what I'd known, and I am dealing with that.' To Achebe, 'one learns as one suffers and one is richer.'[56] In spite of his personal discomfort and struggles to get used to his body, Nigeria was never far from Achebe's mind. He told Jerome Brooks:

> I try as hard as possible not to be pessimistic because I have never thought or believed that creating a Nigerian nation would be easy; I have always known that it was going to be a very tough job. But I never really thought that it would be this tough. And what's going on now, which is a subjection of this potentially great country to a clique of military adventurers and a political class that they have completely corrupted – this is really quite appalling. The suffering that they have unleashed on millions of people is quite intolerable. What makes me so angry is that this was quite avoidable.[57]

Achebe had always felt whatever affected his society keenly; that he continued to do so was a further sign that he was on his way to full recovery.

Achebe's recovery had now proceeded far enough for him to venture out from his Bard College retreat. After receiving his twenty-first honorary degree from the City University of New York he went to the University of Cambridge in January 1993 to deliver the annual Ashby Lecture at Clare Hall on the topic: 'The Education of a "British Protected Child"'. In this lecture, spiced with memories of his childhood in the village and events from his school and university days, he reflects on the selfless service in the areas of education and commerce in colonial Nigeria of people like Lord Ashby, J. M. Stuart Young, William Simpson, James Welch and Robert Fisher. In the lecture Achebe identifies 'the potency of the unpredictable in human affairs' as an important theme: he 'could have dwelt on the harsh humiliations of colonial rule or the more dramatic protests against it' but he is 'fascinated by that middle ground' where 'the human spirit resists an abridgement of its humanity' which 'was to be found in the camp of the colonizer as well as the colonized'. He acknowledges that

> those significant people had reached across the severe divide which colonialism would have and touched many of us on the other side. But more important, far more important, was the fact that even if those hands had not reached across to us we would still have survived colonial tribulations as we had done so many others before it through the millennia. That they did reach across, however, makes a great human story.[58]

Those who heard the lecture applauded a vintage Achebe essay, subsequently published in the *Cambridge Review*.

Achebe's recovery advanced significantly as he commenced work on a new novel. He told Karen Winkler that his novels have steadily included more women's voices and that his next book will focus on women. From time to time in his culture, when things have gone wrong, he says, women have risen up to take action. He wants to write a novel about one such incident in the 1950s, when women protested school fees imposed by the British.[59]

With the novel under way, Achebe also started responding again to invitations to give lectures. As this book has tried to show, the universal respect in which Achebe is held has much to do with the way he has been able to combine these roles: the gifted writer is also the concerned public man. Alastair Niven spoke for many admirers of Achebe:

> We have a column in one of our Sunday newspapers called Heroes and Villains. I have not yet been asked to contribute to it but I have sometimes thought that if I were asked I would write a profile of Achebe as my hero! I not only regard him as one of the greatest novelists of our time [but also as] an extraordinarily fine human being who has contributed to Africa's development with wisdom and foresight. He is a liberal humanist in the best possible sense of those words.[60]

A reminder of the multicultural nature of Achebe's appeal came with the publication of *South Asian Responses to Chinua Achebe,* a collection of essays edited by Bernth Lindfors and Bala Kothandaraman and published by Prestige Books of New Delhi in 1993. The editors noted in their preface that 'Achebe is the consummate translator of African culture, and this quality makes his work as relevant and important in South Asia as it is throughout the African continent'.[61]

As well as a bridge between contemporary cultures, Achebe had now emerged as a living classic. This was the burden of Colgate University's citation when handing Achebe his twenty-second honorary degree on 23 May 1993: 'Chinua Achebe has the distinction of being the only living author represented among 46 works issued in Everyman's Library, the series of World Literary Classics reintroduced by Alfred A. Knopf last fall.' The citation also confirmed that 'in 1991 the *Times* of London listed Chinua Achebe among its 1,000 "Makers of the 20th Century"'.[62] Fitchburg State College, Massachusetts would soon extend his tally of such honours to twenty-three, but Achebe's attention was now turning homewards to Nigeria again – the final sign of his recovery.

Towards the end of 1993 the political situation in Nigeria had degenerated enormously, with the military government cancelling an election in which the results had almost been collated. At the time the results were cancelled Chief Moshood Abiola, one of the presidential candidates, was widely believed to have won. The political controversy that ensued was fierce, even by Nigerian standards, with several prominent people expressing their dissatisfaction in various ways. Achebe, who was in New York, issued a statement condemning the action and calling on the military to hand over to the civilian government. He insisted: 'Abiola must be allowed to take office because Nigerians said so.'[63]

Achebe's life and art can be seen as an attempt to discover and express what Nigeria – at the heart of the continent where human life began – has to say to its leaders and to the world. As this book ends, he was preparing to continue that story. It was, as he once said, the same story – only written from many angles by a masquerader for whom 'there is no such thing as one story'. One more celebration by his well-wishers would speed him on his way. In November 1993 he was awarded the Langston Hughes Medallion at a festival sponsored by the

City University of New York and the Schomburg Center. For that occasion the South African poet Dennis Brutus wrote the following poem:

> Grave teacher, we attend your speech
> the unaffected address that seeks to reach us all;
> generous have been your gifts to us,
> your giving of thoughts and measured words:
> all over Africa men and women walk tall
> and praise you for enhancing their sense of worth
> and through our diaspora wherever we might be
> fragmented, shoaled, scattered across the earth
> often suffused by seemingly ineluctable despair
> your words seep through an inspiring tide
> your bright honest gaze irradiates our thought.[64]

Notes

Page references to Achebe's works are to the edition and year of publication specified in the note. Some editions were reprinted within the same year and may lead to discrepancies in page numbers.

1 THE CATECHIST'S SON (pp. 1–6)

1. Chinua Achebe, *Things Fall Apart* (London: Heinemann Educational Books, (*AWS* 1), 1962), pp. 168–9.
2. Chinua Achebe, 'Named for Victoria, Queen of England', in *Hopes and Impediments,* (London: Heinemann Educational Books, 1988), p. 21; also in *Morning Yet on Creation Day* (London: Heinemann Educational Books, 1975), pp. 65–70.
3. Chinua Achebe, *Things Fall Apart*, p. 34.
4. Chinua Achebe, 'Named for Victoria', p. 21.
5. T. Basden, *Among the Ibos of Nigeria* (New York: Barnes & Noble, Inc., 1966; originally published 1921), p. 45.
6. Chinua Achebe, 'The education of a "British protected child" ', *Cambridge Review,* 114 (June 1993), p. 53.
7. Chinua Achebe, 'The education', p. 53.
8. Chinua Achebe, 'Publishing in Africa: a writer's view', in Edwina Oluwasanmi, Eva Maclean and Hans Zell, eds, *Publishing in Africa in the Seventies* (Ife: University of Ife Press, 1975), p. 44.
9. Personal interview with Augustine Agogbua.
10. Personal interview with Chinua Achebe.
11. Chinua Achebe, *No Longer at Ease* (London: Heinemann Educational Books, (*AWS* 3), 1963) p. 47.

2 STARTING AT THE CROSSROADS (pp. 7–20)

1. Chinua Achebe, 'The education of a "British protected child"', *Cambridge Review,* 114 (June 1993), p. 53.
2. Karen L. Morell, *In Person: Achebe, Awoonor and Soyinka* (Seattle: University of Washington Press, 1975), p. 45.
3. Chinua Achebe, 'The education', p. 54.
4. Chinua Achebe, 'Named for Victoria, Queen of England', in *Hopes and Impediments* (London: Heinemann Educational Books, 1988), p. 23.
5. Personal interviews with Augustine Agogbua and Chieka Ifemesia.
6. Chinua Achebe, 'The education', p. 54.
7. *Ibid.*, p. 55.
8. Chinua Achebe, 'The Igbo world and its arts', in *Hopes and Impediments,* pp. 44–5.
9. Chinua Achebe, 'African literature as restoration of celebration', in Kirsten Holst Petersen and Anna Rutherford, eds, *Chinua Achebe: A Celebration* (Oxford: Heinemann Educational Books, 1991), p. 7.
10. Chinua Achebe, 'The education', p. 55.
11. Personal interview with Augustine Agogbua.
12. Personal interview with S. N. C. Okonkwo.
13. Personal interview with Zinobia Uzoma Ikpeze, née Achebe.

14 Chinua Achebe, 'The education', p. 55.
15. Personal interview with S. N. C. Okonkwo.
16. Chinua Achebe, 'The education', p. 55.
17. Chinua Achebe, 'Named for Victoria', pp. 23–5.
18. Chinua Achebe, *Hopes and Impediments*, p. 24.
19. Personal interview with Chinua Achebe.
20. Felix K. Ekechi, *Tradition and Transformation in Eastern Nigeria* (Kent: The Kent University Press, 1989), p. 162.
21. Personal interview with Obiakonwa.
22. Chinua Achebe, 'African literature as restoration', pp. 2–3.
23. Chinua Achebe, 'The Igbo world', p. 45.

3 THE OGIDI BOY (pp. 21–33)

1. Chinua Achebe, 'Onitsha, gift of the Niger', *Morning Yet on Creation Day* (London: Heinemann Educational Books, 1975), p. 92.
2. Chinua Achebe, 'Tanganyika – Jottings of a tourist', *Morning Yet on Creation Day*, p. 75.
3. Chinua Achebe, 'The role of the writer in a new nation', *Nigeria Magazine*, 81 (June 1964), p. 159.
4. Chinua Achebe, 'The education of a "British protected child"', *Cambridge Review*, 114 (June 1993), p. 56.
5. Robert M. Wren, *Those Magical Years* (Washington, DC: Three Continents Press, 1991), p. 56.
6. Chike Momah 'Reminiscences', in Chinua Achebe, ed., *The Umuahian: A Golden Jubilee Publication* (Umuahia: Government College, Umuahia Old Boys Association, 1979), p. 14.
7. Chinua Achebe, 'The education', p. 56.
8. Chike Momah, 'Reminiscences', in *The Umuahian*, p. 20.
9. Chukwuemeka Ike, 'William Simpson: reminiscences', in *The Umuahian*, p. 24.
10. Chike Momah , 'Reminiscences', p. 16.
11. Chukwuemeka Ike, 'William Simpson', *The Umuahian*, p. 26.
12. Robert Wren, *Those Magical Years* , p. 79.
13. Chinua Achebe, 'The education', p. 56.
14. Personal interview with Chukwuemeka Ike.
15. Robert Wren, *Those Magical Years*, p. 57.
16. Chinua Achebe, 'African literature as restoration of celebration', in Kirsten Holst Petersen and Anna Rutherford, eds, *Chinua Achebe: A Celebration* (Oxford: Heinemann Educational Books, 1991), p. 7.
17. Personal interview with John Achebe.
18. Personal interviews with Chukwuemeka Ike and Chike Momah.
19. Chike Momah, 'Reminiscences', p. 18.
20. Robert Wren, *Those Magical Years*, p. 54.
21. Chike Momah, 'Reminiscences', *The Umuahian*, p. 21.
22 Robert Wren, *Those Magical Years*, p. 57.
23. *Ibid.*, p. 72.
24. Personal interview with Chukwuemeka Ike. Also in *The Umuahian*, p. 26.
25. Chike Momah, 'Reminiscences', p. 15.
26. Personal interview with Ralph Opara.
27. Chike Momah, 'Reminiscences', p. 19.
28. *Ibid.*, pp. 19–20.
29. Chinua Achebe, 'African Literature as restoration', p. 8.
30. Chike Momah, 'Reminiscences', *The Umuahian*, p. 15.
31. Personal interview with Chike Momah.
32. Robert Wren, *Those Magical Years*, p. 57.
33. Chike Momah, 'Reminiscences', p. 17.
34. Chike Momah, 'Reminiscences', p. 21.
35. Personal interview with Chike Momah.
36. Personal interview with Chinua Achebe.
37. Personal interview with Chike Momah.
38. Robert Wren, *Those Magical Years*, p. 58.

Notes

4 THE YOUNG MAN IN OUR HALL (pp. 34–50)

1. Ulli Beier, *In a Colonial University* (Bayreuth: Iwalewa-haus, 1993), p. 6.
2. Personal interview with Chukwuemeka Ike.
3. Robert Wren, *Those Magical Years* (Washington, DC: Three Continents Press, 1991), p. 69.
4. Robert Wren, *Those Magical Years*, pp. 58–9.
5. Robert Wren, *Those Magical Years*, p. 58.
6. Personal interview with Ulli Beier.
7. Robert Wren, *Those Magical Years*, p. 64.
8. Chinua Achebe,'Polar undergraduate', *University Herald* 3,3 (1950), p. 7. Also in *Girls At War and Other Stories* (London: Heinemann Educational Books (*AWS* 100), 1972).
9. Chinua Achebe, 'Philosophy', *The Bug,* 21 February 1951, p. 5.
10. *University Herald*, 4, 1 (1951), p. 13.
11. 'In a Village Church', *University Herald*, 4, 2 (1951), p. 11. Also in *Girls at War and other Stories* (London: Heinemann Educational Books (*AWS* 100), 1972).
12. Robert Wren, *Those Magical Years*, p. 59.
13. Robert Wren, *Those Magical Years*, p. 60.
14. Ulli Beier, *In a Colonial University*, p. 12.
15. Robert Wren, *Those Magical Years*, p. 46.
16. Ulli Beier, *In a Colonial University*, pp. 9–10.
17. Biodun Jeyifo, 'The author's art and role', *West Africa*, 5 (November 1984), p. 2211.
18. Robert Wren,*Those Magical Years*, p. 71.
19. Robert Wren, *Those Magical Years*, p. 66.
20. Ulli Beier, *In a Colonial University*, p. 12.
21. Personal interview with Chike Momah.
22. Personal interview with Chinua Achebe.
23. Robert Wren, *Those Magical Years*, pp. 61–2.
24. *University Herald*, 4, 3 (1951–2), p. 19.
25. Chinua Achebe, 'Where something stands, look well: something else is standing right beside it', in Don Burness, ed., *Echoes of The Sunbird. An Anthology of Contemporary African Poetry* (Ohio: Center for International Studies, 1993), p. 3.
26. *University Herald*, 5, 1 (1952), pp. 12, 14.
27. *The Bug*, 4, 2 (29 November 1952), p. 3.
28. Chinua Achebe, *The Trouble With Nigeria* (London: Heinemann Educational Books, 1983), p. 5.
29. *University Herald*, 5, 2 (1952/3), pp. 4–5. Also in Chinua Achebe, *Girls at War and Other Stories* (London, Heinemann Educational Books (*AWS* 100), 1972).
30. Personal interview with Zinobia Uzoma Ikpeze, née Achebe.
31. Personal interview with Chukwuemeka Ike.
32. Robert Wren, *Those Magical Years*, p. 46.

5 STEPPING INTO THE WORLD (pp. 51–63)

1. Robert Wren, *Those Magical Years* (Washington, DC: Three Continents Press, 1991), p. 62.
2. Chinua Achebe,'The education of a "British protected child" ', *Cambridge Review,* 114 (June 1993), p. 51.
3. Personal interview with Chinua Achebe.
4. Personal interview with B. N. Igwilo.
5. Chinua Achebe, *Things Fall Apart* (London: Heinemann Educational Books (*AWS* 1), 1962), p. 135.
6. Personal interview with B. N. Igwilo.
7. *Ibid.*
8. Chinua Achebe, *Morning Yet on Creation Day* (London: Heinemann Educational Books, 1975), p. 40.
9. Personal interview with B. N. Igwilo.
10. Personal interview with Chinua Achebe.
11. Personal interview with Ralph Opara.
12. Biodun Jeyifo, ed., *Contemporary Nigerian Literature: A Retrospective and Prospective*

Exploration, (Lagos: *Nigeria Magazine*, 1985), p. 9.

13. Chinua Achebe, *No Longer at Ease*, (London: Heinemann Educational Books (*AWS* 3), 1963), pp. 102–3.
14. *Ibid.*, pp. 14–16.
15. Personal interview with Chukwuemeka Ike.
16. Chinua Achebe, *Things Fall Apart*, p. 99.
17. Chinua Achebe, *A Man of The People* (London: Heinemann Educational Books (*AWS* 31), 1966), p. 24.
18. Anon., *Radio Times*, January 1955.
19. Personal interview with Ulli Beier.
20. Yusuf Hassan, 'More fiction than real: interview', *African Events*, November 1987, p. 52.
21. Chinua Achebe, 'The education', p. 52.
22. BBC information booklet, sent by Susan Whyte.
23. Personal interview with Chinua Achebe.
24. *Ibid.*
25. Biodun Jeyifo, 'Interview'.
26. Chinua Achebe, *No Longer at Ease*, pp. 24–5.
27. Personal interview with Chinua Achebe.
28. Michael Awoyinfa, '*Things Fall Apart* was nearly stolen from me', *Sunday Concord Magazine*, 6 November 1983, p. i.
29. Alan Hill, in Kirsten Holst Petersen, 'Working with Chinua Achebe: the African Writers Series; James Currey, Alan Hill and Keith Sambrook in conversation with Kirsten Holst Petersen', in Kirsten Holst Petersen and Anna Rutherford, eds, *Chinua Achebe : A Celebration* (Oxford: Heinemann Educational Books, 1991), pp. 149–50.

6 ON THE PATH OF LIFE (pp. 64–78)

1. Personal interview with Ejike Obumneme Aghanya.
2. Alan Hill in Kirsten Holst Petersen, 'Working with Chinua Achebe: the African Writers Series; James Currey, Alan Hill and Keith Sambrook in conversation with Kirsten Holst Petersen', in Kirsten Holst Petersen and Anna Rutherford, eds, *Chinua Achebe : A Celebration* (Oxford: Heinemann Educational Books, 1991), p. 150.
3. Alan Hill, *In Pursuit of Publishing* (London: John Murray, 1988), p. 120.
4. Back cover, *Things Fall Apart* cloth edition, 1958.
5. *Things Fall Apart* (London: William Heinemann, 1958).
6. Foreword in W. H. Whiteley, ed., *A Selection of African Prose* (Oxford: Clarendon Press, 1964), p. ix.
7. Personal interview with Christie Achebe.
8. *Ibid.*
9. Alan Hill, *In Pursuit of Publishing*, p. 121.
10. Class discussion with E. N. Obiechina, University of Nigeria, Nsukka, 1979.
11. Personal interview with Ulli Beier.
12. Pius Okigbo, presenting Chinua Achebe at The National Merit Award Lecture, September 1986.
13. Diana Speed, *Black Orpheus*, 5 (May 1959), p. 50.
14. G. Adali-Mortty, *Black Orpheus*, 6 (November 1959), p. 50.
15. *Atlantic Monthly*, April 1959. Also in Chinua Achebe, *Girls at War and Other Stories* (London: Heinemann Educational Books (*AWS* 100), 1972).
16. Personal interviews with Chinua Achebe and Chijioke Abagwe. Also in Nwachukwu-Agbada, 'A conversation with Chinua Achebe', *Commonwealth Essays and Studies*, 3, 1 (1990), p. 122.
17. 'Listening in the East', *Radio Times*, January 1959, p. 17.
18. *Ibid.*, p. 18.
19. Phanuel A. Egejuru, *Towards Literary Independence: A Dialogue with Contemporary African Writers* (Westport, Connecticut: Greenwood Press, 1980), pp. 121–2.
20. Alex Olu Ajayi, 'Okigbo, Ajayi and Fiditi', *Daily Times*, 29 August 1992, p. 12.
21. Personal interview with Chinua Achebe.
22. Personal interview with Chinua Achebe. Also in Nwachukwu-Agbada, 'A conversation', pp. 120–1.
23. Thurstan Shaw, *Unearthing Igbo-Ukwu: Archaeological Discoveries in Eastern Nigeria*

(Ibadan: Oxford University Press, 1977).

24. Personal interview with Chinua Achebe.
25. Personal interview with Christie Achebe.
26. *Rotarian*, April 1960.
27. Frances Ademola, ed., *Reflections* (Lagos: African University Press, 1962).
28. Biodun Jeyifo, ed., *Contemporary Nigerian Literature: A Retrospective and Prospective Exploration*, (Lagos: *Nigeria Magazine*, 1985).
29. *No Longer at Ease* (London: William Heinemann, 1960).
30. *Black Orpheus*, 8 (1960), pp. 51–2. It has been revealed that Omidiji Aragbalu was the pen name of Ulli Beier.
31. Personal interview with Chinua Achebe.

7 STRIDING TO THE FRONTIER (pp. 79–94)

1. Chinua Achebe, 'The judge and I didn't go to Namibia', *Callaloo*, 3, 1 (1990), p. 2.
2. *Ibid.*, p. 82.
3. Chinua Achebe, 'Tanganyika – Jottings of a tourist', *Morning Yet on Creation Day* (London: Heinemann Educational Books, 1975), p. 73.
4. Personal interview with Chinua Achebe. Also in Karen Morell, *In Person: Achebe, Awoonor and Soyinka* (Seattle: University of Washington, 1975), p. 32.
5. Chinua Achebe, 'Tanganyika', *Morning Yet on Creation Day*, pp. 71–2.
6. *Ibid.*, pp. 72–3.
7. *Ibid.*, pp. 73–4.
8. *Ibid.*, pp. 74–6.
9. Chinua Achebe, 'The judge and I', *Callaloo*, pp. 82–3.
10. *Ibid.*, p. 83.
11. *Daily Express*, 17 January 1961.
12. Personal interview with Ulli Beier.
13. *Service*, 6 May 1961, p. 15.
14. Personal interview with Chukwuemeka Ike.
15. Chinua Achebe,'The education of a "British protected child" ', *Cambridge Review*, 114 (June 1993), p. 52.
16. Personal interview with Christie Achebe.
17. Olu Awogbenila et al., 'The Master Craftsman', *This Week*, No. 152, 27 November 1989, p. 23.
18. Personal interview with Christie Achebe.
19. Biodun Jeyifo, ed., *Contemporary Nigerian Literature: A Retrospective and Prospective Exploration*, (Lagos: *Nigeria Magazine*, 1985).
20. Anon., 'Voice of Nigeria', *West Africa*, 24 February 1962, p. 201.
21. Chinua Achebe, 'Voice of Nigeria – how it began', *Voice of Nigeria*, 1, 1 (1963), pp. 5–6.
22. Anon., 'Voice of Nigeria', *West Africa*, 24 February 1962, p. 201.
23. *Ibid.*, p. 201.
24. Chinua Achebe, 'Introduction', *The Sacrificial Egg and Other Stories* (Onitsha: Etudo Press, 1962), pp. 3–6.
25. Ezekiel Mphahlele, 'The Makerere Writers' Conference', *Nigeria Magazine*, 76 (1963), pp. 74–6.
26. Personal interview. Also in *Morning Yet on Creation Day*, p. 49.
27. *Daily Times*, 7 July 1962, p. 7; *Radio Times*, 15 July 1962, p. 6.
28. Lewis Nkosi, *Manchester Guardian*, 8 August 1962; Also in *Home and Exile* (London: Longman, 1965).
29. John Nagenda, 'Conference notebook', *Transition*, 5 (1962), pp. 8–9.
30. James Ngugi (Ngugi wa Thiong'o), 'A Kenyan at the conference', *Transition*, 5 (1962), p. 7.
31. Alan Hill, *In Pursuit of Publishing* (London: John Murray, 1988), p. 126.
32. *Ibid.*, p. 122.
33. *Ibid.*, p. 123.
34. Personal interview with Christie Achebe.
35. Chinua Achebe, 'Don't let him die: a tribute to Christopher Okigbo', *Hopes and Impediments*, pp. 77–81.
36. Personal interview with Chinua Achebe. Also in Yusuf Hassan, 'Interview', *Africa Events*, November 1987, p. 53.

37. Alan Hill, in Kirsten Holst Petersen, 'Working with Chinua Achebe: the African Writers Series; James Currey, Alan Hill and Keith Sambrook in conversation with Kirsten Holst Petersen', in Kirsten Holst Petersen and Anna Rutherford, eds, *Chinua Achebe : A Celebration* (Oxford: Heinemann Educational Books, 1991), p. 152.
38. Flora Nwapa, 'Writers, printers and publishers', *Guardian* (Lagos), 17 August 1988, p. 16.
39. Alan Hill, in Petersen, 'Working with Chinua Achebe', p. 153.
40. *Spear* (December 1962), p. 41.
41. 'Where Angels Fear to Tread', *Nigeria Magazine*, 75 (December 1962), pp. 61–2.

8 WALKING UNDER A GATHERING STORM (pp. 95–110)

1. *Spear* (January 1963), p. 41.
2. Personal interview with Christie Achebe.
3. Chinua Achebe, 'On Janheinz Jahn (and Mphahlele)', *Transition* 3, 8 (March 1963), p. 9.
4. *Nigeria Magazine*, 77 (1963), pp. 132–3.
5. 'Replying to Chinua Achebe', *Transition*, 3, 9 (June 1963), pp. 9–10.
6. *Spear* (June 1963), p. 26.
7. Restated in personal interview with Chinua Achebe.
8. Chinua Achebe, 'Postscript: James Baldwin (1924–87)', *Hopes and Impediments* (London: Heinemann Educational Books, 1988), pp. 118–9.
9. Chinua Achebe, 'Publishing in Africa: a writer's view', in Edwina Oluwasanmi *et al.*, eds, *Publishing in Africa in the Seventies* (Ife: University of Ife Press, 1975), p. 44.
10. Chinua Achebe, 'The African writer and the English language', in *Morning Yet On Creation Day* (London: Heinemann Educational Books, 1975), pp. 58–9.
11. *Spear* (December 1963), p. 13.
12. *Transition*, 3, 13 (March/April 1964), pp. 36–7.
13. *Transition*, 4, 15 (1964), p. 5.
14. Chinua Achebe, *Arrow of God* (London: Heinemann Educational Books, 1964).
15. *Times Literary Supplement* (26 March 1964), p. 249.
16. Quoted in publishers' advertisement for *A Man of the People* (London: Heinemann Educational Books (*AWS* 31), 1966).
17. 'Achebe's new novel', *Transition*, 4, 14 (May/June 1964), p. 52.
18. *Black Orpheus*, 16 (October 1964), pp. 59–60.
19. Alan Hill, *In Pursuit of Publishing* (London: John Murray, 1988), pp. 129–30.
20. Chinua Achebe, *Morning Yet on Creation Day*, p. 58.
21. Obi Wali, 'The dead end of African literature', *Transition*, 10 (September 1963), pp. 13–15.
22. See the responses entitled 'Polemics: letters by Barry Reckord, Mphahlele, Soyinka, Gerald Moore and Williams', *Transition*, 3, 11 (1963), pp. 7–9.
23. Chinua Achebe, 'The African writer and the English language', *Morning Yet on Creation Day*, pp. 55–62.
24. *Spear* (August 1964), pp. 43, 45.
25. Chinua Achebe, 'The role of the writer in a new nation', *Nigeria Magazine*, 81 (June 1964), pp. 157–60.
26. Chinua Achebe, 'The novelist as teacher', *Morning Yet on Creation Day*, pp. 42–3.
27. *Ibid.*, p. 44.
28. *Ibid.*, pp. 42–5.
29. Donatus Nwoga, 'Interview with Chinua Achebe' in Dennis Duerden and Cosmo Pieterse, eds, *African Writers Talking* (London: Heinemann Educational Books, 1972), p. 7.
30. Chinua Achebe, 'Keynote address', Zimbabwe International Bookfair, August 1987. Also in Karen Morell, *In Person: Achebe, Awoonor and Soyinka*, pp. 29–30.
31. Letter from John Updike, quoted in 'The writer and his community' in Chinua Achebe, *Hopes and Impediments*, p. 38.
32. Valerie Wilmer, 'Chinua Achebe and the African novel', *Flamingo*, 4, 11 (1965), pp. 27–9.
33. 'The voter', *Black Orpheus*, 17 (June 1965).
34. Bernth Lindfors, *Dem-Say: Interviews with Eight Nigerian Writers* (Austin, Texas: African and Afro-American Studies and Research Center, 1974), p. 35.
35. Personal interview with Chukwuemeka Ike.

36. Personal interview with Chinua Achebe.
37. Chinua Achebe, *A Man of the People*.
38. Robert Wren, *Those Magical Years* (Washington, DC: Three Continents Press, 1991), pp. 65–6.

9 RETREAT TO THE CITADEL (pp. 111–27)

1. Chinua Achebe, 'Uncle Ben's Choice', *Black Orpheus*, 18 (March 1966). Also in *Girls at War and Other Stories* (London: Heinemann Educational Books (*AWS* 100), 1972).
2. John Povey, 'The First World Festival of Negro Arts at Dakar', *Journal of the New Literature and the Arts*, 2 (1966), p. 29.
3. *Chike and the River* (Cambridge: Cambridge University Press, 1966).
4. *Sunday Times*, Lagos, 28 February 1965. Also in A. H. M. Kirk-Greene, *Crisis and Conflict in Nigeria: A Documentary Source Book* (two vols) (Oxford: Oxford University Press, 1971).
5. Personal interview with Chinua Achebe.
6. Peter Enahoro, 'Why I left Nigeria', *Transition*, 3 (5 July 1968), pp. 27–30.
7. Harvey Swados, 'Chinua Achebe and the writers of Biafra', *New Letters*, 40, 1 (1973), pp. 5–13. Also in 'Chinua Achebe on Biafra', *Transition*, 7, 36 (1968).
8. Personal interview with Chinua Achebe.
9. Harvey Swados, 'Chinua Achebe and the writers of Biafra', pp. 5–13.
10. Onuora Udenwa, 'Interview with Chinua Achebe', *Quality*, 10 November 1988, p. 34.
11. Chinua Achebe, *Morning Yet on Creation Day* (London: Heinemann Educational Books, 1975), pp. 87–9.
12. Personal interview with Chukwuemeka Ike.
13. Michael Awoyinfa, 'Chinua Achebe: *Things Fall Apart* was nearly stolen from me', *Sunday Concord*, 6 November 1983, p. xi.
14. Personal interview with Ulli Beier.
15. Colin Legum, 'East Nigeria strikes a defiant note', *Observer*, 5 March 1967.
16. Tony Hall, 'Chinua Achebe Talking to Tony Hall', *Sunday Nation*, 15 January 1967, p. 15.
17. Chinweizu, 'Interview with Chinua Achebe', *Okike*, 20 (1981), p. 28.
18. Jonathan Cott, 'Chinua Achebe: at the crossroads', in Jonathan Cott, ed., *Pipers at the Gates of Dawn: The Wisdom of Children's Literature* (New York: Random House, 1983), p. 183.
19. G. D. Killam, 'Personal note', in Kirsten Holst Petersen and Anna Rutherford, eds, *Chinua Achebe : A Celebration* (Oxford: Heinemann Educational Books, 1991), p. 160.
20. Personal interview with Christie Achebe.
21. *Ibid.*
22. C. O. Ojukwu, *Biafra: Selected Speeches with Journal of Events* (New York: Harper and Row, 1969), pp. 190–3.
23. C. O. Ojukwu, *Biafra: Selected Speeches*, pp. 193–6.
24. Harvey Swados, 'Chinua Achebe and the writers of Biafra', pp. 9–13.
25. Jonathan Cott, 'Chinua Achebe', pp. 180–1.
26. Chinua Achebe and John Iroaganachi, *How the Leopard Got His Claws* (Enugu: Nwamife, 1972).
27. Robert Wren, *Those Magical Years* (Washington, DC: Three Continents Press, 1991), p. 11.
28. Personal interview with Chinua Achebe.
29. Robert Wren, *Those Magical Years*, p. 11.
30. Personal interview with Chinua Achebe. Also in Harvey Swados, 'Chinua Achebe and the writers of Biafra' and in 'Achebe on Biafra', *Transition*.

10 THE IDEA OF BIAFRA (pp. 128–42)

1. Part of a speech by Hassan Usman Katsina, military governor of Northern Nigeria and later chief of army staff. Also in A. H. M. Kirk-Greene, *Crisis and Conflict in Nigeria: A Documentary Source Book* (two vols) (Oxford: Oxford University Press, 1971).
2. Anon., 'Chinua Achebe on Biafra', *Transition*, 7, 36 (5 July 1968), p. 36.
3. An uncle who was a soldier narrated this incident.
4. Chinua Achebe, *Hopes and Impediments* (London: Heinemann Educational Books,

1988), pp. 78–9.

5. Chukwuma Azuonye, 'Reminiscences of the Odunke Community of Artists: 1966–90', *ALA Bulletin*, 17, 1 (Winter 1991), p. 22.

6. Personal interview with Chinua Achebe.

7. Harvey Swados 'Chinua Achebe and the writers of Biafra', *New Letters*, 40, 1 (1973), pp. 9–10.

8. Chinua Achebe, *Beware, Soul Brother and Other Poems* (Enugu: Nwankwo-Ifejika, 1971), p. 12.

9. Chinua Achebe, *Beware, Soul Brother and Other Poems*, pp. 5–6.

10. 'Chinua Achebe on Biafra', *Transition*, 7, 36 (1968), p. 35.

11. Richard Wilson, ed., *Chinua Achebe: Miscellaneous Papers* (mimeographed) (Evanston: Northwestern University Program of African Studies, 1970).

12. Personal interview with Agnes Achebe.

13. Alan Hill, in Kirsten Holst Petersen, 'Working with Chinua Achebe: the African Writers Series; James Currey, Alan Hill and Keith Sambrook in conversation with Kirsten Holst Petersen', in Kirsten Holst Petersen and Anna Rutherford, eds, *Chinua Achebe : A Celebration* (Oxford: Heinemann Educational Books, 1991), p. 154.

14. James Currey, in Kirsten Holst Petersen 'Working with Chinua Achebe', p. 154.

15. 'Chinua Achebe on Biafra', *Transition*, p. 31.

16. *Ibid.*, p. 31.

17. Amma Ogan, 'Pepper Clark: no bitterness', *Guardian*, 14 April 1985,p. B1–B2.

18. *Sunday Times* magazine, 9 June 1968, p. 24.

19. 'The Biafran possibility', *Africa Report*, 13, 2 (1968), pp. 16–19.

20. 'Chinua Achebe on Biafra', *Transition*, p. 37.

21. *Tanzania Government Statement on the Recognition of Biafra* (Dar es Salaam: Government Printer, 1968).

22. Ulli Beier, 'Interview with Obiora Udechukwu', *Okike,* 20 (1981), p. 55.

23. Personal interview with Ejike Obumneme Aghanya.

24. *Ibid.*

25. *Ibid.*

26. 'Chinua Achebe on Biafra', *Transition*, pp. 31–7.

27. Chinua Achebe, 'The African writer and the Biafran cause', *Morning Yet on Creation Day* (London: Heinemann Educational Books, 1975), pp. 78–84.

28. Michael Awoyinfa, 'Chinua Achebe: *Things Fall Apart* was nearly stolen from me', *Sunday Concord*, 6 November 1983, p. xi.

29. Chinua Achebe, 'A Letter [on Stanley Diamond]', In C. W. Gailey, ed., *Dialectical Anthropology: Essays in Honor of Stanley Diamond* (Florida: University Press of Florida, 1992), p. 134.

30. Personal interview with Christie Achebe.

31. Chinua Achebe, *Morning Yet on Creation Day*, pp. 85–6.

32. Personal interview with C. C. Ifemesia.

33. *Beware, Soul Brother and Other Poems*, p. 15.

34. 'Chinua Achebe on Biafra', *Transition*, p. 32.

35. Chukwuma Azuonye, 'Reminiscences', p. 23.

36. Chinua Achebe, 'A Letter [on Stanley Diamond]', pp. 135–6.

11 TO UNDERSTAND WHAT HAPPENED (pp. 143–60)

1. Chinua Achebe, *Beware, Soul Brother and Other Poems* (Enugu: Nwankwo-Ifejika, 1971), pp. 39–40.

2. Conor Cruise O'Brien, 'Biafra revisited', *New York Review of Books*, 8 May 1969.

3. Harvey Swados, 'Chinua Achebe and the writers of Biafra', *New Letters*, 40, 1 (1973), p. 5.

4. *Ibid.*, pp. 10–12.

5. Chukwuma Azuonye, 'Reminiscences of the Odunke Community of Artists: 1966–90', *ALA Bulletin*, 17, 1 (Winter 1991), pp. 24–5.

6. Government of Biafra, *The Ahiara Declaration: The Principles of the Biafran Revolution* (Geneva: Mark Press, 1969).

7. *The Ahiara Declaration*, p. 33.

8. Personal interview with Christie Achebe.

9. Bernth Lindfors *et al.*, *Palaver: Interviews with Five African Writers in Texas* (Austin, Texas: African and African-American Institute, 1972), p. 6.
10. Ulli Beier, 'Interview with Obiora Udechukwu', *Okike*, 20 (1981), p. 55.
11. Chukwuma Azuonye, 'Reminiscences', p. 20.
12. Personal interview with Lyn Innes.
13. Lindfors, *et al.*, *Palaver*, p. 5
14. *Ibid.*, pp. 12–13.
15. Personal interview with Chinua Achebe. Also in Ulli Beier, *The World is a Dancing Masquerade: A Conversation Between Chinua Achebe and Ulli Beier* (Bayreuth: Iwalewa Haus, 1991).
16. Michael Smith and Harry Cowen, 'A man of the people: interview with Chinua Achebe', *McGill Reporter*, 2, 20 (23 February 1970), pp. 1–2.
17. Restated in personal interview with Chinua Achebe. Also in Charles Rowell, 'An interview with Chinua Achebe', *Callaloo*, 13, 1 (1990), p. 99.
18. 'Christmas in Biafra', *Beware Soul Brother and Other Poems*, pp. 13–14.
19. A. H. M. Kirk-Greene, *Crisis and Conflict in Nigeria: A Documentary Source Book 1966–70* (Oxford: Oxford University Press, 1971), Vol. 2, pp. 449–50.
20. *Ibid.*, pp. 451–2.
21. Chinua Achebe, 'A Letter [on Stanley Diamond]', in C. W. Gailey, ed., *Dialectical Anthropology: Essays in Honor of Stanley Diamond* (Florida: University Press of Florida, 1992), p. 135.
22. A. H. M. Kirk-Greene, *Crisis and Conflict in Nigeria*, pp. 457–61.
23. Onuora Udenwa, 'Interview with Chinua Achebe', *Quality*, 10 November 1988, p. 34.
24. Personal interview with Chinua Achebe.
25. Jonathan Cott, 'Chinua Achebe: at the crossroads', in Jonathan Cott, ed., *Pipers at the Gates of Dawn: The Wisdom of Children's Literature* (New York: Random House, 1983), p. 180.
26. Personal interview with Chinua Achebe.
27. Personal interview with Ulli Beier.
28. *The Trouble with Nigeria* (Enugu: Fourth Dimension Publishers and London: Heinemann Educational Books, 1983), pp. 45–6.
29. *Beware, Soul Brother and Other Poems*, pp. 37–8.
30. *Ibid.*, p. 31.
31. *Ibid.*, 'An If of History', pp. 16–17; 'He Loves; He Loves Me Not', p. 55.
32. Personal interview with Ulli Beier.
33. Personal interview with Chukwuemeka Ike.
34. Chinua Achebe, *Morning Yet on Creation Day* (London: Heinemann Educational Books, 1975), p. 51.
35. *Ibid.*, p. 52.
36. Suzanne Hayes, 'An interview with Chinua Achebe (Adelaide 1980)', *New Literatures Review*, 11 (n. d.), pp. 43–52.
37. David Carroll, *Chinua Achebe: Novelist, Poet, Critic* (London: Macmillan, 1990), p. 152.
38. Chinua Achebe, 'The *Okike* story', *Okike*, 21 (1982), pp. 1–5.
39. *Okike*, 1, 1 (April 1971), pp. 1–54.
40. Donatus Nwoga, ed., *Rhythms of Creation: A Decade of Okike Poetry* (Enugu: Fourth Dimension Publishers, 1982).

12 CONSTRUCTING A RELEVANT VISION (pp. 161–76)

1. Pius Okigbo, presenting Chinua Achebe at The National Merit Award Lecture, September 1986.
2. Publishers' back cover blurb, *Beware, Soul Brother and Other Poems* (Enugu: Nwankwo-Ifejika, 1971).
3. Review of *Beware, Soul Brother and Other Poems* in *Okike*, 1, 2 (1971), pp. 37–40.
4. Okey Ndibe, 'Low-profile guru', *Concord Weekly*, 4 March 1985, p. 30.
5. Editorial, *Nsukkascope*, 1 (1971), pp. 1–4.
6. Ikenna Nzimiro, 'Universities, how international are they?', *Nsukkascope*, 1 (1971), pp. 5–9.
7. Chimere Ikoku, 'Where are the laboratories', *Nsukkascope*, 1 (1971), pp. 10–16.
8. Editor's note to Anon, 'The plight of a junior lecturer', *Nsukkascope*, 1 (1971), p. 22.

9. James Currey, in Kirsten Holst Petersen, 'Working with Chinua Achebe: the African Writers Series; James Currey, Alan Hill and Keith Sambrook in conversation with Kirsten Holst Petersen', in Kirsten Holst Petersen and Anna Rutherford, eds, *Chinua Achebe : A Celebration* (Oxford: Heinemann Educational Books, 1991), p. 154.

10. 'Civil peace', *Okike* 1, 2 (December 1971).

11. Editorial, *Nsukkascope*, 2 (1971/2), pp. 1–5.

12. 'Letters to the Editor', *Nsukkascope*, 2 (1971/2), pp. 6–13.

13. *Girls at War and Other Stories* (London: Heinemann Educational Books (*AWS* 100), 1972).

14. Paddy Kitchen, 'A relevant art: Paddy Kitchen talks to Chinua Achebe', *Times Educational Supplement* (14 April 1972), p. 19.

15. Jonathan Cott, 'Chinua Achebe: at the crossroads', in Jonathan Cott, ed., *Pipers at the Gates Of Dawn: The Wisdom of Children's Literature* (New York: Random House, 1983), p. 181.

16. Reprinted in Chinua Achebe, *Morning Yet on Creation Day* (London: Heinemann Educational Books, 1975), pp. 38–41.

17. Citation at Dartmouth College, Hanover, New Hampshire.

18. Chinua Achebe, *Morning Yet on Creation Day*, pp. 30–7.

19. Joseph Bruchac, 'Achebe as Poet', *New Letters*, 40, 1 (1973), p. 23.

20. See inside cover, *Okike*, 1, 3 (1972); also *Okike*, 5 (June 1975), p. 85.

21. Chinua Achebe, 'Africa and her writers', *Morning Yet on Creation Day*, p. 27.

22. Chinua Achebe, 'Sugar Baby', *Okike*, 3 (1972), p. 16.

23. Chinua Achebe, 'Chi in Igbo cosmology', *Morning Yet on Creation Day*, pp. 93–103.

24. Chinua Achebe, 'Africa and her writers', *Morning Yet on Creation Day*, pp .19–29.

25. Restated in a personal interview with Chinua Achebe.

26. Chinua Achebe, 'Preface', *Christmas in Biafra and Other Poems* (New York: Doubleday, 1973), p. 9.

27. Personal communication with Alastair Niven.

28. Suggested by Catherine Lyn Innes.

29. Alan Hill, *In Pursuit of Publishing* (London: John Murray, 1988), p. 143.

30. Personal communication with Don Burness.

31. Interview with Chinua Achebe, by Bill Moyers in *A World of Ideas*, ed. B. S. Flowers (New York: Doubleday, 1989), p. 342.

32. John Agetua, *Critics on Chinua Achebe 1970–76* (Benin: Author, 1977), pp. 32–3.

33. Personal interview with Catherine Lyn Innes.

34. Victoria Evalds, 'An interview with Chinua Achebe', *Studies in Black Literature*, 8, 1 (1977), pp . 16–20.

35. Personal interview. Also in Jonathan Cott, 'Chinua Achebe: at the crossroads', in Jonathan Cott, ed., *Pipers at the Gates of Dawn: The Wisdom of Children's Literature* (New York: Random House, 1983), p. 179.

36. Jane Wilkinson, 'Chinua Achebe', in *Talking with African Writers* (London: James Currey, 1992), p. 56.

37. Karen Morell, *In Person: Achebe, Awoonor and Soyinka at the University of Washington* (Seattle: African Studies Program, 1975), pp. 3–33.

38. Chinua Achebe, 'Thoughts on the African novel', *Morning Yet on Creation Day*, pp. 49–54.

13 AN AMERICAN EXPEDITION (pp. 177–93)

1. George Adams, 'Chinua Achebe in America: a commentary', *Interlink*, 9, 2 (1973),p. 8.

2. Reinhard Sander, 'The Kansas City Institute on Caribbean and African Writing', *Research in African Literatures*, 5, 1 (1974), pp. 73–4.

3. Michel Fabre, 'Chinua Achebe on *Arrow Of God*', *Echos du Commonwealth*, 5 (1979/80), pp. 14–15.

4. *Ibid.*, p. 16.

5. *Ibid.*, pp. 12–13.

6. Personal interview with Lyn Innes.

7. *Ibid.*

8. 'Chinua Achebe, 'Colonialist criticism', *Morning Yet on Creation Day* (London: Heinemann Educational Books, 1975), pp. 7, 8.

9. Personal interview with Lyn Innes.

10. *Okike*, 4 (December 1973), p. ii.

11. Personal interview with Lyn Innes.
12. Chinua Achebe, 'Publishing in Africa: a writer's view', in Edwina Oluwasanmi *et al.*, *Publishing in Africa in the Seventies* (Ife: University of Ife Press, 1977), pp. 41–6.
13. 'Chinua Achebe on literature and commitment in Southern Africa', in Bernth Lindfors, ed., *Black South African Literature: A Symposium* (Washington DC: Three Continents Press and ALA, 1985), pp. 87–8.
14. Quoted by John Agetua, *Critics on Chinua Achebe 1970–76* (Benin: Author, 1977).
15. A. P. J. van Rensburg, 'Seeking a better place', *Donga,* 3 (1976), pp. 3–4.
16. Chinua Achebe, 'Continuity and Change in Nigerian Education', *The Umuahian* (1979), pp. 40–1.
17. Chinua Achebe, 'Colonialist criticism', pp. 3–18.
18. H. H. Anniah Gowda, 'The Association of Commonwealth Literature and Language Studies in Kampala', *Research in African Literatures,* 5 (1974), pp. 219–22.
19. Kirsten Holst Petersen, 'Report on the ACLALS Conference in Kampala in 1974', *Commonwealth Newsletter,* 6 (1974), pp. 4–6.
20. 'Chinua Achebe on literature and commitment in Southern Africa', in Bernth Lindfors, ed., *Black South African Literature: A Symposium,* p. 87.
21. Personal interview with Chinua Achebe.
22. Interview with Chinua Achebe.
23. Personal communication with the academic registrar, University of Southampton.
24. Citation of Chinua Achebe for the award of an honorary degree at the University of Southampton.
25. Chinua Achebe, 'Work and play in Tutuola's *The Palm-Wine Drinkard*', in *Hopes and Impediments* (London: Heinemann Educational Books, 1988), p. 68.
26. Chinua Achebe, 'An image of Africa. Racism in Conrad's *Heart of Darkness*', in *Hopes and Impediments,* p. 1.
27. *Ibid.,* p. 2.
28. Chinua Achebe, Preface, *Arrow of God* (London: Heinemann Educational Books (*AWS* 16), 1974).
29. Bruce King, 'The revised *Arrow of God*', *African Literature Today,* 13 (1983), pp. 68–78.
30. Personal interview with Lyn Innes.
31. *Okike,* 6 (December 1974).
32. *Okike,* 6 (1974), pp. 11–27.
33. See the Chancellor's Lecture booklet, 1974–5, Amherst, University of Massachusetts.
34. Chinua Achebe, *Hopes and Impediments,* pp. 1–13.
35. *Ibid.,* Preface, pp. ix–x.
36. C. L. Innes, review of *Morning Yet on Creation Day, Research in African Literatures,* 7, 2 (1976), pp. 245.
37. Bernth Lindfors (ed.), *Black South African Literature: A Symposium,* pp. 86–9.
38. Charles Nnolim, 'A source for *Arrow of God*', *Research in African Literatures,* 8, 1 (1977), p. 3. Also in C. L. Innes and Bernth Lindfors, *Critical Perspectives on Chinua Achebe* (London: Heinemann Educational Books, 1979).
39. Personal interview with Alastair Niven.
40. Personal interview with Lyn Innes.
41. Jonathan Cott, 'Chinua Achebe: at the crossroads', in Jonathan Cott, ed., *Pipers at the Gates Of Dawn: The Wisdom of Children's Literature* (New York: Random House, 1983), p. 186.
42. Personal interview with Lyn Innes.

14 GOING BACK TO THE ROOTS (pp. 194–211)

1. Brigadier Murtala Mohammed, *Drift and Chaos Arrested,* text of broadcast, 30 July 1975, Lagos, p. 11.
2. Chinua Achebe, *The Trouble with Nigeria* (Enugu: Fourth Dimension Publishers and London: Heinemann Educational Books, 1983), p. 1.
3. *Ibid.,* p. 1.
4. Part of Olusegun Obasanjo's broadcast as head of state, 1976.
5. Personal interview with Charles Owen.
6. Personal interview with Joseph Cary.
7. Interview with Chinua Achebe.

8. William Lawson, 'Chinua Achebe in New England: an interview', *Yardbird Reader,* 4 (1975), pp. 99–110.

9. Citation of Chinua Achebe, University of Prince Edward Island, 1976.

10. Ossie Enekwe, 'Interview with Chinua Achebe', *Okike,* 30 (1990), pp. 129–31.

11. John Agetua 'Interview with Chinua Achebe', *Critics on Chinua Achebe 1970–76* (Benin: Author, 1977).

12. *Ibid.*, pp. 39–44.

13. Jane Wilkinson 'Chinua Achebe', *Talking with African Writers* (London: James Currey, 1992), pp. 55–6.

14. *Research in African Literatures,* 8, 1 (1977), pp. 1–26.

15. C. L. Innes 'A source for *Arrow of God:* a response', *Research in African Literatures,* 9 (1978), pp. 16–18.

16. Bu-Buakei Jabbi, 'Myth and ritual in *Arrow of God*', *African Literature Today,* 11 (1980), p. 131.

17. Citation of Chinua Achebe at the University of Massachusetts, Amherst, 21 May 1977.

18. Chinua Achebe, 'Work and play in Tutuola's *The Palm-Wine Drinkard*', in *Hopes and Impediments* (London: Heinemann Educational Books, 1988), p. 68.

19. *Ibid.*, pp. 68–76.

20. Chinua Achebe, 'The truth of fiction', *Hopes and Impediments,* pp. 104–5.

21. 'Achebe on editing', *World Literature Written in English,* 27, 1 (1987), p. 2.

22. *Ibid.*, p. 3.

23. Tony Eluemunor, quoted in *Newswatch,* 24 March 1986.

24. Personal record of a comment by Rems Nna Umeasiegbu.

25. Chinua Achebe, 'The truth of fiction', pp. 102–3.

26. Personal interview with Chinua Achebe.

27. *Okike,* 12 (April 1978), p. v.

28. Citation of Chinua Achebe at the University of Ife, Nigeria, 1978.

29. Chinua Achebe, 'The truth of fiction', pp. 95–105.

30. Chinua Achebe, 'Preface', Chinua Achebe and Dubem Okafor, eds, *Don't Let Him Die* (Enugu: Fourth Dimension Publishers, 1978).

31. Chinua Achebe, 'The uses of African literature', *Okike,* 15 (1979), pp. 8–17.

32. Interview with Chinua Achebe by Ossie Enekwe, 'Dialogue with Achebe', *New Culture* (August 1979), pp. 40, 42.

33. *Ibid.*, p. 42.

34. Chinua Achebe, *The Trouble With Nigeria,* p. 15.

35. Enekwe, 'Dialogue with Achebe', p. 40.

36. Chinua Achebe, 'Continuity and change in Nigerian education', in Chinua Achebe, ed., *The Umuahian: A Golden Jubilee Publication* (Umuahia: Government College, Umuahia Old Boys Association, 1979).

37. Emmanuel Obiechina, editorial, *Okike,* 13 (1979), pp. v–vii.

38. Chinua Achebe, 'Pine Tree in Spring', *Okike,* 13 (1979), p. 2.

39. 'The bane of Union: an appraisal of the consequences of Union Igbo for Igbo language and literature', *Anu,* 1(1979), pp. 33–41.

40. 'Impediments to dialogue between North and South', *Hopes and Impediments,* pp. 14–19.

41. Biodun Jeyifo, 'Interview with Chinua Achebe', in Biodun Jeyifo, ed., *Contemporary Nigerian Literature: A Retrospective and Prospective Exploration* (Lagos: Nigerian Magazine, 1985), p. 19.

42. 'Writers doomed to be free', *West Africa,* 19 November 1979, p. 2123.

15 SETTING UP MORE STRUCTURES (pp. 212–26)

1. Suzanne Hayes, 'Interview with Chinua Achebe (Adelaide 1980)', *New Literatures Review* 11 (n. d.), p. 51.

2. James Davidson, 'Interview: Chinua Achebe', *Meanjin Quarterly* 39, 1 (1980), p. 41.

3. Rosemary Colmer, 'The critical generation', *Ash Magazine,* 5 (1980), pp. 5–7.

4. Mildred Hill-Lubin, 'Chinua Achebe and James Baldwin at the African Literature Association Conference in Gainesville', *Okike,* 17 (1980), pp. 1–5.

5. Chinua Achebe, 'Postscript: James Baldwin (1924–1987)', *Hopes and Impediments* (London: Heinemann Educational Books, 1988), p. 120.

6. Kalu Ogbaa, 'An interview with Chinua Achebe', *Research in African Literatures*, 12 (Spring 1981), pp. 1–13.
7. Jonathan Cott, 'Chinua Achebe: at the crossroads', in Jonathan Cott, ed., *Pipers at the Gates of Dawn: The Wisdom of Children's Literature* (New York: Random House, 1983), p. 192.
8. Interview with Chinua Achebe.
9. Interview with Chinua Achebe by Suzanne Hayes, *New Literature Review*, No. 11, p. 47.
10. Personal interview with Chinua Achebe.
11. Personal observation as an undergraduate student .
12. Chinua Achebe, *The Trouble with Nigeria* (Enugu: Fourth Dimension Publishers and London: Heinemann Educational Books, 1983), pp. 20–31.
13. Chinua Achebe,'Truth, wisdom and beauty', *West Africa* (22–28 December 1980), pp. 2603–4.
14. *Pan African Book World* Vol. 1, No. 1 (August 1981), p. 2.
15. Interview with C. C. Ifemesia.
16. 'The nature of the individual and his fulfilment', in H. H. Anniah Gowda, ed., *The Colonial and Neo-Colonial Encounter in Commonwealth Literature* (Mysore: University of Mysore, 1983), pp. 205–15.
17. Chinua Achebe, 'Examination cheating: *Expo '77* by Chukwuemeka Ike' (extract from a speech at the Launch of *Expo '77* in Lagos, 28 April 1981), *West Africa*, 25 May 1981, pp. 1172–3.
18. *Okike*, 18 (June 1981), p. 7.
19. Lindsay Barrett, 'Giving writers a voice: an Interview with Chinua Achebe', *West Africa*, 22 June 1981, p. 1406.
20. Anthony Appiah, John Ryle and D. A. N. Jones, 'An Interview with Chinua Achebe', *Times Literary Supplement*, 26 February 1982, p. 209.
21. F. N. Ndili, 'An address', *Okike*, 20 (December 1981), pp. 2–3.
22. P. C. Amadike, 'An address', *Okike*, 20,(1981), pp. 4–6.
23. Chinua Achebe, 'Why an association?', *Okike*, 20 (1981), pp. 7–10.
24. Interviews with C. C. Ifemesia and Chinua Achebe.
25. Chinua Achebe, 'What has literature got to do with it?', *Hopes and Impediments*, p. 110.
26. 'Preface', *African Creations: A Decade of Okike Short Stories* (Enugu: Fourth Dimension Publishers, 1982).
27. Chinua Achebe, 'The *Okike* Story', *Okike*, 21 (1982), pp. 1–5.
28. Citation of Chinua Achebe at the University of Kent at Canterbury, July 1982.
29. Robert Wren,*Those Magical Years* (Washington, DC: Three Continents Press, 1991), p. 54.
30. Chinua Achebe, *The Trouble With Nigeria*, pp. 34–5.
31. Interview with C. C. Ifemesia.

16 THE TROUBLE WITH NIGERIA (pp. 227–45)

1. Anon., 'Aminu picks running mate', *West Africa*, 18 April 1983, p. 966.
2. Anon., 'Aminu Kano – leader from the outside', *West Africa*, 25 April 1983, p. 981.
3. Publishers' blurb for the original Nigerian edition.
4. Chinua Achebe, *The Trouble with Nigeria* (Enugu: Fourth Dimension Publishers and London: Heinemann Educational Books, 1983), p. 1.
5. *Ibid.*, p. 27.
6. *Ibid.*, p. 38.
7. *Ibid.*, p. 50.
8. *Ibid.*, pp. 62-3.
9. Michael Awoyinfa, 'Chinua Achebe: *Things Fall Apart* was nearly stolen from me', *Sunday Concord* magazine, 6 November 1983, pp. i, v, xi.
10. Michael Awoyinfa and Ben Okezie, 'Achebe speaks on Wole Soyinka', *Sunday Concord*, 9 October 1983, p. x
11. Interview with Alastair Niven.
12. Interviews with Chinua Achebe and Arthur Nwankwo.
13. G. G. Darah and Afam Akeh, 'The crossroads of our culture – Achebe', *Sunday Times*, 12 November 1989, pp. 18–19.
14. Alan Hill, *In Pursuit of Publishing* (London: John Murray, 1988), p. 225.
15. 'Presidential Address 1983', *ANA Review*, 1 (1985), p. 7.

16. Quoted in 'What has literature got to do with it?', *Hopes and Impediments* (London: Heinemann Educational Books, 1988) p. 108.
17. Reproduced in S. G. Ikoku, *Nigeria's Fourth Coup d'État: Options for Modern Statehood* (Enugu: Fourth Dimension Publishers, 1985), pp. 166–7.
18. *Ibid.,* pp. 168–71.
19. 'Reflections on Nigeria's political culture', *Guardian,* 11 March 1984, p. 6; 12 March 1984, p. 7.
20. Citation of Chinua Achebe at Mount Allison University, Sackville, New Brunswick, Canada, 1984.
21. G. D. Killam 'A personal note', in Kirsten Holst Petersen and Anna Rutherford, eds, *Chinua Achebe : A Celebration* (Oxford: Heinemann Educational Books, 1991), p. 160.
22. Chinua Achebe, 'Chinua Achebe on editing', *World Literature Written in English,* 27, 1 (1987), pp. 1–5.
23. Quoted in G. D. Killam 'A personal note', pp. 160–2.
24. Citation of Chinua Achebe, University of Guelph, Ontario, Canada, 1984.
25. Benedict Njoku, *The Four Novels of Chinua Achebe: A Critical Study* (New York: Peter Lang, 1984).
26. Personal interview with Don Burness.
27. Chinua Achebe, 'The writer and his community', in *Hopes and Impediments,* pp. 32–41.
28. Chinua Achebe, 'Editorial and linguistic problems in *Aka Weta*: a comment', *Uwa Ndi Igbo,* 1 (1984), pp. 94–5.
29. Chinua Achebe, 'The Igbo world and its art', *Hopes and Impediments,* pp. 42–5.
30. Okey Ndibe, 'Who will save Nigeria?', *Concord Weekly,* 28 January 1985, pp. 34.
31. *Sunday Concord,* 20 January 1985.
32. Michael Awoyinfa, 'Dogs eat dog: professors attack Professor Achebe', *Sunday Concord,* 3 February 1985, p. 1.
33. Chinua Achebe, 'I'm an original professor ... professing literature', *Sunday Concord,* 17 February 1985, p. 2.
34. Interview team of *New Nigerian,* 'Professor Achebe at *New Nigerian* parley', *New Nigerian,* 2 April 1985, p. 1; 5 April 1985, pp. 1–3; 6 April 1985, pp. 5, 8; 8 April 1985, pp. 2, 5; 9 April 1985, pp. 2, 5.
35. *African Short Stories* (London, Heinemann Educational Books, 1985).
36. Citation of Chinua Achebe, Franklin Pierce College, USA, May 1985.
37. Citation of Chinua Achebe, University of Nigeria, Nsukka, 1985.
38. Quoted in Dili Ezughah, Chinwude Onwuanyi and Chuks Iloegbunam, 'Interview with Chinweizu', *Quality,* 4 May 1989, pp. 43–9.
39. Chinweizu, in Ezughah, *et al.,* 'Interview with Chinweizu', *Quality,* 4 May 1989, pp. 43–9.
40. Jane Wilkinson, 'Chinua Achebe', *Interviews with African Writers* (London: James Currey, 1992), p. 50.
41. 'Interview with Chinua Achebe', *Massachusetts Review,* 28 (1987), pp. 273–85.
42. 'Presidential address 1985', ANA Review, 2 (1986), pp. 1–2.
43. Okey Ndibe and C. Don Adinuba, 'Africa is unstable; Nigeria has not been founded; There are oppressors; Not a matter of noise', *African Guardian* 17 July 1986, p. 42; 24 July 1986, p. 34; 31 July 1986, p. 38; August 1986, p. 40.
44. Chinua Achebe, 'Presidential Address', Association of Nigerian Authors, 27 November 1986.
45. Ad'Obe Obe, 'The coup plot verdicts', *West Africa,* 3 March 1986, p. 445.
46. Statement by Chinua Achebe,Wole Soyinka and J. P. Clark for clemency. See Tunde Agbabiaka, 'Execution reactions', *West Africa,* 17 March 1986, p. 553.
47. Anon., 'The Dread logic of power', *West Africa,* 17 March 1986, p. 551.
48. Tunde Agbabiaka, 'Execution reactions', *West Africa,* 17 March 1986, p. 553.

17 WHAT LITERATURE HAS TO DO WITH IT (pp. 246–65)

1. Bernth Lindfors, in Bernth Lindfors and Bala Kothandaraman (eds), *South Asian Responses to Chinua Achebe* (New Delhi: Prestige Books, 1993), pp. i–ii.
2. Patricia Morris 'The politics of language', *African Concord,* 14 August 1986, pp. 19– 21.
3. Robert Moss, 'Writing and politics', *West Africa,* 11 August 1986, p. 1676–7.
4. Pius Okigbo, presenting Chinua Achebe at The National Merit Award Lecture,

September 1986.

5. Chinua Achebe, 'What has literature got to do with it?', *Hopes and Impediments* (London: Heinemann Educational Books, 1988), pp. 106–17.
6. Sina Odugbemi, 'I don't believe an artist needs to be rowdy – Achebe', *Vanguard*, 16 October 1986, pp. 8–9.
7. Chinua Achebe, *The University and the Leadership Factor in Nigerian Politics* (speech reproduced as pamphlet) (Enugu: Abik Press, 1988).
8. Quoted in *African Guardian*, 30 October 1986, pp. 16–17.
9. Presidential address, Association of Nigerian Authors Convention, Lagos, 1986.
10. Personal interviews with C. C. Ifemesia and Chinua Achebe.
11. Reported in *The Guardian* (Lagos) and *Daily Times*, May 1986.
12. Extracts in Anon., 'Achebe dissents', *West Africa*, 8 June 1987, pp. 423–4; Also in Baffour Ankomah, 'Awo: Achebe puts the knife in', *New African*, August 1987, pp. 38–9.
13. *The Guardian* (Lagos), 2 June 1987, p. 3 and 4 June 1987, p. 3.
14. *Sunday Concord*, 12 July 1987, p. 22.
15. Chinua Achebe *et al.*, *Beyond Hunger in Africa: Conventional Wisdom and an African Vision* (Nairobi: Heinemann Educational Books and London: James Currey, 1990).
16. *Anthills of the Savannah* (London: Heinemann Educational Books, 1987).
17. Back cover, reprinted edition of *Anthills of the Savannah*.
18. Emmanuel Ngara, 'Achebe as artist: the place and significance of *Anthills of the Savannah*', in Kirsten Holst Petersen and Anna Rutherford, eds, *Chinua Achebe: A Celebration* (Oxford: Heinemann Educational Books, 1991), pp. 113–29.
19. 'A tale of tyranny', *West Africa*, 21 September 1987, pp. 1828–31.
20. Kaye Whiteman, 'Achebe and the masquerade', *West Africa*, 9 November 1987, pp. 2193–94.
21. Yusuf Hassan, 'More fiction than real', *Africa Events*, 3, 11 (1987), pp. 51–5.
22. Inscribed on a plaque presented to Chinua Achebe.
23. *Campus Chronicle*, 26 June 1987, p. 6.
24. Chinua Achebe, 'Preface', *Hopes and Impediments*, p. x.
25. Chinua Achebe, 'Postscript: James Baldwin (1924-1987)', *Hopes and Impediments*, pp. 118–21.
26. Onuora Udenwa, 'Interview with Achebe', *Quality*, 10 November 1988, p. 37.
27. 'Turning the mind to things that matter', address at the third convocation ceremony of Anambra State University of Technology, Enugu, Anambra State, 1987.
28. Amma Ogan, 'Fiction re-orders society', *African Guardian*, 11 February 1980, p. 29.
29. *Ibid.*
30. Onuora Udenwa, 'Achebe: a chat that bares it all', *Guardian*, 11 November 1989, p. 12; 18 November 1989, p. 12.
31. Lydia Foerster, 'Man of the people', *Daily Texan*, 19 February 1988, p. 11.
32. Enedelia J. Obregon, 'Author chides attitude toward Third World', *Austin–American–Statesman*, 21 February 1988, p. D4.
33. In Jules Chametzky, ed., *Black Writers Redefine Struggle: A Tribute to James Baldwin* (Amherst: University of Massachusetts Press, 1989), pp. 4, 16.
34. Chinua Achebe, 'Spelling our proper name', in Jules Chametzky, ed., *Black Writers Redefine Struggle*, pp. 5–12.
35. Chinua Achebe, 'Panel discussion', in Jules Chametzky, ed., *Black Writers Redefine Struggle*, p. 74.
36. Robert Kimborough, ed., in Joseph Conrad, *Heart of Darkness* (Norton Critical Edition) (New York: Norton, 1988).
37. Karen Winkler, 'An African writer at a crossroads', *The Chronicle of Higher Education*, 12 January 1994, p. A9.
38. Chinua Achebe, 'African literature as restoration of celebration', in Kirsten Holst Petersen and Anna Rutherford, eds, *Chinua Achebe: A Celebration* (Oxford: Heinemann Educational Books, 1991), pp. 1–10.
39. Raoul Granqvist, ed., *Travelling: Chinua Achebe in Scandinavia: Swedish Writers in Africa* (Umeå: Umeå Papers in English, 1990), pp. 22–3
40. 'Interview with Chinua Achebe', *The Guardian*, 11 November 1989, p. 12.
41. Onuora Udenwa, 'Interview with Chinua Achebe', *Quality*, 10 November 1988, p. 31.
42. Patricia Wright, 'Chinua Achebe: bringing the African novel back home', *Contact* 13, 3 (1988), pp. 28, 31.

43. Chinua Achebe, 'The judge and I didn't go to Namibia', *Callaloo,* 13, 1 (1990), pp. 84–6.
44. *Ibid.,* p. 85.
45. Stacy Chase, *Campus Chronicle,* 16 September 1988, p. 6.
46. Bill Moyers, 'Chinua Achebe: Nigerian novelist', in Betty Sue Flowers, ed., *A World of Ideas* (New York: Doubleday, 1989), pp. 333–44.
47. *Hopes and Impediments* (London: Heinemann Educational Books, 1988).
48. Chris Dunton, 'A fine-tuned humanist: a review of *Hopes and Impediments*', *West Africa,* 12–18 September 1988, p. 1675.
49. Raoul Granqvist, ed., *Travelling: Chinua Achebe in Scandinavia.*
50. Okey Ndibe, 'A cry of the heart', *African Guardian,* 28 November 1988, pp. 25–6.
51. Onuora Udenwa, 'Interview with Chinua Achebe', *Quality,* 10 November 1988, pp. 31–3.
52. Onuora Udenwa, 'The Nobel is not an African Prize – Chinua Achebe', *Quality,* 3 November 1988, p. 7.
53. *Quality,* 10 November 1988, pp. 36–7.
54. Onuora Udenwa, *The Guardian,* 11 November 1989, p. 12; 18 November 1989, p. 12. Also in Ulli Beier, *The World is a Dancing Masquerade* (Bayreuth: Iwalewa Haus, 1991), p. 13.
55. Personal record of the ceremony. See also Ezenwa-Ohaeto, 'A literary celebration of the Achebes', *ALA Bulletin,* 15, 2 (1989), pp. 16–18.
56. Chris Searle, 'Achebe and the bruised heart of Africa', *Wasafiri,* 14 (1991), pp. 12–16.

18 THE LEGACY OF AN EAGLE ON IROKO (pp. 266–86)

1. Ezenwa-Ohaeto, 'Celebration for Chinua Achebe', *ALA Bulletin,* 16, 2 (1990).
2. Comment confirmed by Alan Hill, in Kirsten Holst Petersen, 'Working with Chinua Achebe: the African Writers Series; James Currey, Alan Hill and Keith Sambrook in conversation with Kirsten Holst Petersen', in Kirsten Holst Petersen and Anna Rutherford, eds, *Chinua Achebe : A Celebration* (Oxford: Heinemann Educational Books, 1991), p. 152.
3. Ulli Beier, *The World is a Dancing Masquerade: A Conversation with Chinua Achebe* (Bayreuth: Iwalewa Haus, 1991), pp. 14–15.
4. Inscribed on a plaque given to Chinua Achebe.
5. Quoted by Charles H. Rowell, in 'An interview with Chinua Achebe', *Callaloo,* 13, 1 (1990), p. 90.
6. Plaque given to Chinua Achebe by the president of the borough of Manhattan, New York.
7. Citation of Chinua Achebe, Westfield State College, Westfield, Massachusetts, 19 May 1989.
8. Citation of Chinua Achebe by the Open University of Great Britain, 1989.
9. Charles H. Rowell, 'An interview with Chinua Achebe', p. 93.
10. *Ibid.,* pp. 86–101.
11. Ulli Beier, *The World is a Dancing Masquerade.*
12. Interview with Chinua Achebe.
13. Chinua Achebe, 'Our mission', *African Commentary: A Journal for People of African Descent,* 1, 1 (1989).
14. Okey Ndibe, 'Editorial', *African Commentary,* 1, 1 (1991).
15. Chinua Achebe 'Our mission'.
16. Tony Nzotta *et al.,* 'I am a missionary in reverse – Prof. Achebe', *Nigerian Statesman,* 14 November 1989, p. 7.
17. Alvan Ewuzie, 'Academics have ruined University system – Achebe's bombshell at 60', *Daily Champion,* 18 November 1989, p. 13.
18. G. G. Darah and Afam Akeh, 'Achebe at 59', *Daily Times,* 18 November 1989, p. 12.
19. Editorial, *Daily Times,* 18 November 1989.
20. Louis James, in Hene Maes-Jelinek, ed., *A Shaping of Connections: Commonwealth Literature Studies – Then and Now* (Sydney: Dangaroo Press, 1989).
21. Onuora Udenwa, 'Achebe: a chat that bares it all', *The Guardian,* 11 November 1989, p. 12; 18 November 1989, p. 12.
22. Onuora Udenwa, 'Achebe: a chat that bares it all', p. 12.
23. *Ibid.,* p. 12.

24. Lawrence Baugh, 'An interview with Chinua Achebe', *Drum* (Amherst), 5, 3 (1974), pp. 18–22.
25. Chinua Achebe, 'African literature as restoration of celebration', in Kirsten Holst Petersen and Anna Rutherford, eds, *Chinua Achebe : A Celebration,* pp. 1–10.
26. Personal interview with Obi Maduakor.
27. G. G. Darah and Afam Akeh, 'Achebe at 59', *Daily Times,* 18 November 1989, p. 12.
28. Chidi Amuta, 'The Eagle on Iroko', *Daily Times,* 12 February 1990, p. 15.
29. Speeches by Vice-Chancellor Chimere Ikoku and Edith Ihekweazu at the 'Eagle on Iroko' symposium, 11–15 February 1990.
30. 'Editorial – and Achebe at 59', *Daily Times,* 16 November 1989.
31. Eni-Jones Umuko, director, production notes for Emeka Nwabueze, *When the Arrow Rebounds,* University of Nigeria Arts Theatre, February 1990.
32. *Daily Times,* February 1990.
33. Joseph Bruchac's goodwill message, quoted in Ezenwa-Ohaeto, 'Celebration for Chinua Achebe', p. 23.
34. Dimgba Igwe, 'Conversation with Chinua Achebe's wife', *Weekend Concord,* 31 March 1990, pp. 7, 14.
35. Angela Jackson, 'Interview with Chinua Achebe', *Black Books Bulletin,* 8 (1991), pp . 53–8.
36. Get well messages for Chinua Achebe, *Weekend Concord,* 21 April 1991, p. 10.
37. Citation of Chinua Achebe, Georgetown University, May 1990.
38. Gideon Okar's broadcast to the nation, 22 April 1990. Excerpts in 'A bloody attempt', *West Africa,* 30 April–6 May 1990, pp. 696–7.
39. Karen Winkler 'An African writer at the crossroads', *The Chronicle of Higher Education,* 12 January 1994, p. A12.
40. Quoted in *ibid.,* p. A12.
41. Petersen and Rutherford eds, *Chinua Achebe: A celebration,* p. 159.
42. Chidi Amuta and Tunde Olusunle, 'Achebe: eagle above seasons', *Sunday Times,* 11 November 1990, pp. 13–15.
43. G. D. Killam, 'A personal note', in Kirsten Holst Petersen and Anna Rutherford, eds, *Chinua Achebe : A Celebration,* p. 162.
44. Personal interview with Ulli Beier.
45. Amma Ogan, 'Tribute to Chinua Achebe', *Sunday Times,* 16 December 1990, p. 7.
46. Ola Rotimi, 'Achebe: another feather for the eagle', *Daily Times,* 20 February 1991, p. 18.
47. Citation of Chinua Achebe by Skidmore College, Saratoga Springs, New York, 26 March 1991.
48. Citation of Chinua Achebe by the New School for Social Research of New York, 21 May 1991.
49. Karen Winkler, 'An African writer at a crossroads', p. A9.
50. Citation of Chinua Achebe by Hobart and William Smith College, June 1991.
51. Citation of Chinua Achebe by Marymount College, 3 June 1991.
52. Announcement by Heinemann Educational Books.
53. Quoted by Karen Winkler in 'An African writer at a crossroads', p. A9.
54. Quoted in an Anchor Books advertisement.
55. Personal interview with Don Burness.
56. Bradford Morrow, 'Chinua Achebe: An interview', *Conjunctions,* No. 17 (1991), pp. 26–7.
57. Jereme Brooks, 'Chinua Achebe: The art of fiction', *Paris Review,* Vol. 35, No. 133 (Winter 1994), p. 164.
58. 'The education of a "British Protected Child"', *Cambridge Review,* 114 (June 1993), pp. 51–7.
59. Karen Winkler, 'An African writer at the crossroads', p. A9.
60. Personal interview with Alastair Niven.
61. Bernth Lindfors and Bala Kothandaraman (eds), *South Asian Responses to Chinua Achebe* (New Delhi: Prestige Books, 1993).
62. Citation of Chinua Achebe by Colgate University, Hamilton, NY, 23 May 1993.
63. Marguerite Michaels , 'The power of silence', *Time,* 23 August 1993, p. 25.
64. *ALA Bulletin,* 19, 4 (1993),p. 48.

Bibliography

Publications by Chinua Achebe

BOOKS

Things Fall Apart (London: William Heinemann, 1958; New York: Astor Honor, 1959; London: Heinemann Educational Books (AWS 1), 1962).

No Longer at Ease (London: William Heinemann, 1960; New York: Obolensky, 1961; London: Heinemann Educational Books (AWS 3), 1963).

The Sacrificial Egg and Other Short Stories (Onitsha: Etudo, 1962).

Arrow of God (London: William Heinemann, 1964; New York: John Day, 1967; London: Heinemann Educational Books (AWS 16), 1965; revised edition, London: Heinemann Educational Books, 1974).

Chike and the River (Cambridge: Cambridge University Press, 1966).

A Man of the People (London: William Heinemann, 1966; New York: John Day, 1966; London: Heinemann Educational Books (AWS 31), 1966).

Beware, Soul Brother and Other Poems (Enugu: Nwankwo-Ifejika, 1971; revised and enlarged edition, London: Heinemann Educational Books, 1972; Reprinted as *Christmas in Biafra and Other Poems*, Garden City, NY: Anchor/Doubleday, 1973).

Girls at War and Other Stories (London: Heinemann Educational Books (*AWS* 100), 1972; Garden City NY: Anchor/Doubleday, 1973. (Includes in revised versions the stories in *The Sacrificial Egg and Other Stories*.)

With John Iroaganachi, *How the Leopard Got His Claws* (Enugu: Nwamife, 1972; New York: The Third Press, 1973) (children's book).

Morning Yet on Creation Day. Essays (London: Heinemann Educational Books, 1975; enlarged and revised edition, Garden City NY: Anchor/Doubleday, 1975).

The Drum (Enugu: Fourth Dimension, 1977) (children's book).

The Flute (Enugu: Fourth Dimension, 1977) (children's book).

Ed., with Dubem Okafor, *Don't Let Him Die: An Anthology of Memorial Poems for Christopher Okigbo* (Enugu: Fourth Dimension Publishers, 1978).

Ed., *The Umuahian: A Golden Jubilee Publication* (Umuahia: Government College Old Boys' Association, 1979).

Ed., with Obiora Udechukwu, *Aka Weta: Egwu Aguluagu, Egwu edeluede* (Nsukka: Okike Magazine, 1982).

The Trouble With Nigeria (Enugu: Fourth Dimension Publishers, 1983; London: Heinemann Educational Books, 1983).

Ed., with C. L. Innes, *African Short Stories* (London: Heinemann Educational Books, (AWS 270) 1985).

Anthills of the Savannah (London: William Heinemann, 1987; New York: Doubleday, 1988).

Hopes and Impediments. Selected Essays, 1965–87 (London: Heinemann Educational Books, 1988).

Nigerian Essays (Ibadan: Heinemann Educational Books, forthcoming).

Ed., with C. L. Innes, *Contemporary African Short Stories* (London: Heinemann Educational Books, 1990).

Ed., with Göran Hyden, Christopher Magadza and Achola Pala Okeyo, *Beyond Hunger in Africa: Conventional Wisdom and an African Vision* (Nairobi: Heinemann Educational Books and London: James Currey, 1990).

SHORT STORIES

'Polar Undergraduate', *University Herald*, 3, 3 (1950).

'In a Village Church', *University Herald*, 4, 2 (1951).

'The Sacrificial Egg', *Atlantic Monthly*, April 1959.*

'Chike's School Days', *Rotarian*, 96, 4 (1960).*

'The Madman', in Chinua Achebe, Arthur Nwankwo, Samuel U. Ifejika, Flora Nwapa, *et al.,The Insider* (Enugu: Nwankwo-Ifejika, 1971).*

'Sugar Baby', *Okike* 3 (1972).

* These stories appear in the *Girls at War* collection.

POEMS

'There Was a Young Man in Our Hall', *University Herald* (Ibadan), 4, 3 (1951–2), p. 19.

'Flying', *Okike* 4 (1973), pp. 47-8.

'The Old Man and the Census', *Okike* 6 (1974), pp. 41–2.

'The American Youngster in Rags', *Okike* 12 (1978), pp. 3–4.

'Knowing Robs Us', *Okike* 13 (1979), p. 1.

'Pine Tree in Spring' *Okike* 13 (1979), p. 2.

'Agostinho Neto', *Okike* 18 (1981), p. 7.

All but the first of these have been reprinted in D. I. Nwoga, ed., *Rhythms of Creation* (Enugu: Fourth Dimension Publishers, 1982). All other published poems are collected in *Beware, Soul Brother* or *Christmas in Biafra*.

ESSAYS, TALKS & MISCELLANEOUS WORKS

'Philosophy', *The Bug* (Ibadan), 21 February 1951, p. 5.

'An argument against the existence of faculties', *University Herald* (Ibadan), 4, 1 (1951), pp. 12–13.

Editorial, *University Herald* (Ibadan), 4, 3 (1951–2), p. 5.

Editorial, *University Herald* (Ibadan), 5, 1 (1952), p. 5.

'Mr Okafor versus arts students', *The Bug* (Ibadan), 29 November 1952, p. 3.

'Hiawatha', *The Bug* (Ibadan), 29 November 1952, p. 3.

'Eminent Nigerians of the 19th Century', *Radio Times* (Lagos), January 1958, p. 3.

'Listening in the East', *Radio Times* (Lagos), January 1959, p. 17; February 1959, p. 17; March 1959, p. 18; April 1959, p. 18; May 1959, p. 33; June 1959, p. 22 (about Nigerian Broadcasting Corporation programming in Eastern Nigeria).

'Two West African library journals', *The Service*, 6 May 1961, p. 15.

'Amos Tutuola', *Radio Times* (Lagos), 23–29 July 1961, p. 15.

'Writers' conference: a milestone in Africa's progress', *Daily Times* (Lagos), 7 July 1962, p. 7.

'Conference of African writers', *Radio Times* (Lagos), 15 July 1962, p. 6.

Introduction to Delphine King, *Dreams of Twilight. A Book of Poems* (Apapa: Nigerian National Press, n. d., c. 1962), p. 5.

Review of Christopher Okigbo's *Heavensgate*, *Spear* (Lagos), December 1962, p. 41.

Review of Jean-Joseph Rabéarivelo's *Twenty-Four Poems*, *Spear* (Lagos), January 1963, p. 41.

'A look at West African writing', *Spear* (Lagos), June 1963, p. 26.

'Voice of Nigeria – how it began', *Voice of Nigeria* 1, 1 (1963), pp. 5–6.

'Are we men of two worlds?' *Spear* (Lagos), December 1963, p. 13.

'On Janheinz Jahn and Ezekiel Mphahlele', *Transition*, 8 (1963), p. 9.

'The role of the writer in a new nation', *Nigerian Libraries* 1, 3 (1964), pp. 113–19; *Nigeria Magazine* 81 (1964), pp. 157–60.

Foreword to W. H. Whiteley, ed., *A Selection of African Prose*, Vol. 1 (Oxford: Clarendon

Press, 1964), pp. vii–x.

'The African writer and the English language', *Transition*, 4, 18 (1965), pp. 27–30. Reprinted in *Morning Yet on Creation Day*.

'The black writer's burden', *Présence Africaine*, 31, 59 (1966), pp. 135–40.

Editorial, *Nsukkascope* (Nsukka) 1 (1971), pp. 1–4.

Editorial, *Nsukkascope* (Nsukka) 2 (1971–2), pp. 1–5.

Editorial, *Nsukkascope* (Nsukka) 3 (1972), pp. 4–5.

Introduction to Kofi Awoonor, *This Earth, My Brother* (Garden City NY: Anchor/Doubleday, 1972), pp. vii–xii; reprinted as a review in *Transition* 41 (1972), p. 69, and in *Hopes and Impediments*, pp. 82–6.

Introduction to Keorapetse Kgositsile, *Places and Bloodstains [Notes for Ipelang]* (Oakland, California: Achebe Publications, 1975), p. 7.

'An image of Africa', *The Chancellor's Lecture Series*, 1974–75 (Amherst MA: University of Massachusetts Press, 1975), pp. 31–43; reprinted in *Hopes and Impediments* pp. 1–3.

'Publishing in Africa. A writer's view', in Edwina Oluwasanmi, Eva Maclean and Hans Zell, eds, *Publishing in Africa in The Seventies* (Ile-Ife: University of Ife Press, 1975), pp. 41–6.

'Contemporary literature', in *The Living Culture of Nigeria* (London: Nelson, 1976).

'African writing and the problem of translation', *Translation* 3 (1976), pp. 38–43 (panel discussion with Rajat Neogy, Donald Herdeck, Joseph Okpaku and Mazisi Kunene).

'Commitment and the African writer', in Ogbu U. Kalu (ed.), *Readings in African Humanities: African Cultural Development* (Enugu: Fourth Dimension Publishers, 1978), pp. 181–7.

'Work and play in Tutuola's *The Palm Wine Drinkard*', *Okike*, 14 (1978), pp, 25–33; reprinted in *Hopes and Impediments*, pp. 68–76.

'The bane of Union: an appraisal of the consequences of Union Igbo for Igbo language and literature', *ANU Magazine*, 1 (1979), pp. 33–41.

'The uses of African literature', *Okike* 15 (1979), pp. 8–17.

'Impediments to dialogue between North and South', *Okike*, 16 (1979), pp. 8–12; also published in the *Times Literary Supplement*, 1 February 1980; reprinted in *Hopes and Impediments*, pp. 14–19.

'Examination cheating: *Expo '77* by Chukwuemeka Ike', *West Africa*, 25 May 1981, pp. 1172–3 (excerpts from a speech at the launch of *Expo '77*, 30 April 1981.)

'Why an association? Address to the Convention of Nigerian Authors', *Okike*, 20 (1981), pp. 7–10, reprinted in *Association of Nigerian Authors Review (ANAR)*, 1 (1985), pp. 1–2.

'The *Okike* story', *Okike*, 21 (1982), pp. 1–5.

'The nature of the individual and his fulfilment', in H. H. Anniah Gowda, ed., *The Colonial and Neo-colonial Encounter in Commonwealth Literature* (Mysore: University of Mysore, 1983), pp. 205–15.

'The purpose of education', *Guardian* (Lagos), 4 December 1983, p. 8 (excerpts from a speech given at Federal Government College, Lagos, 26 November 1983).

'Editorial and linguistic problems in *Aka Weta*: a comment', *Uwa ndi Igbo*, 1 (1984), pp. 94–5.

Foreword, in Herbert Cole and Chike Aniakor, eds, *Igbo Arts: Community and Cosmos* (Los Angeles: University of California Press, 1984).

'I'm an original professor ... professing literature', *Sunday Concord* (Nigeria), 17 February 1985, p 2. (Letter to editor in response to criticism by Lagos University professors.)

'Reflections on Nigeria's political culture', *Guardian* (Lagos), 11 March 1984, p. 6; 12 March 1984, p. 7 (excerpts from a speech given at the University of Port-Harcourt, Nigeria, 1984).

'Presidential address 1983', *ANAR*, 1 (I 985), p. 7.

'Presidential address 1985', *ANAR*, 2 (1986), pp. 1–2.

'Achebe's letter from Canada', *Concord Weekly*, 5 September 1985, pp. 16–17.

'What has literature got to do with it?' Nigeria National Merit Award Winner's Lecture 1986 (Lagos: Federal Republic of Nigeria, 1986); reprinted in *Vanguard*, 4 September 1986, pp. 8–9; *ANAR*, 2 (1986), pp. 9, 15; and in *Hopes and Impediments*, pp. 106–17.

'Achebe on editing', *WLWE*, 27, 1 (Spring 1987), pp. 1–5.

'James Baldwin, 1924–87: a dedication' (with Esther Terry, Michael Thelwell and John Wideman), *Massachusetts Review* 28, (Winter 1987), pp. 551–60; reprinted in *Hopes and Impediments*, pp. 118–21.

The University and the Leadership Factor in Nigeria Politics (Enugu: Abic Press, 1988) (speech given by Achebe and reproduced as a pamphlet).

'Turning the mind to things that matter', an address at the third convocation ceremony of Anambra State University of Technology, Enugu, 1987. Printed by Anambra State University of Technology, Enugu, 1987.

'Spelling our proper name', in Jules Chametzky, ed., *Black Writers Redefine Struggle: A Tribute to James Baldwin* (Amherst: University of Massachusetts Press, 1989), pp. 5–12.

'The judge and I didn't go to Namibia', *Callaloo*, 13, 1 (1990), pp. 82–4; also published as 'Travelling white', *Weekend Guardian*, 21–22 October 1989, p. 7; and as 'A Nigerian encounters colonial Southern Africa', *Weekly Mail* Literary Supplement, 8–14 December 1989, p. 13.

'African literature as restoration of celebration' in Kirsten Holst Petersen and Anna Rutherford, eds, *Chinua Achebe: A Celebration* (Oxford: Heinemann Educational Books, 1991); reprinted in *Okike*, 30 (1990), pp. 1–10.

'A letter' [on Stanley Diamond and other sympathizers with Biafra], in C. W. Gailey, ed., *Dialectical Anthropology: Essays in Honor of Stanley Diamond Vol. 1: Civilization in Crisis: Anthropological Perspectives* (Florida: University Press of Florida, 1992), pp. 133–6.

'Where something stands look well: something else is standing beside it', in Don Burness, ed., *Echoes of the Sunbird: An Anthology of Contemporary African Poetry* (Athens, Ohio: Ohio University Center for International Studies, 1993), p. 3.

'The education of a "British protected child"', *Cambridge Review*, 114 (June 1993), pp. 51–7.

Other previously unpublished lectures and unrevised essays are collected in *Morning Yet on Creation Day* and *Hopes and Impediments: Selected Essays 1965–87*.

INTERVIEWS WITH CHINUA ACHEBE

Al-Bishak, 'Professor Achebe's window on the writer's world', *Nigerian Statesman*, 13 July 1985, p. 7; 20 July 1985, p. 7; 27 July 1985, p. 7.

Akeh, Afam, 'Achebe flays racists and loud critics', *Daily Times*, 11 November 1989, pp. 1–2.

Anon., 'Voice of Nigeria', *West Africa*, 24 February 1962, p. 201.

Anon., 'Chinua Achebe on Biafra', *Transition*, 7, 36 (1968), pp. 31–7.

Anon., 'BBB interviews Chinua Achebe', *Black Books Bulletin*, 3, 2 (1975), pp. 20–2.

Anon., 'Professor Chinua Achebe at NN parley', *New Nigerian*, 2 April 1985, p. 1; 5 April 1985, pp. 1–3, 5; 6 April 1985, pp. 5, 8; 8 April 1985, pp. 2, 5; 9 April 1985, pp. 2, 5.

Appiah, Anthony, John Ryle, and D. A. N. Jones, 'An interview with Chinua Achebe', *Times Literary Supplement*, 26 February 1982, p. 209.

Agetua, John, 'An interview with Chinua Achebe', *Critics on Chinua Achebe* 1970–76. (Benin: Author, 1977).

Awoyinfa, Michael, and Ben Okezie, 'Achebe speaks on Wole Soyinka', *Sunday Concord*, 9 October 1983, p. x.

— 'Chinua Achebe: *Things Fall Apart* was nearly stolen from me', *Sunday Concord* magazine, 6 November 1983, pp. i, v, ix.

Baugh, Lawrence E., 'An interview with Chinua Achebe', *Drum*, 5, 3 (1974), pp. 18–22.

Barrett, Lindsay. 'Giving writers a voice: an interview with Chinua Achebe', *West Africa*, 22 June 1981, pp. 1405–7.

Beier, Ulli, *The World is a Dancing Masquerade: A Conversation Between Chinua Achebe and Ulli Beier* (Bayreuth: Iwalewa Haus, 1991).

Bosah, Conrad, 'I write for self-expression', *Weekly Star*, 3 February 1985, pp. 8–9.

Brooks, Jerome, 'Chinua Achebe: the art of fiction', *Paris Review*, Vol. 35, No. 133 (Winter 1994), pp. 142–66.

Chinweizu, 'An interview with Chinua Achebe', *Okike*, 20 (1981), pp. 19–32.

Colmer, Rosemary, 'The critical generation', *Ash Magazine*, 5 (1980), pp. 5–7.

Cott, Jonathan, 'Chinua Achebe: at the crossroads', in Jonathan Cott, ed., *Pipers at the Gates of Dawn: The Wisdom of Children's Literature* (New York: McGraw Hill, 1985), pp. 161–92.

Darah, G. G., and Afam Akeh, 'The crossroads in our culture – Achebe', *Sunday Times*, 12 November 1989, pp. 18–19.

— and Afam Akeh, 'Achebe at 59', *Daily Times*, 18 November 1989, p. 12.

Davidson, James, 'Interview: Chinua Achebe', *Meanjin Quarterly*, 39, 1 (1980), pp. 35–7.

Duerden, Dennis and Cosmo Pierterse eds, *African Writers Talking* (London, Heinemann Educational Books, 1972), pp. 3–17.

Egejuru, Phanuel Akubueze, *Towards African Literary Independence: A Dialogue with Contemporary African Writers* (Westport: Greenwood, 1980).

Emenyonu, Ernest and Pat Emenyonu, 'Achebe: accountable to our society', *Africa Report*, 17, 5 (May 1972), pp. 21, 23, 25–7.

Enekwe, Ossie Onuora, 'Dialogue with Chinua Achebe', *New Culture*, 1, 9 (1979), pp. 37–46.

— 'Interview with Chinua Achebe', *Okike*, 30 (1990), pp. 129–33.

Evalds, Victoria K., 'An Interview with Chinua Achebe', *Studies in Black Literature*, 8, 1 (1977), pp. 16–20.

Ewuzie, Alvan, 'Academics have ruined university system – Achebe's bombshell at 60', *Daily Champion*, 18 November 1989, p. 13.

Fabre, Michel, 'Chinua Achebe on *Arrow of God*', *Echos du Commonwealth*, 5 (1979–80), pp. 7–17; *Literary Half-Yearly*, 21, 1 (1980), pp. 1–10.

Felton, M., 'Interview with Chinua Achebe', *Spectrum*, 1, 1 (1967), pp. 4–7.

Foerster, Lydia, 'Man of the People', *Daily Texan*, 19 February 1988, p. 11.

Granqvist, Raoul, 'Achebe interviewed', *Travelling: Chinua Achebe in Scandinavia. Swedish Writers in Africa* (Umea: Department of English, University of Umea, 1990), pp. 43–50.

Hall, Tony, 'I had to write on the chaos I foresaw', *Sunday Nation*, 15 January 1967, pp. 15–16.

Hassan, Yusuf, 'More fiction than real', *Africa Events*, 3, 11 (1987), pp. 51–7.

Hayes, Suzanne, 'An interview with Chinua Achebe (Adelaide 1980)', *New Literature Review*, 11 (n.d.), pp. 43–52.

Iloegbunam, Chuks, 'Achebe: interview', *Newswatch*, 24 March 1986, p. 16.

Imfeld, Al, *Portraits of African Writers: 5 Chinua Achebe*, trans. Jan Klingemann (Cologne: Deutsche Welle Transcriptionsdienst, 1979).

Jackson, Angela, 'Interview with Chinua Achebe', *Black Books Bulletin*, 8 (1991), pp. 53–58.

Jeyifo, Biodun, 'The author's art and role', *West Africa*, 5 November 1984, pp. 2211, 2213.

— ed., *Contemporary Nigerian Literature: A Retrospective and Prospective Exploration* (Lagos: *Nigeria Magazine*, 1985).

Kitchen, Paddy, 'A relevant art: Paddy Kitchen talks to Chinua Achebe', *Times Educational Supplement*, 14 April 1972, p. 19.

Lawson, William, 'Chinua Achebe in New England: an interview', *Yardbird Reader*, 4, 1975.

Lindfors, Bernth, Ian Munro, Richard Priebe and Reinhard Sander, *Palaver: Interviews with Five African Writers in Texas* (Austin, Texas: African and Afro-American Research Institute, University of Texas Press, 1972).

Morell, Karen, *In Person; Achebe, Awoonor and Soyinka at the University of Washington.* (Seattle: University of Washington, 1975).

Morna, Colleen Lowe, 'Chinua Achebe speaks on the role of the African writer', *New African*, November 1987, pp. 47–8.

Morris, Patricia, 'Achebe on leadership and justice', *Concord Weekly*, 5 September 1985, pp. 13–14.

Morrow, Bradford, 'Chinua Achebe: an interview', *Conjunctions*, No. 17 (1991), pp. 7–28.

Moss, Robert, 'Writing and politics', *West Africa*, 11 August 1986, pp. 1676–7.

Moyers, Bill, 'Chinua Achebe: Nigerian novelist', in Betty Sue Flowers ed., *A World of Ideas: Conversations With Thoughtful Men and Women About American Life Today and the Ideas Shaping Our Future* (New York: Doubleday, 1989), pp. 333–44.

Ndibe, Okey, 'Who will save Nigeria?' *Concord Weekly*, 28 January 1985, pp. 34–5.

— 'The low-profile guru', *Concord Weekly*, 4 March 1985, pp. 30–1.

— 'I created the characters 15 years ago', *African Guardian*, 24 September 1987, p. 33.

— 'A cry of the heart', *African Guardian*, 28 November 1988, pp. 22–6.

— and C. Don Adinuba, 'Africa is unstable; Nigeria has not been founded; There Are oppressors; Not a matter of noise', *African Guardian*, 17 July 1986, p. 42; 24 July 1986, p. 34; 31 July 1986, p. 38; 7 August 1986, p. 40.

Nwachukwu-Agbada, J. O. J., 'An interview with Chinua Achebe', *Massachusetts Review*, 28 (1987), pp. 273–85.

— 'A conversation with Chinua Achebe', *Commonwealth: Essay and Studies*, 13, 1 (1990) pp. 117–24.

Nzotta, Tony, Chukwuemeka Okoro, Martin Ebe, Sam Akagha, Tony Ibeh, Uchechukwu Nwafor, Iro Ibe, Jasper Okoro, Ford Ozumba, Macdonald Nwokore, Ogechi Onwuneme, Ndubueze Iroaganachi and Sam Onyema, 'I am a missionary in reverse – Prof. Achebe', *Nigerian Statesman*, 14 November 1989, p. 7; 20 November 1989, p. 7.

Obregon, Enedelia J., 'Author chides attitude toward Third World', *Austin-American Statesman*, 21 February 1988, p. D4.

Odugbemi, Sina, 'I don't believe an artist needs to be rowdy – Achebe', *Vanguard*, 16 October 1986, pp. 8–9.

Ogan, Amma, 'Fiction re-orders society', *African Guardian*, 11 February 1988, p. 29.

Ogbaa, Kalu, 'An interview with Chinua Achebe', *Research in African Literatures*, 12 (1981), pp. 1–13.

Rowell, Charles H., 'An interview with Chinua Achebe', *Callaloo*, 13 (1990), pp. 86–101.

Rutherford, Anna, 'Chinua Achebe: interview', *Kunapipi*, 9, 2 (1987), pp. 1–7.

Searle, Chris, 'Achebe and the bruised heart of Africa', *Wasafiri*, 14 (1991), pp. 12, 16.

Smith, Michael and Harry Cowen, 'A man of the people: interview with Chinua Achebe', *McGill Reporter*, 2, 20 (23 February 1970), pp. 1–2.

Udenwa, Chuzzy Onuora, 'From the corners of Achebe's mind', *Guardian* (Lagos), 20 July 1986, pp. B1, B4, B6.

— 'The Nobel is not an African prize – Chinua Achebe', *Quality*, 3 November 1988, p. 7; 'Interview full text', *Quality*, 10 November 1988, pp. 31–4, 36–7.

— 'Achebe: a chat that bares it all', *Guardian* (Lagos), 11 November 1989, p. 12.

Uzoma, Chidi, 'Chinua Achebe: a novelist as a visionary', *Daily Times*, 11 January 1986, p. 5.

Van Rensburg, A. P. J., 'Seeking a better place', *Donga*, 3 (1976), pp. 34.

Wilkinson, Jane, 'Chinua Achebe', *Talking with African Writers: Interviews* (London, James Currey, 1992), pp. 46–57.

Wilmer, Valerie, 'Chinua Achebe and the African novel', *Flamingo*, 4, 11 (1965), pp. 27–9.

Wright, Patricia, 'Chinua Achebe: bringing the African novel back home', *Contact*, 13, 3 (1988), pp. 28–31.

Secondary Sources

Ademola, Frances, ed., *Reflections: Nigerian Prose and Verse* (Lagos: African University Press, 1962).

Ademoyega, Adewale, *Why We Struck: The Story of the First Nigerian Coup* (Ibadan: Evans, 1981).

Ad'Obe, Obe, 'The coup plot verdicts', *West Africa*, 3 March 1986, pp. 445–6.

Agbabiaka, Tunde, 'Execution reactions', *West Africa*, 17 March 1986, p. 553.

Ajayi, Alex Olu, 'Okigbo, Ajayi and Fiditi', *Daily Times*, 29 August 1992, p. 12.

Amadike, P. C., 'Address to the Convention of Nigerian Authors', *Okike*, 20 (December 1981), pp. 4–6.

Amuta, Chidi, 'Eagle on Iroko', *Daily Times*, 12 February 1990.

— and Tunde Olusunle, 'Achebe: eagle above seasons', *Sunday Times*, 11 November, 1990, pp. 13–15.

Ankomah, Baffour, 'Awo: Achebe puts the knife in', *New African*, August 1987, pp. 38–9.

Anon., 'Profile: the man who looks ahead', *Radio Times*, March 1955, p. 14.

Anon., 'Behind the microphone', *Radio Times*, January 1955, p. 4.

Anon., 'Chinua Achebe', *West Africa*, 19 November 1971, p. 1356.

Anon., 'Writers doomed to be free', *West Africa*, 19 November 1979, p. 2123.

Anon., 'Aminu picks running mate', *West Africa*, 18 April 1983, p. 966.

Anon., 'Aminu Kano – leader from the outside', *West Africa*, 25 April 1983, p. 981.

Anon., 'Achebe dissents', *West Africa*, 8 June 1987, p. 1123–4.

Anon., 'Editorial: Achebe at 59', *Daily Times*, 18 November 1989.

Astrachan, Anthony M., 'Does it take one to know one', *Nigeria Magazine*, 77 (1963), pp. 132–3.

Awogbemi, Olu, Ndaeyo Uko, Amuzie Akpaka, Soji Omotunde and Sanya Ademiluyi, 'The master craftsman: tribute to a thinker and writer at 59', *This Week*, 27 November 1989, pp. 14–17, 20, 22–3.

Awoyinfa, Michael, 'Dogs eat dog: professors attack Professor Achebe', *Sunday Concord*, 3 February 1985, p. 1.

Azuonye, Chukwuma, 'Reminiscences of the Odunke community of artists, 1966–1991', *ALA Bulletin*, 17, 1 (Winter 1991).

Basden, G. T., *Among the Ibos of Nigeria* (London: Frank Cass & Co.), 1966.

Beier, Ulli, 'Interview with Obiora Udechukwu', *Okike*, 20 (1981), pp. 53–66.

— *In a Colonial University* (Bayreuth: Iwalewa Haus, 1993).

Bruchac, Joseph, 'Achebe as poet', *New Letters*, 40, 1 (1973), p. 23–31.

Carroll, David, *Chinua Achebe: Novelist, Poet, Critic* (Basingstoke and London: Macmillan, 1990).

Chametzky, Jules, ed., *Black Writers Redefine Struggle: A Tribute to James Baldwin* (Amherst: University of Massachusetts Press, 1989).

Chase, Stacy, 'Report', *Campus Chronicle*, University of Massachusetts, Amherst, September 1988, p. 6.

Chinweizu, Onwuchekwa Jemie and Ihechukwu Madubuike, 'Towards the decolonization of African literature, Part 1: the case of Nigerian poetry', *Okike* 6 (1974), pp. 11–27.

Dazang, Nick, 'A time to forgive', *Sunday Concord*, 12 July 1987, p. 22.

Diamond, Stanley, 'The Biafran possibility', *Africa Report*, 13, 2 (1968), pp. 16–19.

Dunton, Chris, 'A fine-tuned humanist: review of *Hopes and Impediments*', *West Africa*, 12–18 September, 1988, p. 1675.

Echeruo, M. J. C., 'Introduction' to Chinua Achebe, *The Sacrificial Egg and Other Stories* (Onitsha: Etudo Press, 1962), pp. 3–7.

Ehling, Holger, ed., *Critical Approaches to* Anthills of the Savannah (Amsterdam: Rodopi, 1990).

Ekechi, Felix K., *Tradition and Transformation in Eastern Nigeria* (Kent: The Kent University Press, 1989).

Emenanjo, Nolue, 'After the blackout: editorial and linguistic problems in *Aka Weta*', *Uwa Ndi Igbo*, 1 (June 1984), pp. 89–93.

Enahoro, Peter, 'Why I left Nigeria', *Transition*, 7, 36 (5 July 1968), pp. 27–30.

Ezenwa-Ohaeto, 'A literary celebration of the Achebes', *ALA Bulletin*, 15, 2 (1989), pp. 16–18.

— 'Celebration for Chinua Achebe', *ALA Bulletin*, 16, 2 (1990), pp. 21–3.

Ezughah, Dili, Chinwude Onwuanyi and Chuks Iloegbunam, 'Interview with Chinweizu', *Quality Magazine*, 4 May 1989, p. 43–9.

Farah, Nuruddin, 'A tale of tyranny', *West Africa*, 21 September 1987, pp. 1828–31

Foerster, Lydia, 'Man of the people', *Daily Texan*, 19 February 1988, p. 11.

Forsyth, Frederick, *The Biafra Story* (Harmondsworth: Penguin Books, 1969).

Gikandi, Simon, *Reading Chinua Achebe: Language and Ideology in Fiction* (London, James Currey, 1991).

Government of Biafra, *Ahiara Declaration: The Principles of the Biafran Revolution* (Geneva: Mark Press, 1969).

Government of Tanzania, *Statement on the Recognition of Biafra* (Dar es Salaam: Government Printer, 1968).

Gowda, H. H. Anniah, 'The Association for Commonwealth Literature and Language Studies Conference in Kampala', *Research in African Literatures*, 5 (1974), pp. 219–22.

Granqvist, Raoul, ed., *Travelling: Chinua Achebe in Scandinavia* (Umeå: University of Umeå, 1990).

Hill, Alan, *In Pursuit of Publishing* (London: John Murray, 1988).

Hill-Lubin, M. A., 'Chinua Achebe and James Baldwin at the ALA Conference', *Okike*, 17 (1980), pp. 1–5.

Igwe, Dimgba, 'Conversation with Chinua Achebe's wife', *Weekend Concord*, 31 March

1990, pp. 7, 14.

Ike, Chukwuemeka, 'William Simpson: reminiscences', *The Umuahian: A Golden Jubilee Publication* (Umuahia: Government College, Umuahia Old Boys Association, 1979), pp. 24–7.

Ikoku, Chimere, 'Where Are the Laboratories', *Nsukkascope*, 1 (1971).

Ikoku, S. G., *Nigeria's Fourth Coup d'État: Options for Modern Statehood* (Enugu Fourth Dimension Publishers, 1985).

Iloegbunam, Chuks, 'A man of prose', *Newswatch*, 24 March 1986, pp. 14–15.

Innes, C. L., 'Review of *Morning Yet on Creation Day*', *Research in African Literatures*, 7, 2 (1976), pp. 242–5.

— *Chinua Achebe* (Cambridge: Cambridge University Press, 1990).

— and Bernth Lindfors, eds, *Critical Perspectives on Chinua Achebe* (London: Heinemann Educational Books, 1979).

Irele, Abiola, 'Creative pacesetter', *West Africa*, 10–16 December 1990, p. 2992.

Jabbi, Bu-buakei, 'Myth and ritual in *Arrow of God*', in Jones, E. (ed.), *African Literature Today, 11, Myth and History* (London: Heinemann, 1980), pp. 130–48.

Killam, G. D, *The Writings of Chinua Achebe*, revised edition (London: Heinemann Educational Books, 1977).

Kimborough, Robert, ed., Joseph Conrad, *Heart of Darkness* (Norton Critical Edition) (New York: Norton, 1988).

King, Bruce, 'The revised *Arrow of God*', in Jones, E., Palmer E. and Jones, M. (eds), *African Literature Today, 13* (London: Heinemann and New York: Africana, 1983), pp. 69–78.

Kirk-Greene, A. H. M., *Crisis and Conflict in Nigeria: A Documentary Source Book* (2 vols) (Oxford: Oxford University Press, 1971).

Legum, Colin, 'East Nigeria strikes a defiant note', *Observer*, 5 March 1967.

Lindfors, Bernth, ed., *Contemporary Black South African Literature: A Symposium*, (Washington, DC: Three Continents Press and ALA, 1985).

— *Dem Say: Interviews with Eight Nigerian Writers* (Austin, Texas: African and Afro-American Studies and Research Center, 1974).

— *Early Nigerian Literature* (New York: Africana Publishing Company, 1982).

— ed., *Approaches to Teaching* Things Fall Apart (New York: Modern Language Association of America, 1991).

— and Bala Kothandaraman, eds, *South Asian Responses to Chinua Achebe* (New Delhi, India: Prestige Books, 1993).

Maes-Jelinek, Hena, ed., *A Shaping of Connections: Commonwealth Literature Studies – Then and Now* (Sydney: Dangaroo Press, 1989).

Michaels, Marguerite, 'The power of silence', *Time Magazine*, 28 August 1993, p. 25.

Muhammed, Brigadier Murtala, *Drift and Chaos Arrested: Text of the First Broadcast to the Nation by his Excellency, Brigadier Murtala Muhammed* (Lagos: Federal Ministry of Information, 30 July 1975).

Momah, Christian Chike, 'Class of '44: reminiscences', *The Umuahian Golden Jubilee Publication* (Umuahia: Government College, Umuahia Old Boys Association, 1979), pp. 14–21.

Mphahlele, Ezekiel, ed., *Conference of African Writers of English Expression: Makerere College, Kampala, Uganda, 11–17 June 1962* (Kampala: Dept. of Extra Mural Studies, Makerere College, 1962).

Muoneke, Romanus Okey, *Art, Rebellion and Redemption: a Reading of Chinua Achebe* (New York. Peter Lang, 1994).

Nagenda, John, 'Conference notebook', *Transition* 5 (1962), pp. 8–9.

Ndili, Frank, 'An address to the Convention of Nigerian Authors', *Okike*, 20 (1981), pp. 2–3.

Ngugi (James) wa Thiong'o, 'A Kenyan at the conference', *Transition*, 5 (1962), p. 7.

Njoku, Benedict Chiaka, *The Four Novels of Chinua Achebe: A Critical Study* (New York: Peter Lang, 1984).

Nkosi, Lewis, *Home and Exile* (London: Longman 1983).

Nwapa, Flora, 'Writers, printers and publishers', *Guardian* (Lagos), 17 August 1988, p. 16.

Nwoga, D. I., 'The *Chi* offended', *Transition*, 15 (1964), p. 5.

— ed., *Rhythms of Creation: A Decade of Okike Poetry* (Enugu: Fourth Dimension Publishers, 1982).

Nzimiro, Ikenna, 'Universities, how international are they?', *Nsukkascope*, 1 (1971).

Obiechina, E. N., 'Editorial', *Okike*, 13 (1979), p. 2.

Bibliography

— ed., *African Creations: A Decade of Okike Short Stories* (Enugu: Fourth Dimension Publishers, 1982).

Obregon, Enedelia J., 'Author chides attitude toward Third World', *Austin-American Statesman*, 21 February 1988, p. D4.

O'Brien, Conor Cruise, 'Biafra revisited', *New York Review of Books*, 8 May 1969.

Ogan, Amma, 'Pepper Clark: no bitterness', *Guardian* (Lagos), 14 April 1985, pp. BI-2.

— 'Tribute to Chinua Achebe', *Sunday Times*, 16 December, 1990, p. 7.

Ogbaa, Kalu, *Gods, Oracles and Divination: Folkways in Chinua Achebe's Novels* (Trenton, N.J.: Africa World Press, 1992).

Ojinmah, Umelo, *Chinua Achebe: New Perspectives* (Ibadan: Spectrum, 1991).

Ojukwu, C. O., *Biafra: Selected Speeches with Journal of Events* (New York: Harper and Row, 1969).

Okoye, Emmanuel Meziemadu, *The Traditional Religion and its Encounter with Christianity in Achebe's Novels* (Bern: Peter Lang, 1987).

Okpowo, Blessyn, 'How do you feel about Achebe's plight?', *Weekend Concord*, 21 April 1990, p. 10.

Olojede, Dele, Chuks Iloegbunam and George Otiono, 'The world of Chinua Achebe', *Newswatch*, 24 March 1986, pp. 11–13, 17.

Omotoso, Kole, 'Occasion to celebrate', *West Africa*, 9 November 1987, pp. 2194–5.

Omotunde, Soji, 'Our relationship is profound', *This Week*, 27 November 1989, p. 21.

O. V. O., 'The man who looks ahead', *Radio Times*, March 1955, p. 14.

Petersen, Kirsten Holst, 'Report on the ACLALS Conference in Kampala in 1974', *Commonwealth Newsletter*, 6 (1974), pp. 4–6.

— and Anna Rutherford, eds, *Chinua Achebe: A Celebration* (Portsmouth: Heinemann Educational Books, 1991).

Povey, John, 'The First World Festival of Negro Arts at Dakar', *Journal of the New African Literature and the Arts*, 2 (1966), pp. 24–30.

Ravenscroft, Arthur, *Chinua Achebe* (Essex: Longmans, Green for the British Council and the National Book League, 1969).

Rotimi, Ola, 'Achebe: another feather for the eagle', *Daily Times*, 20 February 1991, p. 18; *Weekend Concord*, 9 March 1991, p. 7.

Sander, Reinhard W., 'The Kansas City Institute on Caribbean and African Writing', *Research in African Literatures*, 5, 1 (1974), pp. 73–4.

Shaw, Thurstan, *Igbo-Ukwu: An Account of Archaeological Discoveries in Eastern Nigeria* (2 vols) (Evanston: North Western University Press, 1970).

— *Unearthing Igbo-Ukwu: Archaeological Discoveries in Eastern Nigeria* (Ibadan: Oxford University Press, 1977).

Shelton, Austin J., 'The offended *Chi* in Achebe's novels', *Transition*, 13 (1964), pp. 36–7.

Swados, Harvey, 'Chinua Achebe and the writers of Biafra', *New Letters*, 40, 1 (1973), pp. 5–13.

Ugah, Ada, *In the Beginning ... Chinua Achebe at Work* (Ibadan: Heinemann Educational Books, 1990).

Wali, Obi, 'The dead-end of African literature', *Transition*, 10 (September 1963), pp. 13–15.

Weekend Concord, 'Get well messages for Chinua Achebe', 21 April 1990, p. 10.

Whiteman, Kaye, 'Achebe and the masquerade', *West Africa*, 9 November 1987, pp. 2193–4.

Wilson, Richard, ed., *Chinua Achebe: Miscellaneous Papers* (Evanston: Northwestern University Program of African Studies, 1970).

Winkler, Karen, 'An African writer at a crossroads', *The Chronicle of Higher Education.*, 12 January 1994, pp. A9, A12.

Wren, Robert M., *Achebe's World: The Historical and Cultural Context of the Novels of Chinua Achebe* (Washington, DC: Three Continents Press, 1980; Harlow: Longman, 1981).

— *Those Magical Years: The Making of Nigerian Literature at Ibadan 1948–1966* (Washington, DC: Three Continents Press, 1991).

Wright, Patricia, 'Novelist Chinua Achebe joins 1987–88 faculty', *Campus Chronicle*, 26 June 1987, p. 6.

Yankson, Kofi, *Chinua Achebe's Novels: A Socio-Linguistic Perspective* (Obosi, Nigeria: Pacific Publishers, 1990).

Index

About the Author

E ZENWA-OHAETO is a Nigerian poet, short story writer, columnist, scholar and critic. He obtained BA Hons (as one of Chinua Achebe's undergraduate students) and MA degrees from the University of Nigeria, Nsukka and a PhD from the University of Benin. He has been at various times at the Kano Campus of the Ahmadu Bello University, Anambra State College of Education, Awka, Alvan Ikoku Institute for Education, Owerri, and the University of Mainz, Germany. He spent 1996 at the University of Bayreuth. His critical and creative works have been published in England, Germany, Nigeria, Hungary, Zambia, France, Trinidad and Tobago, United States of America, Denmark, Russia, India, Cameroon, Canada and New Zealand. Ezenwa-Ohaeto is the author of *A Critical Study of Alkali's* The Stillborn (Longman, 1991), the editor of *Making Books Available and Affordable* (1995), and the poetry collections *Songs of a Traveller* (1986), *I Wan Bi President* (1988), *The Voice of the Night Masquerade* (1996), *Bullets for Buntings* (1989), *If To Say I Be Soja* and *Pieces of Madness*. He has won several prizes, including a BBC Arts and Africa poetry prize, a University of Nigeria, Nsukka Short Story Prize and an Alexander van Humboldt Fellowship. He is a regular columnist on literature and the Orphic Lute Columnist of Literature and the Arts in the Nigerian press. His work has been translated into several languages, including Russian, German, Igbo and French.